D1064924

NEW ART
NEW WORLD
British Art in Postwar Society

New Art
New World

British Art in Postwar Society

Margaret Garlake

Published for
The Paul Mellon Centre for Studies in British Art
by Yale University Press New Haven and London

Copyright © 1998 Yale University

All rights reserved. This book may not be reproduced, in whole or in part, in any form (beyond that copying permitted by Sections 107 and 108 of the US Copyright Law and except by reviewers for the public press), without written permission from the publishers.

Designed by Kate Gallimore
Typeset in Palatino and Gill by Best-set Typesetter Ltd., Hong Kong
Printed in Hong Kong

Library of Congress Cataloging-in-Publication Number 97-51962

CONTENTS

ACKNOWLEDGEMENTS

In working on this book I have been acutely aware of researching my own history, since it begins in the year after I was born. The history that I have written and the society that I have tried to elucidate are, however, very different from the perceptions of history and society that were presented to me as a child. And so, among the many people who have contributed significantly to this book are those with whom I have, for many years, had inconsequential conversations along the lines of 'what was it like then?' Although their names are unrecorded they are among the many people who have given me all kinds of practical help. Others have, equally essentially, given me the encouragement and support without which I would never have finished the book. I thank all of them.

I am particularly grateful to the artists and their families who have allowed me to interview them, in some cases repeatedly, and who have submitted to questioning with unfailing patience and generous hospitality. Without artists there would have been no book to write and so my special thanks to Frank Avray Wilson, Denis Bowen, Rosemary Butler, Lynn and Eva Chadwick, Prunella Clough, Magda Cordell McHale, Robyn Denny, Terry Frost, the late William Gear, William Green, Corinne Heath and the late Adrian Heath, Patrick Heron, Anthony Hill, Rose Hilton, Sheila and Andrew Lanyon on countless occasions, John Latham, Karin Jonzen, Margaret Mellis, Gustav Metzger, Jon Pasmore, John Plumb, Ralph Rumney and Barbara Steveni. To those whom I have inadvertently left out, my apologies.

My colleagues at the Courtauld Institute have helped me in ways of which they are possibly unaware, not least by providing a constantly stimulating atmosphere, and by their belief that this book would, one day, be completed. I thank particularly Christopher Green, who has for longer than I like to remember, encouraged and cajoled me into continuing, who contributed fundamentally to the structure of the book and, not least, read the whole text in a late draft. His comments and his support have been invaluable. I also thank Richard Cork for his incisive comments on a draft of the final chapter and for his encouragement.

I am also much indebted to many students who have contributed through their very polite scepticism, their humour and their comments, but mostly by forcing me to keep thinking. Without some MA dissertations, on which I have been able to draw, there would have been even more gaps in my book. I am particularly indebted to Oliver Barker, Fiona Gaskin, Matthew Imms, Marcy Leavitt-Bourne, Jessica Morgan, Clare Preston, Matthew Rowe, Stacey Tenenbaum and Mary Yule; also to Virginia Button for her invaluable doctoral thesis on neo-Romanticism and to Sally Bulgin for her thesis on the New Generation and 'Situation' artists. James Hyman and Andrew Wilson have been unfailingly generous in sharing ideas and information, albeit sometimes in dissent.

When I was researching my own doctoral thesis, parts of which reappear in chapter two, I made much use of the archives of the Arts Council, then housed at 105 Piccadilly, the British Council and the Institute of Contemporary Arts. I would like to record my gratitude, not only for access to these archives but for the unfailing helpfulness of library staff and for many cups of coffee. More recently the Henry Moore Foundation at Much Hadham allowed me to use their lavish research facilities: I am most grateful for the many generosities of the director and the staff. I would also like to thank the staff of the Courtauld Institute Library, the London Library, the National Art Library, the Tate Gallery Archive, Michael

Sweeney, the Roland Penrose archivist, the Contemporary Art Society and the Greater London Record Office. They have all responded kindly and patiently to my most importunate demands; life would have been a great deal more difficult without their help.

Two private collections of papers have been of enormous interest and benefit to me. Rose Hilton very kindly allowed me to read and copy Roger Hilton's manuscripts and Sheila Lanyon has given me access to her whole archive, as well as allowing me repeatedly to rummage through her personal art collection. Ken Powell has allowed me to visit his splendid private collection on many occasions and I am deeply indebted to him for the insights that this has given me; also to David Brown, Denis Bowen, Richard Morphet and Penelope Rosenberg for showing me their collections.

One of the most pleasurable aspects of writing this book has been the good reason it gave to spend a lot of time in galleries. For showing me works of art that were not on view, for helping me to meet artists and for generously sharing their enormous and esoteric knowledge I am deeply grateful to René Gimpel of Gimpel Fils, Jane England of England and Co., Maggie Thornton and the staff of the Redfern Gallery, Austin/Desmond Fine Art and Madeleine Ponsonby.

Collecting illustrations has been an arduous job. It has been made a great deal easier by the Courtauld Institute's Photographic Department; my thanks to them, to Ron Baxter, and Philip Ward-Jackson of the Conway Library. To Gillian Ayres, Janet Axton, the Bernard Jacobsen Gallery, Denis Bowen, Lynn and Eva Chadwick, Bernard Cohen, Magda Cordell McHale, Diana Eccles at the British Council, Jane England, Peter Garlake, Carlotta Gelnetti at Tate Gallery Publications, René Gimpel, Pamela Griffin at the Hayward Gallery, Anthony Hill, Sheila and Andrew Lanyon, Rachel Patterson, Ken Powell, Mario Rebellato and Michelle Thomas who have all, in various ways, helped me to find reproductions, much gratitude.

There have been others, whose contribution to my project was indirect and unintentional but no less valuable. I especially appreciate having had the opportunity to work with Peter Townsend, whose insights into the art world and the writing of prose gave me far more than I could ever return; conversations over a long period with Anthony Chennells, which have added to my still inadequate grasp of critical theory, and the friends with whom I have discussed art, history and criticism on so many occasions. To Letty Mooring, who has so often restored my sanity by dragging me away from the computer to do a round of galleries, special thanks.

I am immensely grateful to John Nicoll and Kate Gallimore at Yale University Press for their insights into the final form of the book, the discretion and discernment of Kate Gallimore's editing and their guidance in the final stages of production of the manuscript.

And, finally, my family: I thank them for their forbearance, their encouragement, the generosity of their interest in a project which must so often have seemed perversely obsessive. Most of all I thank Peter, the most severe, and the most generously appreciative critic, for occasional reading, much talk and his somewhat irrational belief in my ability to reach the end. I thank him most, though, for many years of shared discoveries, enthusiasms and delights; for insights into ways of looking at art which are the real foundation of this book.

November 1997

In writing this book I have tried to keep in mind Theo Crosby's precept that 'The artist is the eyes, the conscience, the soul of a society, and, when he is neglected, life becomes dimmer.'[1] Artists function within society and their work is in some measure both produced and consumed by society. Yet between the poles of making and reception there is a vast area of slippage, negotiation and disjunction. Consequently the making of art becomes a process as maverick as its consumption, and in attempting to construct linkages and define origins and causes we are faced with an unwieldy structure like an irregular three-dimensional grid. It is untidy; in some places it is densely clustered while elsewhere there are holes; its lines swoop and sag and run off inconclusively into speculative spaces much more often than they are straight and well-defined. Aware of the complexity of this structure, I have not attempted to write an inclusive history of British art in the 1940s and 1950s, but a set of interlinked thematic essays.

The first four are concerned with the context in which art was made and received. Social and political history establish the conditions and nature of what is conveniently called the art support system, which includes state and commercial patronage, publishing and art education, just as, indirectly, they contribute to perceptions of tradition and nationhood and inflect critical readings of art. The remaining chapters address specific areas of artists' practice. Only one, on wartime art, is chronologically defined. I have made this exception because, as I explain in chapter one, I believe that the Second World War was the single most important cultural determinant during the period covered by this book.

Each of these themes deserves a book in itself, rather than a chapter and I am conscious of having left out far more than I have included. My principal reason for attempting to cram so much complexity into so small a space is that there is no general book (however selective) on early postwar art; I hope that this one will encourage others. It may, however, be seen as perverse to have chosen to concentrate on modernist and modernist-related pratices. Many objections can be raised to my approach, not least that a study of modernism can only be historically limiting. Modernism is also seen to be tainted with the evasions of formalism, through which it occludes the human, the social and the political. I believe this to be a misrepresentation and that modernism can be interpreted as more fluid, pluralist and even post-modern than this view allows. I have tried to demonstrate that connections may be found between practices described as formalist and those known as realist, even when these connections must be teased out and depend on ideas rather than visual similarities.

One of the problems of the historiography of modern British art has been a reluctance to admit either ideological or theoretical content in the work; one of my purposes has been to reinstate them. There are other books to be written, about for instance, women's art, the Academy and Realism. I have given very little prominence to Realism, largely because James Hyman has done the primary research in this area. When his book is published it will oblige us to re-evaluate our readings of all art in the postwar period.

I have tried to address the specificities of postwar art: I suggest that its institutional and ideological contexts contribute at least as much to its definition as any notion of style or even subject matter. Twentieth-century art in Britain has been widely considered derivative from French and, later, American models. I have tried to negotiate this issue by acknowledging formal appropriations and discussing the often very different inflections placed on them by British artists. In doing so I am aware of having overstepped the proper limits of the historian. Historically, we can often go no further than to propose congruences between art and its wider context in society.

Theoretically, however, we may travel a little further by acknowledging Homi Bhabha's perception of a 'Third Space', a notional area between proposition and enunciation[2] which is the pivotal process in the formation of cultural identity. It 'represents both the general conditions of language and the specific implication of the utterance in a performative and institutional strategy'.[3]

Bhabha writes of 'disorientation', of the impossibility, today, of cultural definition and of the need, therefore, to focus on '"in-between" spaces', 'those moments or processes that are produced in the articulation of cultural differences'.[4] In 'the Third Space of enunciation', a space of ambiguity and disruption, narratives are overturned in constituting 'the discursive conditions of enunciation that ensure that the meaning and symbols of culture have no primordial unity or fixity; that even the same signs can be appropriated, translated, rehistoricized and read anew.'[5]

This is not to propose a free-for-all in which interpretation may be understood as a random, dissociated activity but rather to acknowledge the 'ambivalence in the act of interpretation'[6] while we remain alert to the specificities within which each work of art is made. To fail to recognise the necessity of ambivalence in the always imperfect translation of the visual into the verbal would, indeed, be to fail to acknowledge the singularity of the makers, the artists. No analysis of discourse, or of the minutiae of cultural or ideological location allows us to enter their minds or to see with their eyes. It is this inability that reveals our need for Bhabha's definition of a space in which imprecision, ambiguity and fluidity are recognised as creative and empowering conditions without which our understanding of historical processes, including the making of art, are wilfully circumscribed.

1940–1960 *Defining a Period*

The unity we give to a past period is always an effect of historical foreshortening. We should think rather of a complex chart with many graphs starting from different points and pursuing their independent ways: a date-line will cross them at an arbitrary level and the 'present', at any one moment, is merely a chance assembly of achievements, outlines, potentialities, 'work in progress'.

Herbert Read, 1953[1]

1954, R. A. Butler remarked, was 'the year when, for the British trader and the British consumer, the war finally ended'.[2] Three years later, Harold Macmillan was to proclaim 'You never had it so good'. 1957 might then be seen as some kind of turning point onto the less bumpy ride towards the Sixties, with its euphoric blend of esoteric and popular culture, symbolised for the visual arts by the opposition between Pop Art and the Destruction in Art Symposium of 1966. This book is concerned for the most part with the art of the immediate postwar years, on the assumption that they constitute a period which was experienced and understood in terms that distinguish it from the Depression that preceded it and the symbolically laden Swinging London phase that followed.

Read's notion of foreshortening is in part responsible for our perceptions of the long years of postwar austerity as a grimy, dun-coloured continuum of bureaucratic restrictions and stifling convention, punctuated by the anomalies of the Festival of Britain and the Coronation. Read's comments on the arbitrariness of historical perceptions suggest also that any attempt to use chronology as a blunt weapon to link historical events to the making of art will be fruitless. There are no easy correlations between the establishment of the National Health Service, the assimilation of the New Look, the Suez fiasco and the art of the 1950s, but these, like innumerable other events, contributed to the context within which art was made, disseminated and received.

To establish links between art and politics, art and social change is a risky process, a matter of perception rather than events, but while artists do not illustrate society, they exist within it and are subject to its restrictions and liberations.

The making of art is controlled as much by the need to earn a living as by the desire to make original statements; as much by what is being talked about as by individual inspiration; as much by what is saleable as by a preference for painting flowers or geometric abstraction. Artists' choices, like anyone's, are informed by education, class, regional custom and the pressure of friends. They are subject to unstated physical, economic, political and moral constraints, which intersect with the wider social and historical pattern. The question is how to discern the joining point; how to admit the eccentricity and whim of the individual into an historical pattern and, finally, to accept that art history embodies contradictions that cannot be neatly smoothed away, that the making of art is both a social and an entirely private act, and that this is a paradox which is frequently not satisfactorily resolved.

If artists' purposes are irrecoverable, the mechanisms through which their products enter the public domain to become social artefacts are more easily traced. The art support system, which underpins production, was so deeply modified in the early postwar years that it changed the status of art in society as well as the way art functioned as a profession. The rapid expansion of art education, state patronage and the commercial sector after 1945 offered opportunities for an unprecedented number of artists to make, show and sell work and for a new public to see it. These developments were bound up with the establishment of the Welfare State and the reformulation of a civilian society.

On the premise that making and experiencing art is no less integral to a civilised society than education or health care, this chapter is an attempt to outline the formulation of the social context within which artists operated. For this purpose I take a period to mean a number of years which can be distinguished from those that preceded and followed them, politically and economically; in attitudes to foreigners, class, race and gender; in national self-perception and in cultural production, which includes the arts and patronage. In a necessarily extremely brief and generalised account, I hope to demonstrate that it is possible to discern an at least partially coherent period.

The two decades 1940–60 saw the waging of and recovery from a global war; an immense economic reorientation and a series of changes in society which seemed to some people to be little less than a social revolution. Until 1954 almost nothing took place of any social or political significance that was not related to the war. In the early postwar years there is a sense of transition, of a time characterised by aspiration rather than achievement, and by a search for identity rather than by confidence. This period was formed as much by experiences and memories of conflict as by social innovations; by xenophobia as well as the international unity proclaimed by the formation of UNESCO and the Council of Europe; by the *leit motif* of 'before the war', with its dual charges of a lost golden age and the determination never again to experience the economic degradation of the Depression. Both attitudes carried connotations of some kind of tradition, of behavioural and intellectual patterning which changed only in the 1960s, with the benefits of a restored economy and social planning.

The early postwar years were also those of the first and most vicious phase of the Cold War, when European politics were realigned and Britain's status and foreign relationships began to be profoundly changed by the break-up of the empire. In this reorientation America played a central role, as provider and sustainer, as unattainable dream, as the unknown pole on an axis with continental Europe. Admission to knowledge, to union with the desired Other, was attainable only after economic regeneration had indicated Britain's suitability as partner; on the American side, desire for the match was encouraged by the exigencies of Cold War politics. The shift which consequently took place in Britain's cultural allegiance, from France to the United States, was one in which art and politics were inseparable, though there was no obvious relationship between them. It set in train a reformulation both of advanced art and, more significantly, a re-evaluation of national identity.

A subject of intense debate, at least with reference to its implications for high culture,[3] even before the end of the war, national identity was continually and fundamentally called into question by the threat of imminent annihilation in another global war. Peter Hennessy writes of 'those six years which began on 2 July 1947 . . . the "high cold war", years of extraordinary peril when hot war was possible at any moment'.[4] While the long-term physical effects of the bombs exploded over Japan in August 1945 were not widely understood until a decade later, imagination and fear created a mythology around them unparalleled in intensity since the Black Death. The conventional weapons of the Second World War had destroyed ancient cities and converted the stable societies of central Europe into a mass of nomads; new methods of warfare seemed to have the power, anticipated by Francis Bacon's *Three Studies for Figures at the Base of a Crucifixion* (1944) (fig. 79), to convert human tissue into mindless mutants. Horror demands relief, escape from nightmare into dream. Just as at the height of the war the West End of London assumed an air of frenetic gaiety and artists and writers constructed the pub and club culture of Fitzrovia, postwar myths dwelt on more benign notions of a changeless landscape, on the imminent wonders of interplanetary travel and elaborations of the American dream.

From January 1940, when Clement Attlee announced Labour's whole-hearted support for the war effort, he equated it with the struggle for social justice[5] and saw its restrictions and regulations as the framework for an equitable distribution of wealth and services in the postwar years.[6] Other politicians, if more circumspect, were equally eager to put social reforms into practice. From 1943, when the progress of the war began to turn, a wide range of social measures was debated under the heading of reconstruction and enacted under a cross-party consensus.

Since the Blitz had destroyed half a million homes in London and left a further quarter of a million severely damaged,[7] reconstruction was finely balanced between the physical urgency of building and the moral compulsion of William Beveridge's *Pillars of Security*. These were to sustain a 'New Britain . . . as free as is humanly possible, of the five giant evils, of Want, of Disease, of Ignorance, of Squalor and of Idleness.'[8]

An unexpected relationship between social reconstruction and the visual arts emerged after 1946 in the form of several important patronage schemes: in Hertfordshire County Council's schools, the New Towns, particularly Harlow and, from the mid-1950s, the London County Council's properties. The political reality of social reform had established the conditions for an expanded art support system, while higher educational standards, full employment[9] and increased leisure contributed to the basis for a more widespread interest in the arts.

Attlee's government has been accused of Utopianism, of trying to bring about a New Jerusalem in which priority was given to welfare, housing and full employment at the expense of the re-establishment of a sound industrial base.[10] Yet it is now a truism that circumstances beyond his government's control prevented it from either pushing through a full-scale nationalisation programme or rapidly re-establishing a sound capitalist economy.[11]

The unexpected and disastrous, if inevitable end of Lend-Lease, announced by President Truman in August 1945,[12] which ensured that Britain would thereafter be obliged to pay for all that the United States supplied, has been seen as the source of much subsequent anti-American prejudice.[13] Maynard Keynes's damage-limitation trip to Washington in September secured an immediate loan on terms acutely disappointing to the government;[14] the people became rapidly aware of the country's economic plight when bread rationing was introduced in July 1946.[15] At the same time 40,000 people rendered homeless by the Blitz moved into disused service camps as squatters.[16]

January 1947 saw the onset of the most severe winter weather since 1881, when domestic electricity was rationed; nearly two million people were temporarily out of work; the supply of newsprint to periodicals was suspended,[17] and the avail-ability of food was more strictly regulated than at any time during the war, with rationing even of potatoes. The economic crisis was to last nearly eighteen months, rendered acute in July, when convertibility came into effect and countries holding sterling flocked to exchange it for dollars in order to buy American goods. By mid-August the loan was rapidly running out and on 21 August convertibility was suspended, with American agreement. As the crisis deepened in July 1947, sixteen western European nations, including Britain, met in Paris to establish the Commit-tee of Economic Co-operation, charged with formulating a plan for economic reconstruction. It was to be carried out through Marshall Aid, which became effective in 1948.[18]

It is widely acknowledged, with varying degrees of emphasis, that the Marshall Plan was devised not only for immediate relief, but to ensure the deflection of western Europe from Communism; the Soviet Union was invited but declined to take part.[19] It is also acknowledged that without American aid, western Europe would probably have collapsed into totalitarianism or anarchy; Hennessy quotes a secret government document of summer 1947, which set out plans for a 'famine food programme' using conscripted agricultural labour.[20] Marshall Aid was seen, in Ernest Bevin's words and particularly by those who knew most about the alternatives, 'like a life-line to sinking men'[21] but it was not received without suspicion. Rumours that the scheme was dependent on modifications to the nationalisation programme turned out to be exaggerated, but the Right felt that American economic domination posed a threat to the Commonwealth, while the new British relationship with the United States was widely seen as intensely humiliating.

At the same time, it would be difficult to overstate the impact of American culture on Europe. Just as American intellectuals had willingly exiled themselves in France in the 1920s and 1930s, in the 1950s European artists turned to the United States for stimulus. Before the war, its isolationist policies had discouraged cul-tural *rapprochement* and first-hand knowledge had been reserved to the very rich. The cinema and the presence of GIs in Europe had changed that situation and aroused violently opposed responses of enthusiasm and rejection. While the American dream was rejected by the far Left, to which it was a form of cultural imperialism, and by the Right, which saw it as a threat to the set of deep-rooted attitudes that may be described as the British tradition, it was acclaimed by millions who, short of food, warmth and comfort, were enraptured by the cin-ematic vision of America.

The cinema was an eloquent messenger of the American dream, conveying a romanticised and uncritical view of the unknowable. Films, particularly those that explored the nexus of fantasy and reality, were to be an important source of stimulus to artists in the 1950s. At the beginning of the decade science fiction and horror movies exercised a powerful attraction; a few years later the wide screen, Technicolor and slick presentation of Hollywood consumer culture made an equally strong impact on a group of students at the Royal College of Art.

By 1960, Hollywood's less outrageous fictions were, ironically, closer to reality for many people than the socialist society which Attlee had hoped to bring into being. His caution and the insuperable problems of restructuring the economy and industry prevented its full flowering, though his government established structures in education, health care, housing and the arts that were modified and developed throughout the 1950s and 1960s.

The creative phase of postwar socialism ended as early as 1948, though the Labour government survived until a few weeks after the end of the Festival of Britain in 1951, which acted as both celebration and threnody for this short-lived period. Poised symbolically at the beginning of a decade and a new government, the Festival offers many readings: a celebration of survival, an efflorescence of romantic nationalism, a quasi-scientific trade fair, a farewell to socialism. It also contained elements of a new vernacular decorative manner which has seeped down as an instant picture of the 1950s and contributes to a sense of period. Asymmetric furniture with splayed legs and spherical finials, fabrics in acid colours and half-tones, complex black linear forms denote the style that became known simply as Contemporary. Co-existing with the staider floral chintzes, reproduction furniture and bulky shapes left over from the pre-war era, Contemporary was the vernacular equivalent of the avant-garde visual arts.

Whatever its failures, the Labour government negotiated the acceptance of a shift from a profound belief in private wealth, private enterprise and philanthropy to a system that acknowledged the state as the final guarantor of income. One of the strands in the art history of the early postwar period plots the means whereby working compromises were reached between the private patrons of the old order and the new state institutions, for except at the fundamental level of health care and education, the state was little more than a guarantor: its provision for the arts was a long drawn out exercise in parsimony.

Nevertheless, the thrust of postwar social policy was nurture of the whole person, intellect as well as body, which allowed the creation of the Arts Council as well as the National Health Service. While the establishment of the NHS was the most widely acclaimed of the three great reform acts of the mid-1940s, the new education policy had equally radical long-term effects, enabling a vast intake of mature students to enter tertiary education on ex-servicemen's grants, with a concomitant expansion of colleges, art schools and, eventually, the foundation of new universities.

The social policies of Attlee's government and cross-party perceptions of their necessity provided the essential first impetus towards a society very different from that of the interwar years; one in which a new consumer class was prominent[22] and in which there was unprecedented educational and class mobility, encouraged by the boom of the late 1950s and 1960s. One wartime promise that remained unfulfilled was the integration of women into the workforce, a failure which conceals a more profound lack of social integration. If women's subservience was never as complete as in the American situation analysed by Betty

Friedan,[23] it was nevertheless possible, as late as 1956, for a book to be published in Britain on the morality of married women working outside the home.[24] Feminism may not have died during the 1950s[25] but once the compulsions of the war, when 'doing your bit' was almost as stringent a demand as conscription, were over, many women were willing to make way for men returning to pre-war jobs. Those who wished to continue to work found nursery provision reduced and National Insurance contributions weighted against them. Official anxiety over a falling birthrate, combined with promotion of maternity and the family[26] and a universal desire to 'get back to normal' after the carnage, meant that for many young women the war changed very little; from society portraits to advertising, images abound of woman's contradictory roles, so seldom her own.

Amid complaints that a centralised bureaucracy would stifle local culture, there were pockets of deep resistance to cultural change, from Yorkshire mining communities[27] to the intellectual elite when it confronted the suburban sprawl known as Subtopia.[28] Though deeply deplored, this promised, for those who sought it, a higher standard of material life than their parents had dreamt of, with consumer durables and spare money for leisure activities.

The sociologist T. R. Fyvel, prompted by a visit to Harlow New Town in 1956, remarked on recent closures of theatres and the lack of demand for serious films and music, despite the availability of money and an increasingly well educated population. He attributed a preference for pop music, television and magazine fiction to the replacement of a minority bourgeois ruling culture by one grounded in mass participation; Subtopia, welcome or not, was a *fait accompli*.[29] Changing patterns of women's employment played a large part in this; targeted as consumers, their earnings provided the extra money to buy household appliances and luxury items, though their jobs tended to remain insecure and low-paid.[30]

The cultural preferences that Fyvel noted had profound implications for the arts. The Arts Council became aware of the drift very early and tried, not entirely successfully, to stem the tide, but by the end of the 1950s young artists responded with delight to the American version of Subtopia, ironically appropriating film, consumer goods and popular magazine imagery into their work. At the same time the consumer ethic became the target of savage attacks by radical artists passionately committed to anti-nuclear and green issues, a trend concealed in the early 1960s by the superficial commercialism of much Pop art, but now recognised as a politically sensitive counter-culture closely associated with the American peace movement.

The victory year of 1945; 1951, identified with the Festival of Britain and 1956, the year of the Suez crisis, all provide important markers of the period. Returning from Canada in September 1956 for a debate on the Suez crisis, Richard Crossman wrote of his perception of a country without purpose or future: '. . . it hit me in the stomach – the sense of restriction, yes, even of decline, of an old country always teetering on the edge of a crisis, trying to keep up appearances, with no confident vision of the future in front of it.'[31]

In the context of the Suez debacle, Crossman's observations were no doubt acute, but cultural conservatism and political weariness were totally at odds with events in the arts in that year. 1956 began with the first significant showing of Abstract Expressionism in England, albeit only a single room at the end of an exhibition of twentieth-century American art. In May John Osborne's *Look Back in Anger* opened at the Royal Court Theatre in London, to signal the end of the long dominance of Christopher Fry, T. S. Eliot and their imitators in defence of the values of upper middle-class conservatism.[32] Colin Wilson's *The Outsider* was published almost simultaneously, an account of the alienation of the intellectual and an important if incoherent expression of the individual impotence so strongly felt during the early years of the peace movement.

The cleavage between a scarcely articulated Existentialism on the one hand, and the Leavis school with Logical Positivism on the other emphasised the diminishing dependence by the mid-1950s of English intellectuals on French culture. The advent of Abstract Expressionism in Europe signalled the end of the French hegemony in the visual arts. By the early 1960s, British artists no longer represented a province of continental European culture but were becoming absorbed into the international mainstream. It is significant that the key book for the sharpest minds at the Royal College of Art in 1956–7 was not by Jung or Sartre but was Marshall McLuhan's *The Mechanical Bride*.

By 1956 the romantic tendency no longer held a central or even an influential position. For writers, artists, politicians and industrialists alike the emphasis was firmly on the present and the future; the impetus to recall a way of life that had underpinned the neo-Romanticism of the war years and the immediate postwar period, when the whole of western liberal culture was under threat, had passed. Its symbolic end was the building, like a 'phoenix from the ashes', of the new Coventry Cathedral to replace the one destroyed by the Blitz in 1940. The interior of Basil Spence's building, commissioned in 1956, was in many respects a final, valedictory shrine to neo-Romanticism, dominated by Graham Sutherland's great tapestry, *Christ in Glory* (fig. 28), which covers the entire east end.

A sense of a period inevitably depends for its characterisation on the reasons for wishing to establish it. An understanding of domestic politics and foreign policy is essential to a formulation of the arts as a social manifestation, but the art historian is not primarily concerned with the minutiae of housing bills or international treaties. And even in a socially oriented study of painting and sculpture, social history will become unbalanced. The establishment of the National Health Service is now seen as the most socially significant and enduring piece of domestic legislation since the war but it is less relevant to this study than the foundation of the Arts Council.

Behind any initiative that contributes to the support of the arts lies the necessity of an economic capability, but the history of the arts in the postwar period is not primarily one of an economy. The history of the arts is one of divergence rather than orthodoxy. The twenty years under scrutiny cover a period which began when established social and intellectual habits were destroyed as thoroughly as the buildings which were their physical symbols, from Coventry Cathedral to the slums of London's East End. It ended with physical reconstruction still far from complete, but with a reformulated society sufficiently creative and confident to reject the tentative orthodoxies proposed by the interim years of 1945 to 1960. The society that was ready to take advantage of the contraceptive pill and the findings of the Wolfenden Commission, that found an easy affinity with the contemporary vernacular of American music, fashion and advertising and an indigenous identity in the Merseyside beat, the shops and coffee bars of Swinging London and the populist political impetus of the Aldermaston marches, was fundamentally different from the one that set out to create the New Jerusalem.

2

BENEFACTORS AND BUREAUCRATS
The Art Support System

In the end, you can't make painters, you can only make opportunities for them.
James Boswell, 1947[1]

For millions of people, demobilisation signalled the opportunity to restart careers abruptly abandoned six years earlier. Time was short and in 1945 opportunities were scarce, though they were to multiply within a very few years to form a sophisticated support system for the visual arts. Vigorously reformed teaching methods, dealers enthusiastic about contemporary art and theoretically searching publications bound artists into the system and established the context in which modernism re-emerged during the early 1950s. The support system provided a structure which facilitated the professionalisation of the visual arts at the same time as it revealed their social functions. As a corollary, when British art, seen for so long as no more than a provincial offshoot of the Ecole de Paris, was finally incorporated into the international mainstream, this was less a product of individual genius than of the activities of the British Council and a gradual shift of the international art market from Paris to London.

Fluidity, flexibility and abrupt changes of focus; ideas and theoretical constructions characterise the support system of the 1950s as accurately as its institutions. They were bound together by the art establishment, an unconstituted, fluctuating group of disparate personalities who seldom met formally, frequently disagreed with one another and were unhampered by corporate accountability.

THE ART ESTABLISHMENT

The power of the postwar art establishment, a small pool of people, derived from plurality: everyone sat on three or four committees in the intervals between writing books and criticism, organising exhibitions, acting as a trustee of one of the national museums, or even making art.[2] Its members included the directors of the national collections; the heads of the visual arts departments of the Arts and British Councils; the principals of the leading art schools; the President of the Royal Academy and a handful of critics and private collectors. Its efficiency depended on the linkage of disparate organisations by multiple member-ship, which was also a system of mutual restraint, a system where power was a matter of nuance, successfully exercised through an informal network of friends and colleagues rather than the more heavy-weight bludgeoning of official positions.

The directors of the national collections, guardians of the historical tradi-tion, were the most powerful and prestigious members. Implicitly extending far beyond the visual arts to indicate an ideal society, the notion of tradition carried an extra charge during and just after the war and was the yardstick against which contemporary art was measured and all too often found defective. The signifi-cance of the national collections outstripped appreciation of their aesthetic value since their primary function was to act as historical symbols which represented the past to the future. In wartime this message had stood for an intellectual commu-nity and an international civilisation whose residue was located in the National Gallery in London. The Gallery itself became a symbol of cultural survival when, though its paintings were stored deep in a Welsh slate-quarry, thousands of visitors regularly came to see a single Painting of the Month and to hear the lunch-time concerts given by Myra Hess.

Kenneth Clark, Director of the National Gallery (1934–1945), Slade Professor, Chairman of the Arts Council's Art Panel (1946–8 and 1951–3) and of the Arts Council itself (1953–60) was the single most powerful figure in the early postwar art world. Graham Sutherland's portrait (1964) (fig. 1), fittingly posed in 'the fifteenth-century Italian tradition of the profile portrait',[3] shows the scholar and socialite who had the ear of ministers and royalty, whose private collection ranged from Michelangelo to Cézanne. It contained many twentieth-century British works,[4] though Clark stopped short of abstract art. After dutifully amassing a collection of Bloomsbury paintings he discovered Sutherland's romanticised mo-dernity and became one of his most enthusiastic patrons.[5]

Generous in the grand manner, Clark supported artists through a private grant system; the allowance that he made to Victor Pasmore in 1938 enabled him to abandon his clerk's job with the London County Council and to turn full-time to painting and teaching. When war broke out, Clark exploited his contacts and mutual obligations to found the War Artists' Advisory Committee, ostensibly to provide a visual record of the war though, since this was more efficiently carried out by photographers, the WAAC was in fact a way, as he remarked, 'to keep artists at work on any pretext, and, as far as possible, to prevent them from being killed'.[6] Appropriately he was also a committee member of the Council for the Encouragement of Music and the Arts, devised by Maynard Keynes to keep performing artists out of the firing line by providing entertainment on the home front for a conscript labour force.

For all his generosity, Clark found human relationships difficult and was handi-capped by a patrician disdain for those whom he considered to be his social and intellectual inferiors. He communicated with and through works of art, rather than people. His lack of interest in experimental contemporary art may have been a product of his unwillingness to address the unestablished and the uncodified;

1. Graham Sutherland, *Portrait of Lord Clark*, 1964. Oil on canvas, $21\frac{1}{2} \times 18$ in. National Portrait Gallery, London.

his social habits as much as his training militated against a close creative relationship with a group of artists.

Herbert Read was quite as ubiquitous as Clark. Patrick Heron's self-consciously modernist portrait (1950) (fig. 2), indicates his visual allegiances as clearly as Sutherland's portrayal of Clark. Variously ceramicist, art historian, critic, anarchist, poet, novelist, publisher and co-founder of the Institute of Contemporary Arts, he owed his position at the core of the art establishment to his intellectual scope and flexibility.

The publication of *Art Now* in 1933 had confirmed his position as the leading protagonist of contemporary art and spokesman for the avant-garde group based around the Parkhill Road studios in Hampstead, where he lived as a neighbour of Henry Moore, Ben Nicholson, Barbara Hepworth, Paul Nash and others. Naum Gabo arrived in 1936, one of the influx of refugee artists, architects, psychoanalysts and scientists from Nazi Germany that briefly transformed Read's 'nest of gentle artists'[7] into an intellectual centre to rival Paris. In 1937 the group was formally

2. Patrick Heron, *Herbert Read*, 1950. Oil on canvas, 30 × 25 in. National Portrait Gallery, London.

united through the publication of *Circle: International Survey of Constructive Art*, an anthology of artists' and architects' texts. It amounted to a manifesto for constructive art and a statement of international unity among certain avant-garde artists. Naum Gabo, one of the three editors, set out the intellectual foundations of the group in his introductory essay, 'The constructive idea in art'. This, Gabo proclaimed, was 'an ideology caused by life, bound up with it and directed to influence its course'.[8] He conceptualised the constructive work of art as a complement to science: 'Science teaches, Art asserts; Science persuades, Art acts'.[9] Though Gabo's text is deliberately non-specific, he was writing about a body of abstract art which made no reference to the visible world but instead proclaimed, through its aesthetic harmony, a wider metaphysical harmony. This was itself an analogy of a desired social system in profound contrast with the society implied by the irrationality of Surrealism and other kinds of abstract art.

After the war Read joined the British Council's Art Advisory Committee where he exerted himself on behalf of the Parkhill Road group, today established as modern masters, as well as assisting a great many younger artists, at a time when he was also deeply preoccupied with founding the ICA. An extraordinarily pro-lific writer, he selected and wrote catalogue essays for well over half the Council's most important modern exhibitions during the next fifteen years.

Before the Hayward Gallery opened in 1968, the Tate housed many of the Arts Council's exhibitions but, relying on them, generated correspondingly few of its own. When John Rothenstein became Director of the Tate in 1938[10] the gallery had no purchase grant and until 1946, when it first received a regular income from the Treasury, only two small funds provided for acquisitions.[11] Finding a collection that almost totally ignored both English and continental modernism,[12] he set out, according to his own account, to fill the more glaring gaps in the modern European collection, though many were to remain, notably in twentieth-century German art. Though the Tate reopened in April 1946, after its wartime closure, on the high note of the Braque–Rouault exhibition,[13] because of its poverty and the inadequacy of its collection, its efforts were largely confined to mounting rare solo shows for eminent British artists, often organised by the Arts Council.[14] The Tate itself played a minor part in the support system until the 1960s, though Rothenstein exerted himself privately on behalf of artists, intervening with archi-tects to obtain commissions in new buildings, not least the great symbol of national survival, the rebuilt Coventry Cathedral.[15]

As a champion of tradition, especially as manifested by the Camden Town painters, and a fervent proponent of 'the oldest and most consistent of European traditions, namely realism',[16] Rothenstein was unenthusiastic about abstract art,[17] attacking Read's advocacy of it.[18] He based his argument on selective quotations from Read's essay on Ben Nicholson in *A Coat of Many Colours*,[19] and concluded: 'the philosophy of abstract art, in all the inflation of its currency and the high-flown and tense seriousness of its diction, is unsound from top to bottom'.[20] Read, he maintained, was more concerned with the philosophy of art than with 'the aesthetic or representational content of works of art themselves'[21] on which Rothenstein relied. His writings present an educated version of the widespread mistrust of critical theory and innovatory art that permeated early postwar society, an attitude which sat uneasily on the director of the national collection of modern art. It is not insignificant in this context that just as Read's ideas can be seen to infuse the British Council's exhibitions, so can Rothenstein's be traced in the conservatism and quest for populism of the Arts Council's.

Until well into the 1960s the Tate's shortcomings were compensated by Bryan Robertson's programme at the Whitechapel Art Gallery. Director from 1953 to 1968, he transformed it from a philanthropic educational resource for East Enders into the country's leading centre for contemporary art. A Whitechapel exhibition, with one of the gallery's well-documented and illustrated catalogues, was a defini-tive marker in the career structure of an ambitious artist and a shortcut to critical recognition.

Robertson's taste was confident, eclectic and independent. Convinced that if British art were to be seen as more than a tributary of the Ecole de Paris, it must be set in an international context, his exhibition programme[22] wove between well-established artists like Hepworth, rising stars like Jack Smith, and leading conti-nental and American modernists, from Piet Mondrian to Jackson Pollock.[23] Since these were often the artists' first substantial exhibitions in this country, the gallery can be seen as virtually constituting an independent support system within the wider structure.

Robertson's tenure culminated with the promotion of the New Generation, characterised by uncompromisingly abstract paintings and coloured sculpture in steel and fibreglass. Though they were unattractive to private buyers, with the notable exception of Lord McAlpine, Robertson's collaboration with the Peter Stuyvesant Foundation[24] was an early and extremely successful instance of the corporate patronage that was to flourish in the 1970s.

PRIVATE PATRONS AND COLLECTORS

Long before corporate sponsorship became widespread, Eric Gregory, chairman of Lund Humphries, commissioned the architect Jane Drew to redesign his firm's premises; she in turn commissioned Patrick Heron's spectacular *Horizontal Stripe Painting: November 1957 – January 1958* (fig. 3), to hang in the entrance hall. His most enduring support for artists was to be found in the catalogue–monographs published by Lund Humphries. Like Peter Watson, the backer and art editor of Cyril Connolly's magazine, *Horizon*, Gregory was also a founder member of the ICA, which both men discreetly subsidised in its early years.[25]

Watson had sought out artists, musicians and writers in pre-war Paris, re-enacting the role of the aesthete dandy, a knowledgeable, trusted insider and confidant. On his return to England in 1939 he turned his energy to the English art world; Michael Shelden, the historian of *Horizon*, considers that 'the only person who did more to promote British art in the early 1940s was Kenneth Clark'.[26] He gave way to Connolly's pleas to collaborate on an arts review and the first issue of *Horizon* was published in December 1939. Watson's formal undertaking was to cover printing and distribution, but informally he agreed to pay salaries, contributors, advertising and other miscellaneous costs.[27] The magazine brought him into contact with young painters like Lucian Freud and John Craxton, whose drawings he published. Like John Lehmann's *New Writing*, the magazine became a conduit for bringing new art to a public cut off from any means of seeing it at source.[28]

Colin Anderson, chairman of the Orient Line, later P&O, was an energetic member of the network of committees predicated on voluntary lay participation that were the central structure of the art establishment.[29] He was also responsible for 'an astonishing record of artistic patronage'[30] which transformed his ships into floating galleries of modern art and design, commissioning, through his architect Brian O'Rorke, artists whose work he also bought for his own collection.[31] In 1953, P&O played a less glamorous but essential role in the Arts Council's exhibition '12 Australian Artists' when Anderson arranged concessionary rates for the transport of the paintings.[32]

The Contemporary Art Society exhibition '17 Collectors',[33] was drawn from the collections of members of its executive committee, who included Anderson. Eric Gregory's statement in the catalogue would probably have stood for most of them: 'I have no particular policy. I seem to form quite sudden, emotional likings, and they enlarge and enrich my experience of life.' Few had collections as grand as Kenneth Clark's, which extended from the Renaissance to Claude, Turner and Matisse. In 1947 he gave fifty-six works to the CAS[34] for distribution to museums, including twelve paintings by Sutherland, ten by Pasmore and three by Nicholson.

One of the most important private collections was E. J. Power's, which was toured by the Arts Council not long after it was first assembled. The critic Lawrence Alloway had advised on its formation, which had taken place, as he remarked, 'while the paint is still wet'.[35] Concentrated on the recent interactions

3. Patrick Heron,
*Horizontal Stripe
Painting: November
1957–January 1958*.
Oil on canvas, 110
× 60 in. Tate
Gallery, London.

between European and American painting that Alloway called 'other art', it contained names known only to a few artists in Britain, most of them assiduous visitors to Paris. The Clark and Power collections, equally important as exemplars to different generations of artists, act as symbolic markers of the period. One represented, on a grand scale, the collector as expert and arbiter of taste, while Power's approach was experimental, idiosyncratic and closely focussed on a single strand in postwar art.

Without the diverse interventions of informed private patrons, the state support system, especially for marginal organisations like the ICA, would not have been viable. Critics' assessments of the new system ranged from horror to acknowledgement of an appropriate role for the state in a socialist society, but they were united in accepting that the burden of support could no longer be reserved to the private patron.

THE STATE AS PATRON

The state's role as patron remained minimal until after the Second World War, when an unprecedented centralisation of effort and resources established the necessary conditions for official patronage. Abroad this was conducted by the British Council, founded in 1934 by industrialists,[36] while at home it was in the hands of the Arts Council, which appropriated the existing structure of CEMA, though with significantly different intentions. CEMA, as conceived by Keynes, was a wartime makeshift,[37] but when the Arts Council was formally established in 1946 it was as a permanent, modern and ambitious organisation, the cultural arm of the Welfare State.

During the war the British Council was absorbed, because of its propaganda potential, by the British Overseas Information Services, and funded through the Foreign Office. After 1945 it became clear that with greatly diminished coercive power, national status would increasingly be defined by culture. Consequently the Council became an unacknowledged arm of foreign affairs, supporting foreign policy through a velvet glove of high culture, which it promoted as a metaphor, sometimes a substitute, for political action. Cultural creativity, manifested by the modernity of contemporary art forms, was a crucial indicator of national survival and continuing vitality after the ravages of war.

The political significance of culture was recognised much earlier in Germany, France and Italy where international exhibitions had been scenes of intense rivalry since the late nineteenth century. The Venice Biennale had a unique position among them as the only one devoted exclusively to the fine arts, though it was relegated to fellow-traveller status between the wars as a forum for fascist aesthetics.[38] Re-established in 1948, it became the leading showplace for contemporary art, closely emulated by the São Paulo Bienal. The biennials and other international cultural events had immense symbolic significance at a time when governments were desperate to cement the fragile political reconstruction of Europe. The network of festivals, open-air sculpture exhibitions and biennials for paintings and prints which sprang up in western Europe during the postwar decade, with or without prizes, but nearly always with national sections administered by official agencies, were important acts of cultural diplomacy as well as aesthetic events. The exhibitions that the British Council organised for Venice were also extremely significant for the artists' careers as they were subsequently toured to three or four capital cities where they received close critical scrutiny.

Any doubts about the primary role of the British Council in these years must be dispelled by the letter written by a member of the Foreign Office to one of his colleagues, stating that 'The "cold war" is in essence a battle for men's minds. The British Council is one of our chief agencies for fighting it.'[39] At a grassroots level the Council addressed the issue through language teaching and libraries; its exhibitions, concerts and theatre tours were icing on the cake, designed to appeal to a much smaller but more influential public. Like other specialist sections, the Fine Art Department devised its own programmes but it was foreign policy that determined where they would be put into practice. Consequently its efforts were concentrated on the newly liberated European countries, including France, that the Foreign Office held to be most susceptible to Communism. These conditions favoured the Fine Art Department, with its heavy emphasis on building a close relationship with the French art world, a process that was considered so crucial that the Council employed a full-time Fine Art Officer resident in Paris to sustain it.

Frank McEwen, who held the post until he was succeeded by Roland Penrose in 1956, interpreted his job as a remit to reverse a widespread perception that British artists were essentially provincial and rated well below their French colleagues in critical estimation. A forceful, outspoken personality, McEwen was devoted to professionalism and scathingly impatient with intermittent suggestions from the Foreign Office and the Council's Executive that its exhibitions should be oriented towards generalist rather than expert reception, a situation that would have turned the British Council into an Arts Council abroad.

Without any evidence of direct interference, aesthetic prejudice occasionally presented a formidable challenge to the Fine Art Department's ferociously guarded autonomy. Alarm bells sounded when a Foreign Office official expressed the view that the Council might more profitably concentrate on activities 'with a quick return in the political field', like lectures, visits and language teaching, rather than 'exhibitions of modern painting' whose political benefit was unquantifiable and which the writer correctly perceived as being 'of interest to the intellectuals rather than the wider public'.[40] His suggestions were easily deflected,[41] but the incident illustrates the fragility of the much lauded independence of the official patronage system.

The head of the Fine Art Department from 1948 to 1970 was Lilian Somerville, a rare woman in the male-dominated network of the art establishment.[42] A powerful, difficult, but entertaining woman, affectionately remembered as Diamond Lil who, as her successor John Hulton recalled, 'loved the smell of gunpowder',[43] she had been trained as a painter, so her sympathies lay with artists, as opposed to bureaucrats. Maintaining that her job was 'to do honour to British artists',[44] she exploited her position at the core of the art establishment to assemble an Advisory Committee so powerful that it was virtually unassailable.[45] The members protected her from the Executive and, equally important, were strong enough to withstand her.

Read dominated the Advisory Committee throughout the 1950s. His *Contemporary British Art* (1951) virtually amounts to a manifesto for the British Council's exhibitions, to the extent that the point at which text and exhibiting policy diverged, particularly in the Council's emphasis on sculpture, can be taken to represent Somerville's sphere of influence. Her strong response to sculpture was echoed in the prominence given to the group of young artists whose work Read later described in a famous essay as 'the geometry of fear'.[46]

Both Read and Somerville favoured Sutherland and the painters often described as the middle generation – those born about 1920.[47] They were less enthusiastic about process-dominant art, which received less support until the late 1950s.[48] Moore, an international name since his exhibition at Curt Valentin's Bucholz Gallery in New York in 1944, represented the old avant garde,[49] together with Hepworth, Sutherland and Nicholson. They all showed in the early postwar biennials[50] but Moore's triumph in 1948, in competition with leading members of the Ecole de Paris, remained unique.

Politics and aesthetics dovetailed at Venice and São Paulo; they were the principal events in Somerville's calendar and were rigorously scrutinised by the foreign press to discern the precise status of British art, particularly in relation to the Ecole de Paris. The constant question was whether it was genuinely innovatory and a threat to French hegemony, or whether 'British painting was lagging along behind Paris in a fairly unremarkable way'.[51] When the Executive decided in 1956 to abolish the all-important Paris post in order to realign resources towards the Third World[52] and even suggested that participation at Venice might become an occasional event[53] on the grounds that Lynn Chadwick's sculpture, due to be shown in 1956, lacked general appeal and would reflect badly on the Council, members of the Fine Art Department were outraged.

After bitter recrimination they were conclusively vindicated when Chadwick in turn won the Grand Prize for Sculpture, shortly after one of the founding fathers of the Council and a member of the Executive, W. E. Rootes, had offered to fund the Paris post on a part-time basis for three years. After this absurd episode the visual arts still played a minor role in the Council's global activities, but the Department's financial situation improved,[54] and Somerville's long years of preparation began to be repaid by its prestige and success in the early 1960s.[55]

Many artists acknowledge the significant – if occasional – part the British Council played in establishing their careers, because although there were no financial benefits to be selected for an exhibition was prestigious and often offered opportunities to meet foreign dealers and critics. In the late 1950s many British artists began to show in New York commercial galleries, taking part in a transatlantic dialogue comparable to that between the studios of Paris and London in the 1930s.

The Arts Council presents a very different aspect of state patronage, eloquently summarised by a character in Angus Wilson's novel *Hemlock and After* who, rationalising the processes that have brought into being a new writers' centre, remarks: 'We can't bring the patrons back; we don't, God knows, want the State; so we have a nice little mixture of the two.'[56] Along with CEMA's structure, the Arts Council adopted its aspirations to populism, though without considering the problems of attempting to popularise high culture in competition with normal peacetime entertainments. The enthusiasm of conscripts, vividly described by Edward Ardizzone: 'Theatre packed to the door with troops which gave the company a tremendous ovation. It is amazing how the soldiers appreciate the "highbrow" ballet, opera, etc . . . Big argument for a state-run opera and ballet',[57] was to prove ephemeral once they were demobbed.

The new Council adopted the motto 'The best for the most', proposing to invest the arts with the popularity of the vicarious dreamworld of the cinema. Benevolent, philanthropic, patrician, Maynard Keynes, who died before he could become its first chairman, established an institution grounded in the ideology of the private patron[58] rather than the model of cultural democracy appropriate to a socialist administration.[59] An intractable problem was that mass participation in the production of art would have demanded the recognition of mass vernacular culture. Richard Hoggart's affectionate analysis of working class visual culture confirms that the taste of the majority was infinitely remote from Keynes's understanding of aesthetic quality: 'It loves the cornucopia, all that is generous and sprawling, that suggests splendour and wealth by sheer abundance and lavishness of colour. It loves the East, because the East is exotic and elaborate . . . the basic furnishings of the home are surmounted by articles whose main charm is their high colour and suggestion of splendour.'[60]

Most compellingly, Keynes's construction of the artist as privileged, unmediated and independent[61] precluded direct or creative patronage, since that would have amounted to interference in creative autonomy. The Council's officers were acutely aware of their accountability to the public and, beyond that, to a vociferous minority of right-wing critics who consistently sought to present the Council as repressive and reductive, asserting that, following the example of the Soviet Union, it would take over the direction of the arts in the name of state ideology. Since the press provided virtually the only means of assessing public opinion, the Council's staff was bound to pay attention to it, with the result that policy was formulated with an exaggerated caution which severely handicapped positive action. Consequently the Arts Council played an almost passive role as a conduit between artist and public until the late 1950s, following a policy apparently designed less to inspire than to avoid giving offence.

Clark's attitude, given his pivotal position, could scarcely have been less encouraging. Convinced that contemporary art was too 'esoteric and specialised' for general acceptance, he wanted the Council to concentrate on exhibitions of reproductions and loans from the national collections,[62] and although he failed to impose his restrictive ideas, there can be little doubt that had he been more supportive, the Art Department would have been able to act more positively. Instead, operating on the same arm's length principle that governed the Council's relationship with the Treasury, it depended on a network of client organisations to provide the bulk of its exhibitions while it rigorously avoided direct intervention with individual artists. These policies effectively maintained the privileged status of the high arts, since if the arts engaged with science, commerce and entertainment they might do so only on terms which underlined their separation, lest they lose their autonomy to become simply another strand in the social nexus.

Caution and conservatism were most effectively countered within the ICA, where Wilson's 'nice little mixture' appeared at its most fruitful. Founded in 1948, after a decade of preparations, it was Read's dreamchild, an unlikely outpost of Surrealism in a publicly funded organisation[63] which retained the quirky eccentricity of a private club in the down-to-earth austerity of postwar London.[64] Perpetuating old surrealist interests, its early meetings took place in a flat over Edward Mesens's London Gallery.[65] Mesens, who may have hoped to find a home for his large collection, proposed the foundation of a 'Museum of Modern Art'[66] but the consensus that emerged over the next few months was in favour of a flexible, non-aligned organisation that 'would be concerned not with the achievements of art but with the stimulation of production'.[67]

The founders included, besides Read, Penrose and Mesens, Peter Watson, Eric Gregory, the critics Robert Melville and Geoffrey Grigson, the film maker J. B. Brunius and George Hoellering, proprietor of the Academy Cinema in Oxford Street. They were soon joined by J. M. Richards, editor of *The Architectural Review* and Douglas Cooper, collector and historian. Cooper resigned before the end of the year, describing the Institute in a petulant letter to Read as 'a wildly impracti-cable hair-brained scheme'.[68] The ICA's founders mistrusted state patronage as restrictive, inclined to promote compromise and exclude innovatory art. Instead they envisaged an organisation that was experimental, international and capable of unifying all the arts.

The early ICA was ineluctably elitist; it represented a microcosm of intellectual history which originated in the Parkhill Road avant garde. Its public was an intelligentsia formed by the Spanish Civil War, the Artists International Associa-tion and *Circle*, by the ethos of Surrealism and the Euston Road School alike. It was idealistic, powerless, intellectually exclusive, neither seeking nor possessing a common touch. Yet it owed its existence to the Arts Council, without whose financial assistance it would never have progressed beyond the Brook Street flat.

The Council welcomed the ICA; as Philip James, Director of the Art Depart-ment, remarked: 'They arrange their own exhibitions, many of which relieve the Arts Council of a certain responsibility, especially in the field of avant-garde art.'[69] James, encouraged by Kenneth Clark, was to be one of the Institute's strongest supporters.[70] He realised that the ICA had a licence to practise a creative irrespon-sibility that the Arts Council, visibly dependent on public money, could never claim, whereas the ICA offered a unique stimulus to creativity.

It would initiate and provide a locus for a wide range of activities, not all obviously connected with the arts, which would soon broaden and diffuse its surrealist affinities. By stimulating cross-disciplinary encounters which focussed on science and anthropology, Read may even have seen in the ICA a practical application of his anarchist beliefs.[71] It would be the leaven in the dough of an industrial society in which, particularly during the war, the freedom of the indi-vidual creator had necessarily been subordinated to the needs of the state.

As well as focussing on the visual arts, lectures, discussions and films were concerned with psychoanalysis and anthropology, the latter encouraged by Penrose's friendship with William Fagg, then Deputy Keeper of Ethnography at the British Museum.[72] Film, drama and poetry were important components of the Institute's programme and in the early 1950s it was well known as a jazz centre. After the opening of the Dover Street premises, designed by Jane Drew, which included a members' bar, library and small gallery, the eclectic exhibition pro-gramme provided a focus for debates on contemporary art, particularly the rap-idly developing forms of abstraction.[73]

The Institute celebrated its formal foundation in February 1948 with the opening of '40 Years of Modern Art' in the basement of the Academy Cinema. An interna-tional exhibition of paintings made between 1907 and 1947, drawn from British collections, it was criticised within the Institute as over-conservative,[74] since the organisers had decided to steer clear of controversy in order to avoid alienating potential supporters. Nevertheless it was theatrically signalled by the surreal presence, among the bomb-damage of Oxford Street, of F. E. McWilliam's *Sculp-ture 1948*, which belonged to Penrose.[75] The exhibition attracted considerable critical attention and many visitors, successfully announcing the Institute and initiating what would become a central policy of setting British artists alongside their foreign contemporaries.

The second exhibition, '40,000 Years of Modern Art', which opened in Decem-ber the same year, was very different: a juxtaposition of ancient, tribal and modern art, it courted controversy, was praised for its conjunction of art and science and is said to have attracted 20,000 visitors.[76] Its centre-piece, shown for the first time in Britain, was Picasso's *Demoiselles d'Avignon* (1907), lent by the Museum of Modern Art, New York in a gesture of generosity by Alfred Barr to his friend Penrose.[77] When the painting reached Oxford Street it was found to be too large to manoeuvre down the basement stairs, so a hole was knocked through a side wall into the street and embellished, in an authentically surreal spirit, to match the adjacent bomb damage.

As the Institute had no premises until December 1950, its activities were severely limited for its first three years. Lack of money was a constant problem, only partially alleviated by regular contributions from the wealthier members of the Management Committee. Poverty meant that a curiously random sequence of exhibitions was taken as fillers, often from American sources,[78] but the organisers managed to maintain a uniquely international policy, focussing predominantly on contemporary art from France and the United States, with exhibitions like 'London-Paris' (1950)[79] and 'Opposing Forces' (1953) which included the first paintings by Pollock to be shown in Britain.[80] The selection of 'Opposing Forces' precipitated John Berger's resignation from the Institute's exhibitions committee in protest at the rejection of his counter-proposal for a group of artists who had 'retained their indigenous characteristics'.[81] After he was overruled he wrote to Penrose: 'I do feel that the ICA and myself – for better or for worse – are on different sides of the fence.'[82] A few years later, when the Institute was established as the creative and intellectual centre of the London art world, solo exhibitions of Jean Dubuffet (1955), Georges Mathieu (1956),[83] Wolfgang Wols (1957),[84] Henri Michaux and Jean Fautrier (1958) provided access to gestural painting at the moment when it emerged from the studios to become the dominant preoccupation of the avant garde.

Recently the ICA has been overshadowed by interest in its progeny, the Independent Group. The significance of the Independent Group's reassessment of the place of art and architecture in society should not conceal the fact that it was one of several disparate groups that emerged from the parent body, nor that the Institute was the only organisation capable of providing the conditions in which it could develop.

Artists were not the only beneficiaries of the ICA; the opening of the Dover Street rooms transformed a private organisation into a society with ever-increasing obligations to its lay members. Essential for their financial contributions, they fulfilled Read's vision of the Institute as a *foyer* where artists, writers, musicians, actors, scientists and creative thinkers could meet. Though the 'laboratory' could not function without such an exchange, these conditions were also the Institute's weakness; the precarious balance between intense private activity, public exhibitions and mundane fund-raising was all too easily disturbed, and when the ICA moved to Carlton House Terrace in 1968 it was transformed into a more robust but less sensitive organism.

EXHIBITING SYSTEMS

In 1945 the exhibiting system was reduced to a skeleton that would not be fully fleshed out until the 1960s.[85] Since the Tate was unable to promote contemporary art adequately, this function was parcelled out between exhibiting groups and commercial galleries in a makeshift accomodation which failed to acknowledge the distinction between the artist-led societies, headed by the Royal Academy, and profit-making dealer galleries. Many artists belonged both to the London Group[86] and the Artists' International Association, the principal non-academic exhibiting societies. In that both were open to an extraordinarily wide range of practice, they were potentially equally attractive, though contemporaries and historians are united in seeing them as politically polarised. For the Left, associated with the AIA, the London Group in the 1930s was 'largely . . . the epitome of faded, Bloomsbury aesthetics'.[87] A decade later the critic Roger Marvell described its annual show as 'what the Royal Aacademy exhibition ought to be':[88] an area between academicism and stylistic proscription.

Founded in 1933, the AIA's purpose was to promote peace by furthering the cause of the working class and opposition to Fascism. It was active during the war, with touring shows and print schemes, but its political impetus diminished after 1945, as a result of hostility to the Left during the Cold War and a sense that with the victory against Fascism and the social innovations of the Labour government its political aims had been fulfilled.[89] A right/left split developed within the organisation, with the right led by the art critic of *The Guardian*, Stephen Bone. In 1952 the split was transposed into visual terms in an exhibition called 'The Mirror and the Square'. Athough this purported to have no political purpose and simply to be a survey of contemporary art, polarised between social realism (the mirror) and constructive abstraction (the square),[90] the dichotomy marked the end of the AIA's endeavour to transcend ideological difference in support of common causes. The following year, as is well known, the political clause, which had formally defined the Association as a strong and active left-wing organisation, was dropped from the constitution[91] and the AIA, which since 1945 had been a club with premises in Lisle Street, became simply another exhibiting society.

As Roger Marvell's comment suggests, by 1945 the Royal Academy was surviving on its reputation and its ability to supply what Andrew Brighton has called consensus art to conservative, middle-class patrons.[92] Yet although the Summer Exhibition represented, well into the 1950s, a norm both for the critics who accorded it more column inches than any other exhibition and the public who flocked to it, the Academy was perhaps less monolithic than Brighton's account suggests. Sir Alfred Munnings, its President from 1944 to 1949, chose the occasion of the first postwar Academy Banquet, in April 1949, to deliver a drunken diatribe against modernism and, especially, Picasso and the 'School of Paris'.[93] This social occasion of splendour and high formality was attended by Field Marshall Montgomery, the Archbishop of Canterbury, and Munnings's friend and admirer Winston Churchill. Since the speeches were broadcast, the occasion was transformed from a private dinner to a public event, a strand in the debate about the relationships between art, artists and the public. Numerous listeners felt sufficiently involved to write in support of the President's views.[94]

After his resignation, defiantly anticipated in his Banquet speech, Munnings kept up a barrage of protest against the modernist works which began to appear in the Summer Exhibition, if only in token numbers, under his successor, the impeccably orthodox portraitist, Sir Gerald Kelly (President of the Royal Academy 1949–54). In 1956 Munnings himself submitted a satirical painting, *Does the Subject Matter?* (fig. 4), which shows, gathered round what he described as a Hepworth sculpture in the Tate, a caricatural group of Rothenstein, Humphrey Brooke, Assistant Director of the Tate, John Mavrogordato, the Professor of Greek at Oxford, Thomas Bodkin, then a vociferous right-wing critic and Patricia Pooter, a model.[95] In the year when Abstract Expressionism arrived in London, it was a pathetic rather than a defiant gesture.

4. Alfred Munnings, *Does the Subject Matter?*, 1956. Oil on canvas, 31 × 42$\frac{1}{2}$ in. The Sir Alfred Munnings Art Museum, Dedham, Essex.

After Munnings's departure, Kelly presided over several important historical loan exhibitions and, more significant to modernists, the 'Ecole de Paris 1900–50' (1951), the first such exhibition in London in a non-commercial space. A year later Nicolas de Staël's first British show, at the Matthiessen Gallery,[96] of paintings made between 1946 and 1952, dramatically proclaimed the return of contemporary French art to London's commercial galleries.[97] His paintings had an immense impact on artists in Britain.[98] They established a model for abstract painting between lyrical abstraction which, as the phrase suggests, was harmonious and somewhat unfocussed, often taking its themes from nature or religion and the hard-edged, geometric precision of the very different kind of abstract imagery closely associated with the Galerie Denise René, which was its centre in 1940s Paris. In 1953, the Arts Council toured 'Young Painters of the Ecole de Paris',[99] a complement to the Academy show and an acknowledgement of the extent to which the postwar Ecole de Paris had become the focus of interest for British contemporaries.

Thematic shows originated by artists and critics, which had previously been rare, spectacular events like the 1936 International Surrealist exhibition, rapidly began to displace the eclectic presentations of the exhibiting societies. None took place at the Tate; instead 'Space in Colour', organised by the painter–critic Patrick Heron, 'Nine Abstract Artists', 'Dimensions' and 'Metavisual, Tachiste, Abstract' were all held in commercial galleries.[100]

None of these equalled the impact of the two exhibitions of modern American art housed by the Tate in 1956 and 1959. Both were organised by MoMA, New York and were seen in London in the course of European tours. The first, 'Modern Art in the United States', contained a single room, the only section that is remembered today, devoted to Abstract Expressionism, whereas 'The New American Painting' was entirely given over to Abstract Expressionism and Post-painterly abstraction. Although 'The New American Painting' has long been supposed to have been originated by the USIS as an ideological weapon in the Cold War cultural machine, Stacey Tenenbaum has demonstrated that on the contrary, it was organised by MoMA in response to requests by the directors of prominent western European museums.[101] Both exhibitions had a profound impact on virtually every artist who saw them; they were among the most significant exhibitions the Tate had ever mounted and certainly the most important for contemporary artists since 'Picasso and Matisse'. That had attracted huge crowds to the Victoria and Albert Museum when it opened in December 1945, a response that acknowledged the symbolic reforging of links with France after six years of isolation. 'Picasso and Matisse' aroused intense controversy and, despite its attraction for artists, it underlined their indebtedness to France, whereas 'Modern Art in the United States' indicated the begining of a new relationship with the New York School.

THE COMMERCIAL SCENE

The first important development in the postwar art trade was the emergence of dealers like Gimpel Fils and the Redfern Gallery[102] who could negotiate between a conservative clientele and advanced artists by laying off losses on contemporary art against a secure trade in nineteenth-century French painting and prints.[103] Gimpel Fils, hailed as the champion of young artists, drew on its long experience in Paris to become an important source of information on contemporary French art,[104] balancing it with the prestigious annual 'Gimpel's Young Contemporaries' selected from the larger show at the RBA Galleries.[105] Discussing modern-oriented galleries in 1957, Basil Taylor singled out Gimpel Fils as 'the most authoritative purveyors of the art of the avant-garde'.[106] The Redfern played a central role at the start of the postwar print boom, founding the London Society of Painter-Printers in 1948 with the sisters Caroline Lucas and Frances Byng Stamper. As the first dealers to support process-dominant art, which was widely felt to be visually and theoretically intractable, and the hosts to exibitions like 'Nine Abstract Artists' and 'Metavisual, Tachiste, Abstract', Taylor gave the Redfern a much rougher ride, remarking that the gallery had 'recently fallen for action painting and fallen in a most uncritical spirit'.

All dealers, even long-established galleries like the Lefevre and the Leicester, were affected by the import regulations, relaxed in 1949 but only fully rescinded in 1954, which imposed 100 per cent duty on foreign works of art if they were retained for longer than six months.[107] As a result very little French art – the London dealers' staple – was to be seen in commercial galleries and British artists benefited from a brief monopoly in the supply of contemporary work.[108] The relationship between contemporary art and the Lefevre and the Leicester Galleries, long-established markers of wealth and social status, underlines the complexity of the commercial scene. Neither was an avant-garde centre; their contemporary artists were modern masters like Moore and Nicholson or, those, firmly in the mainstream, like John Minton and Keith Vaughan, yet inclusion in the galleries' group exhibitions, particularly the Leicester's twice-yearly 'Artists of Fame and Promise', was eagerly sought as a seal of approval.[109]

As the exhibiting societies became more flexible, the commercial system expanded in response to the number and variety of artists demanding exhibition space. A clutch of small, idiosyncratic galleries, where profit-making took second place to the promotion of innovatory art, announced a new way of mediating between artists and the public. Two of the most distinguished, run by women, were models for an approach which involved the steadfast support of a few artists carefully chosen on the basis of personal taste. Erica Brausen was the champion of Francis Bacon and Reg Butler and the conduit to a London public of such luminaries as Alberto Giacometti and Jean Arp. Her Hanover Gallery (1948–72) is particularly associated with artists concerned with the human body, a focus that, unusually, meant that sculpture was as prominent as painting in its exhibitions.

Helen Lessore's Beaux Arts Gallery was the first of the 'small polemical' galleries[110] that existed for the term of an individual's interest, energy and financial capability. Best known for having nurtured the Beaux Arts Quartet – John Bratby, Derrick Greaves, Edward Middleditch and Jack Smith – it was identified with realist painting at the Slade and the Royal College, from which Lessore drew most of her artists.[111] The Quartet was chosen to show at the 1956 Venice Biennale and subsequent emphasis on it has had the effect of marginalising Lessore's centrality in the development of the group of painters now known as the School of London, who were committed to the imagery of the body and the city. Lessore is acknowledged as one of the most discriminating and perceptive dealers of the period, though her intensely personal and proselytising gallery, in which she also lived, was much less commercially successful than the Hanover.

Victor Musgrave conducted a comparably idiosyncratic operation at Gallery One,[112] which progressed from 'a tatty upper room in Lichfield St'[113] to 'snow-white walls and expensively simple fittings'[114] in North Audley Street and was distinguished for promoting art outside the mainstream, including the first London showings of Enrico Baj's 'nuclear paintings'[115] and of the French Nouveau Réaliste, Yves Klein, in 1957. Musgrave also showed artists, like Frank Souza, from the Indian subcontinent who, though well established in their own countries, experienced immense difficulty in penetrating the western art system.[116]

Less smart, completely non-commercial but as tightly focussed as the Beaux Arts was the New Vision Centre Gallery. Described at the end of its first year as 'Fiercely non-figurative, violently tachiste, remarkably international',[117] it was founded in 1956 by three painters, Denis Bowen, Halima Nalecz and Frank Avray Wilson, housed in two basement rooms in Seymour Place and funded by its directors. Its policy of mounting solo shows by young, unknown, often foreign artists was only possible because it was a non-profit making organisation.[118] Since it was exclusively devoted to non-figurative art at a time when Action Painting was the biggest joke since Moore's holes it received a good deal of sensationalist press coverage but it performed a unique role, in which it was the complement to Gallery One, by promoting international gestural art.

Both galleries spanned a period when the status of British art was widely debated. Their contribution was to set it in an international context in which common interests were more important than the preservation of national differences. It was also a time when exhibiting conventions changed profoundly, in response to the first Happenings and performance art, and the critical redefinition of the art object. It is axiomatic within modernism that the way a work is shown determines its significance, but within the mainstream commercial system, even the most radical exhibitions were conventionally hung. Only in situations where selling was not the primary imperative was it possible to devise exhibition formats that encouraged unorthodox readings of work already singled out as mould-breaking. At the Symon Quinn Gallery in Huddersfield in 1955 Roger Hilton's paintings were hung not on the walls, but between steel poles, regularly disposed throughout the gallery, so that they could be read as elements within architecture rather than canvases on a wall.

ART PUBLISHING

The diversification of the exhibiting system was paralleled by developments in art publishing that were equally essential to the growth of a postwar vanguard. Galleries depended heavily on the press for publicity, but writers were slow to respond to the challenges posed by artists by providing an arena for theoretical debate, though art publishing expanded rapidly once wartime restrictions on the use of paper were eased. Reviews, not subject to paper rationing, kept alive the tradition of the eccentric, specialised journals known as little magazines and supported innovative, high quality writing. *Horizon* was the doyen of reviews, individual and as unpredictable as Gallery One. Its leading competitors operated within jealously demarcated areas of interest, indicated by Denys Val Baker's reference to 'a large group of young poets barred by political outlook from *New Writing*'.[119] John Lehmann's enormously popular review[120] had a more restricted editorial policy, grounded in socially conscious realism, though its illustrations, which ranged from war art to theatre design, are among the most succinct indicators of the eclecticism of visual art during the war.

Those excluded from *New Writing* found opportunities in *Poetry London*, the prestigious if irregular magazine founded in 1943 by Tambimuttu, which carried covers and illustrations by Moore, Sutherland and their contemporaries. Beyond its literary merit, *Poetry London* became, as the personification of its eccentric and exotic editor, an emblem of the literary and artistic sub-culture of Fitzrovia, in whose pubs and clubs poets and painters met almost nightly and which provided the nearest equivalent to an avant-garde milieu during the war.

In the diversification that followed the years of restriction, *The Studio* remained the leading contemporary art magazine, despite often dull writing and mediocre colour reproduction and ever-increasing competition from more specialised, small-circulation journals. The postwar *Studio* aspired to broad coverage and a centrist critical position until 1960 when its editor, G. S. Whittet, transformed its appearance and extended its scope, adding 'International' to the title.

The indispensable source of information on young artists, new galleries and innovatory work was *Art News & Review*, founded in 1948 by Richard Gainsborough, a retired medical doctor, in order to provide, as no other magazine did, full coverage of London exhibitions from historical surveys to studio shows.[121] Edited until 1954 by Bernard Denvir, *Art News & Review* was a tabloid format, low-cost fortnightly, published entirely without colour. Its contributors included most of the leading critics of the period, though they were fewer than is suggested by the contents page: one eminent art historian began his career by writing for the magazine under no less than four pseudonyms, each with an individual literary style.

The little art magazine, often edited by an artist or critic, gradually revived during the late 1940s. *Eidos*, edited by E. H. Ramsden and Margot Eates, included among its contributors Rudolph Wittkower and Henri Breuil; *London Broadsheet*, devoted to promoting Tachisme,[122] and *Other Voices*, founded, edited and written by the painter Ralph Rumney,[123] which survived for six issues before he succumbed to exhaustion, were, like the small, specialised galleries, polemical, personal organs of expression financed by their editors. One of the most distinctive artist-run magazines was *The Painter and Sculptor*,[124] founded and edited by Patrick and Barbara Hayman to publish strongly individual writing rather than up to the minute information. The magazine drew much of its content from artists in St Ives and was the first to publish articles such as Peter Lanyon's analysis of the relationship between landscape and action painting.

Roger Coleman edited *ARK*, the Royal College student magazine, from November 1956 to the following August, transforming it from a college-based publication more interesting for its typography than its content into essential reading for architects and art professionals.[125] With its emphasis on the contemporary vernacular of film and communications, its intimations of Pop, its slick professionalism and disregard for academic convention, Coleman's *ARK* signalled the end of austerity and the advent of the youth culture of the 1960s.

Art books played little part in the publishing boom of the war years,[126] though the Penguin Modern Painters series established a hierarchy, which closely reflected the taste of its general editor, Kenneth Clark, based on artists prominent in the 1930s, from William Nicholson to Moore. With rare exceptions, the series focussed on British artists. Ambitious plans were laid for a worldwide series, but 'only the two Americans, Ben Shahn and Edward Hopper were published',[127] together with Douglas Cooper's *Paul Klee* (1949). In drab brown paper covers, the books were cheap and intended for a wide readership.[128] After the war, studies like the *Documents of Modern Art* series, which presented modernism as a revolutionary, pioneering force, were in great demand by young artists trying to slough off a rigidly academic training. Tiranti's artists' shop in Charlotte Street and Zwemmer's Bookshop were the rare, renowned outlets for these and sought-after foreign books and periodicals such as *Cahiers d'Art*, *Cimaise* and *L'Art d'Aujourd'hui*. When currency regulations restricted foreign travel these copiously illustrated magazines became indispensable substitutes for visits to Paris.

By the end of the 1950s advances in reproductive technology and colour printing had transformed both magazines and exhibition catalogues, which developed from small folders with a list of works and sparse monochrome reproductions, into lavishly illustrated, lengthy critical texts, culminating in the book-length productions published by the Whitechapel Art Gallery. Conversely, those published by the NVCG were eye-catching confections of colour and texture, with often arcane texts, written by the artists.

ART EDUCATION

Rodrigo Moynihan's celebrated *Portrait Group (The Teaching Staff at the Royal College of Art, 1949–50)* (1951) is as revealing in its straightforward sobriety as Heron's portrait of Read and Sutherland's of Clark. Moynihan showed himself holding a palette, the only suggestion that this is a portrayal of painters; only John Minton's defiant isolation from the main group suggests anything more dynamic than a group of small-town businessmen. In 1948, when Robin Darwin became Principal and Moynihan was appointed Professor of Painting, the College was associated with realist painting, from Ruskin Spear's street scenes in a belated post-impressionist manner to Minton's history paintings. Nothing suggested that within eight years it would see student-led confrontations with dominant orthodoxies which were to play a central role in the assimilation of American painting. They were part of the process of reversal of pedagogical certainties that profoundly changed both art schools and art production during the postwar decade.

Many of those who became art students after six years in the forces would not have been able to afford their training without the ex-servicemen's grant,[129] though this much valued scheme brought its own problems. John Plumb has recalled the overcrowding that resulted from this educational largesse in 1947, with students at the Byam Shaw School sitting on the floor and sharing donkeys.[130] Mature students, all too aware of lost time, rejected authoritarian teaching and old disciplines of meticulous life drawing and tonal painting, the formal skills essential to the academic artist. Acceptance of these conventions would have suggested that the war had changed nothing, that the new Labour government would have no impact. Just as in Russia and Germany after earlier conflicts, artists responded to new social formations with radicalised art forms that would, they hoped, demonstrate art's centrality to the majority that had hitherto ignored it.

Though these conditions applied only to a small number of art schools, mostly in London, they were 'the country's primary support system for contemporary art, providing not only a basic income but also places and occasions for debate'.[131] Some of the most radical developments, which profoundly affected the course of avant-garde art, took place in the craft-based schools where the demands of multi-disciplinary and multi-media teaching had a liberating effect on the imagination of those who designed courses. The new methods were first developed during William Johnstone's terms of office as Principal successively of Camberwell School of Art (1938–47) and the Central School of Art and Crafts (1947–62).

Towards the end of the war Pasmore, then a part-time Visitor at Camberwell, persuaded Johnstone to appoint Claude Rogers, William Coldstream and Lawrence Gowing as colleagues.[132] Camberwell thus reunited a group of painters devoted to perpetuating the Euston Road approach to painting,[133] grounded in accurate, unmediated recording, aided by a rigorous system of measurement from fixed points, invented by Coldstream.[134] Euston Road realism was exemplified by the painting, *Bolton* (1938), which he made during a Mass Observation exercise to which Tom Harrison had invited him, together with Graham Bell.[135] Coldstream's dark, factual painting, apparently a view from the roof of Bolton Art Gallery,[136] amounted to a visual equivalent of Harrison's and Charles Madge's quasi-anthropological recording methods.

In the late 1940s Pasmore, Kenneth Martin and some of their students at Camberwell began to investigate proportional systems. While these offered intellectual flexibility and were to be the basis of their constructive art, the extent to which Pasmore himself, Coldstream's pursuit of measured accuracy or the new availability of certain mathematical texts[137] was responsible for this interest remains an open question, though Camberwell certainly provided an atmosphere in which such things could be discussed.

When Coldstream was appointed Slade Professor in 1949 he took with him the system of measurement which is still the yardstick of what is widely recognised as a Slade style. Before his arrival, the School's didactic rigidity had caused William Turnbull and Eduardo Paolozzi to break off their courses and depart precipitately for Paris. Their contemporary Adrian Heath considered the requirement that he learn 'to draw the nude like Ingres'[138] equally anachronistic and though he completed his course he valued the Slade's teaching only for providing a sound technical training. They all fared better than women students: the life-room was Coldstream's territory, only to be entered at his invitation, which was only extended to men.[139] During his long term of office[140] the Slade was associated with an empirical aesthetic of truthful appearance which some critics, notably the late

Peter Fuller, have seen as the central British tradition. Robert Medley's *The Antique Room at the Slade: Niobe and Hermes*, (1952)[141] in which classical casts were casually sketched against an undefined space, cogently emphasised the liberalisation that Coldstream introduced to an institution dominated by nineteenth-century precepts. The figurative European tradition remained central, but the way in which it might be interpreted shifted forward significantly.

By the early 1950s a formidable group of young artists, who not long before had been disillusioned students, were installed on the staff of the Central School[142] where teaching intermeshed with radical practice, encouraging open-ended experiment rather than didacticism.[143] Paolozzi, a sculptor and printmaker, was in the textile department; a painter, Alan Davie, taught jewellery-making; Nigel Henderson ran a course in creative photography. The close links between the School, the ICA and the Independent Group[144] underline the pivotal position of the Central School at a point when artists were reaching out for conceptual tools to explore modernism.

A similar revolution in teaching took place in the Department of Fine Art at King's College, Durham, where Pasmore was appointed Master of Painting in 1954. With Richard Hamilton he devised a basic design course involving carefully constructed exercises[145] in which students progressed from simple mark making to complex three-dimensional constructions. Together with Tom Hudson, lecturer in charge of basic design at Leeds College of Art from 1956 to 1960, they formulated their teaching at summer schools in Scarborough, developing interests in microscopy, popular culture and process,[146] which had been widely discussed by the Independent Group.

Basic design courses, drawing on Bauhaus methods and early twentieth-century art history[147] sought to make students aware of their own expressive potential and that of their materials through 'step-by-step teaching beginning with rectangles and developing with exercises in abstract shapes, textures, form and colour'.[148] As much an enquiry into the nature of art and creativity as a pedagogic method, basic design provided insights into process and the physical formation of a work of art without itself claiming aesthetic status, but by the mid-1960s it had lost its inventive edge and was sometimes seen as a formula for making abstract art. Though this is absurdly reductive, the exact nature of its relationship with the development of abstraction is still disputed. Richard Hamilton has written of the 'major distortion' inherent in 'the implication that basic design can teach art students to become Modern Artists, that Abstract Art is the objective of basic design studies',[149] but in general Jessica Morgan is probably correct in concluding that basic design was a crucial component in the development of abstraction.[150]

Despite their diversity, teachers of basic design were united in rejecting the methods developed by Clifford Ellis at the Bath Academy of Art at Corsham[151] to stimulate intuitive, gestural painting.[152] Ellis derived much of his methodology from Marion Richardson, the pioneer educationalist in children's art, particularly his deep belief in the importance of an unconditioned, empathetic response to sensory phenomena.[153] His unorthodox approach was constructed within an attitude to landscape painting in which the purpose was to evoke its characteristic colours, scents, weather and terrain, a transformative process which Peter Lanyon, who saw teaching as 'a dangerous journey',[154] described as 'starting in an extreme awareness of oneself in a place, ends in an extreme awareness of oneself in painting'.[155]

Ellis insisted that his staff teach according to the evolution of their own practices and felt that they would be stimulated by teaching subjects in which they did not specialise, with the result that Robyn Denny and Adrian Heath, both established abstract painters, taught photography and life drawing. Heath acknowledged this as a valuable experience since it coincided with his decision to break away from the restrictions of geometric painting. He developed a method of teaching life drawing as an extension of art history classes on Cubism and Futurism. A long roll of paper was attached to the wall of the studio, where the models wandered around, never holding a formal pose, while the students drew repeated images of their continuous movement, without raising their hands from the paper.

The reformulation of an avant garde was intimately linked with changes that took place in art education, publishing and patronage. The support system of the 1960s, which encompassed the events of 1968, the granting of state subsidy for the wilder shores of the Destruction in Art Symposium and an explosion of publishing, contributed, in its stylish diversity, to a perception of the postwar years as a specific period, albeit an interim one, a time of profound change and increasingly confident experiment, which had ended by 1961.

3

CRITICAL DILEMMAS

Art is a bloodsport and not a ball-game.
David Sylvester, 1952[1]

When, in 1950 Patrick Heron, already a prominent member of a new generation of critics, painted the man he described as 'the Philosopher of Modern Art', Herbert Read (fig. 2), he was alluding to his sitter's ability to draw together psycho-analysis, art history, children's art, the Modern Movement, Surrealism and poli-tics. Read was almost alone among his contemporaries in addressing art as a complex, plural, challenging phenomenon not to be contained by propriety, con-vention or tradition. With an enormous output of books, exhibition catalogues, reviews and articles, he became known, David Thistlewood comments, 'as an (occasionally reckless) defender of the emergent'.[2] It was one of many factors that set him apart from the critics on the daily broadsheets whose remit was to make accessible to the general reader an extraordinary range of art, from the contempo-rary Ecole de Paris to ancient Mexico, from Augustus John to Victor Pasmore, from the Royal Society of Sculptors to children's drawings.

John Minton's portrait of Nevile Wallis (1952) (fig. 5), art critic of *The Observer*, shows the thoughtful critic in the studio, in scrupulous examination of an easel painting. Art, this portrayal suggests, has its place and its limitations and they are as precisely delimited as the studio itself, lightly touched by a modernising clarity that corresponded to Wallis's cautious but enquiring attitude to contemporary art. A wary, slightly suspicious liberalism, detailed attention to the work of art as a physical object and disregard for philosophical content characterised many of Wallis's fellow critics for the broadsheet dailies.

Their colleagues on the weeklies were able to address more theoretical issues, though Patrick Heron recalls that his frequent references to space in painting finally drove the editor of *The New Statesman & Nation* to seek out a critic less concerned with formal issues, which were felt to be too arcane for the average reader.[3] Heron's replacement was the Marxist John Berger who ironically proved to be an equally sharp thorn in the editorial flesh, though for different reasons.

David Sylvester, who wrote regularly first for *The Listener* and later for *Encounter*, turned the demand for versatility to extraordinary creative account. His enthusiasms were always passionate, committed and partisan. His first important article was a poetic reverie on Paul Klee for the American magazine, *The Tiger's Eye*, written in 1948 when he was caught up in the implications of Existentialism. It was followed by commentaries on current art in Paris and especially Alberto Giacometti; a long and important series of articles on Henry Moore which extended throughout the 1950s; reviews of Francis Bacon's work which constituted virtually the only early analytic writing on the artist and later, perceptive comments on the young realist painters championed by Berger.

As mediators between artists and the public, critics spoke with conflicting voices, addressing many different publics whose knowledge of and engagement with art were as diverse as its creators. There is a slippage from one writer to another, one journal to another, in which trends and generalisations are contradicted as soon as they emerge; only extreme positions are relatively easily defined. Within a body of writing that all too often seems committed to the safety of well-worn ideas there are hints of a discourse which embraced themes such as Primitivism,[4] Existentialism and tradition, though references have to be teased out and inferred, only to remain inconclusive. The dilemmas that confronted critics lay in these ill-identified theoretical issues, in their constructions of artists and readers, in attempts to define an avant garde and, most acutely, in the inflection of art by politics.

5. John Minton, *Portrait of Nevile Wallis*, 1952. Oil on canvas, 48 × 60 in. The Royal Pavilion, Art Gallery & Museums, Brighton.

THE CRITIC AND THE PUBLIC

A perceived gulf between writers and readers was a source of much concern to socially-conscious critics in the late 1940s. Art had suddenly become a political issue; dismissing metaphysical connotations, it made ideological claims; it appeared in utterly unfamiliar forms with an obscure theoretical content and demanded a new language with which to discuss it.

The compound of rumour and prejudice known as public opinion is notoriously difficult to assess. We seldom understand how it is formulated, though the unnamed 'they' is often the agent that acts as a catalyst to a summary, by a third party, of general opinion. They are powerful and malevolent, contributors to a sense of paranoia, of being 'got at', which may be a constituent of rumour and prejudice.[5]

In an attempt to discern the mechanisms of public opinion Harry Hopkins suggested that *The Daily Mirror* ignored diversity or contradiction and simply presented readers with a consensus which was to be accepted as normative. The paper was 'a mirror whose first necessity was to reflect . . . a collective image or *persona* of its readers . . . and out again was projected a bright, sharp, larger-than-life image which had a considerable, if elusive, effect on the evolution of post-war society.'[6] On this model, editorial policy was to repackage the assumed prejudices, fears and affections of a collective readership, to reinforce its loyalty to the paper by appearing to act as its mouthpiece.

This collective voice was seldom heard directly, since though people flocked in thousands to important exhibitions, they were rarely invited to record their reactions. When they did so, notoriously at the 'Unknown Political Prisoner' exhibition in 1953, they expressed outrage on finding that art did not precisely mirror their experience; that Reg Butler's winning maquette (fig. 106) showed few signs of conventional skill, or the use of expensive materials and that there was no well-established precedent for the way in which its symbolic content was articulated. The artist, in short, had failed as a communicator of commonly held values. For a brief time in the spring of 1953 Butler became a popular demon. Over a much longer period his work epitomised the unpopular face of the visual arts: difficult, esoteric and defiant of convention, it was also labelled abstract and avant-garde, both sensitive triggers to indignation.

Popularity was reserved for paintings like those of the neo-Impressionist Ruskin Spear (fig. 6), whose combination of accessible subject matter, style and luscious paint led Nigel Gosling to conclude that he 'succeeds in bridging the gulf between the specialist's and the public's fancy; and that, today, is as rare as it is heart-warming'.[7] Expectations that artists and viewers might be drawn together through activities at arts centres or the beneficient effects of state sponsored exhibitions were short-lived. As early as 1949 a *Times* leader writer asked plaintively why critics, hitherto 'on the side of general opinion', were 'so often with the advance guard, leaving the ordinary man to his bewilderment'.[8] Phrases like 'the ordinary man' indicated both an awareness of a lingering, rigid class structure which restricted access to high culture, and a desire to see that structure's demise. Following a change of government and the retrenchment of the Arts Council's early aspirations, the ordinary man was less often invoked and the divergence suggested by the *Times* leader became increasingly obvious, forcing a wedge between the critic's roles as explicator of the arcane and champion of the creator.

6. Ruskin Spear,
Hammersmith Café,
c.1945. Jonathan
Clarke Fine Art,
London.

The problems raised by the Unknown Political Prisoner competition were not new but the event brought an unusual prominence to the relationship between critics and the public and to the seething cauldron of attitudes concealed by the phrase abstract art. The gradual transformation of the relationship between writers and readers can be plotted through the language of criticism and the attitudes implicit in it. Fired by social idealism, some writers adopted the accessible language but patronising tone with which Maynard Keynes had introduced the Arts Council in his broadcast in 1946, using the words of teacher to pupil or initiate to outsider. A few years later Nigel Gosling loftily advised a hypothetical reader, confronted with contemporary French painting at the Royal Academy, in very similar terms: 'let him forget his usual ideas of a picture, let him respond simply, as he would in front of a poster, to the display of colour and invention'.[9]

A formidable bar to an informed discussion of modernism and, in particular, abstract art, was the lack of a common terminology. 'The vocabulary of so-called "abstract art" is in appalling condition', wrote Lawrence Alloway in 1953, 'But this is no justification of the aesthetic evasions of dealers, critics, and artists who are lost in semantic chaos.'[10] The constructionist artists with whom he was closely associated achieved a degree of semantic clarity by distinguishing different types of process. Pasmore's *Spiral Motif in Green, Violet, Blue and Gold: the Coast of the Inland Sea* (1950) (fig. 36) and Robert Adams's *Apocalyptic Figure* (1950) (fig. 38)[11] both represented the very large category of art conventionally called abstract, 'by which we mean', Read explained, echoing Alfred Barr, 'an art derived from nature, the pure or essential form abstracted from the concrete details'.[12]

Despite Read's confidence, abstraction was clearly not a simple category. Alloway distinguished Read's phenomenological perceptual abstraction from the more precise concrete art, by which he meant 'paintings without external reference', [13] like Kenneth Martin's *Composition* (1949). This painting was reproduced, with the title 'Abstract', on the first page of the now legendary avant-garde publication, *Broadsheet No.1 Devoted to Abstract Art*, where it illustrated the artist's article, 'Abstract art', in which he first set out the distinction between abstract and concrete reiterated by Alloway:

> What is generally termed abstract is not to be confused with the abstraction from nature which is concerned with the visual aspect of nature and its reduction and distortion to a pictorial form . . . abstract art has . . . become a construction or concretion coming from within. The abstract painting is the result of a creative process absolutely the opposite to abstraction.[14]

Martin's painting introduced his preoccupation with chance, change and movement, which he explored through process, in distinction to the images made by Pasmore and Adams and reproduced on subsequent pages.

Broadsheet No.1 was produced to coincide with an exhibition of abstract art at the AIA Gallery in the summer of 1951.[15] It was a manifesto, explanation and proclamation of a multi-media, international approach to art now in its second generation. The diversity of material in this very slender publication[16] and its sense of a common purpose among fine artists, architects and planners inevitably recall *Circle*, the declamatory publication of the pre-war international avant garde. It is easy to forget that the AIA exhibition was the first entirely abstract group show of the postwar years and that the organisation, many of whose members also belonged to the Communist Party, was a locus for politically committed art. A perception of political radicalism was transferred, not always justifiably, to the proponents of an aesthetically radical abstract art.

The semantic chaos that Alloway deplored was not so much alleviated as bypassed: as non-figurative art[17] became more familiar, *ad hoc* verbal conventions developed through which writers made themselves understood while simply evading intractable theoretical points. Constructive art remained misrepresented and little understood until the latter part of the decade, when it received a sudden elevation in critical esteem with the advent of Action Painting (fig. 32).

'"Abstract", Eric Newton stated in 1958, 'is no longer a word with a useful critical meaning.'[18] The crisis in communication had been rekindled by what was popularly known as Action Painting, an umbrella term applied to various process-based approaches to painting. A reviewer of the Arts Council's 'New Trends in Painting', a selection from the E. J. Power collection, summed up the dilemma, describing it as 'the first representative collection to be seen in this country devoted to what has variously been called "tachisme", "l'art brut", "action painting", and even, in a mood of semantic desparation, "l'art autre"'.[19] If anything was clear it was that little or nothing had been learnt from the efforts of exhibition organisers, principally at the ICA, or of a few careful critics, over the past half decade.

The Guggenheim Prize exhibition in Paris at the end of 1956[20] gave John Golding the opportunity to attempt to clarify a very murky area by emphasising the crucial shift from iconography to the act of painting. Between the traditional canvas and its full-blooded action equivalent, he suggested, lay the 'technique' of Tachisme which allowed the incorporation of accidental drips and marks into the larger image. If his summary did not quite convey the essence of the individual *tache*[21] as the 'phenomenological presence'[22] familiar from Nicolas de Staël's painting, it convincingly differentiated painting as image from painting as event, where the canvas was 'an arena in which to act'.[23]

As modernist practice diversified into Action Painting, the creation of environments and auto-destructive art, critics who were conscious of the need to locate practice in theory communicated with an ever narrower circle, leading Roger Coleman to write that

> The critic communicates by one set of signals, the public, if and when they listen, use an apparatus conditioned to receive another set of signals. Whether the public will ever react to fine art in the manner of the informed is a difficult question to answer. On the face of it, without some major changes in the social set-up it seems very unlikely.[24]

Commentators on avant-garde art adopted the exotic, obscure, luxuriant language of space travel, technology and visceral physicality associated with young urban artists inspired by American popular culture. This language is exemplified by Alloway's 'Word-list suggested by Magda Cordell's paintings' in the catalogue for her exhibition at the Hanover Gallery in 1956: 'solar, delta, galactic, amorphous, ulterior, fused, far out, viscous, skinned, visceral, variable, flux, nebular, irridescence, hyper-space, free fall, random, circulation, capacious, homeomorphism, variegated, reticular, entanglement, multiform, swimming pool, contraterrene.'[25] Beguiling though this language was, it was essentially superficial, descriptive rather than theoretical. Yet its significance was more than merely fashionable: it indicated that the relationship between critics, artists and readers had become one of complicity between initiates, confirming the rupture between artists and a non-specialist public. Critics were no longer able to present art in terms of a 'community of interest'[26] either acknowledged or transgressed, since the new modern art appeared to be an entirely private undertaking, neither relevant to nor aware of the community.

When Nigel Gosling advised his readers to surrender to colours and shapes, he also made a statement about abstract art. The phrase was a shorthand for a raft of prejudices against aesthetic innovation, intellectual effort and foreign ideas. It concealed disturbing questions about the function of art and artists: was the making of art, as John Berger passionately argued, a social act to be assessed according to the values of the community, or was it an entirely personal enterprise?

Keynes's broadcast in July 1945 contained an authoritative pronouncement about the place of artists in the postwar world: they would be the leaven in the dough of an efficient, industrialised, egalitarian but inevitably regulated society. His agenda was to reassure listeners that a modest provision of sponsorship for the arts by the state would not turn into domination of artists' production. Artists and politics had, he said, no connection with one another:

> whatever views may be held by the lately warring parties . . . about socialising industry, everyone, I fancy, recognises that the work of the artist is, of its nature, individual and free, undisciplined, unregimented, uncontrolled. The artist walks where the breath of the spirit blows him. He cannot be told his direction; he does not know it himself. But he leads the rest of us into fresh pastures . . .[27]

Beyond Keynes's emphasis on artists as leaders of a revitalised culture was a subliminal message about their symbolic position in a socialist state in the opening phase of the Cold War. This position required that they be seen to be non-political, to exist in a condition of edenic creative innocence, to fulfil Heron's precept, 'Art is autonomous'. The much reiterated demand that art reveal its 'inherent originality' and 'individual expressive strength'[28] was as much the product of an ideologically grounded perception of individual liberty as the highest value of western society as it was of modernist progress.

Abstract implied modern:[29] the words were sometimes interchangeable. Since abstraction was seen as a threat to received values, right-wing writers were apt to use it as a term of abuse for art that departed from the academic norm. Widely mistrusted, it was condemned as left-wing, intellectual and thus inimical to cultural democracy, foreign in inspiration, inhuman and a denial of individual creativity. Conversely the left might equate abstraction with capitalism.[30] For both sides, abstraction had replaced Surrealism as an object of scandal and, like Surrealism, was treated as difficult, alien and slightly embarassing. A long, confused, often acrimonious debate on the validity of all kinds of abstract art began, paradoxically, with an exhibition of paintings by two of the acknowledged masters of twentieth-century painting. The first important exhibition of contemporary art from abroad after the war, 'Picasso and Matisse', arousing enormous curiosity and controversy, focussed on Picasso's wartime paintings. Epitomes of the modern, these too were described as abstract[31] because of Picasso's cavalier attitude to the human body which he distorted in a way that undermined more than simply physical integrity, calling into question the moral status of a universe constructed on human values. His paintings provoked furious hostility and stimulated a debate on the morality of modern art.

The tone was self-righteous, the phrases used revealing: references to 'healthiness', 'deviations' and 'normal experience'[32] suggest a climate of moralising, timorous repression hostile to experimental creativity.[33] Only a few months after 'Picasso and Matisse' closed, Thomas Bodkin condemned Moore and Graham Sutherland on the grounds that in their new work 'Representation is either deliberately suppressed or barely recognisable'.[34] The implication was that modern or abstract art, like its protagonists, sought to deceive: 'artists, critics, dealers, and others who assert their interest and partisanship in these non-traditional departures from truth are untrue to their real convictions', raged the inappropriately named *Art and Reason*.[35]

The duplicity of the modern threatened to subvert the normal and traditional and even the aesthetic status of the Academy, which represented them. As a member of the Communist Party, Picasso was seen as a particularly dangerous model, but the 'deliberate malformations' of Moore's much-discussed *Three Standing Figures* (1948) (fig. 98) were also taken to have 'a political significance. It is bound up with the desire to destroy the traditional wherever it is met in order that the way may be cleared for the peculiar variety of Heaven which it is nowadays fashionable to preach.'[36]

As the tensions of the Cold War multiplied, uninformed and irrational parallels were drawn between socialism at home and the tyranny of Stalin's USSR, where art was a weapon of the state and creative freedom was denied.[37] Given that the status of Socialist Realism and the fate of the old Soviet avant garde were well-known, the equation between abstraction and the Left is initially puzzling. Although partially explained by the energy with which modernists, including Moore, took part in the AIA's politically inflected pre-war activities, there was a gulf in art and politics between the late 1930s and the mid-1940s.

On 7 July 1938 an exhibition of modern German art opened at the New Burlington Galleries, strongly supported by Read, as a counter to the National Socialist categorisation of *entartete Kunst*.[38] Read also wrote the introduction to Peter Thoene's[39] *Modern German Art*, deploring British ignorance of contemporary art in Germany, and its relatively low status in comparison with the products of the Ecole de Paris.[40] Published to coincide with the London exhibition, the book carried on its cover the proclamation that 'It treats art, not as something isolated from contemporary events, but as a mirror of its time in which one can learn to understand oneself and society'. After the war though, it was not the engagement of protest that was remembered, but Thoene's concluding warning that 'art, if it is to live, needs freedom. Its dreams with their abundance of solace cannot flourish in the arid atmosphere of duress'.[41]

Memories of the revulsion aroused by the labelling of so much art as degenerate must finally have counted as much as Cold War passions in forcing a wedge between art and politics and forming an implausible link between events at the Hofgarten in Munich in 1937 and the foundation of the Arts Council in London nine years later. The knowledge of what might result from a perverted coupling of art and politics was simply transferred onto other hostile forces, as when the strength of the Italian and French Communist Parties became apparent at the end of the war, bringing also the perception that they posed the threat of a further struggle with totalitarianism.[42] Consequently realist painting that was, or was believed to be, politically inflected became a focus for intense suspicion.

In this context it was unlikely also that constructive art, with historical connections with the revolutionary Left in Germany and the Soviet Union, would escape condemnation. Historical parallels no doubt encouraged critics who castigated Pasmore's and Martin's three-dimensional work (figs 31 and 40) as 'doctrinaire' or 'puritan', implying, against all the evidence, a continuation of old political links. They juxtaposed these qualities with the humanism[43] imputed to Moore's sculpture and, especially, the Shelter drawings which had made him Britain's best-known contemporary artist. His work was consistently seen as ideologically innocent[44] yet little attention has been paid to the appropriation of his sculpture as a soft, if potent, weapon by the British Council, while his extraordinary schedule of exhibitions with the Council has been seen only as an acknowledgement of the country's leading artist.

Discussing the Contemporary Art Society's exhibition 'Twentieth-century Form' Nigel Gosling regretted the 'breakaway', evident in constructionist art, 'from the European tradition of a humanist art based on visual appearance'.[45] Geometric and gestural art were condemned as meaningless, unworthy of any 'symbolic, poetic and metaphysical significances' which might be read into them, 'of which they are almost as innocent as a modern curtain material'.[46] Derided as being of no more significance than decoration or design, constructive works[47] were appropriate only as adjuncts to contemporary architecture, successors to the florid architectural sculpture that adorned so many of London's buildings.

Gosling consoled himself with the conclusion that though 'Totally abstract, non-figurative art is indeed a revolutionary idea',[48] it was likely to be short-lived. Even before 'Modern Art in the United States' heralded the apotheosis of gestural painting, it was clear that he had miscalculated. As formulations of abstract art became more sophisticated and discriminating, its case was clinched by the demonstration of individual creativity on every Action Painter's canvas. Belief in the autonomy of the gesture even extended to perceptions of the social role of artists; no longer constructed as symbolic cold warriors, they were transformed into flesh-and-blood Bohemians, living out the engagement of their art in their private lives.

A 'FEROCIOUS SQUABBLE'

Between 1951 and 1953 a 'ferocious squabble about abstract art',[49] otherwise known as the abstraction versus realism debate, enlivened the correspondence columns of *The Listener* and *The New Statesman and Nation*. Initiated by Basil Taylor's review of a pioneering survey exhibition of contemporary British abstract art at Gimpel Fils,[50] the first, inconclusive round was conducted with variable awareness of the complexity of the issue, though it provides a summary of the prejudice, legitimate confusion and alienation expressed by many professional writers.

Bernard Boles, a reader infuriated by Taylor's review, wrote four letters in little over five weeks[51] in which, further aroused by measured responses from artists,[52] he identified an abstract-traditional dichotomy; hinted at a conspiracy, involving the Arts Council, to support abstraction; castigated the Council for 'its sterility, its lack of direction and its use of funk-hole terms' and finally dismissed the totality of abstract art as decoration of foreign origin which had been rejected by the 'English art public'.

The second round focussed on a confrontation between Patrick Heron and John Berger which coincided with the furore over the Unknown Political Prisoner competition. In response to Heron's provocative remark that 'the alleged "new return to realism"' appeared to be no more than 'a fiction in the mind of . . . Mr. Berger',[53] the latter proposed realism as an attitude seeking 'to interpret art in relation to life as a whole', in contrast to the prevalent formalist emphasis on style.[54] Heron's reply set out the essence of their differences: Berger's understanding of realism originated in an idea 'which has deeper roots in familiar political and social theory than in art'. His argument led inevitably to a point where 'art and propaganda are one', whereas for Heron, '"to hell with any audience" is the only attitude for a painter at work. Art is autonomous.'[55]

The debate reveals a concentration and polarisation of attitudes. It enabled Heron and Berger to oppose notional, or ideal, situations: an engaged art of the Left against the ideological innocence of all other artists. Both were valuable as theoretical positions from which more pragmatic critical arguments might be evolved.

Seven years later, in the preface to *Permanent Red*, Berger described his position at the time of the exchange, writing 'at the height of the Cold War in a period of rigid conformism', when he had to fight for every article 'line by line, adjective by adjective, against constant editorial cavilling', so that it seemed that his comments had been 'coded'.[56] No doubt this was so: the *New Statesman* would not have tolerated overtly Marxist sympathies from a critic about whom the editors were accustomed to receive complaints,[57] yet Berger's views on contemporary art were not conventionally Marxist. The artists whom he admired ranged from Guttuso to Matisse, Léger to Lanyon, and it was perhaps because he looked at art as a painter as well as a committed critic that he had such difficulty in formulating his criteria in terms of ideology. The qualities that Berger sought focussed on the trans-formatory power of art to enhance 'our awareness of our own potentiality':[58] a valid work of art was one that encouraged betterment, whether social, moral or political; it was to be truthful, analytic and specific.

Berger's responses to individual works were mercurial, now echoing left ortho-doxy, now the most unthinking right-wing prejudice, to underline the difficulty of trying to establish a stable position on the treacherously shifting ground of advanced practice. It is not surprising that he dismissed the vapid qualities of naturalist painting, but his enthusiasm for much modernist art was less predict-able. It is exemplified by his comment on Peter Lanyon's *Trevalgan* (1951) (fig. 7), which he perceptively acknowledged as 'a painting, not of the appearance, but of the properties of a landscape',[59] of essentials not obscured by the superficial. The 'Unknown Political Prisoner' display had, however, prompted one of his most scathing reviews and the conclusion that '"official" modern art' was 'bankrupt'. Butler's maquette (fig. 106), which Berger equated with abstraction and an interna-tional style that he deplored, represented the vast range of ideologically vague, modernising art shown in state-sponsored exhibitions.[60]

Berger's virulence was principally directed at art without specific and signifi-cant content, particularly as manifested by Action Painting. Reviewing the ICA's 'Five Painters' in 1958,[61] he castigated Action Painting in general for meaningless solipsism and the exhibition in particular for 'protests [that] are emotional rather than intellectual' and 'incomprehensible'. Yet despite its inarticulacy, he inter-preted the exhibition, as few critics did, as a passionately political protest fol-lowing the foundation of the Campaign for Nuclear Disarmament: 'The fact that thousands of works are painted in this spirit ought to shake the faith of those who believe that all is well with our so-called free, individualistic culture.'[62]

PATRICK HERON, THE SCHOOL OF LONDON AND THE MIDDLE GROUND

One result of the intensely chauvinist atmosphere of the late 1940s was a demand for a convincingly modern alternative to the dreamy poets of neo-Romanticism. As the Tate reopened with a token half-dozen rooms, Michael Ayrton excitedly proclaimed 'England is just about to emerge from a century of pictorial mediocrity into a period of great painting'.[63] Not long after this outburst of optimism Ayrton left *The Spectator*, where he had been the regular art critic since 1944.

His departure overlapped Heron's two years with *The New English Weekly*.[64] Only twenty-five when the war ended, Heron set out to re-establish the continuity between British and French painting, situating himself, in acute contrast to Ayrton, as the most determined and articulate disciple of the old Ecole de Paris, modelling his own painting on Bonnard, Matisse and Braque.[65] Having formed

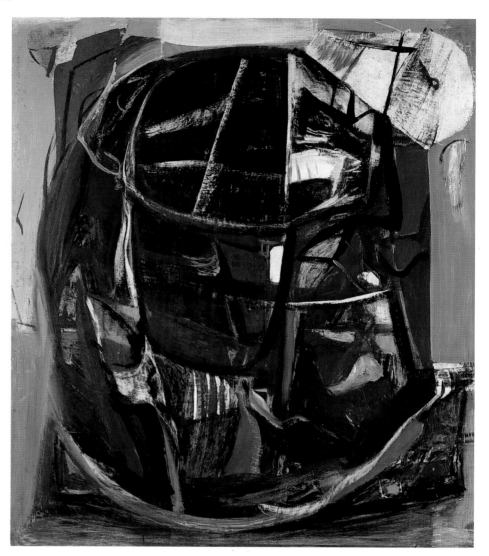

7. Peter Lanyon,
Trevalgan, 1951.
Oil on masonite,
48 × 45 in. Witte
Memorial Museum,
San Antonio, Texas.

close links with Adrian Stokes, Naum Gabo, Ben Nicholson and their circle when he worked at the Leach pottery towards the end of the war, he was in the rare position of being equally familiar with art events in London and in St Ives, the Cornish outpost that seemed likely to become the home of a new avant garde. In his first review for *The New English Weekly* Heron set a pattern for his writing by measuring Nicholson's recent work against the paradigm of French art. He concluded that Nicholson's Mondrian-inspired paintings and reliefs had 'perpetuated in a succession of refinements the most theoretical moment in modern French painting'.[66]

Heron has insisted that Matisse's *Red Studio*, which he remembers as having hung during part of the war in the Redfern Gallery, was 'the most influential single painting in my entire career',[67] but it was the linear complexity of Braque's post-cubist painting that had the greatest impact on his own early work. His reverential review of Braque's 1946 Tate exhibition[68] revealed an impact that was renewed when, during a visit to Paris as an exhibitor in the 1949 Salon de Mai, he went to Braque's studio, where he saw some of the late *Ateliers*.[69]

Shortly before this visit Heron had outlined a possible School of London. As eclectic as the Ecole de Paris and geographically much wider, since it included 'constructivists' working in Cornwall,[70] as well as London-based artists, its title inadvertently emphasised the metropolitan bias of the art world and paid tribute to its parent, the Ecole de Paris. Following the French model, Heron nominated a group of older artists – Matthew Smith, Ivon Hitchens, Moore, Sutherland and Percy Wyndham Lewis – who had acted as conduits for the transmission of French art and, as representatives of a modernising trend which avoided extreme avant gardism were natural leaders of younger artists. Among the latter he named Sutherland's followers as particularly significant, while 'less linked' contributors included Pasmore, David Jones, Lucian Freud and Bacon: 'the School of London is remarkable for its variety'.

Heron's attempt to identify a focus for critical attention was not taken up by other writers, nor did he return to the theme himself. Instead, he attempted to demonstrate the existence of a practice that was modern, crossed the abstract/figurative divide and was concerned with the fundamentals of painting. Acutely aware of contemporary developments, Heron may have felt that constructive artists, who had produced publications and held a number of exhibitions, were stealing the thunder of those who had remained painters.

With 'Space in Colour', the group exhibition which he organised at the Hanover Gallery in July 1953, he took the opportunity to show that far from being an alien imposition that had ruptured the western tradition of painting, abstraction had enlarged and reinforced it. Heron's theory of abstraction was essentially visual and non-theoretical; as early as his Nicholson review in *The New English Weekly*, he had argued for the retention of the object within modernist painting. The emphasis was congruent both with the complex linearity that he adapted from Braque and with his painterly theory, which hinged on the well-rehearsed ability of juxtaposed colours to create a pictorial effect of space, a central tenet of the western tradition. While this was the basis of his own early work, like *The Piano* (1943), by the time he painted *Balcony Window with Green Table: St Ives: 1951* (fig. 8), the balance between linearity and colour had lost its resolution and Heron was soon to develop a more consistently abstracted approach.

He seems also to have learnt from his friend Ivon Hitchens, of whom he wrote 'The study of landscape in terms of near-abstraction is Hitchens's special contribution'[71] and one which Heron himself began to explore in 1955. It seems that Hitchens provided Heron with the means to verbalise his theory succinctly and memorably,[72] but it was de Staël who offered a model for a kind of painting that might create spatial effects without objects. In *The Changing Forms of Art*, the compilation of his writing which Heron published in 1955, which contains a reproduction of de Staël's undated *Painting*,[73] Heron announced that the French artist stood 'at the beginning of a new development in painting'.[74] In the summer of 1952, after the Matthiessen Gallery exhibition, Heron's own work took a startling new turn as he briefly abandoned object-based painting for images made up of clustered blocks and small planes of colour that were clearly related to de Staël's work.

'Painting', Heron wrote in the catalogue for 'Space in Colour', 'is essentially an art of illusion . . . the illusion of forms in space . . . Colour is the utterly indispensable means for realising the various species of pictorial space.'[75] To demonstrate this was the purpose of the exhibition and in his introductory essay Heron cast a rare light on the variations within abstraction, extending the division, recently elucidated by Kenneth Martin, between abstract and constructive artists.[76]

8. Patrick Heron,
*Balcony Window with
Green Table: St Ives:
1951*. Oil on canvas,
35 × 17 in. Private
Collection.

Hitchens and Vaughan, he wrote, 'disturb natural configuration very little' and Hitchens's painting retained, even in the long horizontal *Winter Walk* series[77] 'a single viewpoint as their basic vision', whereas Lanyon's experiential approach to landscape painting[78] required a 'coalescing of a number of viewpoints including aerial ones'.[79] Turning to colour, Heron wrote of the 'vibration of colour without which there could be no pictorial space', a familiar proposition except that he argued that it could be effected 'in blacks, whites and greys – no less than the full chromatic range'. He had therefore included three photostat collages by Pasmore in the exhibition.[80]

Heron trod an uneasy line with his constructive colleagues, deploring the 'pictorial heresy'[81] of their theorised process, since all painting was rooted in visual perception,[82] though he admired Adrian Heath's work (fig. 34),[83] which he could interpret in terms of colour relations, and praised Pasmore's first fully abstract exhibition, seeing in the work pure, intense statements of light and space (fig. 33).[84]

'Space in Colour' helped to clarify the opposition between perceptual and process-based art and the unexpected elisions between them. It also opened up an arena for the reconciliation of modernism and convention, the 'middle way between pure abstraction and abject representation'[85] to which Heron had been calling attention for some time before the exhibition, and which he found in the work of his friends and colleagues in St Ives and those other artists whom he enumerated as forming the School of London.

Extrapolated from factors considered desirable in modernising painting and expressed as mediations between imagination and fidelity to the subject; between modernism and tradition and advanced art and majority taste, the arena that Heron sought to define stood for a *juste milieu* or middle ground. The phrase was not used, yet this inferred practice became a near obsession for critics seeking to reconcile the inevitability of innovation with the conservatism of taste. It finally provided the accomodations which would enable them to accept process-based art.

The quintessential artist of the middle ground was Alan Reynolds, described by G. S. Whittet as 'that phenomenal artist . . . the modern and the traditional at once'.[86] His *Summer – Young September's Cornfield* (1954) (fig. 9) is clearly modern; its colour is bright though still within the bounds of the natural, while it is spatially plausible and easily deciphered. The reason for Whittet's superlatives was perhaps Reynolds's combination of intense precision and bold, spontaneous marks: a simultaneous demonstration of traditional skills and modern virtuosity.

Vitality and spontaneity were highly valued well before Abstract Expressionism made them fashionable; they connoted truthfulness, a concern for life and humanity, in contrast with the cold refinement attributed to geometric abstraction. Particularly in association with landscape painting, they underlined the authenticity of the individual author in the unmediated relationship with nature demonstrated by Hitchens's paintings of the woods and waterways of rural Sussex. As gestural abstraction developed outside this relationship, appreciation of paint as a metaphor for nature was transformed into a taste for the texture and sensuality of oil-paint, with the canvas as a field to be scraped, quarried and rebuilt.

Bright colour, encouraged by the Matisse and van Gogh exhibitions, was a signifier of modernity, though artists trained in a tonal tradition were slow to adopt it. It indicated a positive attitude and the belief that art should be pleasurable rather than provocative, whereas colour that could be characterised as drab was vigorously condemned. Ceri Richards's palette was so attractive that it even

9. Alan Reynolds, *Summer – Young September's Cornfield*, 1954. Oil on board, $40\frac{1}{4} \times 61$ in. Tate Gallery, London.

outweighed the distortions and flat, uptilted surfaces of his *Trafalgar Square* (1951–3) paintings, which were widely praised for their topicality and cheerfulness (fig. 10).[87]

The pluralism of the middle ground is revealed by the inconsistency with which colour was read. The centrality of Heron's space and colour theory is underlined by the dismissal of canvases like his *Christmas Eve*, made for '60 Paintings for '51', as decorative because of their intricate, flat linearity. Though his palette was brighter than many of his contemporaries', a suggestion of three-dimensionality was required since flatness indicated mere pattern or design, without significant content.[88] William Gear's colour was often interpreted as an indicator of the landscape origins of his paintings, compensating for the absence of a recognisable subject and suggesting that much attention should be paid to their titles. As an adjunct of bright colour, heavy impasto might contribute to a literal reading of it. Like gesture it signified individuality and, perhaps, a release from wartime austerity.

Ultimately the middle ground is predicated on the presence of a definable subject as much as on its accomodations with modernism. Perhaps its least explicit characteristic, a corollary of the centrality of the subject, was an insistence on the atmosphere of a painting. The distaste that critics expressed for the mechanical appearance of constructive art indicated a desire for some more luxuriant quality, through which the viewer might make an imaginative identification with the work. It was such a quality that was exemplified by Richards's Trafalgar Square paintings.

FROM EXISTENTIALISM TO LOGICAL POSITIVISM

Existentialism, rooted in Paris under the German occupation, had no direct equivalent in Britain. What filtered across the Channel was a rationale for a new attitude to portraying the body, in which both narrative and emotional engagement were rejected on the grounds that life was a pointless absurdity. If we acknowledge a corpus of ideas passed largely by word of mouth and visual example, a syncretic echo of Existentialism proper offers a way to read some of the work of Bacon and Reg Butler (figs 85 and 86). The links are too loose for this to be constructed as a monolithic existential art: it is better expressed as the category of 'Existentialist related art' defined by David Mellor.[89] Direct exposure to Existentialism was a rare experience for English artists, yet the term was broadcast by writers with a familiarity that suggests a ready conversion into an indigenous intellectual category.

Postwar Paris attracted foreign artists by its diversity rather than a still-obscure philosophy. Adrian Heath, who made regular visits in the late 1940s, gravitated to the Galerie Denise René, centre for geometric abstraction, while Gear, who lived in the city from 1947 to 1950 and was familiar with many aspects of the postwar Ecole de Paris, aligned himself with the lyrical abstraction or *paysagisme abstrait* of young painters like Jean Bazaine and Alfred Manessier.[90]

Much depended on contacts and introductions; much also on chance. William Turnbull's *Game* (1949) is an assemblage of schematic figures which can be moved around their base-board to invoke the haphazardness of relationships within a crowd, or the anonymity and loss of intentionality experienced by the individual. Turnbull made it during a two-year stay in Paris, having joined his former fellow-student at the Slade, Eduardo Paolozzi. They came into contact with a vast range of artists and ideas, including the surrealist poet, Tristan Tzara, Constantin Brancusi, Jean Dubuffet and the Foyer de l'Art Brut. However, it was Giacometti who made the most immediate impact on Turnbull, who began to construct wire armatures coated in rough, knobbly plaster bearing the imprint of his hands. Within a short time Turnbull turned to the near life-size, leaf-shaped bronzes that

10. Ceri Richards, *Trafalgar Square*, 1951–3. Oil on canvas, 32 × 39 in. Private Collection.

11. William Turnbull,
Idol 2, 1956. Bronze,
$64\frac{3}{4} \times 17 \times 19\frac{3}{4}$ in.

he often called Idols (fig. 11), which were modelled both on Cycladic marbles and, as is evident from their immense bases, on Giacometti's sculpture. When Theo Crosby reproduced many of them in *Uppercase*, in 1961, they were photographed in such a way as to underline Turnbull's allegiance to his mentor by replicating the way in which Giacometti's work was photographed in the studio, as if in a transitory form.[91]

Early in 1948 Turnbull lent David Sylvester the catalogue of Giacometti's recent exhibition at the Pierre Matisse Gallery in New York,[92] with a text by Sartre. It was accompanied by the facsimile copy of a letter from the artist, also published as a statement in the catalogue.[93] These were among a handful of texts[94] that represented not so much a philosophy as an invitation to abandon the comfortable certainty of received ideas for an uncharted sea of invention and enquiry.

At the end of this extraordinary year, Sylvester published 'Auguries of experience', the brief, poetic, prescient essay on the late works of Paul Klee[95] in which he referred to the disruption of 'perceptual habits' and the continuous and continually enquiring nature of process,[96] soon to obsess constructive and gestural artists alike. Klee's compositions were unfocussed, 'allover', 'an organism, not a constructed form' or 'a landscape through which you journey . . . [as] a participant'. Sylvester aligned Turnbull and Paolozzi with Giacometti, late Klee and André Masson as producers of work that was to be approached 'not by confronting it as a scene detached from himself, but by entering it and moving about in it'.[97]

Prophetic though Sylvester's writing was, the distance between the intensity of postwar Paris and London a decade later was too great to claim any close connection. He stood apart from the many English writers on art who made passing references to Existentialism, interpreting it, unlike their literary colleagues, always in terms of anguish rather than absurdity and offering no equivalent to Samuel Beckett's black comedy. Writing about Bacon, Sylvester suggested that the painter understood Existentialism as embodying a challenge to humanity and an attitude 'expressed in the closing words of *Huis Clos*, when Garcin, having recognised that there is no way out and that frustration is endless, says, *"Eh bien, continuons"*. The attitude that life *is* hell and we had better get used to the idea.'[98]

Read's famous essay, 'New aspects of British sculpture', written for the 1952 Venice Biennale, which included Turnbull and Paolozzi, has attained the status of an *ad hoc* existential declaration. In a reverie on the condition of the individual in a post-atomic age, Read invoked an impotent social responsibility through references to 'excoriated flesh', 'iron waifs' and 'collective guilt', implying that there was no route out of despair. There were no parallel verbal declarations by artists, though Roger Hilton eloquently voiced the dilemma of the artist as creator in his statement in *Nine Abstract Artists*:

> The abstract painter submits himself entirely to the unknown . . . he is like a man swinging out into the void; his only props his colours, his shapes and their space-creating powers. Can he construct with these means a barque capable of carrying not only himself to some further shore, but with the aid of others, a whole flotilla which may be seen, eventually, as having been carrying humanity forward to their unknown destination.[99]

In a letter to Lawrence Alloway three years later, he moved forward the discussion of the existential act, relating it to Action Painting, the most compelling issue of the moment. In doing so he set out the rationale for the new gestural painting, proclaiming that

> The act is its own meaning . . . But it is not enough to say that. You must say that the act can *only* occur when there is no longer any meaning. In this way the act *makes* the meaning. The meaning could not precede the act. In any case there is no difference between a painter and any other kind of creative individual. They are all engaged in a life and death struggle with *existence*.[100]

In the three years between Hilton's statement in *Nine Abstract Artists* and his letter to Alloway, Colin Wilson's *The Outsider* was published. Claimed by its author as an existential work of criticism, it was instantly mythologised, its tone of impotent *ennui* taken as the authentic voice of a society trapped in a long descent into a shabby senility. A mishmash of philosophy, personal religion and quotations, it reaffirmed the status of individual creators who, in becoming Outsiders alienated from social convention, were rendered free. Wilson hoped that writers and artists might become spiritual leaders, a quest in which 'we have, to guide us, two discoveries about the Outsider's "way": [1] That his salvation "lies in extremes". [2] That the idea of a way out often comes in "visions", moments of intensity.'[101] In his demand for the extreme experience lies the faint link between Existentialism and the beat generation of the 1960s, for which *The Outsider* became a key text.[102]

Not long after it was published Paolozzi began to make free-standing bronze figures, among which *The Philosopher* (1957) (fig. 12) is perhaps the most impressive. Apparently tacked together from workshop and household scraps, *The Philosopher* proclaims the jauntiness of a streetwise survivor rather than intellectual agony, and the primacy of the maker over the theorist. It can be

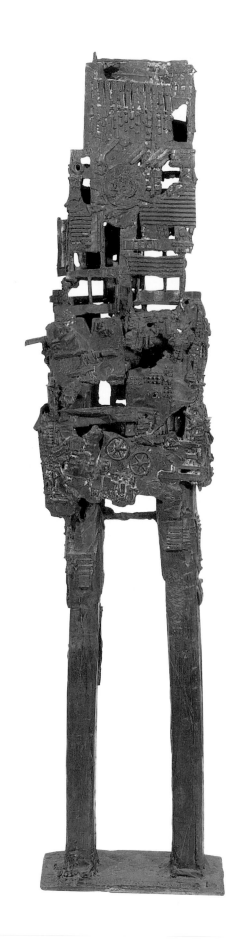

12. Eduardo
Paolozzi, *The
Philosopher*, 1957.
Bronze, 74 in. high.
British Council
Collection.

seen as poised symbolically between the antitheses of Existentialism and Logical Positivism.

In *Language, Truth and Logic*[103] A. J. Ayer set out the principles of Logical Positivism, later dismissed by Wilson as a 'pseudo-philosophy',[104] in terms of robust common sense. Ayer's rejection of metaphysics as senseless and his dismissal of ethics and aesthetics were influential far beyond his actual readership, a popular philosophy to suit the notion of the common man. Like Existentialism, it affected literature more directly than the visual arts, particularly the Movement poets. Philip Larkin, Kingsley Amis and Donald Davie were the most prominent members of the group first identified by the publication of the anthology *New Lines* in 1956, and later characterised by Blake Morrison as seeking 'rationalism, realism, empiricism',[105] qualities emphasised in Robert Conquest's introduction to the anthology. The poets themselves, type-cast in the 1950s as 'provincial, lower-middle-class, scholarship-winning', philistine and prejudiced against foreigners, represented populism and democracy in opposition to the upper-middle-class attitudes of the pre-war generation.[106]

While the Movement has been seen as an aspect of the 'strategic retreat of the Left' under Cold War pressures, facilitating the re-establishment of a class-based, reactionary orthodoxy,[107] its closest parallels lie in attitudes to art. Its populism echoed the concern of the well-meaning dispensers of culture for the predicament of the man in the street, while its emphasis on syntax and clarity was a refinement of critics' demands for accessibility, a reassertion of the centrality of the moralising, democratising territory marked out historically by Hogarth and upheld by members of the AIA.[108]

Urban representatives of populism and democracy, the Movement poets have been associated with the Beaux Arts Quartet, the young realist painters promoted by John Berger and so named because they showed very early in their careers at Helen Lessore's gallery. In their paintings they converted the minutiae of urban poverty into aesthetic objects. John Bratby's clumsily painted, chaotic tables, spilling over with chip fryers, cornflake packets and tea mugs, represent the daily life experienced by millions (fig. 52). To set his work beside the cerebral, disengaged elegance of Nicholson's contemporaneous post-cubist still-lifes is to juxtapose not only different generations but different cultures.

Despite their astonishing achievement in being selected to show in the British Pavilion at Venice in 1956, the members of the Beaux Arts Quartet were very young artists whose work did not offer a close parallel to the sophistication of the Movement poets. The transient nature of an identification between painters and writers was soon to become evident in the very different approaches to realism seen in the work of Frank Auerbach, Bacon and Leon Kossoff, for whom clarity, empiricism and populism were irrelevant terms.

PERCEPTIONS OF THE PRIMITIVE

In the late 1940s the great swathe of art contained within the term primitive became a significant factor in the discourse of modernism to an extent that was unprecedented in Britain, though it had, of course, long been accessible and familiar to artists working in Paris. Equally well-known were Moore's personal discovery of ancient and tribal art[109] in the British Museum and Jacob Epstein's own magnificent collection of tribal art. After the war individual discoveries of arcane ethnographic objects were displaced by a political process in which the notion of primitive societies, and their art, became part of a wider political discourse.

Colonial Office policy moved rapidly away from the defiant attitude expressed by Churchill during the war: 'I have not become the King's first minister in order to preside over the liquidation of the British Empire'.[110] Labour policy had long been enshrined in Stafford Cripps's unequivocal declaration that 'It is fundamental to socialism that we should liquidate the British Empire'.[111] After 1945 a 'vague idea of ultimate self-rule'[112] was replaced by the policy set out by Arthur Creech-Jones.[113] Committed to colonial independence, he dismissed 'economic imperialism' and called for a relationship of partners without racial discrimination.[114]

For the electorate of 1945, socialist policy was expounded in a set of Fabian Society essays published that year.[115] They combined political pragmatism with ethical socialism, expressed in language that closely echoed Beveridge's in *The Pillars of Security*. Their central theme was the urgent need, particularly of the African colonies, for immediate, large-scale capital investment. This was accepted by the authors as an ethical requirement, while pragmatism also recognised that fully productive colonial territories within the sterling area could provide essential support for the fragile British economy.

Externally, the government was subject to constant pressure, particularly from the United States, to dismantle the empire.[116] A different set of issues was raised by the electorate, resistant to change, sensitive to a perceived reduction of national status and, not least, reluctant to see people who had recently fought on its behalf apparently cast off to fend for themselves. Reason also suggests the likelihood of strong opposition to faraway colonies taking economic priority over domestic reconstruction.

History, political habit and sentiment were the combined objections to the loss of the colonies. Their loss would remove both a power base for British political recovery after the end of Marshall Aid and, with the inevitable end of empire preference, the obvious means of alleviating long-term domestic economic problems.[117] The situation was exacerbated and further confused by strong undercurrents of racial prejudice and the electorate's manifest ignorance of the colonies.[118] It was not a scenario that seemed to offer a prominent place to the visual arts, yet in the period immediately after the independence of India, which heralded the imminent loss of the remainder of the empire, tribal art was seen to be a powerful signifier of disparate British attitudes to subject populations. For the liberal Left it connoted different but parallel high cultures; for others it indicated either barbarism or a condition of child-like simplicity. Neither appeared to demonstrate the fitness of indigenous politicians to take over the government of colonised territories.

However indirect and peripheral the role of the arts in postwar colonial politics, the prominence of tribal art in the late 1940s offered contemporary British artists a visual stimulus perfectly in accord with the recent revelation of Picasso. For the early ICA, anthropology was as consuming an interest as psychoanalysis; anthropological research, particularly in West Africa,[119] stimulated curiosity about tribal art, which was easily acculturated under sub-headings like 'art from the colonies'. Most of the young artists involved in the development of a post-surrealist discourse of primitivism were closely connected with the ICA. Founder members, well aware of the impact of French ethnographers on Surrealism, were eager to explore links between the modern and the primitive, which of course included prehistoric art, a subject of renewed interest since the discovery of Lascaux in 1940.

Late in 1948, the ICA's second exhibition, '40,000 Years of Modern Art' brought together ancient, tribal and contemporary works lent by private collectors and museums, including the Musée de l'Homme and the Ashmolean.[120] It was, on many counts, one of the most significant exhibitions held in London in the late 1940s: it relocated an ill-defined notion of the primitive in an expanded, trans-cultural and transhistorical context heavily inflected by Jungian theory. This underlay Read's belief in 'the universality of art', demonstrated by the exhibition, proving that ancient, modern and primitive shared, in Thistlewood's words 'a vitality, a challenging potency, an active, sensually satisfying, even shocking symbolism'.[121] Politics, aesthetics and scholarship apart, Read had a further comment on the congruence of primitive and contemporary: '. . . like conditions produce like effects . . . conditions in modern life . . . have produced effects only to be seen in primitive epochs . . . they are archetypal and buried deep in the uncon-scious. But generally they can be described as a vague sense of insecurity, a cosmic anguish (*Angst* . . .) feelings and intuitions that demand expression in abstract or unnaturalistic forms.'[122]

The facilitator of the loans for '40,000 Years' and source of invaluable expert advice was William Fagg, Secretary of the Royal Anthropological Institute, Keeper of Ethnography at the British Museum, editor of *Man* and an early member of the ICA.[123] He was 'especially interested in promoting the study of art by anthropolo-gists and anthropology by artists'.[124] Fagg was particularly active within the Insti-tute during the 1950s, when he was closely involved with two more of its exibitions,[125] as well as debates and panel discussions.[126] For the Festival of Britain the RAI mounted a large exhibition, 'Traditional Art from the Colonies', at the Imperial Institute and Fagg was again among the speakers in a related discussion at the ICA in July 1951. Two years later he was a member of the selection com-mittee for the ICA's 'Wonder and Horror of the Human Head', where the exhibits had the same effervescent eclecticism as in 1948 (fig. 13).

The Institute offered him the opportunity to work with tribal art unfettered by the academic restraints of a museum, while it also brought him into close contact with artists, which he valued greatly. Unusually among ethnographers at this time, Fagg focussed on the artist as an individual creator, rather than an anony-mous producer of artefacts; it was an attitude to which Read and his colleagues would have been fully sympathetic. In return, Fagg was able to give the Institute intellectual support and a degree of validation, as well as practical help in the form of exhibition reviews[127] and contacts with the RAI.[128] In 1949 he organised 'Tradi-tional Art of the British Colonies'[129] as the RAI's contribution to a series of events that went under the general title of Colonial Month.[130] Through Fagg and the RAI, and their connection with this government initiative, the Institute was linked into a discourse of primitivism profoundly inflected by current politics.

Early in 1949, the Central Office of Information, reeling from the results of a survey which had indicated that 50 per cent of respondents were unable to name a single colony, while three per cent believed that 'America is a British colony',[131] embarked on a national education programme of which the main feature was to be Colonial Month. It took place in London from 21 June to 20 July 1949. It was opened with some pomp by George VI, though it was little publicised except for a pamphlet produced by the COI, which listed twenty-three exhibitions and a programme of films.[132] The main event, announced as 'Colonial Exhibition 1949 –

13. Installation shot, 'Wonder & Horror of the Human Head', Institute of Contemporary Arts, London, 1953.

Focus on Colonial Progress', took place in what was described as a COI exhibition hall near Marble Arch.[133] *The Times* covered the exhibition's most widely reported feature in some detail:

> Visitors begin their tour by passing through a replica of West African jungle, heated to a native temperature, and complete with even the hoarse croaks and shrieks of jungle life. The massive brutality and oppressiveness of real jungle is well depicted in this short stretch before the cool of a modern African House is reached. There is a collection of effigies of the surprising and often alarming aboriginals of the Colonies, notably one of a Masai warrior standing on one leg . . .[134]

The bulk of the exhibition was nevertheless devoted to trade,[135] while the living tableau, long a staple of colonial exhibitions, was roundly attacked by a Nigerian journalist for its falsification of colonial history.[136] Perhaps because of its appeal to popular stereotypes, the exhibition apparently satisfied the expectations of its target audience; it was extended for some weeks and in 1950 a smaller version was toured to major regional cities, in a series of Colonial Weeks.

Since Colonial Month placed very little emphasis on art, attention focussed on the RAI show, 'Traditional Art of the British Colonies'. For many people its greatest attraction was a group of brass and terracotta heads from Ife, in western Nigeria (fig. 14).[137] Beautiful though they were acknowledged to be, they were already embedded in a controversy that illuminates the core of the primitivist debate. Lacking the stylisations that conventionally denote African art and were understood as its makers' natural means of expression,[138] these serene, sophisticated heads were considered to have closer affinities with Greek or renaissance art than with tribal carvings.[139]

Integral aspects of primitive art, Fagg wrote in the catalogue for 'Traditional Art of the British Colonies', were its spontaneity, lack of intellectual content and the unmediated directness of the artist's vision, which was formulated in response to an internal tradition. Identified with a community, and thus of profound social significance, this tradition contributed to the production of anonymous and unindividualised art that changed very slowly,[140] a condition often described as timeless. It was widely agreed that all tribal art was in some way religious, which was consistent with its expressive qualities and the emphasis on community. Fagg recognised the impossibility of reconciling the art of Ife with simplicity or spontaneous expression: 'modern artists are loath to believe that the pure well of Negro art can have been defiled by such naturalism except by alien importation',[141] though he subsequently fully accepted the African origin of the Ife heads.

In the nuances of language of the three heavily illustrated, popular books on West African art written by Leon Underwood[142] we find what amounts to a revision of Fagg's careful essay. Underwood attributed tribal art's appeal to modern artists to its non-classical qualities,[143] which measured the extent to which it might be constructed as spontaneous, non-intellectual and even child-like.[144] For

14. Terracotta head, Ife, Nigeria, National Museum of Nigeria, Lagos.

Underwood, the threat posed by incomprehensibly alien cultures might be less-ened by collapsing their diversity into a unitary vision of edenic communities of simple people living close to nature,[145] their art uncontaminated by contact with a sophisticated world. He therefore proposed a category of 'pre-logical' artists,[146] implying an extension of the phrase to entire cultures, which might then be understood as blank spaces for the inscription of western values.

The Ife heads denied such a possibility, for they conformed neither to a model of savagery nor one of pre-lapsarian innocence and we may surmise that they failed also to signal a culture compliant with Colonial Office policy. Confronted with this problem, Underwood conveniently attributed their anomalous style to an 'unknown event in history', adding that there was little prospect of their being found to originate in Africa.[147]

Discussing the ways in which contemporary artists had addressed any of the many facets of primitivism through their work, Fagg identified a serious limita-tion in their 'preoccupation . . . with the visible forms of the tribal sculptures [while] little or no account was taken of their content or the nature of the carver's inspiration.'[148] His distinction is illustrated by the disparity between Moore's 1929 *Reclining Figure*, famously inspired by the Mexican Chac Mool figure, William Turnbull's *Idols* or Paolozzi's bronze figures. *The Philosopher* (1957) (fig. 12), con-structed with a *bricolage* technique, suggests an understanding of the primitive as an alternative cognitive system, while the figure itself is the result of a cultural synthesis more complex than formal appropriation.[149]

Discussed overwhelmingly in formal terms, no art was more foreign, further removed from current social and political issues than the perception of the primi-tive presented by Underwood. Yet while the primitive was seen as alien when it represented a colonised culture, closer to home it might be equated with the innocence imputed to so-called naive artists like Alfred Wallis (fig. 59) and Mary Jewells. A mythic prehistory was to remain the model for an ideal condition, echoed occasionally by writers on St Ives. Denys Val Baker suggested that the 'art colony by the sea' was a place apart, an echo of the island depicted in Keith Vaughan's Festival of Britain mural, *At the Beginning of Time*, while there is more than an echo of the natural savage in Sven Berlin's famous biography of Alfred Wallis.

The remote otherness of prehistory, unlike that of anthropology, required no naturalisation; rather it was seen to speak directly to the contemporary artist.[150] The prehistoric standing stones, hill-forts and barrows of southern England had had a particular fascination for Paul Nash and others in the pre-war *Axis* milieu, an indigenous alternative to French ethnographic Surrealism. John Piper pub-lished an article on the benefits of aerial photography to archaeology in *Axis*,[151] a factual account of a technique that, by revealing traces of ancient activities invis-ible at ground level, poetically converted the landscape into a palimpsest of superimposed activities. Later, under the stress of war, this same landscape was seen as a refuge in which modern town dwellers were identified with ancient Celts.[152]

After the war it was the paintings of the French and Spanish caves, together with fragments of engraved bone and obese little Venus figures, that fascinated artists. Although many of the caves were known by the early twentieth century, the recently discovered Lascaux caves provided a fresh lure for contemporary artists. Prehistoric painting appeared to connect directly with the intuitive process

of the gestural artist. The attraction of 'the Sorcerer, the Shaman . . . the isolated celebrated enigma out of the past'[153] that enthralled Geoffrey Grigson at Les Trois Frères in the Dordogne was that it revealed the perhaps magical origins of a process of creativity towards which the modern artist had painfully to struggle past the barriers of logic. It set a precedent also for the artist as energiser, a mysterious if powerful agent of change.

15. N. H. (Tony) Stubbing, *Coral Variations*, 1956. Oil on canvas, 79 × 127 in. Tate Gallery, London.

Henri Breuil, whose copies of paintings at Lascaux were exhibited at the Arts Council Gallery in October 1954[154] wrote of the cave as a 'temple' filled with art made as 'magic' and first evidenced by 'the imprint of human hands'.[155] The artist N. H. (Tony) Stubbing, who had lived in Madrid from 1947 to 1954 and was familiar with the paintings at Altamira in northern Spain, took the handprint as his main technique and image, either randomly superimposed in different colours or carefully arranged in radiating patterns (fig. 15). His adoption of such a widely recognised and fundamental human sign has been connected with his member-ship of a group of artists called the School of Altamira who often met in caves. These artists, who included Joan Miró, shared a postwar sense of fracture and dislocation, of needing to retrieve common human origins.[156]

Other artists saw prehistoric painting as a model for abandoning conventions of finish and context as William Scott did when, after visiting Lascaux in 1954, he began to paint women's bodies, in thick paint, with heavy black outlines and little or no setting (fig. 16). Like tribal art, prehistoric art is most revealing in relation to twentieth-century artists when it is discussed as an intellectual construction rather than formally copied.

16. William Scott, *Reclining Red Nude*, 1956. Oil on canvas, 36 × 60 in. William Scott Foundation.

A CRITICAL STRATEGY

Early in 1956 'Modern Art in the United States' opened at the Tate Gallery. Although Jackson Pollock's huge painting, *One: Number 31, 1950*[157] had been seen at the ICA in 'Opposing Forces' three years earlier, this was the first opportunity for British artists to see a range of contemporary American art. Overwhelmingly, they focussed on the single room of Abstract Expressionism, in which seventeen artists showed twenty-eight works.[158] This inspired painters, shook critics and forced a re-evaluation of the nature and status of British modernism. Abstract Expressionism had its most passionate advocate in Lawrence Alloway; while nearly all his colleagues addressed the exhibition with circumspection, he recognised the enthusiasm it aroused in artists and began to examine how this could be turned to account to align them with advanced practice in America and continental Europe.

Alloway's dual strategy was to define a vanguard practice with which British artists might engage and to identify the individuals most likely to undertake this process. His rapidly shifting perceptions of the modernist mainstream were revealed in a cluster of exhibitions that he organised or for which he wrote catalogue essays, though he was careful never to claim a group or practice as representative of a current avant garde, but only of innovative approaches.

As a still relatively inexperienced critic, he was invited by the constructive group to write the book published as *Nine Abstract Artists*.[159] Its core consists of artists' statements and reproductions of work but it is prefaced by a long and pre-emptive essay which Alloway may have envisaged, with the exhibition that followed a few months later,[160] as a riposte to 'Space in Colour'. Differentiating between 'pure geometric art' and 'a kind of sensual impressionism without things',[161] Alloway set constructive art beside proto-gestural painting as elements of a potential vanguard. Both would be hostile to the perceptual abstraction which he associated with St Ives and dismissed as a compromise between modernism and traditional landscape painting. He compared the work of Terry Frost, Roger Hilton and William Scott, the three painters among the nine artists, with 'expressionistic action painting'[162] and proposed them as prophets of gestural abstraction.

While his annexation of their work is no longer convincing, it is clear that a case could be made for expecting it to develop in a non-referential mode. Conversely, by emphasising the centrality of the act of painting and reproducing a very early tachiste painting by Anthony Hill[163] he avoided a dogmatic assertion that constructive art constituted the only avant-garde trend or the only process art.

'Statements' opened at the ICA in January 1957.[164] Subtitled 'a survey of British art in 1956', it implicitly acknowledged that profound changes were to be expected in the wake of 'Modern Art in the United States'. 'Statements' consisted of one work each by twenty-one artists, all of whom wrote a brief statement for the catalogue, which provided a summary of current preoccupations. Barbara Hepworth wrote a poem, Alan Davie a short reverie on Zen Buddhism; Gear boldly proclaimed 'the creative act is the important thing'; Heron foresaw a 'brand-new figuration' and Kenneth and Mary Martin discussed the role of mathematics in their art. Peter Kinley no doubt spoke for a large constituency when he dismissed '"constructivist" art' as 'only of academic interest' and Action Painting as philosophically inadequate.[165]

Alloway's stance, faced with so much evidence of individualised, intuitive practices, was to downgrade constructive art[166] even while he emphasised a new wave of 'American-influenced' art, apparent in St Ives no less than among gestural painters like Alan Davie. Though Alloway was mistaken in supposing that geometric abstraction had passed its creative peak, by the end of 1957 he had cleared the way for a comprehensive reformulation of gestural painting. Dominant defining factors were a fresh awareness 'of the physical means of painting' and 'an existential definition of the artist' as one who dismissed the past to dramatise the present 'with a startling rigour and intensity'.[167] In 'Dimensions',[168] a larger, more ambitious survey, subtitled 'British Abstract Art 1948–1957', Alloway proclaimed gestural painting as the cutting edge of current practice and explored its relationship with current French and American painting.

The 'Dimensions' catalogue, which contained an extensive bibliography and a succinct history of abstract art since 1945, again identified the basic distinction as being between 'geometric and painterly', though the latter, which included both perceptual and gestural abstraction, outnumbered geometric works by nearly three to one. The effect, ironically, was to ratify rather than to marginalise constructive art, which was increasingly seen to possess an intellectual clarity lacking in its counterpart. Confirming that the former *enfant terrible* of contemporary practice had ceded its position to the new trend, John Russell wrote that Pasmore, Heath, Kenneth Martin and Nicholson, 'so long ignored or derided, are beginning to have the laugh on their adversaries', whose work he described as 'commotion-in-paint'.[169]

During the period of the survey exhibitions, Alloway wrote a series of catalogue essays[170] in which he sought to locate the European origins of Abstract Expressionism and secondly, American painting itself as a source for images like Turnbull's palette-knifed heads,[171] that returned to those origins in their insistence on the retention of the image. In a series of articles for *Art News & Review*,[172] Alloway provided a brief history of the assimilation of Abstract Expressionism, emphasising the role of Dubuffet and the primitivising COBRA artists who had offered solutions for artists engaged in 'a search for images'.[173]

Although he had firmly stated that in American Action Painting the marks 'though evocative, do not refer to a subject outside the picture',[174] this accorded neither with the work being made by his artist friends nor with the origins of the new art. It was an issue to which he hoped that Monet might hold the key, if paintings like the Rouen Cathedral series, 'objects of terrific material density' might be seen as proto-gestural and reconciled with a reception process in which 'the spectator completes the configuration of the artist's gesture'.[175] In 'Abstract Impressionism', an exhibition which he arranged with the painter Harold Cohen, Alloway presented a continuum of American, British, French and Italian artists concerned with allusions to natural phenomena and the emergence of an image from a 'bed of paint'.[176] However, the argument depended too heavily on the rigorous selection of artists to be widely convincing and Alloway abandoned this line of enquiry to turn to a more overtly American-oriented painting practice.

'Situation', organised by a committee of artists which he chaired,[177] took place at the RBA Galleries in September 1960[178] and evolved from a need to provide an opportunity for artists to exhibit paintings too large for normal commercial spaces.[179] No work was to measure less than thirty square feet and all were to be totally non-figurative, but within these limitations there was enormous variety, from the exuberance of Gillian Ayres's *Cumuli* (1959) (fig. 17), in thin, splattered pigment, to the hard pink teardrop shape that subverts the ordered geometry of Bernard Cohen's *Painting 96* (1960) (fig. 18). 'Situation' had many sources: the development of basic design teaching, the unprecedently large and tranquil canvases seen in 'The New American Painting',[180] the stimulus of an urban environment and the possibility of working within a professionalised and international milieu. All these factors contributed to what Turnbull called 'the situation in

17. Gillian Ayres, *Cumuli*, 1959. Oil on board, 120 × 125 in. Artist's collection.

18. Bernard Cohen, *Painting 96*, 1960, in the 'Situation' exhibition, 1960. Oil on linen, 96 × 132 in. Walker Art Gallery, Liverpool.

London now', from which the exhibition took its title.[181] In more complex and sophisticated terms it replicated the geometric/painterly duality that Alloway had first identified in *Nine Abstract Artists*. At the same time, it represented a real synthesis between European and American models, albeit at the cost of excluding large areas of British practice concerned with landscape and perceptual painting, as well as constructive art, by now poised on the verge of a more secure and prominent phase.

After 'Situation', Alloway emigrated to the United States, driven by what he saw as a continuing provincialism in England. He had worked to negotiate a *rapprochement* between British, continental and American painting, an enterprise that can be compared to Bryan Robertson's at the Whitechapel Art Gallery and which took place on a very similar aesthetic territory. For both men, 'Modern Art in the United States' was a springboard in the enterprise of simultaneously stimulating artists and persuading the public to accept a difficult and revolutionary art form.

4

NATION AND TRADITION

Those who are dissatisfied with the culture in which they live and would like to alter it will naturally try to construct a new canon. The past, however, is not infinitely malleable; it frustrates many of our efforts to change it. Tradition is resistant. On the other hand, it is not monolithic; it is, in fact, continuously being reshaped. Nevertheless, tradition has to appear to cooperate with the reshaping.

Charles Rosen, 1996[1]

English artists were, or were to be, rugged individuals rooted in nature, free from the pedantry, mystery and mannerism critics found in continental culture.

Stephen Daniels, 1993[2]

THE NATIONAL TRADITION

Naum Gabo's *Spiral Theme* (fig. 19) and Alfred Munnings's *Does the Subject Matter?* (1956) (fig. 4) illustrate the polarities of the debate on tradition that developed after 1940. Gabo stood for analysis, engagement, renewal; Munnings for the perpetuation of an ill-defined *status quo*.

In his Trowbridge lecture, read in 1948 to great acclaim at the Leach Pottery in St Ives, Gabo denounced the 'demand of some of these self-appointed public critics of ours, that unless we stick to the ancient, to the naive, anthropomorphic representation of our emotions, we are not doing serious art; we are escapists, decorators, abstractionists, murderers of art, dead men ourselves.'[3] As far as the St Ives artists were concerned, Gabo spoke for the avant garde, against an Academy sustained by a rigid, unchanging notion of tradition. Between the two lay an area of caution, of thus far, no further, where the middle ground represented the leading edge. Although a consensus existed on the meaning of tradition, there was little agreement on its significance to artists or the manner in which it was to be perpetuated.

Raymond Williams assumed the existence of a 'central, effective and dominant system of meanings and values', which is constantly amended by incorporation. Far from being random, this process is subject to choices made in the light of theory and experience. Williams described the area of choice which operates within a dominant system as 'the selective tradition: that which, within the terms of an effective, dominant culture is always passed off as "*the* tradition", "*the* significant past"'.[4] For a culture to survive it must renew itself and tradition provides a mechanism for change, one recognised as so important that it is often presented as inviolable.[5] Few writers in the 1950s considered the way in which traditions are examined, appropriated and reformulated, though John Berger, exceptionally, recognised their capacity to adapt, describing tradition as a 'stable but constantly developing' phenomenon.[6]

Against the model of assimilation and development stood a perception of a monolithic tradition, grounded in craft-based skills and requiring no theoretical justification.[7] In his infamous Royal Academy Banquet speech in April 1949[8] Munnings expounded this view through an attack on modern art, for which he received a great deal of public support. The Academy acted as a bulwark against the dangers of innovatory practice, from abstraction to social realism. The Summer Exhibition represented a datum point for comparison, sustained by popular faith in the Academy as a setter of standards and centre of excellence. The solid centrism of the Summer Exhibition of 1951 was aptly captured by Nevile Wallis: 'a surer index of the national character, certainly a far clearer picture of our scene, than all the inventive murals on the South Bank.'[9] As an old, respected national institution devoted to the maintenance of established values, the Academy was a repository of national virtues and an indicator of that which was typically British. Yet it was more eclectic and more aware of the need for self-renewal than Munnings's much publicised activities would suggest.

Analysing the art of the Academy, Andrew Brighton found it non-theoretical, predicated on 'common sense', taking the 'natural' as its datum point.[10] The unstated canons of academic art are formulated by a consensus taste among purchasers. It operates in the wide space between reproductions of famous historical works and, at the other extreme, avant-garde art,[11] with a centrist area which, in the late 1940s, favoured the naturalised Impressionism[12] of such painters as Ruskin Spear (fig. 6).

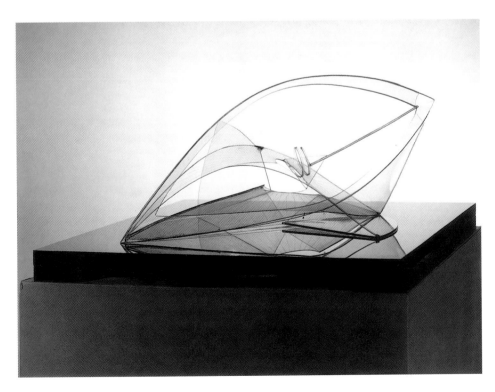

19. Naum Gabo, *Spiral Theme*, 1941. Plastic, $5\frac{1}{2} \times 9\frac{5}{8} \times 9\frac{5}{8}$ in. Tate Gallery, London.

If the Summer Exhibition was a convenient catch-all, which contained an up-to-date version of tradition, the word itself conceals a much more diverse set of codings. In early postwar culture it bore the weight of nationalism, for which high and popular culture offered contradictory forms of expression. To elicit readings of nationalism from the visual arts is at best an elliptical process, often only tenuously related to political events. Such readings may nevertheless contribute to the 'structuring of consciousness' that Patrick Wright has defined as a constituent of nationalism. It has 'among its most fundamental elements . . . a historically produced sense of the past which acts as ground for a proliferation of other definitions of what is normal, appropriate or possible'.[13]

By the end of the 1950s cultural cross-currents were so complex that a brief account will inevitably be highly selective. I have chosen to concentrate on high culture and the status of modernism, since modernism provided the narcissistic pool from which an aesthetic national image was selected for dissemination.

Early postwar interpretations of tradition bordered on xenophobia; they scarcely engaged with French popular culture, though the high culture of France presented a potent challenge. As regards the United States, the situation was reversed: American high culture was virtually unknown until the late 1950s, while its popular culture was both resented and deeply desired.

In a number of books published during the 1940s, critics sought to define the British historical tradition in the visual arts in relation to national character.[14] Its sequential development was understood to have begun with Hogarth, who was characterised as sensible, straightforward, 'defiantly insular'[15] and a man of the people.[16] There followed, in sharp contrast, Reynolds, who provided an intellectual foundation for the British school, and Gainsborough, distinguished by the key words 'lyrical' and 'spontaneous'.[17] Some writers traced the roots of what was often called a native tradition back to the early mediaeval period, citing the Book of Kells and later the Winchester Bible which, by leapfrogging several centuries, might be linked, through their 'linear quality', to William Blake and thus to the proto-modern period.[18] Blake was a revered maverick who defied simple definition but provided a theoretical model for twentieth-century artists like Stanley Spencer and Cecil Collins who defy easy categorisation and are, therefore, seen as eccentrics. Connected with Blake but less problematic, was Samuel Palmer (fig. 25), with his Shoreham associates. Seeking simple definitions, postwar commentators settled on Gainsborough, Blake, Turner and Constable as evidence that 'British art has always been predominantly romantic',[19] with individual informality and spontaneity as its distinguishing characteristics. William Gaunt unexceptionally situated the tradition of British painting 'somewhere between the illustrative genius of Hogarth, the linear rhythm of Blake, the romantic love of nature of Turner, the gentle poetry of Gainsborough'.[20]

How was this corpus to be read by contemporary artists? By describing Hogarth's art as 'illustrative', Gaunt signalled its low status, underlined by Herbert Read, for whom the painter was 'but a deformed creature' because of his concern for social *mores*.[21] An important article by Frederick Antal, titled 'The moral purpose of Hogarth's art',[22] which was published a year after *Contemporary British Art*, casts some light on Read's attitude. Hogarth 'belonged to the core of English philanthropists': he supported Henry Fielding's campaigns, carried out in his capacity of Justice of the Peace for Westminster, to reduce casual robbery and murder on the streets. Politically conscious and active, Hogarth was imbricated in the social structure; it is difficult to imagine an artist more alien to the vanguard sensibilities of the early 1950s.

In the complex negotiation between perceptions of the native artist and one indebted to foreign sources, Hogarth presented a further problem. Though foreign influences were morally suspect, they conferred a stamp of authority on artists who assimilated them creatively. Hogarth, as Antal demonstrated, was such a painter: '[he] had to create a pictorial art out of nothing, for in England the Protestant middle-class . . . from the Reformation until Hogarth's day had produced practically no art at all for religious reasons. Thus Hogarth . . . was obliged to take up and summarize in himself, within his early development, the entire previous continental evolution.'[23]

Unlike the socially engaged Hogarth, the contemporary artist of the 1950s was ideally to focus on nature and its poetic content, for which history provided models of international status. Nature meant landscape, almost invariably qualified as romantic, though the privileging of the romantic in British art-historical writing of the last half century is at the expense of a large part of the historical tradition.

Early postwar accounts of British art history are almost unanimous in their distaste for the classical, ignoring Richard Wilson,[24] Reynolds and Romney.[25] Correspondingly, modernist artists disregarded history painting and portraiture. Rare exceptions are Patrick Heron's portraits of Read and T. S. Eliot and John Minton's historical subject pictures. It is not easy to account for the occlusion of classicism, though perceptions of it as a foreign and southern European corpus of knowledge and taste[26] and the style recently associated with Fascism, were no doubt significant.[27] Landscape painting moved into the vacuum left by classicism, which had previously been inadequately filled by supposedly truthful naturalism.

Readings of landscape conformed closely to historical models. Geoffrey Grigson's work on Palmer encouraged historicism, as did John Piper's *English Romantic Artists*, published in 1942, in a series of illustrated books on aspects of British culture, which amounted to a statement of the values for which the war was being fought. Piper conflated romanticism with early nineteenth-century antiquarianism and thus with the Gothic Revival: 'the still growing passions for old churches and old castles, for rustic cottages and sylvan dingles'.[28]

An updated Picturesque was at the core of the modernising strand of painting led by Piper, whose work was filled with the incident and variety described two hundred years earlier by Uvedale Price as central to the Picturesque.[29] The circumstances of the agrarian revolution to which Picturesque theory responded were remote from wartime urban destruction, though there are ideological parallels between the eighteenth-century theorists and the artists of the 1940s. The effects of the Picturesque are dependent on the passage of time: change, as opposed to the stasis of classicism, is inherent in it. The neo-Picturesque of the 1940s contained both nostalgia for a lost past and a hope that a new social order might grow from the ruins.[30] It found its necessary artifice in antiquities, from prehistoric hill-forts to mediaeval churches and barns, and finally the great country houses of the seventeenth and eighteenth centuries, in whose parks the theory had been put into practice.

Much of Piper's postwar work retained the nostalgia and grief evident in the paintings of bomb-damaged historic buildings that he made as a war artist. The theme was echoed in Keith Vaughan's wartime watercolours of time-encrusted Yorkshire houses, but by the end of the decade the impetus provided by the conjunction of loss and renewal was waning, and with it, the moment of the neo-

Picturesque. Nevertheless, ideas of liberty associated with eighteenth-century aesthetics continued to resonate in mid-twentieth-century formulations of landscape art, constructed as an arena in which the autonomous creator, protected by the authority of a beneficient state, was supreme.

In the gardens at Rousham, among the grandest of their kind, William Kent had created a Claudian landscape, with classical sculpture and pavilions within the garden, while beyond it, vistas terminated in eye-catching 'Gothic' ruins.[31] Denis Cosgrove understands the Rousham gardens to combine metaphors for Roman authority and British liberty, since the visitor's 'eye was led over a scene associated with the Roman *campagna*, but into an unmistakeably English landscape, consciously alluding in its architectural ruins to the traditional freedoms of Britain.'[32] He conflates nature, Gothic allusions and Picturesque informality into a metaphor for individual liberty:

> English liberty . . . threw the weight of judgement on to individual taste and sensibility, in Shaftesbury's words 'that which is dictated by the senses as opposed to the reasoning faculties; it implies the spontaneous, instinctive, imaginative, the directness of emotional experience and also the aesthetic pleasures derived from sensory response'.[33]

It is not, then, surprising that the Picturesque celebration of high civilisation within the rural should have been the subtext of the wartime Recording Britain scheme. Between 1940 and 1943 this project demonstrated 'exactly what we are fighting for – a green and pleasant land, a landscape whose features have been moulded in liberty, whose every winding lane and irregular building is an expression of our national character.'[34]

Another, less well-defined metaphor for freedom, which also contributed to the formulation of the autonomous modernist, is connected with interpretations of the 'prospect'. Seventeenth-century writers equated the breadth of a distant view with a 'wide-ranging political survey' and 'a vision of transcendant truth'.[35] A century later, a taste for an idealised, panoramic landscape – at the opposite pole from Shaftesbury's intuitive pleasures – indicated a man fit for public life, able to think in general and abstract terms, for the public good. Against this elevated taste stood the 'occluded landscape', with much incidental detail but no long view. The implications of such a landscape were that its inhabitants would lack the education and intellectual ability to qualify them for political office.[36]

In the eighteenth-century poetry of John Clare the prospect became a more flexible metaphor that offered a promise to be set against the miseries brought about by enclosure: 'when the moors are thought of as open, they are emblematic of the freedom of the villages before the enclosure; when they are thought of as boundaries, they express the possibility of a movement *towards* freedom.'[37] A similar ambiguity establishes an atmosphere of melancholic desire in Minton's drawing, *Surrey Landscape* (1944) (fig. 20). A spiky branch bars access to a lane, the route to distant hills, though since the way is obscured by foliage, it is not clear whether the couple resting in the lane will manage to complete their journey. The motif of a distant view, sometimes obscured, illuminated only at its furthest point, was a recurrent one during the war, a metaphor for the slow progress towards liberty, the hills at the end of the prospect an echo of Churchill's 'distant sunlit uplands'.[38] A decade later, such metaphors had become unfashionable in a society which esteemed artists principally for their intuition. Gestural abstraction, which answered demands for spontaneity as a sign of the free, creative individual

20. John Minton, *A Surrey Landscape*, 1944. Pen, ink and wash on paper, 21 × 29 in. Arts Council Collection, Hayward Gallery, London.

appeared to relegate the prospect to history, but in chapter eight I suggest that Peter Lanyon's gliding paintings may be approached through a modern reading of the prospect which turns on the relationship between the state and the individual creator.

If a metaphoric reading of the prospect concerns the content of painting, an extension of the theory allocates an equal significance to form. James Turner suggests that the clarity and lack of artifice characteristic of topographic painting indicate a desire to project those qualities onto the state, which would then appear to be 'innocent, self-renewing and inviolable'.[39] The history of the association of these qualities with landscape is a long one,[40] fundamental to an account of tradition and particularly pertinent in the early postwar years.

Landscape's innocence, its historical prominence, a perception of British art and landscape as inherently romantic, together with a conflation of romanticism and the individual, were the basis of readings of tradition current in the late 1940s.[41] From a construction of the artist as an innocent inspired by communion with nature and untouched by social intercourse, it is only a short step to the construction of all landscape as natural and divorced from ideology. The perceived ideological emptiness of landscape art, which assisted readings of its codes in terms of atmosphere and intuition, made it a prime vehicle for the assimilation of modernist forms. New work could be set off against the old and familiar: Graham Sutherland against Palmer, Piper against the Picturesque, Lanyon against Turner.

The modern contribution to tradition was extended to a reassessment of a core concept in English landscape art: the spirit of place or *genius loci*. Alexander Pope's exhortation to 'Consult the Genius of the Place in all'[42] was not so much a plea to leave nature alone as to order it, through landscape gardening, with the utmost sensitivity. For the picturesque gardener, nature stood in a symbiotic relationship with artifice and the boundaries between the two were not readily drawn: the ha-

ha or boundary ditch was as much a sign of the division between the artifice of the garden and the untouched, natural territory beyond it as a physical barrier. By 1810, when Wordsworth published his *Guide to the Lakes*, his concept of nature was much closer than Pope's to the modern understanding of a fragile alternative order. Deploring the fashion for exotic plants, Wordsworth besought gardeners to cultivate only the immediate environs of their homes, as they would then realise that 'after this natural desire has been provided for, the course of all beyond has been predetermined by the spirit of the place'.[43]

Mid-twentieth-century artists attempted to address landscape more directly by redefining the 'Genius of the Place'. The *genius loci*, revived by Paul Nash,[44] implies a non-interventionist attitude coupled with the ability to discern the unique quality of a place.[45] It was a reversal of the generalised concept of landscape familiar to the eighteenth-century connoisseur, which 'expressed itself in a specialised vocabulary and a grammar, as it were, of landscape patterns and structures, established so thoroughly in his language and imagination that he became less and less able to separate any one landscape from any other.'[46] In contrast, their successors, two centuries later, were to *interpret* places, leaving them physically unaltered but creating images of such singularity that locality and artist became identified. Sussex became peculiar to Ivon Hitchens,[47] Dorset to Nash, and Suffolk to Patrick George, just as Cézanne, van Gogh and Bonnard had been identified with specific locations in the south of France.

Nash, writing more than twenty years earlier, when his enterprise had been to define the terms of an English avant garde as distinct from the French one, claimed the *genius loci* as a British characteristic, aligning it with a cool, rationalised 'national idiosyncrasy'. He discerned 'behind the frank expressions of portrait and scene, an imprisoned spirit: yet this spirit is the source, the motive power which animates this art . . . If I were asked to describe this spirit I would say it is of the land . . .'[48]

By conflating contemporary nationalism with tradition and invoking Blake as one who had expressed a national spirit through non-naturalistic art,[49] Nash established a model for modernist painting about places in which the ordering intellect of the individual is paramount and the place is invented by the artist, acting as the Genius of the Place, in order to express some aspect of the relationship between landscape and humanity. In Nash's own paintings such as *Nocturnal Landscape* (1938) (fig. 21), where lumps of flint take on the magnitude and menace of animated megaliths, this approach is disruptive, suggesting a dislocated spirit of place. Like most other aspects of landscape painting, the invented landscape was also historically sanctioned. Gainsborough, despite his attachment to east Suffolk, had painted anonymous, unidentifiable landscapes which investigated 'an unmediated and organic relationship between man and nature, as though isolation from urban culture were an essential prerequisite for such a relationship'.[50] It seems that for some of the artists who extended Nash's concept of place, like Piper in north Wales and Lanyon in Cornwall, for whom landscape was as often as not an unmediated terrain of rock, vegetation and weather, it was of primary importance to exclude the urban.

The range of interpretations of place offered by cultural geographers parallels the variety of approaches by artists, and extends from people to places the value placed on the individual.[51] Geographers have assessed place as an experiential phenomenon;[52] as a product of biological conditioning in which preference is always given to a sheltered habitat overlooking a wide prospect,[53] or as metaphor and social construction.[54]

21. Paul Nash, *Nocturnal Landscape*, 1938. Oil, 30 × 40½ in. City of Manchester Art Galleries.

Within the ethos of the *genius loci*, a memorable locality, worthy of the artist's attention, was assumed to be rural and idealised, an idyllic alternative to the city.[55] Thus the impetus towards regionalism that emerged shortly after the end of the war rode on the back of tradition. Essentially conservative, deeply suspicious of the encroachments of a centralised bureaucracy, it sought to promote regional cultures as counterweights to the international culture that seemed to be politically inevitable. Denys Val Baker's short-lived review, *Voices*, was a mouthpiece for regionalism, calling for 'a cultural effort which attempts to endow a specific region with all that is unconsciously its own. The artist must look at Sussex, Devon or Cornwall to see it as it is; to give the half-buried lore and custom a true shape and reproduce the spirit of the area.'[56]

The development of the small Cornish town, St Ives, as a centre for modernist art, which took on a fresh impetus at the end of the war, was an apt model for Val Baker's regionalism. Its remoteness from metropolitan sophistication and its strong but alien culture of fishing and tin mining facilitated the construction of St Ives as an exotic place, beautiful and elemental. Notions of the primitive and of landscape unsullied by human intervention have been more readily expressed in connection with Cornish artists than with any other group. Cornish landscape can 'be simultaneously an idyll and a model, an escape or a solution'[57] and evokes the 'purity of identity' associated with expressions of nationalism in cultures under stress.[58]

In recent British art history, St Ives is one pole on the axis of the representation of place. The other is occupied by the generic city. Whereas the elevated historical status of landscape painting is inseparable from a class and property-owning system,[59] the art of the city has been less highly regarded, conflated with genre or satire, associated either with realism and the Left or with a conservative rejection of modernism. The realist artists promoted by John Berger were extraordinarily eclectic and, as a result, proposed no coherent urban alternative to the central romantic–pastoral tradition.

During the early postwar years much critical energy was spent on attempts to define coherent patterns, explicable in historical terms, within the plethora of fresh approaches to making art. At the same time a searching debate was conducted on the modernisation of tradition and the status of British artists in an international, western context. Their relationship with the French art world was intensively scrutinised.

THE FRENCH CONNECTION

The isolation and introspection that characterised neo-Romantic art during the war was brought to a climax by the young painter–critic, Michael Ayrton, when he wrote in July 1945 that 'nothing has done more good to my own generation of English painters than being entirely cut off by the war from the Continent and from Paris for five years'.[60] It had forced them 'to fall back not only upon British art but upon British landscape'.[61] Ayrton, whose own work ranged from adaptations of northern sixteenth-century figure painting to meticulously detailed lyric landscape, saw modernism, personified by Picasso, as the greatest threat to his generation.[62] Through his virtuosity Picasso had abused tradition, appropriating and rejecting it at will,[63] though his principal crime for Ayrton was the ubiquity of his impact on western visual culture, which lay like a dead weight over young artists.[64]

Ayrton followed his attack by a series of four articles in *The Studio*, pre-emptively titled 'The heritage of British painting', in which he extended his animosity to embrace the contemporary Ecole de Paris. Examining the British tradition, he concluded that it revealed particular characteristics,[65] transmitted by some sort of genetic national inheritance that enabled it to disregard foreign models. However, the achievements of British art had been appropriated by French artists and assimilated into their own tradition. The twentieth century had seen the 'French domination of British painting', with the result that English artists were often held to be subordinate to their French colleagues[66] though the hiatus of the war had made it possible to reassess the Ecole de Paris as an historical phenomenon whose period of power had passed.[67] Contemporary British artists, reviving poetic and satirical trends,[68] were in a better position than any others in Europe to carry forward its central tradition, possibly, though Ayrton was vague on this point, because they had not suffered the cultural rupture of occupation. Today, Ayrton's case reads like the special pleading of an insecure young artist; in 1946 when peace-time culture had not yet been established, when the sense of national identity was undergoing an enforced and profound change, it probably had a much greater impact.

He seems, however, to have made little impression on his close colleagues, who departed for France, Italy and southern Europe as soon as possible after the war. Paris, where so many artists had studied in the 1930s, was the favourite destination; the Ecole de Paris remained a magnet even for those too young to have known it before the war. While he was still a student, Eduardo Paolozzi sold enough work at his first solo exhibition at the Mayor Gallery in 1946 to enable him to spend four years in Paris discovering the emergent generation of French artists, thus laying the groundwork for much of his work within the Independent Group.

The most fervent proponent of the contemporary Ecole de Paris was, as we have seen in chapter three, Ayrton's near-contemporary and fellow painter–critic, Patrick Heron. He was deeply opposed to Ayrton's isolationism,[69] though determined that British art should develop independently and avoid being drawn into a bland internationalism.[70] His hypothetical School of London was intended primarily to counter such an attitude. Emphasising the diversity of the artists he named as its members, he claimed as their only common characteristic, an awareness 'of what might be called the spiritual landscape of our time',[71] in which a consensus on tradition and the significance of its legacy to contemporary artists played a large part.

THE AMERICAN RELATIONSHIP

Cinema, the pre-eminent popular entertainment before television ownership became widespread,[72] had made American popular culture far more familiar than the daily life of France, even while it retained the allure of an unattainable dream. The early postwar period was one of record cinema attendances, which reached a peak of 1,635 million in 1946,[73] when one-third of the population went to the cinema once a week,[74] generally to see American films, though the quota system stipulated that at least 20 per cent must be British. Although usually seen as a move to protect the British film industry, the quota system articulated an acute perception of the ideological power of film: 'the screen has great influence both politically and culturally over the minds of people. Its potentialities are vast, as a vehicle for the expressions of national life, ideals and tradition, as a dramatic and artistic medium, and as an instrument for propaganda.'[75]

Both French and American culture had profound implications for the visual arts throughout the 1950s. The Left saw American capitalism, manifest in Marshall Aid, as a threat to the people's culture fostered by the war and symbolised by state patronage of the arts. Writers in the communist journals *Our Time* and *Arena* spoke for a constituency far wider than Party membership when they described the cultural effects of cold war-mongering, supporting the suspicions of many Europeans faced with a new world power.[76] American wealth and military might had undoubtedly saved the West from Nazi tyranny, but a question remained as to whether Europe would retain its own cultures and national status or become an outpost of an Americanised international culture.

The Left press, vocal and committed to analysis, expressed grassroots prejudice as well as the views of those concerned with high culture. Both constituencies can be recognised in Frances Pohl's comment that 'Europe's impressive cultural heritage made it especially critical of that of the United States. The view, held by a large number of Europeans [was] that America was materialistic, barbarous, and uncultured.'[77] Marcia Vetrocq has described a parallel situation in Italy, where Cesare Brandi maintained that 'American interventionism' was essentially a matter of 'needing that which it could not create: "the originality, the spontaneity of European individualistic culture"'.[78]

Late in 1947 reports began to emerge of the activities of the House of Representatives' 'Un-American Affairs Committee'. They were reported in *Our Time* under the heading 'We want to be un-American'. The writer commented on the long-running 'Hollywood witch trial' as a diversion from 'much more serious infringements of thought, constituting a cold war against intellectuals in America' and saw the possibility of a similar threat in Britain. Expressing a vulnerability more potent than a political attitude, he deplored the Arts Council's apparent decline in status since the days of CEMA and called for artistic production to be safeguarded as 'part of a national plan', 'creating British works for British leisure'.[79]

The same issue of the magazine offered an explanation for the often inarticulate suspicion of American political intentions, citing a 'cold censorship', 'red-baiting and war-mongering stories' which had placed unstated but quantifiable restrictions on expression in journalism and the arts while alienating 'the ordinary American'. The result was that 'Ignorance of what Americans are really like today, what decent Americans are doing, and how much, is inevitable because these Americans themselves are blocked off from nearly all means of expression.'[80]

A much longer attack occupied a whole issue of *Arena* in 1951, raising the vexed question of film quotas, the bad influence of American comics and magazines and the ubiquity of American popular music. The 'profoundly humanist', national high art tradition of Constable, Turner, Hogarth (the people's painter) and Rowlandson was under threat from American culture; it was urgently necessary to 'popularise and re-discover our cultural heritage' – and to foster social realism.[81]

No similar threat was seen to issue from contemporary American high culture, which remained an object of benign curiosity until 1956. Hard on the heels of the 1945–6 'Picasso and Matisse' exhibition, followed a historical survey of American painting, for which John Rothenstein's catalogue introduction accorded the modern works 'one evasive paragraph'. Louis Crombeke, writing in *Our Time*, commented that the historical 'origins of American art are not only extremely dull but quite unrelated to contemporary developments'. In contrast, he found that contemporary transatlantic painting revealed 'a vigorous social protest' exemplified by Ben Shahn's *Liberation*.[82]

Shahn, a social realist painter, was one of very few non-British artists to be the subject of a Penguin Modern Painters monograph.[83] In 1954 he was chosen, with Willem de Kooning, to represent the United States at the Venice Biennale. Frances Pohl has emphasised that Shahn was an ideal choice in the context of American attempts to promote liberalism and Christian Democracy in Italy, since he 'was a strong advocate of the liberal policies of both the Truman and Eisenhower administrations, openly attacking McCarthyites and communists alike in America'.[84] J. T. Soby's text had long since identified the attraction of Shahn's work for early postwar Britain, describing him as a satirical realist, a 'humanist' and 'the opposite of the "pure" painter'.[85] Most important, Shahn was an ideological bridge-builder, 'appreciated by both Left and Right' for his aesthetic independence, who bore testimony to America's 'willingness to treasure the artist who speaks with sincere authority, in whatever idiom he alone prefers'.[86]

Shahn and the romantic painter, Morris Graves, were the only artists considered worthy of individual attention in the all-American issue of *Horizon* published in 1947. While Soby was careful to emphasise the distinctions between his two subjects,[87] an uncritical notion of realism nevertheless dominated British perceptions of American contemporary painting until the mid-1950s.

In 1947 neither Soby nor Clement Greenberg was prepared to claim full autonomy from foreign sources for contemporary American painting. Greenberg recognised that in casting off provincial isolation and entering the international arena, American high culture had been appropriated, like any commodity, from available stocks.[88] The future of American painting lay not in Shahn's realism but in the hands of the students of Hans Hofmann; only Jackson Pollock showed real achievement and David Smith was 'the only other American artist of our time who produces an art capable of withstanding the test of international scrutiny'.[89]

The most striking aspect of Greenberg's article was its emphasis on the international identity of the new American art, derived as he made clear, entirely from European sources and principally from Paris.[90] Internationalism was neither a goal nor a threat; rather it signposted the route out of provincialism. While it is now clear that no American government initiative lay behind the 1956 and 1959 exhibitions in London,[91] their impetus, confidence and hegemonic status ran parallel to the thrust of American postwar foreign policy. Confronted with the dynamism of the world's richest superpower, Europe went on the defensive, promoting its own diverse national identities.

THE FESTIVAL OF BRITAIN

The introspection fostered by the war and the scarcely less embattled years of recovery has no more telling illustration than the Festival of Britain. Nature, tradition and city came together in the South Bank Exhibition, the largest and most prominent section of the nationwide multi-site Festival, in a burst of euphoria which concealed a more serious intent. First mooted in 1943, when serious planning for postwar reconstruction began, it was initially intended as a national festival and commemoration of the Great Exhibition of 1851.[92] Scarcely two years later the editor of the *News Chronicle*, Gerald Barry, proposed what was soon conceived as a 'Universal International Exhibition'. Lack of money quickly reduced Barry's scheme to a more manageable domestic celebration, but its message remained intact: it was to 'demonstrate to the world the recovery of the United Kingdom from the effects of the war in the moral, cultural, spiritual and material fields'.[93]

Once this principle was established, the many misfortunes that befell the organisers, from shortages of building materials to the appalling weather of the summer of 1951, could be turned to advantage as obstacles overcome by a nation of plucky survivors. The South Bank Exhibition, the heart of the nationwide celebrations, was enormously popular: crowds thronged to the engineering and industrial exhibits, as they did to the Battersea Pleasure Gardens, delighting in the colour, freshness and inventiveness. Today it is easy to dismiss the organisers as naive utopian socialists or quaintly period designers; to interpret the Festival, with its emphasis on education through pleasure, as a class-ridden gesture to social rhetoric. It was both celebration and threnody: a few weeks after it ended the Labour government was defeated in the General Election of October 1951. The Conservative Minister of Works, David Eccles, found no reason to reprieve pavilions always intended as temporary structures, so with the single exception of the Royal Festival Hall the entire site, the first large-scale building project of the postwar years, was demolished.

The architecture of the South Bank was eclectic; no grand plan imposed an order on buildings or layout, and the concept of a Festival Style has been dismissed as a combination of disparate innovations by continental architects.[94] Rejection of a formal, symmetric 'grand manner layout' was an early decision taken by the Design Group led by Hugh Casson.[95] Casson's role in co-ordinating the twenty architects who worked on the pavilions with the overall design of the exhibition can scarcely be overrated, not least for the opportunities he offered to young architects whose careers had been interrupted by the war. Visually the exhibition was held together, if not always with great conviction, by its emphasis on linearity, which extended from Ernest Race's wire chairs to the Skylon designed by the architects Powell and Moya, testimony to the architects' and designers' origins in the Modern Movement aesthetic of revealed structure and the relationship between form and function.

Behind the trade fair and the floodlit dancing the South Bank exhibition concealed deeper, subliminal themes. They are summed up in an advertising spread from Iain Cox's official guidebook. On the right, the planet Saturn, masquerading as a space ship, presents technological expertise as the key to the future. On the left an avenue of mature trees, conveying in their bare branches a promise of regeneration more poignant than full-blown foliage, evokes a changeless pastoral landscape which fuses past and present, tradition and renewal. 'This England', a chunk of the natural world, is juxtaposed with the advances of science and culture, a dichotomy in which both parts are interdependent.[96]

Interplanetary travel was the obsessive vision of the period, promising opportunities for heroism, lands to conquer and sexual gratification.[97] It was a vision about to be realised, brought within sight by the Skylon. Functionless and unclassifiable, at once sculpture, architecture and a feat of engineering, the apparently weightless aluminium pod, soaring floodlit into the night, high above the crowds, rapidly became the unofficial symbol of the Festival. Undefinable, it was an apt symbol of the unknowable: it was everyone's future and the vehicle of every space odyssey.

The planning of the South Bank was based on another dichotomy, of technology versus culture. Upstream of the dividing Hungerford Bridge, in the section titled 'The Land', the focus was on natural resources and the physical world, while downstream the theme was 'The People', with their homes, schools and pastimes, from new and glamorous television to the Women's Institute. The first pavilion in the visitor's sequence, 'The Land of Britain', proposed a powerful equation between geological longevity and national survival. This was circulated beyond the confines of the exhibition by a popular geological history of Britain, *A Land*,[98] written by Jacquetta Hawkes, the archaeological advisor to the Festival. Narrated as a recollection of time past, it is a plea for the values of a natural, rural society over those of the industrial modern city. Her theme was endurance, timelessness and the inseparability of the present from an unimagineably ancient past. The physical structure of the land, from impenetrable subterranean rocks to pastoral outer skin, had become a potent metaphor for the survival and regeneration which the Festival celebrated.

Geology was poetically glossed by Sutherland's mural, *The Origins of the Land*. Arranged in a tripartite form suggesting rock strata, it acted as the visual counterpart to Hawkes's book, emphasising the longevity of organic life. Three forms at the base recalled the artist's mutant forms, which he called personages, in the process of metamorphosis from molten matter to a plant or animal condition. A pterodactyl, a 'hint of prehistory',[99] drawn from a model in a natural history museum,[100] served as a reminder of time and mortality[101] and was painted, as befits a fossil, in a flat grey. The rocks on the earth's surface, which indicated weathering and decay, might alternatively be read as rudimentary human figures.

In 1951 the metaphor of the skeletal structure was no doubt less apparent than it is today, though it was undogmatically echoed by the art and architecture of the South Bank. John Berger's painting, *Scaffolding – Festival of Britain* (1950) showed Ralph Tubbs's Dome of Discovery under construction, exposing the ring girder which supported the span of the dome, a graphic illustration of the stark structural core of these steel-framed buildings.[102]

Modernist revelation co-existed on the South Bank with an obsessive interest in the fundamentals of natural and human form. Edward Mills's abacus screen, one of many that marked off the arena of the Exhibition from the dereliction of the surrounding streets, was made of brightly coloured spheres strung on a framework of thin wires. It extended a decorative theme characteristic of the South Bank, derived from microscopy and crystallography. Fed by geological and archaeological discoveries and the popular diffusion of scientific knowledge, this interest became one of the defining characteristics of a modern visual culture in which artists found a new set of references to nature, where the microscopic structure became a signifier of the larger world.[103]

Sculptors also turned to skeletal notations of form and to the shapes hidden by their containing skin. Henry Moore's *Reclining Figure*, (1951) set in the Fairway outside the Country Pavilion, which was largely devoted to displays of rural handicrafts, takes its place within this aesthetic of natural structure. One of the starkest of his monumental reclining figures, it offered a variation on the identity between a woman's body and the folds of landscape, proposing a metamorphic dichotomy between rocks and the human skeleton. It contrasted sharply with the frontispiece which Moore had provided for Hawkes's book, a lithograph showing four serene and gently rounded reclining figures, apt metaphors for timeless landscape. The curves of Moore's sculptures, Hawkes wrote, 'follow life back into the stone, grope round the contours of the woman he feels there, pull her out with the accumulating layers of time, the impressions of detailed life, marking the flesh of her universal existence.'[104] The *Reclining Figure* of the South Bank was, however, an acutely urban form, taut, angular and tense, her erect head peering anxiously over the jostling crowds.[105]

The linear structure of a fantastic skeleton was also the basis of Reg Butler's *Birdcage*, (1951) which stood near the Regatta Restaurant. A notation for a human figure far above human scale, it proclaimed the enduring power of the intellect through an antenna-like head, probing the sky like a radio beacon. Other, more decorative sculptures, such as Lynn Chadwick's *Cypress* (1951) and Paolozzi's fountain (1951), highly praised as an example of the new public art,[106] also sustained the metaphor of structural endurance, though it would be misleading to claim that such works were not in a minority, since most of the sculptures which adorned the site were unambiguously figurative.

In 1946 the Victoria and Albert Museum had played host to an exhibition, called 'Britain Can Make It', of manufactured goods intended for export. Viewed with longing by a large number of visitors, it had been rapidly renamed 'Britain can't have it'. Five years later a dream promised to become reality. The architecture and imagery of the South Bank exhibition suggested a burgeoning prosperity, a message which would be the dominant theme of the New Elizabethan Age of 1953. The subliminal message of national survival is a tenuous thread, often submerged beneath demonstrations of technological prowess, cultural diversity and pure aesthetic pleasure, yet powerful precisely because of its elusive quality.

'O MY AMERICA! MY NEW-FOUND-LAND'

In his 1955 Reith lectures, given under the title 'The Englishness of English art', Nikolaus Pevsner remarked that 'None of the other nations of Europe has so abject an inferiority complex about its own aesthetic capabilities as England.'[107] As a result, British artists were unlikely to be among the 'principal contributors' to the art of the future and 'most English painting today . . . is a reflection of continental movements'.[108]

Two points are important here: Pevsner, whose definition of the tradition conformed to the majority view cited earlier, also echoed a well-established position regarding British aesthetic subservience. He deviated from the consensual view of tradition only in his lack of nostalgia: as a naturalised immigrant he wrote not out of regret for a lost way of life but in awareness of the totalitarian horror that had almost replaced it. Secondly, he saw British artists as still dominated by their continental colleagues; America found no place in the thinking of this most European of historians.

Pevsner outlined a model of unitary culture that was out-dated by 1955, despite his acknowledgement of 'modern communications . . . keeping everyone all the time in touch with all other parts of the world',[109] with the potential to diminish a sense of difference based on nationalism. The impetus to cultural unity evident throughout the 1940s, on which his model was based, was not sustainable in the long term, if only because the conformity that it implied posed a deadening threat to creativity.

Many writers have described a cultural *malaise* in the late 1950s. Anthony Hartley wrote of 'a narrowing of horizons and a sense of frustration'[110] brought about by disillusion with the 'imperfections . . . especially its cultural imperfections' of the Welfare State, a situation exacerbated by the consequences of the end of empire and Britain's declining status as a world power.[111] He recognised the attendant danger 'of a provincialism which has little to teach the rest of the world and is inclined to complacency',[112] emphasising the insularity embedded in conventional readings of tradition. By the mid-1950s high employment and a modest increase in prosperity had contributed to the provincialism of the New Towns and Subtopia.[113] Here the cautious, comfortable, middle-class high culture offered in the Arts Council's bid for populism and so acutely parodied in Angus Wilson's *Hemlock and After* had become irrelevant, overtaken by the lure of a consumer ethos within which surplus money was spent on a television set rather than a theatre-going habit, a down-payment on a car rather than concert tickets.

Yet in retrospect, the events of 1956 can be seen as having begun a reversal of Pevsner's perception of the status of contemporary English art, a reversal in which the visual arts played a prophetic role as metaphors for the social and political shifts of the 1960s. 1956 saw the Soviet invasion of Hungary and a new crisis for the old supporters of the USSR, while the Suez crisis, which divided Left and Right, families and classes,[114] brought a resurgence of anti-American sentiment among those who supported the intervention. Deploring the ubiquity of this undercurrent in cultural relations,[115] Hartley attributed it to a combination of envy for a visibly glittering material culture and a mistrust of capitalism.[116] Clearly it was an ambiguous attitude, at least among the intelligentsia, for whom 'a common attitude . . . has been to enjoy America thoroughly, to accept its material advantages, but with a subtle nuance of superiority which let it be understood that one was dealing with a society without "roots" and/or social democracy.'[117]

Hartley wrote of the impact of American literature, of its music and popular culture, from Hollywood to 'horror-comics', much of which provided 'at a high level of adequacy for perfectly respectable needs'. Conversely he saw the visual high arts as 'the one field where there seems to have been relatively less transatlantic communication'.[118] Although this may simply have reflected the ubiquity of the popular in the mass-media, it echoed Lawrence Alloway's observation, a few years earlier, of a 'resistance' to American visual art among his colleagues, who had long acquiesced in French domination.[119] On the one hand there was an implicit acknowledgement by the late 1950s that the cultural centre of gravity had shifted: that high culture occupied a place apart, respected but not essential, and that within it the visual arts were the furthest removed from general consciousness. Simultaneously there was a detectable desire to retain the status of the visual arts, to oppose the blurring of high and low boundaries that might result from the impact of American culture.

For some young artists, the America of 1956 offered a renewal of the dream in the form of a youth culture evinced by music, clothes, cars and the vitality of its cities, conveyed in a glamourised form through the cinema. On a practical level, American dealers and critics, Greenberg among them, were beginning to pay regular visits to St Ives at a time when British artists had benefitted from a decade of exposure to European and, especially, French modernism. This reached a spectacular apogee with Georges Mathieu's painting performance at the ICA in 1956. The artist made all the works *in situ* in two days, to avoid the expense of importing them from France, an undertaking described by Toni del Renzio as 'convulsive lyricism'.[120] The phrase hints at the emphasis on image, spectacle and style that was to characterise not only the art of the avant garde in the late 1950s but also its wider culture, formulated from such diverse sources as the infant CND, fashionable Bohemianism and Left politics.

Robert Hewison has seen in the realignments that formulated these sources a 'model for a theory of culture which depends on the opposition between an elite "high culture" and inferior "popular" one . . . in both politics and culture the elite controls the mass, through the institutions of the corporate state, and the control of mass communications by corporations run by elites.'[121] In this context the populist aspirations of the Labour government and its institutions appear simplistic, grounded in the relics of a class system rendered obsolete by economic expansion. In 1956 Alloway and other promoters of high art were no longer concerned either with populism or a unitary culture.

The assimilation of American popular – or junk – culture into high art was initiated by Paolozzi's 'Bunk' lecture at the ICA in April 1952 when, in images like *Meet the People* (1948) (fig. 22), he combined Hollywood, power and consumption in a single statement of yearning desire. For a few years the Independent Group and the ICA remained the locus of serious enquiry into all aspects of American art and culture, but this situation changed abruptly in January 1956, with the opening at the Tate Gallery of 'Modern Art in the United States'.

It is evident from Holger Cahill's introductory essay to the exhibition catalogue that it was conceived in some respects as a challenge to European art, both as an homogeneous category and as an institutional marker of national identities. 'One thing', he wrote, 'is certain. Whatever direction American art is to take, it will be taken primarily in reference to the American situation. After its long tutelage to Europe and its turn toward Asia, American art today has the courage and the will to choose itself.'[122]

In contrast to 1945, when Picasso's wartime paintings penetrated the closed circle of British art with the 'shock of the new', artists active in 1956 converged on contemporary American work informed by a decade of experience of French innovation. They were familiar with Matisse, Jean Dubuffet, Nicolas de Staël, the

22. Eduardo Paolozzi, *Meet the People*, 1948. Collage on paper, $14\frac{1}{8} \times 9\frac{1}{2}$ in. Tate Gallery, London.

lyrical abstraction of the new Ecole de Paris, the Tachisme of Sam Francis and Mathieu and the sculpture of Alberto Giacometti and Germaine Richier. In this context, Abstract Expressionism, with its deep European roots, was as much a catalyst to further development, a confirmation of the validity of experiments already under way, as a revolutionary innovation.

The critical reception of the exhibition implicitly acknowledged this point, though the understated disdain with which it was expressed[123] underlined firstly the mean-minded anti-American sentiment later castigated by Hartley and secondly, the continued dependence of critics on a self-sufficient, historically specific tradition. Yet disoriented though they were by an invasion for which they had no critical model, most commentators reluctantly acknowledged a turning-point: 'the illustration, in the last room, of the tendency towards abstract expressionism, may well have important consequences'.[124]

Alloway took his colleagues to task for their lack of enthusiasm in an article in which he analysed the gestural painting of Pollock, de Kooning and Franz Kline in such a way as to incorporate it into the nexus of European humanism. He pointed out that within Abstract Expressionism 'a picture is not painted according to pre-existing ideas but . . . it is a structure that results from the activity of its making. The tracks of these actions are not primarily decorative but charged with the humanity of the man who makes them.'[125]

The American critic Meyer Schapiro, writing in *The Listener*, offered a conventional interpretation of Abstract Expressionism within the rhetoric of the artist as autonomous hero. Asking whether the movement's confidence was 'merely a reflex of national economic and political strength', he concluded that, on the contrary, its success lay in demonstrating 'the self-sufficiency of the artist on the canvas'. As a result 'The artist's freedom is located more narrowly and more forcefully than ever before within the self, and opposed to the set, impersonal order of the external world.'[126]

In one of the rare enthusiastic reviews of 'Modern art in the United States', Patrick Heron hailed it as evidence of 'the most vigorous movement we have seen since the war', promising: 'We shall now watch New York as eagerly as Paris for new developments.'[127] The exhibition, as Heron indicated, was to prove as great an inspiration to the artists who flocked to it as had 'Picasso and Matisse' a decade earlier and although a second, larger show in 1959, 'The New American Painting', inspired more direct imitation and has therefore been claimed as more influential, nothing in its reception could equal the impact of the recognition that New York had replaced Paris as the centre of the western contemporary art world.

The balance had shifted from a generation of artists dominated by France to one that was receptive to all things American; from the residue of neo-Romanticism and a reverence for landscape and the pastoral tradition to an urban-based, gestural, abstract practice. As Robyn Denny remarked, looking back on this period: 'Suddenly art was future-oriented; it was no longer historically oriented.'[128] For those artists able to respond to it, 'Modern Art in the United States' initiated a period when their acceptance of the formal qualities of American modernism – gesture, large scale, flatness and the centrality of the mark as image – brought them into the international mainstream.

Prominent among them was the small group of painting students at the Royal College who were already obsessed with American culture. Robyn Denny, Richard Smith and Roger Coleman shared Alloway's perception of the modern city as the creative centre of cultural renewal, manifested in the advertisment hoardings, cars, wide cinema screens, Technicolor, fashion and music of urban north America. By the beginning of the 1960s Smith was regularly making paintings over six feet wide. With small, delicate paint marks he magnified inconsequential objects like cigarette packets and coins to a vast scale, like a cinemascape close-up, so that they became unrecognisable. *Formal Giant* (1960) (fig. 23), a shimmering, Rothko-like expanse of red on which is posed a much magnified bow-tie, exemplify the merger between a high painting tradition and the urban consumer culture revealed in glossy magazines. In the scale and the marks of these artists' work there is an emphasis on gesture as an extension of the whole body that is diametrically opposed to Pevsner's belief in the impersonality of English art, which he had connected with its famed linearity and identified as 'an unconcern with the solid body and a watchful interest in the life of line instead – zigzag at first, undulating later; violent at first, tender later but always line, not body'.[129]

'Metavisual, Tachiste, Abstract', mounted at the Redfern Gallery in 1957 and subtitled 'Painting in England Today',[130] offered a prescient summary of this moment of transition from an introspective historicism to a still unfocussed vitality. The exhibition suggested that old categories had been rendered obsolete by the international synthesis known as Action Painting: 'the hybrid child of the Frenchman Dubuffet, the German Ernst, the American Jackson Pollock'.[131] Dismissing old groupings and tradition alike, its only allegiance was to the fresh vision, reformulated on every canvas to posit the supremacy of the existential individual.[132] Though all but one of the artists in the exhibition was British,[133] it was clear that they were riding an international wave; the exhibition marked the

23. Richard Smith, *Formal Giant*, 1960. Oil on canvas, 84 × 90 in. Berardo Collection, Sintra.

end of defensive insularity, with the result that it was 'no longer necessary to confess . . . that the English artist is averse to experiment'.[134]

Less obvious is the rapid expansion of artists' connections, through group and individual exhibitions, with continental and north American art institutions. Sandra Blow, Alan Davie, Lanyon and Gear all had solo exhibitions in New York in 1956/7, building on reputations already promoted by the British Council, which had also formed strong connections with Germany and the Scandinavian countries,[135] in a pronounced shift away from the London–Paris axis.

While Royal College students explored American bourgeois culture, American contemporary art flooded into London. In 1958 the Whitechapel Art Gallery was host to a Pollock retrospective, the prelude to a series of one-person exhibitions at the gallery by contemporary Americans which ended only in 1969 with Helen Frankenthaler. These exhibitions provided the fullest source of information on the New York School to be found anywhere this side of the Atlantic.[136] The ICA, which had a history of eclectic American exhibitions, showed Adolph Gottlieb's recent work in 1959 and a year later, the Californian parallel to Abstract Expressionism in 'West Coast Hard-Edge'.[137]

A celebrated but poorly documented series of exhibitions also took place in the USIS Gallery at the American Embassy,[138] under the auspices of the popular and knowledgeable Cultural Affairs Officer Stefan Munsing, who befriended many artists while he worked in London and was well-informed about contemporary British art. William Green, who was married to Munsing's secretary, recalls that after graduating from the Royal College in July 1958, Munsing gave him occasional work hanging exhibitions, tried to sell his paintings and introduced him to visiting American artists, among them Sam Francis, Gottlieb and Franz Kline.[139]

In November 1958 *Art News & Review* devoted an entire issue to American art. It carried a review of '17 American Painters', then on view in the recently opened embassy gallery.[140] Most of the artists, who included Ellsworth Kelly, Richard Diebenkorn and Ad Reinhardt, were new to Britain and lay outside the Action stereotype with which American painting was already identified. After this impressive opening, USIS exhibition policy seems to have been to provide a varied programme emphasising the typical as much as the spectacular, so that visitors might find 'New England Area Artists', alongside Stefan Knapp's mural scheme for the Seagram Building,[141] or 'Modern American Painting', which was assembled in 1961, entirely from English sources.[142] The fact that it was possible to do so demonstrated the magnitude of the change that had taken place in the art world in the previous five years for, as Alloway wrote, 'New York is now as firmly established as, at least, the rival of Paris and, for some people, as the successor to Paris. English dealers visit New York and the West Coast of America, as once they only visited Paris.'[143]

The intensive preliminary period of assimilation of American art culminated in 'The New American Painting', held at the Tate Gallery early in 1959, and 'Situation', the British response, which opened in September 1960. Drawn from MoMA, commercial galleries and private collections and selected by MoMA officials with Munsing's assistance, 'The New American Painting' was a celebration of recent abstract painting, which it promoted as the dominant contemporary art movement.[144] Although twelve of the seventeen artists had been in 'Modern Art in the United States', the new scale of their work, particularly that of Barnett Newman and Sam Francis,[145] astonished critics and led many of them to equate it with mural painting.

The European tour of 'The New American Painting' confirmed the shift, foreseen by Schapiro, in aesthetic leadership from Paris to New York. The exhibition was received with varying degrees of acclaim. British critics, perhaps wary of being caught in a second error of judgement, were more generous if not always more perceptive than in 1956: 'Enormous, stunning and shocking' was one much quoted response.[146] John Russell expressed admiration for paintings that he understood to be outside the western tradition and probably spoke for many of his colleagues when he admitted that in 1956 'I made the error, as it now seems to me, of judging them according to the canons of traditional aesthetics'.[147]

Summarising the reception of 'The New American Painting', Alloway again castigated his colleagues for their lack of enthusiasm, accusing them of 'anti-Americanism' and inherent 'anti-modernism'.[148] If such a show had been assembled from contemporary British art, he wrote, '. . . the sense of discovery and purpose, power and vitality that marks the American exhibition would be, to put it mildly, missing . . . No other country in the world could put on an exhibition of post-war painting to equal "The New American Painting"'.[149]

Whether Alloway's attack on his colleagues was justified is of less interest than his perception of a persistent Little England attitude to culture which would dismiss the new because it came from that strand of international high culture that was American-led. A context existed by 1959 in which Dubuffet's work might be situated with reference to his peers, whereas that of Gottlieb and Kelly remained unassimilated, unexplored territory. The solution, Alloway considered, lay in a selective appropriation of American practice. More or less coinciding with the moment when the limitations of Action as a pure painting process became apparent, an eschatological alternative was announced by John Latham's *Burial of Count Orgaz* (1958) (fig. 57). His violent but potent image, a relief which contains several black-painted books, redirected Action Painting into a more closely defined ideological context as a protest against the categorisation of human experience symbolised by the book and, more generally, by the notion of a central tradition.

Alloway was to write an introduction to Latham's exhibition at the ICA in 1960, but although he represented the new wave of vanguard art, he was still, as Alloway noted, an isolated figure,[150] not one who might be seen as a cultural bridge-builder. Alloway also detected this role in the artists responsible for the exhibition called 'Place'. Its identification as environment rather than exhibition, its references to American art, through the organisers' insistence on large scale and the interpretative role of the viewer, offered a starting-point for a re-identification of painting 'in ways that are British, or, better, European and not just a retreat to the usual lousy definitions of our national capacity (the Picturesque, linearism, love of country, the light of St Ives).'[151]

The fresh start came a year later, with 'Situation', which established an opposition to perceptual abstraction and, with the exclusion of all St Ives-based artists, also to the updated landscape tradition. Entirely concerned with a radically reformed abstract painting, Alloway poured scorn on contemporary landscape art, recognising that the monolith of tradition could only be overturned by undermining this central stronghold. Introducing 'Situation', Roger Coleman placed its origins firmly in recent transatlantic painting: 'the values that have been accepted are the outcome of the influence of the Americans'.[152] His phrasing contained more than an acknowledgement of formal assimilation, for American art and culture were understood as almost exclusively urban and, despite their diversity, the paintings in 'Situation' emerged, with a few exceptions, from an urban aesthetic. There was no place within a pastoral tradition for Gwyther Irwin's immense collages of paper torn from hoardings,[153] for John Plumb's works in coloured PVC tape or William Green's bitumen paintings (fig. 35).

Central as Alloway's activities were to the assimilation of American painting,[154] his intense focus led him to disregard many of the complex cross-currents at the turn of the decade. An emergent counter-culture, which took the form of Happenings and auto-destructive art, had dual roots in American beatnik culture and the European peace movement. By the middle of the decade it was to constitute a challenge to the conventions of an avant garde. At the same time, the St Ives-based artists known as the middle generation and scorned by Alloway, assumed a position that can best be described as an official avant garde, supported by the British Council and frequently represented in New York's commercial galleries. They continued to denote a central tradition mediated but not dominated by American formal innovation and extended by the urban, body-centred painting of Lucian Freud and Francis Bacon who, like the rising stars Frank Auerbach and Leon Kossoff, offered a more viable counterpart to the pastoral than the unfocussed realism of Berger's young artists a few years earlier.

New Generation sculpture, bright, modish and strongly American in its references, was soon to deflect attention from the older, intensely European and existentially-oriented welded metal sculpture exemplified by Butler's and Chadwick's work (figs 86 and 87). While constructive art entered on its second and more overt phase, Pop Art was identified at the 'Young Contemporaries' exhibition of 1961. It enjoyed an instant commercial success which suggests that it offered a high cultural equivalent to the hugely popular music and clubs of Merseyside.

The long years of austerity were over and the timorous, introverted nationalism of the late 1940s had given way to the consumer culture heralded by Richard Hamilton's collage *Just What Is It that Makes Today's Homes so Different, so Appealing?* (1956) (fig. 55). National survival and the fine balance between the demands of the community and the rights of the individual that had been issues of intense concern in the early postwar period, were negligible fifteen years later, when the ideology of a national community was replaced by that of the individual creator-consumer.

The first, much acclaimed group of Pop artists included an American, R. B. Kitaj, though the origins and forms of British Pop Art had little in common with that of the United States. Witty and slick, British Pop celebrated youth, consumption, the city and unprecedented sexual liberty. Its values were utterly at variance with the national myths that had sustained early postwar society and we may see in its ascendancy a symbolic end to the obsessive search for a national identity. Pop Art bore within itself the disruptions of post-modernism, the negation of categories and the reversal of notions of hierarchy and progress. In the plurality of the post-modern, Pop and modernism co-existed, reinforcing one another. It was the brash and confident face of Pop that led David Thompson to announce in 1964 that 'British art in particular has suddenly woken up out of a long provincial doze, is seriously entering the international lists and winning prestige for itself.'[155]

5

REBUILDING ARCADIA *Art in Wartime*

In this country never before such an interest in painting as to-day – and not only in London. In country places where a decent picture, old or new, has never been seen, crowds flock to good contemporary shows. Expensive French pictures have fled, giving at last a fair chance to native artists, who sell remarkably. If they survive, the English School in twenty years should hit a new level.

Raymond Mortimer, 1940[1]

We are fighting for a new Britain, for the rehousing of our fellow countrymen in a humane way, for the rebuilding of cities bombed by our enemies and bedevilled by ourselves, for the relocation of industry, for the preservation of our heritage of ancient buildings, and for the rehabilitation of the countryside.

Towards a New Britain, 1943[2]

In March 1942 an ambitious exhibition called 'New Movements in Art' opened at the London Museum, then situated in Lancaster House.[3] While it determinedly ignored the war, it may be seen as heralding the thrust to reconstruction which was to become prominent in domestic politics the following year when the first proposal was made for a commemorative festival in 1951. The war, surprisingly, was a rich period for art when, though modernism temporarily ceased to be an active force, it represented a model of dynamism and confidence to be retrieved when the rebuilding began. While the war lasted, many artists were engaged with some aspect of recording while, at the other extreme, a small but significant group, which included John Minton, was principally concerned with an overwhelming, private sense of loss. Both kinds of activity concealed complex, even conflicting sub-texts concerned with the preservation of the historic and the rural, with an arcadian way of life and a class order that no longer existed. Beside these themes stood the need to modernise agriculture, industry and urban housing – indeed, to restructure an entire society. While this was initiated at a practical level with the establishment of the Welfare State, the aspirations and dreams that complemented legislation were often most potently expressed by architects, who were at the forefront of the reconstruction debate.

Introducing 'New Movements in Art', E. H. Ramsden boldly claimed that it provided both 'the refreshment as of a dream remote from the cares of the common day' and a demonstration that 'the art of today is playing no inglorious part in keeping alive those qualities by which alone a nation can ultimately survive'.[4] Though a patriotic sub-text was normal, even expected, of art during the war, one of the paradoxes of the period is that hard propaganda was confined to posters and photographs. In terms of subject matter, painters, other than those employed by the WAAC, often seemed to be unaffected by the conflict, though many of them were forced to restrict their practices to making works on paper after losing their studios.

For sculptors, deprived of both studio space and materials, the situation was more difficult, though not inevitably disastrous. As an official war artist in London, Henry Moore produced the Shelter drawings, perhaps the most familiar and certainly the most mythologised icons of the entire home front. At the same time, in remote St Ives, Barbara Hepworth was working on her immaculate Crystal drawings, abstract visions of metaphysical perfection which constitute a profound rejection of engagement with the war.

While official war art was required to be informative and not likely to spread alarm, no guidelines were laid down for its production. There is, therefore, often no intrinsic evidence that a given work was made during the war, unless it is dated. Is it possible then, to see any patterns, any recurrent themes in the art of the war period, or is it more plausible to accept the eclectic diversity of conflicting voices as the authentic echo of a period of chaos?

As a survey of vanguard British art made during the previous five years, the painting and sculpture in 'New Movements in Art' focussed on Constructivism, with smaller sections devoted to Surrealism and what Raymond Mortimer tentatively identified as a new 'neo-romantic' trend.[5] Graham Sutherland, Frances Hodgkins and Ivon Hitchens were neo-Romantic artists, their paintings 'the expression of an identification with nature'. Works as dissimilar as Minton's *The House* (1941) and Sutherland's *Red Monolith* (1958) could be understood, 'in a world of waste, wickedness and idiocy' as irrational, emotional counterparts to the 'protest and the expression of a particular hope or ideal' that Mortimer found embodied in constructive art.[6] Surrealism, the third thematic strand of the exhibition, was dismissed as irrelevant, given the chaos of the times.[7] The importance of Mortimer's review lay in his identification of a movement sufficiently coherent to be distinguished from the avant-garde groups of the 1930s. Neo-Romantic artists formed the only equivalent to an avant garde in wartime England after the dispersal of the Surrealists.

It was Herbert Read who identified the most pressing question raised by the exhibition: 'is any of this art . . . or any art visible anywhere, prophetic of things to come?'[8] Seeking to perpetuate the earlier dialectic between Surrealism and Constructivism, Read was unable to find an answer within the exhibition, despite his praise for Naum Gabo's *Construction in Space – Spiral Theme* (1941) (fig. 19) – 'the highest point ever reached by the aesthetic intuition of man' – since in 1942 a critic could only discuss art 'in terms of social reconstruction. These activities which we call art are social activities, they are communal activities'.[9]

Read wrote more prophetically than he could know, given the social idealism of postwar constructive art. Retrospectively however, it is neo-Romanticism, which he all but ignored, that has been understood as the dominant trend in wartime art and the one that most comprehensively expressed the diverse emotions of a nation at war.

Reviewing the period in 1977, the poet Derek Stanford wrote of 'an allied front of "goodies" – Apocalyptics, Surrealists, Neo-Romantics and Anarchists – against that old popular front of the "baddies" consisting of Marxists and Social Realists.'[10] The polarity between romanticising and documentary ideologies, the latter the

24. John Craxton, *Dreamer in a Landscape*, 1942. Ink and chalk on paper on board, 21 × 30 in. Tate Gallery, London.

legacy of the AIA and the Euston Road School and including official war art, has obscured the strong thematic and formal links between them. Yet these links are as apparent in the inherent romanticism of the Recording Britain project, with its emphasis on village societies, as in Paul Nash's *Totes Meer* (1940–1), a painting that was as definitive an icon of war as his *Menin Road* (1918–19) had been two decades earlier.

NEO-ROMANTICISM: 'A CERTAIN STRANGENESS'[11]

While recent writers have provided diverse and detailed analyses of neo-Romanticism,[12] Stanford's 'fronts' represent a dual ideological thrust within a chaotic, fecund flux of ideas and attitudes. Read, who was already committed to anarchism, which he understood as a form of cultural expression rather than a political reality, was described by Stanford as the founding father of neo-Romanticism.[13] This was a poet's view which acknowledged Read's support at Routledge for the young poets who became known as the Apocalyptics. Their elusive identity emerged in little magazines and three anthologies published in the early 1940s.[14] In his introduction to *The White Horseman*, G. S. Fraser sought to make a case for the Apocalypse as a 'dialectical development' of Surrealism, although he rejected the Surrealists' insistence on the primacy of the unconscious, emphasising instead the individual imagination.[15] The war, he wrote, had brought about an inevitable dependence on 'our own uncorroborated imaginings. Withdrawn from the public world . . . we are thrown back on the erratic judgements and uncertain impulses of a few intimate friends.'[16]

Though there were no formal links between the apocalyptic poets and the neo-Romantic painters, there is a striking consistency between the luxurious linear complexity of John Craxton's *Dreamer in a Landscape* (1942) (fig. 24) and the heaped-up verbal richness of J. F. Hendry's verse:

Heaven and the stars may roof the mind we own
Within, but this forever white light's constancy,
A bright, sharp foam whose miracle is grace, is all we
Know we lack and never yet have grown.
Therefore I pace the choked roads of the heart
Praying its wilderness of secret flowers
Preserve their root there; master a hard and plaster hate
Bred in the bone and stone; drenching with showers'
Mystery dark lives, dark toils of evil
And ancestral dreams wherein we shelter as in pits
Until above us, on the morrows level,
Roar the wild beasts bursting out of night,
Tilting the hourglass of the conscience as they roam and fight
Beside the tigers, tearing apart this street, this heart.[17]

The philosophy of Personalism[18] represented a further conceptual bond between poets and painters. Expounded as a theory of 'responsible anarchy' by the poet, D. S. Savage, it offered a compelling counter to the voluntary totalitarianism of a society given over to war.[19] Writers and artists should work for the ideal society represented by Personalism; it would be classless and would recognise the primacy of the individual and the artist, who would formulate its values.[20] Given the centrality of the individual within neo-Romanticism, the links between Personalism and the visual arts are indirect but compelling.

The cultural antecedents of neo-Romanticism and the extent to which its artists may be seen aesthetically and ideologically as a coherent group, has been much debated.[21] While Personalism and the Apocalyptic poets offer a theoretical context which suggests that neo-Romanticism may be most convincingly understood as an ideological construction stimulated by the war, the term conceals a complex mesh of sources and readings.

Contemporary artists' texts contribute to our understanding of the common, if ill-defined ethos within which neo-Romantic artists worked. Nash's statement in *Unit One* (1934) was the *locus classicus* for a modern romantic perception of landscape. In *English Romantic Artists* (1942) John Piper situated neo-Romanticism historically, as the modern manifestation of the central impulse in British art. Geoffrey Grigson provided one of the most perceptive, if indirect interpretations of the neo-Romantic ethos in his acclaimed biography of Samuel Palmer[22] and his somewhat premature autobiography, *The Crest on the Silver* (1950), where he identified an individual, empathetic relationship with a nurturing landscape as its dominant element.

The young Grigson, who apparently saw himself in the mould of Palmer, as 'a Christian, a visionary, and a mediaevalist',[23] recalled the garden of his father's Cornish vicarage as a personal Eden. Later he extended this private centre to include the whole Pelynt valley, from which he derived a sense of a locality and its history, knowing it 'as thoroughly as one comes to know the body of a woman'.[24] Palmer's Shoreham paintings, where pastoral innocence was mediated through 'visionary excess', were a model for Grigson's sense of personal place. At the same time they concealed a political content with poignant implications for England in the 1940s: Grigson understood Palmer's paintings as the passionate protest of a High Tory against the riots which preceded the 1832 Reform Bill and threatened the survival of the artist's 'earthly Paradise'.[25]

Sutherland was one of a group of students at Goldsmith's College who had rediscovered Palmer's etchings in the 1920s and obsessively imitated their technique and heavily textured, visionary pastoral imagery.[26] Though Sutherland had abandoned historicism by the end of the 1920s, his intense, anthropomorphised perceptions of landscape and places, initially stimulated by Palmer, had a profound impact on the development of neo-Romanticism. In the 1930s, Sutherland's paintings of Pembrokeshire, Nash's mediations of Surrealism through landscape and Piper's and Nash's antiquarian passions, together with the formal impact of French neo-Romantic painting,[27] provided the basis for the work of the young artists who acknowledged Sutherland as a *chef d'école* during the war.

Though the enormous diversity of work produced by these artists – and others sometimes described as neo-Romantic[28] – tends to defy attempts to define a common style, certain thematic and formal motifs double as ideological markers. Moonlight, intense solitary figures sunk into a landscape and dense, writhing marks, typically in black ink over paint, recur across a wide range of imagery. To take one example, tiny figures are to be seen in Sutherland's *Pembrokeshire Landscape with Roads* (1935) as well as his illustrations to David Gascoyne's *Poems*,[29] while in Keith Vaughan's illustrations for Rimbaud's *Une Saison en Enfer* a minuscule human body appears at the centre of a vortex. Minton adapted the motif, slightly enlarged, in drawings where the figures are subsumed into the landscape, buried in dense ink marks. In each instance the signification of the body is very different: whereas Sutherland's figures seem to propose an identification with natural forces, Vaughan's suggests intense psychological alienation from both nature and culture. For Minton, as we have seen, the body seems to have stood as a metaphor for events beyond human control.

Palmer's watercolour, *A Cornfield by Moonlight with the Evening Star* (1826–32) (fig. 25), which belonged to Kenneth Clark, may well have been familiar to Sutherland and the younger artists; it certainly contains motifs that they shared. It shows a man among corn sheaves in moonlight, with the background, which

25. Samuel Palmer, *A Cornfield by Moonlight with the Evening Star*, 1826–32, British Museum.

26. Graham Sutherland, *Red Landscape*, 1942. Oil on canvas, 26 × 39 in. Southampton Art Gallery.

occurs so frequently in Sutherland's early landscapes, of folded hills. The emphatic pen drawing which overlies the watercolour and the heavy body colour which forms a halo to the moon were neo-Romantic leit-motifs, though Sutherland's younger colleagues were as likely to have known Palmer's imagery through the mediation of the print revival of the late 1920s as from direct experience of his work.

The artists of the 1940s appropriated the disjunctions in scale so characteristic of Nash's Dorset paintings, such as *Nocturnal Landscape* (1938) (fig. 21) where the ambiguous relationship between gigantic anthropomorphised stones and their setting suggests a landscape where the natural order is reversed and no longer dominated by rational human agency. The discordancies in Nash's landscapes are underlined by the clarity of his forms and his high, light colour, which imply a certain logic and moderation. Distinctive, elaborate drawings and occasional paintings by Minton and John Craxton in which, typically, figures are enmeshed in writhing foliage, also carry intimations of nature animated by an overwhelming and alien force. These artists, however, ignored Nash's clarity, preferring the apocalyptic drama of Sutherland's Pembrokeshire landscapes, where rich half-tones are heightened with dense black (fig. 26).

Within the diversity and apparent incoherence of neo-Romantic visual art, which extended to theatre design and book illustration,[30] certain images stand out as particularly potent thematic signifiers. Writing about Sutherland late in 1940, Mortimer discerned 'a romantic self-identification with Nature',[31] an insight which the artist himself elucidated:

> . . . the landscape painter must almost look at the landscape as if it were himself – himself as a human being . . . I'm interested in looking at landscapes . . . so that the impact of the hidden forms develops in my mind . . . Thus follow forms which because of the excitement connected with their discovery, assume in their pictorial essence what one might call a certain strangeness.[32]

27. Graham Sutherland, *Gorse on Sea Wall*, 1939. Oil on canvas, $24\frac{1}{2} \times$ 19 in. Ulster Museum, Belfast.

Gorse on Sea Wall (1939) (fig. 27)[33] was the prototype both for Sutherland's own transformations of insignificant roots and plants into images infused with intense, hostile vitality and for the luxuriant, spikey vegetation which was a definitive neo-Romantic motif. The twisted gorse, which has sprouted menacing prehensile terminals, suggests a mutation between plant and animal or human organisms, a dissolution of the barriers between species.

An equally far-reaching painting was Sutherland's *Entrance to a Lane* (1939),[34] the visual model for the favoured neo-Romantic image of a tunnel without an exit, a metaphor for danger and the loss of personal freedom. Such a tunnel was the central image of Geoffrey Household's novel *Rogue Male*. First published in 1939, it has been described as the 'closest literary parallel' to neo-Romanticism.[35] A blocked tunnel, formed out of a deep lane between open fields and concealed by undergrowth, provides a refuge for a fugitive obliged to hide for reasons of honour. Freedom lies beyond the fields, but the proximity of his enemies prevents him from crossing them. The grimly prophetic message was transformed by painters into an imaginary landscape, a notation for England and their own sense of loss and longing.

Henry Treece articulated an important paradox in neo-Romanticism when he wrote about the significance of the city to an ethos principally expressed through the nuances of landscape imagery: 'Out of the city . . . will come an art of complexity, even of chaos, of nostalgia and sentimentality. The tired city dweller yearns for the country, for peace and quiet, for other periods of time and other places. His art will be private . . . Cities give opportunities to the brain; they neglect the spirit, which may only be perfected in solitude.'[36] Neo-Romantic artists either spent most of their time in London or served as non-combatants; their relationship with an arcardian landscape was in any case severely limited, so it is not entirely surprising that urban and rural themes appear to be interchangeable in their work. Their motifs, but especially the way they portrayed the human body under constriction or in mental anguish, suggest that their imagery emerged from a common experience of the effects of war, rather than a commitment to a particular kind of subject matter. Yet despite the quantity of poignant urban paintings produced by Minton alone, despite the emphasis on bomb-damaged cities in Sutherland's and Piper's work for the WAAC, or such specific and personal images as Vaughan's barrack-room drawings and Robert Colquhoun's angular, neurotic women, there was a constant thrust in neo-Romanticism towards landscape,[37] if only as an unattainable desire.

In 1941, as an official war artist commissioned to record bomb damage, Sutherland extended the theme of transformation from the natural to the man-made in the richly detailed drawings of his *Devastation* series, where shattered machinery and buildings take on the rebarbative vitality of his earlier plant forms.[38] Rather than straight-forward damage, the series recorded a transformatory process in which a once orderly and productive city had become a territory released to savagery, where, as Ronald Alley remarked of *Devastation 1941: City, Twisted Girders (2)* (1941) 'the girders rear like a mortally wounded animal'.[39]

Whereas Sutherland's images emerged from the details of real places, younger neo-Romantic artists treated landscape as a metaphoric construction.[40] Michael Ayrton's *Entrance to a Wood* (1945), which drew directly on Sutherland's painting,[41] and Minton's *A Surrey Landscape* (1944) (fig. 20) are key images which reveal the fundamental themes and motivations of neo-Romanticism. Conspicuous in the foreground of both is a tortuously twisted fallen branch, lying across a path leading to distant open hills. Dense, writhing foliage fills much of the picture surface and, in Minton's drawing, creates a bower for two resting youths. The lane is thus both route and refuge, a place of safety as much for the homosexual as for the beleagured civilian. In the far distance a line of brightly lit hills promises both the 'earthly paradise' and the release of the war's end.

Craxton's pen drawings, *Poet in a Landscape* and *Dreamer in a Landscape* (fig. 24), both made in 1941, acutely summarise the desperation of that year and its remoteness from Palmer's edenic society. Craxton described his solitary figures, enmeshed in barbed and twisted foliage, as self-portraits, studies of a man mentally detached from a hostile landscape.[42] Appropriately enough, the model was a German Jewish refugee, though Craxton's figure recalls the soldier determinedly reading *Horizon* or *Penguin New Writing* on the battlefield.[43] Retrospectively, Craxton made explicit the neo-Romantic elision between nightmare and idyll, or city and country: 'Like Palmer I painted dark sombre pictures with moons and mysterious atmospheres, but these were as much the outcome of my experience of the blackout and the tensions of wartime London as anything else.'[44]

Minton found wartime London an equally rich source for the construction of an imaginary environment. In 'New Movements in Art' he showed a single painting, *The House* (1941), an opened-out bird's-eye view of a roofless, ruined building, set beside a rocky bay and painted in the blue–green tones that he had adopted while working in France before the war.[45] Minton found the shattered buildings and rubble-strewn streets of London subjects as apt for imaginative transformation as any rural landscape. His *London Street* (1941), an extremely dark oil, is as topographically anonymous as *A Surrey Landscape* and an equally atmospheric evocation of alienation. Like many of Minton's city paintings, *London Street* resembles a stage-set, with receding theatrical flats on each side.[46] Theatre provided a frame of reference for artifice and excess, as well as a compositional structure, but the city itself had a more fundamental role in the construction of a neo-Romantic ethos. As a signifier of alienation and destruction it constituted a denial of the fecund countryside, and thus revealed the fragility of the 'earthly paradise'.

Though many artists continued their careers apparently remote from any intimations of conflict, today we read almost every image produced between 1939 and 1945 as having some bearing on the war: from the official art of record and its informal echo, the paintings and drawings of internees, to the Bloomsbury painters' gentle reminders of better times. Though the immediate antecedents of neo-Romanticism lie in the 1930s, its brief apotheosis occurred during the war, of which it was as much a product as the art of record. It expressed ideas necessarily excluded from official war art, of fear, longing and desolation, looking back, with elegiac regret, to the irretrievably lost, whereas the art of record was implicitly optimistic, assuming victory. At the core of neo-Romanticism was an unstated rejection of propaganda, of a common cause, of pulling together for victory and a better society. Once released from wartime restrictions, the artists had no shared goals; they dispersed and rapidly diversified their practices.

The 1945 Picasso exhibition was a potent stimulus to change, while printmaking and book illustration proved to be more secure sources of income than painting, especially for Minton, the most successful and prolific illustrator of all the former neo-Romantics. His adoption of a more academic way of painting in the 1950s, manifested in portraits and grand manner narrative paintings like *The Death of Nelson* (1952), indicated that the attitudes brought into focus by the war were no longer relevant and no longer had the power to hold together a group of artists.

In March 1948 Grigson attacked neo-Romanticism in *Horizon*, condemning it as self-indulgent, nostalgic and naive. Most damagingly, he saw it as 'a new provincialism', obsessed with the past and without any worthwhile purpose. Lacking this, he concluded that neo-Romantic painters would 'reach into a "heart of darkness"; and there each mystery may well resolve itself at last – at last – into a stale puff of flatulence.'[47] The qualities that made neo-Romanticism so apt a means of expression during the war also made it irrelevant once the fighting ceased. The promise of social reconstruction and full employment was more concrete and attractive than an arcadian myth, which had never had the allure for popular consciousness of the dream-world of the American cinema.

CODA: COVENTRY CATHEDRAL

Basil Spence's design for the new Cathedral of St Michael in Coventry, which replaced a mediaeval church destroyed by bombing in November 1940, was a grand romantic gesture of survival, rather than the sign of a new order. Its interior, dominated on the main east–west axis by Sutherland's enormous tapestry, *Christ in Glory* (1962) (fig. 28), which hangs behind the high altar, and on the transverse axis by Piper's Baptistery window, amounts to a last flourish of neo-Romantic themes and imagery.

The tapestry, commissioned in 1952 and completed a decade later, just in time for the consecration of the Cathedral on 25 May 1962, was controversial, attracting criticism particularly for the iconography and pose of the figure.[48] Enclosed in a

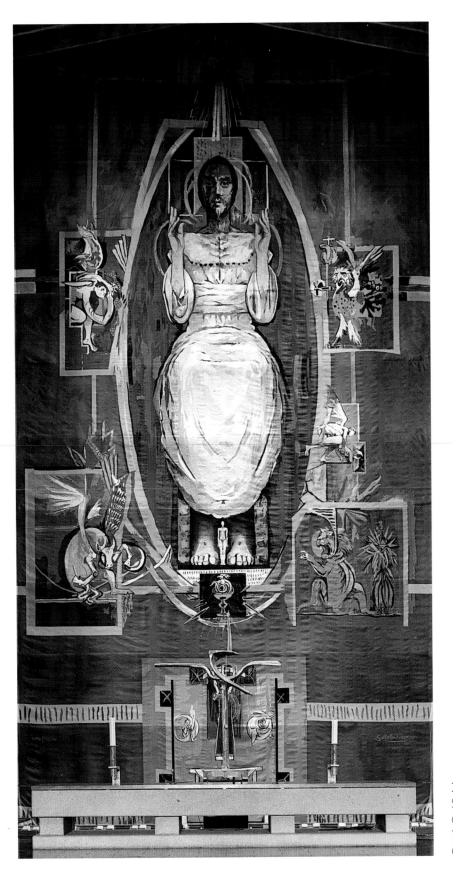

28. Graham Sutherland, *Christ in Glory*, 1962. Tapestry, 74 ft 8 in × 38 ft. Coventry Cathedral.

golden mandorla, it is almost colourless, though the grey–white expanse of the robe is amply compensated for by the glowing reds and purples of the surrounding symbols of the Evangelists, which recall both the resonant colour of the artist's Pembrokeshire landscapes and the mutant forms of the *Devastation* series. Between Christ's feet stands a tiny human figure, a close relation to the fragile bodies that are the focus of some of Sutherland's most poignant earlier works.

There are certain striking visual, if not historical correspondences between the mutant organisms and spiky thickets of neo-Romantic imagery and the jagged anthropomorphic forms of the 'geometry of fear' sculptors. Among them was Geoffrey Clarke who, a decade after Read defined the aesthetic, was seen to have the strongest sculptural impact on the interior of Coventry Cathedral. Clarke made the gilded silver cross (1962) which stands on the high altar, in front of Sutherland's tapestry, where it replicates the convoluted curves of the woven symbols of the Evangelists; the soaring aluminium *Flying Cross* on the flèche and a candelabrum, *The Crown of Thorns*, for the Chapel of Industry.[49]

The complexity and surface detail of these pieces are in startling contrast to the monumental ceramic candlesticks by Hans Coper, which flank the high altar. Together with Piper's and Patrick Reyntiens's great bowed Baptistery window, a dramatic backdrop of abstract colour for the font, which it notionally encloses, Coper's candlesticks are the only convincingly modernist works inside the building. Consequently, by the time it was consecrated, the interior of Spence's cathedral, with its mass of detail and incident, was something of an anachronism. However, this seems to have been inherent in his design concept, which he summarised in the phrase a 'Phoenix rising from the Ashes'.[50] In formulating his concept for the third church on the site, Spence set out programmatically to proclaim its links with the past,[51] particularly the recent past when the old building was destroyed. Most clearly demonstrated in the plan which joins the new church to the ruins of the old one with a great open-sided entrance porch, this concept permeates the interior which looks back to the apocalyptic period of the war, to which it constitutes a most convincing memorial, rather than to the optimism of the postwar reconstruction.

'. . . AN ALLIED FRONT'

Writing in the catalogue of the 1936 International Surrealist exhibition, Read, motivated by the political situation in Germany, had proposed an elision between Surrealism and Romanticism. Inseparable from a liberal political attitude, Romanticism most fully revealed its position in the dialectic with Classicism: 'There is a principle of life, of creation, of liberation, and that is the romantic spirit; there is a principle of order, of control and of repression, and that is the classical spirit.'[52]

However, the liberating influence of British Surrealism collapsed early in 1940 when E. T. Mesens, editor of its house magazine, *The London Bulletin*, and director of the London Gallery, called a meeting at the Barcelona Restaurant to discuss ways of refocussing the group's activities, which showed signs of becoming submerged in the programme of the AIA. Mesens urged members to 'adhere to the proletarian revolution' and demanded that they avoid membership of any other organisation, the better to exercise their singular identity.[53] Read, with a few others, raised strong objections and was evicted from the group, though he was later reinstated.[54] The aftermath of the episode was to be a still deeper fracture, though the meeting achieved enough unity for those who complied with Mesens's demands to show in 'Surrealism Today' at Zwemmer's Gallery in June 1940, together with some specially invited artists who had not been present in the Barcelona Restaurant.

The Zwemmer's exhibition was a relatively sober event, without any of the associated activities that had distinguished the 1936 event, apart from a characteristically distinctive window display, which involved 'a miniature bed, its rumpled sheets transfixed by a dagger. Near it was a full-size chair, upholstered in the shape of a fat negro mammy.'[55] Reviews of 'Surrealism Today', which opened a week after the evacuation from Dunkirk, show that critics, intent on elucidating its relationship with the war, were deeply divided in their reactions. While some found it 'tragically contemporary', 'prophetic', even realistic in its evocations of the chaos of Dunkirk, others were angry or concluded 'nothing that you can do on canvas will stand up to what is going on in the world'.[56] Despite the united political front that British surrealist artists had briefly presented in the late 1930s, through actions and declarations,[57] the very nature of the surrealist enterprise made it impossible to transfer their ideological unity into the production of art: the Zwemmer's exhibition demonstrated primarily what Michel Rémy has called 'the *resistivity* of surrealism in wartime'.[58]

Just over a year after 'Surrealism Today', in July 1943, the first Recording Britain exhibition opened at the National Gallery. As David Mellor has demonstrated, it was a 'hybrid',[59] as much one of Clark's schemes to ensure that artists were in a position to make art rather than war, as an attempt to fix traditional culture in a freeze-frame at a time of maximum vulnerability. Devised by the Committee for the Employment of Artists in Wartime, with the Council for the Preservation of Rural England, its purpose was to record, in 'topographical watercolour drawing',[60] the buildings and, more rarely, landscapes, deemed to be most characteristic of Britain in the early 1940s. On the whole, artists concentrated, as was intended, on the vernacular, and on 'buildings and places that were little known and previously overlooked',[61] though the remit also included 'the elegance and dignity of country houses in their last phase'.[62]

The scheme combined nostalgia with thoroughly contemporary nationalist sentiment, though it was not only German bombs that were seen to threaten the old order. Recording Britain was set up in opposition also to the casual damage caused by oversight, modernisation and bureaucratic regulations,[63] a thrust that was to be echoed in *The Architectural Review*'s impassioned 'Outrage' campaign a decade later. Not only the themes of Recording Britain but its medium and style were located in a strong sense of a national visual tradition. While few of the works produced for the scheme were as consciously archaising as Walter Bayes's *The Yard of the White Hart Inn, Middlesex*, in which a coach and pair stands incongruously beside a sign announcing 'Restaurant', modernism had only a minor impact on the imagery of Recording Britain. Modernism in art could be all too readily identified with industrialisation and the state bureaucracy that commanded modernisation as an aspect of the war effort;[64] for traditionalists, no equation was to be made between the wartime state and the real life of Britain.

Kenneth Rowntree, much praised by contemporary writers,[65] was one of very few artists to extend the conventions of topographic watercolour, introducing an element of modernising *faux-naiveté* into his *Underbank Farm, Woodlands, Ashdale, Derbyshire* (1940), with its mauve roof and blue highlights. Piper, also widely acclaimed for his part in the scheme, made some of its most familiar images, which tellingly invoked neo-Romantic sensibilities, in the pen and wash drawings of the

Windsor Castle series. Piper had established himself as an artist with a passion for decay, preferably in architectural detail, which he fully indulged in his painting of tombstones at Holy Trinity, Hinton-in-the-Hedges. He converted the soft, crumbling stones, set in uncut grass against dark, theatrically lit foliage, into a dramatic metaphor for human frailty, unlike Rowntree who, commissioned to paint the Livermore tombs at Barnston, set down a briskly factual record. Rowntree celebrated the pathetic eccentricity of the subject but suggested, through his meticulous rendering of the inscriptions, that the tombs, in their neatly tended churchyard, would survive.

The Recording Britain scheme was wound up in 1943, after three exhibitions at the National Gallery and the production of well over 1,500 works. These were dispersed all over the country and the scheme was rapidly forgotten for nearly fifty years. It was, nevertheless, a central aspect of art produced in response to war and very much more than the pure record that it purported to be. Its alliance between factual topography and a passionate desire to stop the clocks of progress mark it out as a prelude to the extended postwar dialectic between modernism and tradition.

WAR ART

The War Artists' Advisory Committee was set up in November 1939, chaired and to a large extent instigated by Kenneth Clark. Until it was disbanded in December 1945 its purpose was to 'purchase and commission works of art to form an historical record of the War'.[66] A rolling exhibition of war art occupied the National Gallery from July 1940 until the end of hostilities, while smaller shows toured regional centres;[67] both sets of exhibitions proved immensely popular and were widely discussed in the press. The range of official war art was enormous: it encompassed multiple battlefields as well as the home front; artists were employed from Sicily to Hong Kong, from the Normandy beaches to Tobruk. No images were grimmer than the paintings made by Leslie Coles after the liberation of Belsen; few were more cheerfully relaxed than Edward Ardizzone's scenes in bars and cafés.[68]

Brian Foss has convincingly argued that the formation of 'an historical record' is a less than adequate explanation of the WAAC's activities; that a deeper and more pressing concern was its role in defining a sense of national identity, specifically in opposition to National Socialism.[69] War art thus had a dual thrust of soft propaganda[70] as well as information, while it was clearly also of engrossing interest to a wide public. Above all, both in reception and subject matter, it was a communal, public art; the national identity that it proposed was one that proclaimed its freedom from political control.[71] Freedom was demonstrated by the value placed on diversity and therefore tolerance, which encompassed Ardizzone's barmaids as well as Eric Kennington's stiffly heroicised portraits.[72]

Not all work submitted to the WAAC was accepted; the Committee exerted a certain amount of censorship, since some subjects were considered too sensitive or controversial to be addressed.[73] In the country at large, labour was conscripted and directed, while the lives of civilian women were dominated by the daily grind of queueing long hours for scarce necessities. A sense of community was achieved by a fine balance of coercion and shared purpose; the unanimity that war art proposed was less complete than it may have apppeared in the National Gallery.[74] There was, for instance, a cleavage between war art and the neo-Romantic ethos, which was articulated by G. S. Fraser: 'The New Apocalyptic will be on the side of . . . the myth, the living and organic expression of human need, against the "object-machine" – the attempt by newspapers, government rhetoric, and systematic organization to manipulate men as mere parts of a huge (but quite silly and unproductive) State Machine.'[75]

That a primary function of war art was the formulation and expression of communal values was underlined by the WAAC's deliberate exclusion of what Clark described as 'pure painters . . . interested solely in putting down their feelings about shapes and colours'.[76] Abstract art, like Ben Nicholson's, though theoretically consistent with the aims of official war art, was unlikely to fulfil the demand for information, but Clark considered even the work of Matthew Smith, Victor Pasmore and Ethel Walker overly formalist. Anticipating an ideal that was to dominate the early Arts Council, official war art was required to communicate both with initiates and people who had never previously visited an exhibition, since it was understood to be 'an important index of our democratic spirit'.[77]

The WAAC's decision, perhaps prompted by Clark, to commission such radical artists as Sutherland, Piper and Moore was a very bold one, amply justified by the acclaim with which their work was greeted: 'these three artists are united in this that their work is never commonplace, never obvious and has nothing of the banal . . .'.[78] It was Sutherland, though, the acknowledged romantic, who was repeatedly singled out for his ability to convey the sensations that lay beyond the facts of war. Tellingly, A. C. Sewter judged his paintings to be 'intensely romantic and full of a spiritual agony which makes them the finest tragic expression I know . . . of the suffering of a society at war.'[79] Other writers emphasised the metaphorical, fantastic and anthropomorphic nature of Sutherland's images, whether they were of bombed buildings or of tin-miners in Cornwall. Similarly, Nash's *Totes Meer* and Moore's Shelter drawings were held to embody a more literal, documentary truth than is suggested by their highly individualised form. Moore's drawings have come to occupy a place apart in accounts of the civilian war, contributing, as Adrian Lewis has argued, to a perception of national identity grounded in 'collective endurance and solidarity'.[80]

An important result of the Blitz was to diminish the distance between civilians and the fighting forces and between artists of the home front and those on the battlefields.[81] Several artists were commissioned to record the underground air-raid shelters and all except Moore made factual representations which emphasised the squalor, overcrowding and discomfort in which exhausted Londoners spent their nights.[82] These were overwhelmingly working-class East Enders, shown in drawings by Ardizzone and Peter Peri inelegantly and casually huddled against walls and bundles.[83]

Images of the home front dwelt on social equality and humour in straightforward representations that emphasised labour and productivity over atmosphere or allusion. Much greater weight was placed on the role of women than in the official art of World War I, although there was only a single official woman war artist, Evelyn Dunbar.[84] She was the painter most closely associated with the Women's Land Army, often seen as one of the more comic aspects of the war. However, a painting such as Dunbar's *A Land Girl and the Bail Bull* (1945) (fig. 29), a scene of dairy farming in an idyllic landscape, indicates the urgency of the georgic tradition in wartime, when it represented the survival of the entire nation. That it was also a national industry is suggested by the extent of Dunbar's landscape, filled to the horizon with orderly fields. There is no nostalgic gesture to

29. Evelyn Dunbar, *A Land Girl and the Bail Bull*, 1945. Oil on canvas, 36 × 72 in. Tate Gallery, London.

tradition; no class differentiation, no leisure, no dark symbolic corner to suggest that 'the sweets of life are reserved for the rich, the sweats for the poor' as they were in the eighteenth century.[85] The most startling feature of Dunbar's painting is the gender reversal of the agricultural labourer: no longer relegated to the quasi-decorative status of shepherdess or milkmaid,[86] her task is a real one as she confronts the bull, an enounter in which she is clearly dominant.

The Blitz meant that all aspects of civilian life had a prominence in the official art that is lacking in the equivalent record of the Great War,[87] though the occupations of war workers formed the focus of home front commissions. The grandest, most eccentric and long-lasting of these projects was Stanley Spencer's *Shipbuilding on the Clyde*, a series on which he worked, with diminishing enthusiasm, from May 1940 to March 1946.[88] The artist envisaged a vast scheme involving sixty-eight panels and an entire room, in which he would also explore the sexual and religious connotations with which, as so often, he found the subject imbued.[89] He achieved fourteen paintings, the largest of which are 228 inches wide, as well as numerous working drawings, which record in meticulous detail most of the principal skills involved in ship building.[90]

Spencer's cycle records both the travails of the workers and the material quali-ties of the product: the long, sinuous lines of the wooden template for a ship's hull and the hard, resistant slipperiness of new rope. The central section of *Shipbuilding on the Clyde: Welders* (1941) (fig. 30) shows the men as individuals in features and dress, while the treatment of their bodies, bent and distorted in order to perform their work, vividly illustrates the extent to which war had diminished personal liberty, particularly for working-class men. There is an acute contrast between Spencer's ant-like welders and Dunbar's land girl, who fills the height of the canvas and is the active protagonist and focus of the painting.

War art was required to be factual and informative to an even greater degree than the paintings made for Recording Britain. There, artists were encouraged to seek out the eccentric and quirky, in order to emphasise the singularity of the national character. With official war art, this was the exception rather than the rule, though neo-Romantic artists, especially Piper and Sutherland, provided some of the most highly acclaimed images of the entire home front, with their apocalyptic and fantastic renderings of bomb damage. Critics acknowledged the diversity of official war art in reviews of the National Gallery exhibitions but, beyond commenting on genre – illustration, portraiture, action images – they had little to say about the content of the work. This, the reviews imply, was understood to be a comprehensive range of exposure to every aspect of war, filtered through an individual aesthetic sensibility. War artists had an obligation to record, as did those who worked for Recording Britain, though there the opportunity for diversity was much greater. Both programmes were, finally, exercises in underpinning a sense of national identity without overt propaganda.

'. . . THAT OLD POPULAR FRONT'

A brief skirmish on the perennial subject of the viability of abstract art took place in *The Listener* in September 1940, between Grigson and Read. Grigson circumspectly welcomed the prospect of artists 'returning to nature'. He hoped that this might hasten the disappearance of 'the astonishing intellectual and spiritual dullness and littleness of English artists at present', though 'Whatever happens politically in Europe, I should not be surprised if, in the urgency of other things, much of the best art once more goes underground.'[91] In response to this Read quoted Clement Greenberg's 'Towards a new Laocoon' in support of 'the abstract principle' which, he maintained, underlay 'that desire for coherence, for unity, for an objective basis in universal law, which is the secret of the greatest art the world has seen'.[92]

Read's gentle artists of Hampstead, the Surrealists and Constructivists of 'New Movements in Art' were all dispersed, some to the war, others to Cornwall. There was little evidence of the continuing vitality of abstraction in wartime. Propaganda, factual record and poetic allusion were all better expressed, it seemed, in figurative terms.

30. Stanley Spencer, *Shipbuilding on the Clyde: Welders*, 1941 (central section). Oil on canvas. Imperial War Museum, London.

Like other organisations, the AIA was intent on supporting artists' careers and livelihoods during the war,[93] through print schemes[94] and travelling exhibitions. Sometimes organised in association with CEMA, the latter were held in factory canteens and British Restaurants, as well as the more conventional municipal galleries. Many other AIA shows were mounted in various venues in London, notably 'War Pictures', in Charing Cross underground station, where it not surprisingly had enormously high attendance figures.[95]

The AIA's most celebrated wartime exhibition was 'For Liberty', held between 13 March and 11 April 1945 in a new basement canteen near the bombed John Lewis store in Oxford Street. In his foreword, Misha Black[96] claimed that the exhibition demonstrated an under-exploited role for art in wartime, as a branch of propaganda, distinct from 'the written word and the poster. Both make their appeal to reason, but here is a new kind which appeals to the imagination, differing from poster art in the same way as poetry and song differs from written propaganda.'[97] He emphasised the Association's role in bringing art to 'people who do not normally have the opportunity of enjoying pictures' and, in a measured dismissal of modernism, deplored the dissociation of art from society. This had led to artists becoming 'absorbed in technical problems and methods of expression which result in new forms which are often beyond the understanding of the public'.[98] For art to be truly democratic, easel painting must give way to murals, which should be combined with texts in order to maximise their propaganda function.

In the event, only a handful of the 170-odd works in 'For Liberty' were mural panels or designs for murals. However, the fifteen paintings made especially for the exhibition, on the theme of 'the four Freedoms',[99] all conformed to a stipulated large format of four by five feet.[100] 'The four Freedoms', set out in the catalogue beside a reproduction of Hans Feibusch's *Resurrection*, were those of the Atlantic Charter,[101] their urgency underlined by the participation of many refugee artists, including Oskar Kokoschka and Feibusch himself.[102] Many of the smaller works were thematically arranged under such headings as 'This is how we are fighting', the ominous 'This will happen here unless . . .' and 'This is what we are fighting for', which included a work by Mary Hoad with the title *The Triumph of Social Security, Over the Beveridge Giants – Want, Disease, Idleness, Ignorance, Sloth*.

The constructive, surrealist and neo-romantic artists of 'New Movements in Art' were conspicuously absent from 'For Liberty'. Mortimer's review of the earlier exhibition had hinted at the reason: 'Obviously art has no place in total war, along with the pursuit of truth and the cultivation of friendship'.[103] He felt that access to art presented no problem to the working class, who chose wilfully to ignore it, while the exhibiting pattern of most of the 'New Movements' artists, with regular shows in West End galleries, indicated that they were uninterested in a populist approach and considered their work destined for the old-established private patron market.[104]

While war art strictly denotes work commissioned by the WAAC, an expanded reading of the term suggests any art that is imbued with a sense of the conflict. Where else should we situate the art made by refugees who had been designated aliens and interned on the Isle of Man? As a deeply felt emotional and ideological construct, war art has no formal definition, except that its populist thrust inclined it strongly towards figuration. Yet the Temple Newsam trio: Moore, Piper and Sutherland,[105] who were deeply appreciated for their sensibility to the war, showed work between 1939 and 1945 which remained heavily inflected by modernism.

Painting was arguably not the most appropriate medium for an art of record; its inability to compete with the photography of *Picture Post* meant that it was relatively unsuccessful as documentation. Its achievement, as Foss has argued, was to promote a sense of national cohesion; beyond that, the most acclaimed works, like Nash's *Totes Meer* and Moore's Shelter drawings combined emotional outpouring with a sense of common purpose. Yet very little war art – 'For Liberty' is one of the rare exceptions – looked forward to constructing the future.

'REBUILDING BRITAIN'

In 1943 the National Gallery mounted an architectural exhibition arranged by Jane Drew.[106] Titled 'Rebuilding Britain', it amounted to a proposal for the architectural infrastructure of the New Britain, an exacting visionary exercise with a practical purpose. Optimistic, modernist and socialist, it made a significant contribution to the reconstruction debate, drawing its social ethos from the Beveridge Report.[107] Prophetically warning that 'The people of Britain will get the reconstruction they deserve',[108] the accompanying text emphasised the democratic, participatory quality of reconstruction and the need to ground architecture in both social and town planning.[109] This would combine the radical vision of Le Corbusier's abstract schemes for great modern cities with sensitivity to local needs.

'Rebuilding Britain' cited the recent achievements of Modern Movement architects on the Continent and in Britain and a project by Architectural Association students 'for a new town in Berkshire'.[110] It also commended 'the atmosphere and [a] human scale' of English market towns.[111] It was as much concerned with the countryside and country towns as with London. Impington Village College was a model for rural community centres which, like National Parks, should proliferate, to fulfil the leisure requirements of the future rather than to preserve the past. Only London was to be radically rebuilt, for 'Judged by either aesthetic or humane standards, the parts of London genuinely worthy of preservation are relatively very small.'[112]

Though no grand plan for rebuilding London was put into effect, since even the extensive reconstruction of the blitzed East End was fitted into surviving streets and buildings, 'Rebuilding Britain' formulated an architectural and social ethos which had a visible legacy in new housing and schools and the New Towns. In practice, physical reconstruction was a piecemeal process of compromise, handicapped as much by timidity[113] as by lack of money, but when the Welfare State became effective at the end of the war, it brought about the democratic social revolution to which 'Rebuilding Britain' had been a rallying call. If relatively little of its architectural radicalism was translated into buildings, its ideology contributed significantly to a restructuring of social consciousness that was only cut off by the Conservatism of the 1980s. The arcadian dream that sustained the neo-Romantics dissolved in the hard realities of the postwar world, when progressive artists chose to respond to the vision of the New Britain rather than the lost Eden.

6

GEOMETRY AND GESTURE
Process-Dominant Art

It is the process, the method of development that is the life of the painting, and this that absorbs my interest rather than the attractions of any particular form or colour. The forms themselves, their size and position are born from the process. In fact all forms should witness clearly to their evolution. The colour and shape of their past is responsible for their present which is richer for these transitions.

Adrian Heath, 1954[1]

Art is a subjective process of individuation and its products are metamorphic, illogical. Art is variety; art is adventure.

Herbert Read, 1948[2]

Tom Hudson, the constructive artist and teacher, drew an arresting parallel between the Renaissance and the modern world when he defined, as a distinguishing mark of both periods, 'the same instinctive desire to dominate the physical universe'.[3] As in the Renaissance, art, science and technology were often to be found working in parallel to produce similar results, though contemporary artists were no longer interested in the illusions generated by single-point perspective. Even if constructive artists, most of whom had abandoned paint on canvas to make three-dimensional, sculptural objects, seemed to offer the most resolved alternative to perspectival space, Hudson could also recognise satisfactory variations in geometric and tachiste painting.[4]

Hudson wrote his article in 1957, when constructive art had already passed through its first tentative years of trial and experiment and had given way, as an art scandal and focus of vituperation, to gestural painting. Both come under the heading of what David Thistlewood has called process-dominant art.[5] The term denotes an intellectual approach rather than a procedural method, indicating that the final form of a work is determined, conceptually and physically, by the course of its fabrication and not, as in earlier periods, by sketches, working drawings or an envisaged end.

The two forms of process art, mathematical and gestural, that emerged in the late 1940s, established a confrontation that lasted more than a decade and echoed what Read had described as 'a polar axis, with transcendental metaphysics at one end and an intense self-awareness of physical vitality at the other end'.[6] The first, which became known for a few years in the 1950s as Constructionism,[7] was a non-

31. Victor Pasmore,
White Relief, 1951.
Painted wood, $40\frac{1}{2}$
$\times$ $18\frac{1}{4}$. Artist's
estate.

perceptual abstract art grounded in geometric and proportional systems, deliberately depersonalised to exclude extrinsic associations (fig. 31). The complementary form, which became known as Tachisme or Action Painting,[8] (fig. 32) was personal, asocial, intuitive, a physically inflected art which found expression through the interaction of gesture and materials.

Kenneth Martin analysed the constructive approach in 1951, when he wrote in *Broadsheet No.1* that 'Proportion and analogy' were the fundamental principles of

32. Denis Bowen,
Galactic 1, 1961. Oil
on canvas, 52 $\times$
92 in. Artist's
collection.

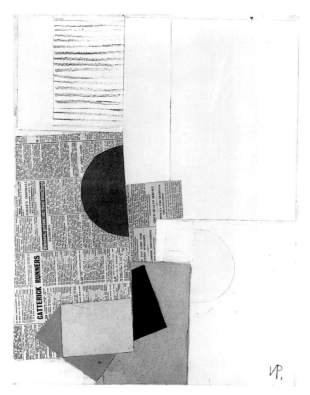

33. Victor Pasmore, *Abstract in White, Grey and Ochre*, 1949. Collage on canvas, 20 × 16 in. Tate Gallery, London.

34. Adrian Heath, *White Collage*, 1954. Oil and collage on canvas, 20 × 16 in. Tate Gallery, London.

a process which did not seek to reproduce 'the illusory and transient aspects of nature, but which copies nature in the laws of its activities'.[9] Victor Pasmore's collage, *Abstract in White, Grey and Ochre* (1949), which was reproduced in the same publication,[10] combines drawing, newsprint and coloured paper cut in geometric shapes (fig. 33). In that it does not reproduce anything, but simply presents its constituent parts for scrutiny, it is consistent with Martin's central point that 'The object which is created is real and not illusional in that it sets out to represent no object outside the canvas, but to contain within itself the force of its own nature.'[11] In a later text Martin emphasised the experimental nature of constructionist practice. He effectively refuted the recurrent objection that it produced a formulaic art and pointed out that 'it is difficult to predetermine a system for forms whose properties one is in the way of discovering . . . it is process that one is inventing.'[12]

The best contemporary summary of the constructionist approach remains Adrian Heath's statement in *Nine Abstract Artists*, part of which is quoted at the head of this chapter. His early geometric paintings exemplify the kind of process art that is determined by a theoretical programme. *Composition White and Yellow* (1953)[13] is laid out in the static format of a root-two rectangle on which Heath superimposed a 'moving format', shown as a fan-like succession of shapes which form a track around an axis.[14] While the process implied a certain severity, the basic geometry did not have to be programatically displayed: colour and the texture of paint and canvas could provide aesthetic interludes of drama and contrast. *Composition White and Yellow* is, like *White Collage* (1954) (fig. 34) one of many that works Heath made between 1952 and 1955 that are strongly reminiscent of the work of Serge Poliakoff, a Russian artist settled in Paris. Poliakoff's paintings may well have provided visual models for the repertoire of forms and modulations of the surface which helped Heath to translate his process into a pictorial language.[15]

William Green, a 1958 graduate from the Royal College of Art, briefly became the epitome of the Action Painter, the gestural artist driven by intuition. While still a student, he abandoned colour and conventional paint and canvas for bitumen, which he threw over large sheets of hardboard laid on the floor. He then modified his paintings by riding a bicycle through the wet pigment, setting it on fire or etching it with acid, to leave a dull grey bloom which faded into areas of small, burst bubbles like sand, or a thick, black shiny medium (fig. 35). Though Green later became intensely interested in Jackson Pollock,[16] his immediate model was presumably Georges Mathieu, who gave a much publicised painting performance at the ICA in July 1956.[17] However, the myth attached to Pollock no doubt gave his paintings an extra edge in Green's estimation. One of the artists designated 'Mythmakers' by his friend Mark Rothko,[18] Pollock had himself been mythologised, firstly by photographs of his spectacular technique and then by his early death in a car accident. Alcoholic and unstable, the implication is that the painter was consumed by the overwhelming demands of his art, a monster out of control.

The young William Green was a promising model for a native avant-garde myth. Ken Russell, who met him in 1957, made a film which was shown on the

35. William Green, *Painting 1958*. Bitumen on board, 35 × 35 in. England & Co., London.

36. Victor Pasmore,
*Spiral Motif in Green,
Violet, Blue and Gold:
the Coast of the
Inland Sea*, 1950. Oil
on canvas, 32 ×
39¹/₂ in. Tate Gallery,
London.

BBC's *Tonight* programme[19] in which Green set alight a bitumen-covered board in an act of ritual aesthetic violence. The film was immensely successful; Green became an instant living legend, a delight to journalists, for whom his spectacular activities signalled the outer reaches of the avant garde. In reality, his bitumen-fire-bicycle process rapidly became a formula to which he was tied by his reputation as a beat artist. Unable to extend his practice and hounded by publicity, he retreated into teaching and gave up painting for many years.

The examples of Heath and Green, at the polarities of process-dominant art, confirm that it is as open to interpretation and as rich in content as any other aspect of contemporary practice and that to read it solely in formal terms is as limiting as the judgements of critics who dismissed it as 'bathroom fittings' or 'wallpaper design'. Objections to gestural painting focussed on the fact that each work of art resulted from a spontaneous, unpremeditated act; its theoretical grounding in Jungian philosophy, surrealist automatism and Zen Buddhism only slowly became apparent. Constructive art was condemned for being rigidly programmatic, or over-theorised, a verdict that ignored its explicit social idealism and the courage of artists who risked ridicule and professional failure by rejecting the weight of training and tradition.

The extraordinary difficulty that artists encountered in abandoning perceptual painting emerges from accounts of the ICA's first Public View debate, held on 9 January 1951, which focussed on Pasmore's recent exhibition at the Redfern Gallery.[20] Discussing his painting, *Spiral Motif in Green, Violet, Blue and Gold: the Coast of the Inland Sea* (1950) (fig. 36), which was displayed during the debate,[21] Pasmore tried to explain his new imagery through a musical analogy. He aligned himself with a kind of painting that had broken with tradition to replace perceptual images by 'formal elements which, in themselves, have no descriptive qualities at all'.[22] Following this principle, *The Coast of the Inland Sea* had, Pasmore maintained, evolved from a simple spiral, though he conceded that he had also begun to see it 'as rocks, coast, sea and sky'.[23] It was, in fact, one of a group of paintings in which he had worked out variations on a dividing horizontal with spirals and small, Klee-like forms above and below it, which he later acknowledged as generalised 'landscape themes' unrelated to locations.[24]

In his account of constructionist exhibitions and publications Alastair Grieve has emphasised the centrality of *Nine Abstract Artists*, a small book published late in 1954.[25] The pivot between geometric and gestural practices, it contains a long introduction by Lawrence Alloway, followed by statements and reproductions of the work of the nine artists involved, at whose request he had edited the book. While Alloway's text transcends formalism, he was largely concerned with antecedents and affinities, with establishing the institutional relations of a group of artists.

An alternative approach to process is through the themes that are the rationale of the work. While critics characterised process-dominant art as either uniform, programmatic and reductive, or conversely as threatening in its subjectivity and lack of discipline, it was apparent by the mid-1950s that in practice the two strands overlapped.

ART AND SCIENCE

Although apparently irreconcilably opposed, art and science are, as Thistlewood has demonstrated, theoretically linked through certain texts and activities at the ICA in the early 1950s. Artists claimed to construct their work according to organic principles,[26] acknowledging an analogy with the development of natural growth patterns from a single cell to a complex organism. A much-discussed model for this was d'Arcy Wentworth Thompson's *On Growth and Form*, copiously illustrated with reproductions of cellular structures. Thompson's thesis was that except in extremely rudimentary organisms, physical form is determined by the forces that produce growth and that in every instance this is unique and unpredictable.[27]

The book was a primary visual resource for a number of artists, including Richard Hamilton when he was devising the ICA's 'Growth and Form' exhibition in 1950–1. Its catalogue carried a reproduction of his previously unpublished etching, *Heteromorphism*, on the cover.[28] More significantly for Hamilton, whose early imagery evolved from an initial mark which set off a chain reaction of responses, Thompson demonstrated that an apparently random configuration might actually result from a rational intellectual pattern,[29] dominated by a perception of process in which biology and aesthetics were coterminous.

Thompson showed also that the growth of spirals in, for instance, shells, could be expressed mathematically, in terms of ratios, thus effecting an elision between natural processes and the disengagement of mathematical laws. This was particularly significant for constructive artists, who chose to order their work according to ratio and proportion, since these were models that could transcend the barriers between scientific and aesthetic perceptions. Just as William Green's bitumen paintings might be understood as the imprint of his personality on a transient situation, Heath's *White Collage* (fig. 34) was the counterpart of a morphological process. Both were unique, organic developments from an initial impulse or mark.

The possibilities of common ground between artists and scientists were strenuously debated, culminating in C. P. Snow's 'Two Cultures' lecture and the controversy which it engendered in 1958, a decade after discussion of a lecture by Giedion had highlighted the difficulty of effecting a synthesis of art and science.[30] In his Trowbridge lecture at Yale in 1948, Naum Gabo, who had trained in medicine, the natural sciences and engineering, developed the ideas he had first formulated in the 'Realistic Manifesto'. He spoke of art as a conduit to bring scientific concepts into general consciousness with a sensual and emotional charge, so that they could be intuitively grasped by those with no scientific training. Formal arrangements of shapes and colours had no more validity than naturalism as an art form, since neither could represent the reality of science, but abstract, constructive artists might create fresh images and 'convey them as emotional manifestations in our everyday experience'.[31]

At the turn of the decade two texts, one by an art historian, the other by a scientist, traced different routes through which this situation might be brought about and incidentally also provided justifications for constructive art. In a parallel argument to Tom Hudson's, the art historian, Rudolph Wittkower found a *rapprochement*, and an echo of renaissance philosophy, in the tendency of both periods to form 'a simple and synoptic image of the surrounding world'. Art, he wrote, must have a theoretical grounding; without this it could only be considered as craft; with it, however, art might be regarded as one of the 'liberal arts', or sciences. Painting should therefore be grounded in mathematics, which would enable it to reveal the harmonic structures of all natural phenomena; failure to achieve this objectivity, which was demonstrated by abstract art, would result in a reprise of formalism.[32]

Lecturing at the ICA in 1951, the scientist, Jacob Bronowski reminded his audience that science was not simply a collection of facts but an arrangement of facts that made sense: 'The order of the structure is, in fact, the content of science. Now we have all grown up in a generation in which all think of the arrangement, the order, the structure, as being the content of a picture, the content of a piece of sculpture, or art.'[33] A 'search for internal structure' and the difference between that structure and external appearance had formed the 'essential content' of both science and painting since the 1890s. Bronowski found a cogent illustration of that difference in the 'disorderly scribble' of Henry Moore's Shelter drawings, which nevertheless created coherent forms. Bronowski's argument about 'essential content' is well illustrated by Kenneth Martin's *Composition* (1949), a seemingly formalist study of colour and balance which was, the artist explained, actually derived from the pattern of venation in a dragonfly's wing, taken from an illustration in *On Growth and Form*.[34]

Art and science was a favoured theme for debates at the ICA, much encouraged by Herbert Read and his multi-disciplinary circle. Participants in a symposium titled 'Aspects of Form' included, alongside the art historian Ernst Gombrich, a neurologist, plant and animal experts, psychologists, a crystallographer and an astronomer.[35] Its organiser was Lancelot Law Whyte, 'a physicist who had been conducting a one-man campaign, from as early as the 1920s, for recognition of a single discipline embracing subjects as apparently diverse as physics and psychology, biology and art.'[36]

Some months later, on 3 July 1951, Hamilton's exhibition, 'Growth and Form' opened at the Institute, a demonstration of the possibility of bridging the art–science divide. Hamilton had designed a thematic exhibition, still a rarity in an aesthetic context, an installation ahead of its time, where the physical form was identical with the content.[37] His own brief account indicates that design and content had equal weight in his planning.[38] Inspired by Thompson's book, his media were photography, models, scientific drawings and diagrams, free-standing or arranged on a three-dimensional metal grid. Additional information was conveyed by projection onto the walls: photographs show a gigantic skeletal hand thrown over the whole exhibition, while strobe lights and mirrors added physical disorientation to intellectual discomfort.

ART AND INTUITION

Just as d'Arcy Wentworth Thompson's exposition of biological development had an impact on constructive artists, in alliance with their knowledge of proportional systems and geometry, so did Jungian concepts, particularly of the archetype, inflect the work of gestural painters. Read was the conduit for the entry of Jungian theory into contemporary art both as the psychoanalyst's English publisher[39] and through his own writing.[40] Thistlewood cites a definition of the modern artist given by Jung in a letter to Read, which is a key to understanding the gestural painting of the late 1950s. This artist was able 'to dream the future by attending to the images and forms from the unconscious, accepting responsibility to reveal them *without modification*, avoiding temptation to make them conform to the familiar. The creative act was to be regarded as an event *visited upon* the artist by virtue of an ability to tap the creative unconscious.'[41] An understanding of the artist as medium, one able to convey images in a pure, primaeval form, rapidly became a fundamental and, in some quarters, fashionable tenet of avant-garde thinking, following the first impact of Abstract Expressionism.

While Read was completing the first volume of Jung's complete works, he wrote a succinct essay on Jung, the kind of summary more likely to have popularised his philosophy than the Routledge edition. The human unconscious, Read explained, possessed an 'innate bias' for forming symbols with some kind of communal significance: 'symbolic images or moulds of thought by which the hopes and aspirations of mankind can be expressed and shaped'. Dreams might reveal the unconscious, but Jungian dreams, unlike their Freudian counterparts, were nei-ther fully explicable nor consistent with the conscious mind; rather they emerged from an unconscious continuum 'which by chance we interrupt', and were echoed in the products of human culture.[42] Finally, Read summarised the concept of the archetype: certain mental sets established patterns for unconscious image-building and a predilection for certain kinds of imagery, but this understanding carried with it the warning that 'the archetype is not a ready-made image. It is merely an inherited predisposition or tendency to fabricate definite types of imagery'.[43]

The Jungian archetype provided a rationale for art which bypassed social inten-tionality, always suspect as possibly *dirigiste*, as well as the banalities of formalism and academic naturalism, while it accomodated an emotionally intense approach. For artists who had identified gestural abstraction as a vanguard practice, for instance those associated with the New Vision Centre Gallery, Jungian theory amounted to a shorthand for avant-garde status: it denoted abstract and therefore not surrealist, as well as contemporary rather than pre-war. Unlike the surrealist espousal of Freud, however, Jungian theories were not taken as a model for practice. This was, perhaps, part of their attraction; in a less prescriptive milieu than that of the Surrealists, psychoanalytic theory might underpin and justify a practice, rather than dominate it.

Consciousness of Jung coincided with enthusiasm for Zen Buddhism. While Zen, like Jungian philosophy, may have had few knowledgeable followers, for many, including artists, the quest for a higher state of consciousness was a vague if compelling goal.[44] Congruences might readily be found between the unwilled emergence of the Jungian archetype and the intuitive, irrational insight characteristic of *satori*, or enlightenment: 'an intuitive looking into the nature of things in contradistinction to the analytical or logical understanding of it'.[45]

The New Vision artists, who included at different times a member of the Situationist International, the Dutch Zero group and the comedian Charlie Drake, as well as sculptors and photographers, defy simple definition, though certain dominant interests can be discerned. Many of them shared a sympathy for Zen, while they believed in the primacy of intuition and emphatically proclaimed their allegiance to Jung as opposed to Freud. The gallery records confirm Denis Bowen's account of it as a locus of tachiste painting more closely aligned with French artists than with Americans.

Bowen's own practice represents this trend. He insists that each of his paintings was made in one session, since to return to a canvas would destroy its integrity, which depended on its being the product of a single, unpremeditated act. Less obviously calligraphic than Mathieu's paintings, Bowen's work also contained strong, central forms and splashes of paint on heavily impasted surfaces (fig. 32). Gestural marks replaced connotative signs, since it was an article of faith that imagery should evolve exclusively out of the conjunction of gesture and surface. Bowen maintains that though he later gave titles like *Landscape* or *Flying City* to his early paintings, they were entirely non-representational. However, like Pasmore, he found non-figuration an elusive goal and some early works of the 1950s appear to be notional land- or seascapes, with horizon lines.

Bowen emphasises the importance of the Jungian archetype to tachiste painters. Tachiste and surrealist artists vigorously proclaimed their mutual disdain. Their protestations echo as a refrain of the larger abstract–realist debate, but the gesturalists' physical engagement with the act of painting is inescapably linked to surrealist automatism. Yet Tachisme lacked both the political content and the ironic wit of Surrealism and its accidental paintmarks were considerably less calculated. In many ways its emphasis on the irrational, emotional and personal relate it more closely to neo-Romanticism than to Surrealism, while its contradictory dependence on chance and the quest for order within random dispositions confirm its position as the obverse of constructionist rationality.

In *Art as Understanding*, published in 1963, Bowen's colleague, Frank Avray Wilson, a biologist turned painter, proposed a theoretical model for British tachiste artists comparable to the Bergsonian notion of dynamism.[46] He suggested that art exists in a continuum of knowledge to which it contributes as much as science, while both undergo the profound redefinition demanded by modern physics.[47] A characteristic image, repeated in many of Avray Wilson's paintings, was an irregular, nuclear shape from which criss-cross lines radiated, formed by applying thick paint with a knife, or his fingers. Its frequent repetition would weaken the case for total spontaneity even had he not emphatically distanced his practice from gestural painting: 'Pepping up paint in splashes or dripples [sic] as in much of "tachisme" is visibly connected with a naturalistic emotion: nature is tachiste in many of its effects. The only way that paint can be validly used in a spotty, dribbly manner is when it is part of a synthetic structure.'[48]

While Avray Wilson's attempt to distinguish between dynamism and gestural

37. Alan Davie, *The Altar of the Blue Diamond*, 1950. Oil on board, 71 × 95 in. Private Collection.

painting is unconvincing, since it depends on the artist's desire to achieve spontaneity, his text underlined the obstacles to developing an exclusively gestural practice and the anxiety inherent in an approach that critics dismissed as meaningless. Even those who accepted the validity of gestural painting were far from unanimous in their interpretations. Read understood it as a protest against the atom bomb,[49] while Kenneth Coutts-Smith, later a director of the New Vision Centre Gallery, took it as an assertion of individuality and a rejection of collective social policies.[50]

The ascendancy of gestural painting lasted for only a very short time: well before the New Vision Centre Gallery closed in 1966 Pollock's legacy of action had been transformed into an overtly politicised, auto-destructive event art, fulfilling Read's perception of radical content. Though gestural painters maintained and diversified their practices, they no longer formed an avant garde; that role passed, just as their mild Bohemianism gave way to the harsher and more politically radical underground culture of the 1960s.

A handful of artists who travelled to Venice for the 1948 Biennale were able to see paintings by Pollock in Peggy Guggenheim's collection, when they were exhibited in the Greek pavilion.[51] Among them were Peter Lanyon on a brief visit and Alan Davie, in the course of an extensive scholarship tour of Europe. Davie sold a painting to Peggy Guggenheim and took the opportunity also to see her early works by Rothko and Robert Motherwell.[52] Pollock's primitivism and its echoes of Jungian theory[53] resonated with Davie's own interest in non-western art and his preferences for conceptual rather than material sources: for creation myths and magic rather than African carvings.

Until 1956 Davie was the only British artist consistently described as a Tachiste, though his work diverged significantly from the general understanding of Tachisme. In *The Altar of the Blue Diamond* (1950) (fig. 37) Davie combined a dominant geometric form with calligraphic scribbles and other, more recognisable motifs, suggesting that while automatism was a constituent of his painting, he stopped short of pure process.[54]

For almost ten years after his Venetian visit, Davie experimented with different types of imagery and ways of balancing gesture with stasis, and undifferentiated, all-over imagery with emblematic motifs. About 1957 he began to use less ambiguous signs, like the wheels and columned building that appear through a dense mass of writhing marks in *The Creation of Man or Marriage Feast* (1957). This adoption of familiar symbols, which led Bowen and his colleagues to reject Davie's work, was in fact its critical salvation, since rather than being purely spontaneous, his painting was understood to be securely grounded in real objects.[55]

In 1958 Bryan Robertson gave him a solo show at the Whitechapel Art Gallery. In the notes that he wrote for the catalogue Davie emphatically rejected the vulgarisation of Action Painting and described his own practice in terms of an intuitive 'activity of painting', which called on 'enigmatic and non-rational symbols'. His references to a Zen-inspired quest for enlightenment[56] and the increasing prominence of symbols and static structure in his work of the late 1950s suggest that at a time when many of his colleagues were still coming to terms with American painting, Davie had already replaced his Pollock-inspired process with a more contemplative approach grounded in Zen.

THE STRUCTURE OF AN AVANT GARDE

The publication of *Nine Abstract Artists* marked the culmination of several years of intensive effort by a small group of artists. The diversity of their work is startling, given the cohesion of their group identity in exhibitions and publications. In practice it proved impossible to sustain their coherence for more than a few years, so that *Nine Abstract Artists* records the beginning of the dissolution of the group as much as its triumphant emergence.

The Constructionists constituted a significant section of the tiny postwar avant garde. Faced with incomprehension and hostility, they found it psychologically essential to have a sense of belonging to a group and, as Mary Martin later acknowledged, a degree of isolation had a positive benefit: '. . . one was surrounded by Romanticism, English provincialism, Paris school abstract art and the first waves of Tachism and Action Painting. Without some detachment one could not have survived.'[57]

By the time Alloway's book was published, the artists concerned had developed theoretically sophisticated practices. They had already collaborated in some important group shows[58] and then, because commercial galleries were unwilling to show their work, in a series of three weekend exhibitions in Heath's studio, where they invited sympathetic colleagues like Eduardo Paolozzi, William Scott, Roger Hilton and Terry Frost to join them. In addition they had produced two documents to elucidate their work. With *Broadsheet No.1*, published by Lund Humphries in 1951, they set out their principles in what amounted to a manifesto, though unlike those produced by the Futurists and Surrealists, it was deliberately non-exclusive and sought to make connections with other modernist practices.

An article on some of the more conspicuous collaborations between artists and architects in the South Bank exhibition of 1951[59] outlined the developing field of commissioned public art in which these artists ultimately aspired to work, as well as underlining their wide affiliations. A second *Broadsheet*, published a year later to coincide with the first studio show, extended the theoretical debate but was less ambitious in format.

One of the paradoxes of the group was Pasmore's emergence as its dynamic central figure, since he was not the most conceptually advanced of the artists. Although he was the first to make and show concrete art, that is paintings with no reference to the external world,[60] his early reliefs were still formulated pictorially and he seldom adopted any more complex mathematical system than the Golden Section. It was more important perhaps that Pasmore was persuasive, determined and experienced in the theoretical debates surrounding the development of new practices, having been involved in the 'Objective Abstractions' exhibition at Zwemmer's Gallery in 1934 and subsequently with the Euston Road School. His experience gave him a certain authority among younger friends like Heath, for whom he became a mentor, as did Heath himself for Terry Frost.[61]

A year after his own abstract debut, in 1949, Pasmore coaxed Heath into exhibiting his first, small, untitled abstract painting with the London Group. It was a hard won, aesthetically unsatisfactory panel that nevertheless amounted to a significant challenge and a signal of intent. At this time other members of the constructive core group were also meeting one another and abandoning figurative practices. Kenneth Martin made his first abstract paintings in 1949–50 and Mary Martin reached the same turning point in 1950, when they both met Anthony Hill, the only member of this first, intense grouping never to have made figurative works.

Robert Adams, who began to teach at the Central School with Pasmore in 1949, was deeply sympathetic to the group's ethos and aspirations. He took part in all the early exhibitions and was one of the nine abstract artists, though his practice was anomalous in the constructive context. His *Apocalyptic Figure* (1950) (fig. 38), a wood carving reproduced in *Broadsheet No.1*, corresponds far more closely to the painted structures that Roger Hilton and William Gear were making in 1950–1 than to any constructive work. Like their paintings, Adams's early work was associative and open to readings in terms of rudimentary human forms. His sculpture was also consonant with the Modern Movement principles of revealed structure that were so emphatically reinterpreted on the South Bank in 1951.[62]

During that year, when the Skylon signalled a celebration of technology, Pasmore made his first construction, Mary Martin her first relief and Kenneth Martin his first mobile. The impetus that pushed them from paint on canvas into three dimensions has been exhaustively discussed by Grieve. It came partly from Charles Biederman, whose long, convoluted and idiosyncratic book, *Art as the Evolution of Visual Knowledge*, was passed round among the artists[63] and intensively analysed.[64] They were also stimulated by Alfred Barr's pre-war catalogues, and new or recently republished books such as the Wittenborn Documents of Art series, which included reprints of texts by the de Stijl artists and Mondrian.[65] Amédée Ozenfant's *Foundations of Modern Art*, Wassily Kandinsky's *On the Spiritual in Art* and D. H. Kahnweiler's monograph on Juan Gris were also important testimony to earlier avant gardes. Tiranti's artists' shop in Charlotte Street, a convenient source for these books, also stocked the texts on proportion and measurement that effectively became the Constructionists' technical primers.[66]

While they acknowledged historical affinities with Russian Constructivism, Neo-Plasticism, Cubism, German utopian architecture and Gropius's Bauhaus,[67] emphasis on the formal properties of their work, which they strongly encouraged, has often obscured its political implications, though these were clear enough to the

38. Robert Adams, *Apocalyptic Figure*, 1950. Ash, $122\frac{1}{4} \times 36 \times 38\frac{1}{2}$ in. Arts Council Collection, Hayward Gallery, London.

39. Mary Martin, *Climbing Form*, 1954–62. Perspex, stainless steel and wood, $21\frac{3}{4} \times 13\frac{1}{2} \times 3\frac{1}{4}$ in. Tate Gallery, London.

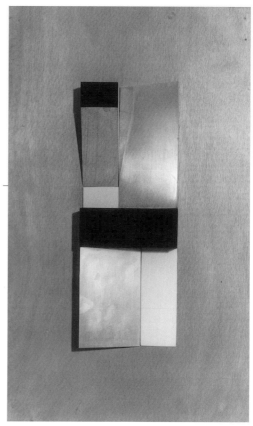

contemporary critics who sneered at 'doctrinaire products'.[68] Constructionism was a revolutionary art form without a revolution, its media so unfamiliar and its messages of social renewal so radical that it was seldom directly identified with a political cause. The situation was exacerbated by the rapid diminution of the British Communist Party after the war and its failure to achieve any significant place in government, so that there was no natural focus for a radical, politically oriented art, as there was in France.

Nevertheless, as whole-hearted supporters of the Labour government and the Welfare State, political and social idealism were important, if largely unstated factors in formulating the ethos of constructionist artists. The old academic traditions of representation and tonal painting, in which most of them had been trained, were no longer appropriate: as Pasmore wrote, 'Today the whole world is shaken by the spirit of reconstruction . . . In painting and sculpture, as also in architecture, an entirely new language has been formed.'[69] There could have been no more appropriate model than the revolutionary public art that had briefly flourished in Germany and the Soviet Union at the end of the First World War: an uncompromisingly new art was a metaphor for social change as applicable to Britain in 1948 as to Russia in 1917, whereas academic art, like social division and grinding poverty, belonged to the past.

Constructionism asserted a reformist role in the lineage of William Morris and John Ruskin, proposing that access to art was a citizen's right, which would bring social benefits through the impact of an aesthetically educated population on housing and design. Mistrusted though it was, the new art was recognised as a signifier both of the Left and of modernity; it denoted the urban and the technological and an intellectual stringency which demanded essentials without superfluities. Formal process and ideological progress were as inseparable here as they had been for Gabo's utopian projects. Like de Stijl, postwar constructive art aspired to synthesis, in which painting, sculpture, architecture and decoration would become a single entity.[70] Closely associated with architects and designers, the artists envisioned forms to complement the clean functionalism of postwar public sector housing. Their references, always oblique, were to technology and the machines that would transform the conditions of labour.

Once the artists had developed a theoretical process they had to find the most apposite materials in which to put it into practice, for, as Kenneth Martin wrote: 'Concept and material go hand in hand. Material can inspire – concept dictate material – material qualify concept.'[71] The cold-cast plaster from which Mary Martin laboriously carved her first relief, *Columbarium* (1951), with which she introduced her characteristic chequer-board and tilt, was no more appropriate to the aesthetic than the amateur carpentry with which Pasmore assembled *White Relief* (1951) (fig. 31),[72] his first painted relief. Recognising this problem, the artists dismissed the conventions of uniqueness and handcraft and replaced paint and canvas with plastic, metal and wood. Kenneth Martin called these 'kitchen material', to emphasise their ordinariness, their distance from conventional studio practice and their status as signals that the artists had rejected 'the old individualist humanism'.[73]

Such modest modern materials would help to ensure the erasure of the individual hand and were, at least in theory, the first step towards a low-cost, mass-produced art, though in practice this was not achieved. There was, indeed, an irresolvable paradox in the artists' desire to exclude all traces of the natural and individual. Heath used no blue or green colours for several years lest they might suggest landscape. In a similar spirit Anthony Hill made his constructions as far as possible from unmodified ironmongery and found objects, yet their work remains instantly recognisable. Anonymity was metaphor rather than reality. It stood for a perception of the artist's role close to that outlined by Gabo in 1948, when his implicit demand was that artists subordinate their individuality[74] to collective action, to ensure, as he had written in another cataclysmic period more than a quarter of a century earlier, that 'Art should attend us everywhere . . . in order that the flame to live should not extinguish in mankind'.[75]

To turn from materials to imagery is to find the paradox reiterated. Thompson's revelations of morphological patterns, which paralleled and were convertible to mathematical ratios, strongly inflected constructionist work. Whereas Biederman and Power provided visual models, Thompson added a poetic, organic element that was still reassuringly grounded in scientific principles. For the Martins, as for Pasmore, the spiral was a rich stimulus to invention.

One of Mary Martin's first reliefs, *Spiral Movement* (1951), combined a notional chequer-board 'and a spiralling system of golden section rectangles that move within it'.[76] Though she made her earliest reliefs in wood or board, by the mid-1950s she had begun to use perspex and stainless steel which, in conjunction with the tilt, allowed her to exploit the reflections and contrasts of light and dark that characterise *Climbing Form* (1954–62) (fig. 39). The tilt holds the surface and the highest point of the relief in tension, linking positive and negative, or light and dark areas. Its implicit movement, together with the bright colours and mirror glass that Mary Martin adopted in the 1960s, ensure that her reliefs are among the most dynamic constructionist works.

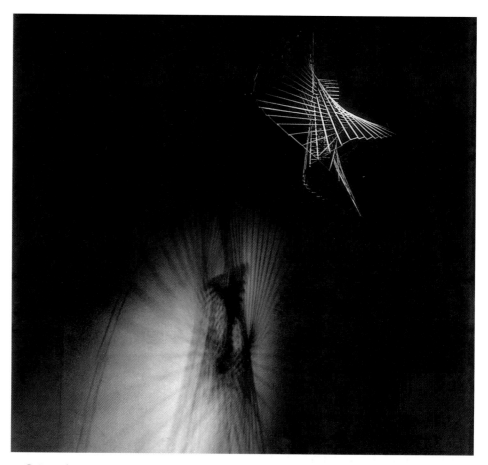

40. Kenneth Martin,
Screw Mobile, 1956–
64. Phosphor
bronze.

Grieve has commented on 'a sense of structured events taking place through
time, of organic development' in Kenneth Martin's early abstract painting, *Composition* (1949–50).[77] His first mobile, made in 1951, initiated a long period of experiment with spiralling forms. Martin first constructed it with wooden dowel rods,
which protruded horizontally from a central, vertical rod, to terminate in small tin
plates. Their weight unexpectedly caused the rods to bend downwards, which, he
said, forced him to acknowledge that all systems are subject to chance. In future
his mobiles were to be made of metal, while his process became to some extent a
matter of testing how far it might be submitted to chance and retain its validity as
a systematic working method. Most importantly, Martin's mobiles were 'kinetic'
pieces, 'form unfolding in space and time'.[78] They were analogues for human
experience,[79] rich in symbolic content[80] and remote from the aridity of formalism.

Martin's work not only displays an extraordinary formal range, from the wiry
Lines in Space, reproduced in *Nine Abstract Artists*, to the flamboyant complexity of
the 1956–64 *Screw Mobile* (fig. 40), but also reveals the flexibility and the intellectual paradoxes inherent in this apparently rigorous and austere art. As he so
frequently emphasised, while the arrangement of his work was always systematic,
the choices available within a given process were made empirically.[81]

Pasmore's first reliefs, made in 1951 and confined to white with small areas of
black, look more austere than Martin's glinting brass mobiles, while his process
was far simpler. His principle concern, carried over from painting by way of the
photostat collages that he had shown in 'Space and Colour', was with the interaction and mutual modifications of light and space. Pasmore maintained that

through its extension from the wall plane, however slight, the relief would intervene in and thus modify the physical and psychological territory occupied by the viewer.[82] Consequently, though the *White Relief* (1951) (fig. 31) projects only a very short distance forward from the plane surface, the extension of its vertical fin below the support has great symbolic significance. It indicates that the fin is to be read as an element of the wall and is therefore situated in actual architectural space, rather than in the illusionary space of a moveable work of art.

The transparent reliefs which Pasmore began to make in 1953 are more convincing in this respect. Consisting of a sheet of glass attached by vertical fins to a backing board, with further fins projecting from the front of the glass, they depend for their effect on the activity of viewers. People moving past see shifting reflections in the glass and thus themselves become agents of change in the spatial relationships that exist within the works and between themselves and the reliefs. The artwork might thus be theorised as simultaneously integral to its containing architecture and a source of subversion within it, with the capacity profoundly to alter visual perceptions of volume. As Kenneth Martin wrote: 'this real concrete object . . . need no longer be solid or rectangular. It can expand into and pierce space; open space and light can enter into it. It need no longer be still but can move, linking space with time.'[83]

Anthony Hill was later to formulate the group's central problem as how to 'make works which are not works of Art'.[84] He found a model in Marcel Duchamp's pioneering use of the ready-made, his adoption of materials foreign to conventional fine art and abandonment of painting. An untitled collage made by Hill in 1950 suggests, in retrospect, the direction in which he was moving. It reveals his debt to Gris and Picasso, as well as his delight in the use of found materials, since he made a punning appropriation of a Pears soap wrapper.[85] A year later, in 1951, Hill began to correspond with Duchamp and with the Swiss concrete artist, Max Bill, whom he considered to be the pre-eminent interpreter of the early twentieth-century modernists.

The concrete art defined by Bill was to be profoundly important as a model for establishing an inclusive, as opposed to a restricted constructive process, since it was not necessarily mathematically grounded and could function through organic as readily as through geometric forms. That though, was for the future. For the moment Hill, like Heath, was intent on achieving the appearance of mechanical perfection demonstrated in the hard-edged forms in *Jeux* (1951) (fig. 41).[86] His work, more mathematically sophisticated than that of his colleagues, became increasingly rigorous. He restricted himself to black and white between 1953 and 1956, when he abandoned painting for reliefs constructed from ready-made industrial components, ranging from enamel stove backs to aluminium angle pieces (fig. 42).

In his introduction to *Nine Abstract Artists* Alloway sought to situate the radicalism of constructionist work in an historical and European context, emphasising its affiliations with the concrete artists Richard Lohse and Max Bill, as well as with compatible contemporaries like Alan Davie. Alloway differentiated between 'pure geometric art' and 'a kind of sensual impressionism without things',[87] a category in which he placed most non-figurative painting. The three painters, Hilton, Scott and Frost, who were included alongside the core Constructionists, were described as approaching 'expressionistic action painting',[88] which suggests that Alloway saw them as prophets of gestural abstraction. While his annexation of them is no longer convincing, when he was writing the nature of their work meant that it might have been expected to develop in a theoretical, non-referential manner.

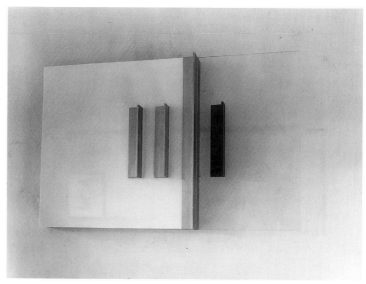

41. Anthony Hill, *Jeux*, 1951. Ripolin on cardboard, 30 × 25¼ in. Artist's collection.

42. Anthony Hill, *Relief Construction 1956–60*. Aluminium, plastic and wood, 18 × 29 × 3¾ in. Private Collection.

Frost had adopted Pasmore's use of the Golden Section and the melon-slice motif seen in *Movement: Green, Black and White* (1951) (fig. 43),[89] with which he conveyed dynamic movement within a constraining structure. Frost's much-quoted statement, with the explanation that 'The subject matter is in fact the sensation evoked by the movements and colour in the harbour',[90] illuminates the extent to which his painting diverged from pure process art. The harbour at St Ives inspired a series of at least nine paintings, all titled *A Walk Along the Quay* (fig. 63). An early collage version, *Moon Quay* (1950) was hung in the first studio show, testimony to the ease with which a rigorous process might be converted to purely pictorial ends.

Hilton more radically maintained that paintings that he made in 1953–4, like *August 1953* (fig. 44) or *February 1954*[91] were 'space-creating mechanism[s]'[92] implying that they articulated space in a similar manner to Pasmore's glass reliefs. Here Hilton's intentions were at least briefly consistent with constructionist process. Moreover he understood process to be the locus of a work's meaning, describing it as 'a communication between an idea and possible ways of saying it'.[93] Yet the work itself renders Hilton's aspirations and self-assessment problematic: while *July 1953* (fig. 45)[94] falls within the category of concrete art, it is difficult to read *August 1953* or *February 1954* as other than a woman's torso. When he painted them, Hilton was moving out of his brief abstract phase and back to figuration, a shift that he was soon to acknowledge in his letters to Terry Frost.[95]

Scott, similarly, had a visual rather than a theoretical relationship with Constructionism. His schematic linear painting, *Figure into Landscape* (1953) (fig. 46)[96] is inexplicable without its title, but retains traces of a phenomenological origin. For many years Scott had made still lifes which, in the early 1950s, he progressively reduced to flat rectangles bearing rudimentary marks or the minimal protrusions seen in *Still-life: Coffee Pot 1 (Black Composition)* (1952/3) (fig. 47).[97] As he explained, these residual still lifes might also be conflated with a body or landscape: 'I may begin a picture as a careful recording of a special sensation evoked clearly at a remembered time and place and by a continuous process of work, obliteration, change, an expression of an entirely different thing grows, a "figure into landscape" or into a still life, "a man into a woman".' Scott dismissed 'space construction', remarking firmly 'I have no theory'.[98] In fact his rich, allusive impasto aligned him with an emergent gestural aesthetic, as Alloway recognised when he wrote 'There is no paraphrasable meaning in Scott's new work, only a meaning dependent on the act of painting.'[99]

Alloway's introduction to *Nine Abstract Artists* reveals an ambivalence or, perhaps, a desire to keep his options open for as long as possible. His emphasis on the act of painting and accidents of the surface, together with the reproduction of a very early tachiste painting by Anthony Hill, meant that he was able to avoid a dogmatic assertion that constructive art was the sole focus of the avant garde, or the only kind of process-dominant art. Consequently, when, not long after publication of the book, the artists began to modify their practices, Alloway was able to amend his position without having to develop a fresh theoretical stance.

Pasmore's return to painting, Heath's adoption of a freer technique and brighter palette, Hilton's reprise of figurative imagery were changes in degree rather than kind: their work remained process-dominant, while its increasing distance from constructive art was naturally attributed to the impact of the 1956 American exhibition. Process-dominant art soon came into clearer focus in a series of exhibitions which charted the development of abstraction since the war. Early in 1957 'Statements. A review of British Abstract Art in 1956' opened at the ICA. Organised by the ubiquitous Alloway, this was a survey of twenty-one artists, each of whom showed one work. It brought together constructive, gestural and perceptual artists, including representatives of St Ives, despite Alloway's recent, brutal dismissal of the 'art colony by the sea'.[100]

In the 'Statements' catalogue, he followed the format of the book, presenting his own analysis, followed by brief artists' statements. Many of them emphasised the

43. Terry Frost, *Movement: Green, Black and White*, 1951. Oil on canvas, 43 × 33½ in. Tate Gallery, London.

44. Roger Hilton,
August 1953. Oil on
canvas, 24 × 20 in.
Private Collection.

internal dynamic of the work of art: 'the painting begins with opening the cans of colour, and ends when *it* has decided so' (Magda Cordell); 'I combine a sense of disciplined growth with the free discoveries made in the actual process of painting' (Terry Frost). Today, the most startling feature of 'Statements' is its reversal of the relative status of gestural and geometric process since 1954; only two years after the Redfern exhibition of the abstract pioneers, Action Painting had displaced construction to become the dominant radical practice.

Alloway continued to insist on the prevalence of improvisation in his introduction to 'Dimensions', a more ambitious, didactic and analytic sequel to 'Statements', which opened only eleven months later, in December 1957. 'The artist's relation to his materials', he wrote, 'is the dominant factor. The forms of the picture cannot be predicted ahead of the action of the artist in making the work of art.'[101] All the members of the constructionist core group, together with painters from St Ives and the Independent Group were among the forty exhibitors. For William Green and his fellow students from the Royal College, Robyn Denny and Richard Smith, it was their first important group exhibition.

Alloway became closely involved with the Royal College group, which included Roger Coleman who, between the autumn of 1956 and the following summer, edited three seminal issues of *ARK*, the college magazine. With its passionate emphasis on American films, music, fashion, cars and style, its rejection of the traditional and conventional, *ARK* acted as a running manifesto for these artists. It probed issues in contemporary culture, such as the semiotics of advertising, which fascinated the artists so much that, in the form of packaging, it soon became the principle stimulus for Smith's paintings. Like the constructive group, the Royal College artists were intensely urban and, though their aspiration to make large scale, public works was more quickly fulfilled, they also confronted critical derision. Just as the first, hermetic phase of constructive art culminated in *Nine Abstract Artists*, gestural painting emerged from relative obscurity in 1960

45. Roger Hilton, *July 1953*. Oil, 40 × 36 in. Stedelijk Museum, Amsterdam.

46. William Scott,
Figure into Landscape,
1953. Oil on canvas,
45 × 60 in. William
Scott Foundation.

with 'Situation', a seminal exhibition organised by Alloway and a committee of artists.

ARK 19, published in the spring of 1957, set out many of the issues that preoccupied the Royal College group. In a 'Personal statement' Alloway wrote of a new

47. William Scott,
*Still Life: Coffee Pot 1
(Black Composition)*,
1952–3. Oil on
canvas, $26\frac{1}{2}$ × 32 in.
Private Collection.

way of conceptualising art, 'freed from the iron curtain of traditional aesthetics which separated absolutely art from non art'. A more permissive attitude would allow art to function as one method of communication in a polymorphous field where it would have parity with popular media such as film and advertising. Such an approach, which would 'see art in terms of human use rather than in terms of philosophical problems', would emphasise 'The new role of the spectator or consumer, free to move in a society defined by symbols'.[102] This notional consumer, at loose in an urban world of abstract signs, was Alloway's focus and passionate interest.

Addressing a single instance of 'human use' in the same issue, Coleman commented on the immediacy of modern mass-media images that could be absorbed without conscious effort.[103] Fashion photography, in particular, had the ability both to create a dream world 'that is fabulously strange by very familiar means' and to assimilate fine art into popular culture.[104] In effect, photographs in magazines like *Vogue* fulfilled Alloway's desire for art to extend laterally across the gamut of available media, while retaining a fine art aura. Despite their passion for film and popular music, neither Alloway nor Coleman could envisage a worthwhile art, in any medium, that abandoned itself to the intellectual banality of magazine imagery.

Coleman used his editorial to castigate *The Architectural Review*'s 'Outrage' campaign against the uncontrolled, creeping urbanisation of the countryside.[105] For Coleman, Smith and Denny, the 'Outrage' articles represented an allegiance to tradition, nostalgia and the pastoral that quickly became a focus for their contempt. While Denny respected John Minton, who exemplified such attitudes and was his tutor at the Royal College, as a larger-than-life figure, he deplored his painting, just as he deplored that of John Bratby and Stanley Spencer, who was held up as a model by tutors at St Martin's. Denny's aesthetic heroes were William Turnbull, whom he had met at the Royal College and Alloway, whose writing, especially on the American exhibitions of the late 1950s, he greatly admired.[106]

Alloway and Denny were at one on the importance of the city as the locus of the modern. 'Language, symbol, image, an essay in communication' was the title of Denny's Royal College thesis, presented in 1957. Its cover carries a photograph of a San Francisco street, its buildings all but obscured by signage. Denny's essay, copiously illustrated with signs and symbols, from ancient rock engraving to modern graffiti, sought to show how signs construct the human environment and behaviour. The theme reverberated in the paintings that he made in 1957, four of them selected by Nevile Wallis for his 'Critic's Choice' exhibition.[107] The central image of *Painting, March 1957* (fig. 48) is a head-like shape, the human reference confirmed by the word 'MAN' incised into wet paint up the left-hand side. Blue and red vertical marks and drips are overlaid by thick bituminous pigment in the midst of which is a small patch of scorched newsprint.

The incorporation of torn paper and burning into paintings signalled a cultivation of the deliberate accident. Though the popular press appropriated Denny to Action Painting, making much of the fact that he worked on the floor, with pop music on the radio,[108] his engagement with process was clearly very different from that of the nine abstract artists. The use of materials like fragile newsprint, coloured paper or bitumen was almost a defining feature of the developing avant garde in the late 1950s and, as Robert Kudielka has commented, a peculiarly European phenomenon;[109] American contemporaries used conventional oil paint on canvas. Denny was concerned with the way in which unfamiliar materials

48. Robyn Denny,
Painting, March 1957.
Oil on board, $37\frac{5}{8} \times 22\frac{1}{2}$ in. Private
Collection.

might be used to construct an image that was deliberately difficult to read and obviously divorced from traditional painting.

The finger-painted word in *Painting, March 1957* quickly developed into stencilled letters and fragments of words, truncated and superimposed, overlaid with paint and scraps of collaged paper in a process where, as Kudielka has noted, 'interest in the act of perception took precedence over interest in the act of painting'.[110] To acknowledge this shift was to acknowledge the transformative role of the viewer, just as to appropriate the signage of city streets was to formulate an imagery from anonymous public information systems.

FROM THE PAINTED GRID TO THE BUILT ENVIRONMENT

Among the reproductions of Anthony Hill's works in *Nine Abstract Artists* is *Free Orthogonal Composition* (1953): a freehand grid superimposed on an indeterminate mass of scumbled paint.[111] Subsequently destroyed, this canvas is a reminder of the centrality of the grid to earlier avant gardes[112] and of the fluidity between different kinds of practice. The grid allowed, as Rosalind Krauss has written, the expression of 'a contradiction between the values of science and those of spiritualism to maintain themselves within the consciousness of modernism, or rather its unconsciousness, as something repressed.'[113] Constructive artists, following Mondrian, recognised the grid, albeit in many manifestations, as a fundamental principle with a symbolic value, while gestural painters adopted it as a practical way of imposing order on the formlessness of intuitive painting. When Bryan Wynter turned away from landscape painting in the mid-1950s, suggestions of a grid structure became apparent in his large, abstract canvases. Reviewing his recent work in 1956, Patrick Heron described a 'grille, or network of brushsigns' that formed a 'horizontal-vertical grid'.[114] Heron read Wynter's marks in terms of foreground and horizon, though a less literal perception of metaphorised space is also plausible.

Ralph Rumney's first solo show in London, at the New Vision Centre Gallery in 1956, included paintings in oil and Ripolin on newsprint, with the pigment applied in dribbles and splashes which all but obliterated the underlying text. Rumney's choice of support may have been prompted by poverty, but it also expressed his disdain for the conventions of the fine art market. Always more interested in art as a political or cultural intervention than in the production of objects, Rumney's practice has from time to time come to rest within current modernist norms, before it once again veers away. His gestural phase culminated in a group of paintings made up of small clusters of colour against a sketchy grid,[115] which included *The Change* (1957) (fig. 49). The lines of the grids extend notionally beyond the canvas, the areas between them crossed and infilled by marks which form an undifferentiated and similarly boundless field.[116] Rumney recalls that the grids became apparent roughly halfway through each painting. He maintains that he manipulated, rather than submitted to chance, because even with a drip and splatter technique, 'You have to know where it's going'.[117]

Such paintings occupied an area between the chance emergence of an ordering structure and the plotted disorder of a gestural technique. In the statement that Rumney wrote for his 1956 exhibition, he sought to express this ambiguity, emphasising the priority given to the subject over individual personality. Since his paintings offer no sense of an external subject, we must conclude that Rumney's preoccupation was with the potential of process to act as revelation:

49. Ralph Rumney,
The Change, 1957.
Oil, Ripolin and gold
leaf on masonite, 60
× 78 in. Tate
Gallery, London.

An act of creation must be autonomous and independent of the creator...a
work of art...must not rely on the personality of its creator for its
impact...The artist seeks to eliminate his personality in his work...The
power of a work of art rests in its subject. The subject is independent of all
formal qualities and becomes a violent and powerful entity in its own right. The
artist cannot be objective ... We have no intrinsic concern with drawing, colour,
matière, surface or finish.[118]

By rejecting personality Rumney aligned himself with constructionist theory, yet
he was considered to exemplify gestural painting. The unresolved status of chance
in his work, his combination of grid and gesture and his apparently subjectless
imagery were fully consistent with developments in the wake of 'Modern Art in
the United States'.

John Plumb showed at the New Vision Centre Gallery in October 1957 and June
1959. He was characterised as 'an "action" counterpart to Bratby',[119] though
Richard Smith's catalogue introduction less predictably linked his work to the
mass-media preoccupation with violence. Plumb showed a group of paintings on
a red ground in which *taches* of blue and white were separated and regulated by
a loosely drawn orthogonal grid. In one painting, areas of dense marks were
connected only by a few verticals which appear to form the neck of a rudimentary

figure. Another, predominantly blue and purple, had a central white, head-like shape, overlaid with thick black markings.[120]

As a student at the Central School between 1951 and 1955, Plumb worked in the Painting Department under William Turnbull, who first directed him towards abstraction. Plumb's first abstract work, some newspaper collages made in 1952–3, were followed by images based on a figurative interior scene, built up in de Staël-like slabs of pigment. Turnbull then suggested that Plumb divide and modulate the blocks of colour with thin black lines, forerunners of those in the 1957 paintings. Plumb concedes that these were indebted to Pollock, though he did not feel that he was a fully gestural painter, since he was prepared to rework a canvas over several months.[121]

In 1957 he showed a newsprint collage, which incorporated words, in a mixed exhibition at the AIA. It marked the beginning of a deliberate move away from action-oriented painting, which was underlined when, in his second New Vision exhibition, he showed a group of paintings in which heavy impasto was replaced by smooth, matt black surfaces relieved only by a roughened area in one corner. They were described as 'orderings of space . . . both inside and outside the picture surface'.[122] Commenting that 'The absence of frames causes these works to "grow" outside of their own immediate area', the reviewer incidentally recalled the effect of Pasmore's glass reliefs a few years earlier and, once again, raised the issue of environmental space, reasserted as a burning theoretical issue by recent American art.

Rumney was briefly a founder-member of the Situationist International in 1957, though he was precipitately expelled after six months.[123] Three consecutive issues of *ARK* carried his photo-essay, 'The Leaning Tower of VENICE', presented in strip-cartoon format in fold-out sections. To make it, Rumney had followed his highly self-conscious subject, the writer Alan Ansen, through the city, recording his actions, which were annotated in captions. Ansen's progress, which Rumney described as a 'play-pattern',[124] was a typical Situationist psychogeographical *dérive*[125] which combined an ostensible investigation of behavioural determination, of randomness or play in adult activities, with a heavily shock-horror tone: '"A" now recrosses the Canal Grande by gondola and enters an extremely sinister zone frequented by cats and men with Tommy guns. Even some of the canals in this sector are dry.'[126] Although A's course through Venice was prearranged, his peripheral activities could not be fully predicted: an unexpected meeting with a friend, encounters with children and cats, the onset of rain, were factors beyond control, essential to the notion of the *dérive*.

A more structured, abstracted and less ironic variation on the *dérive* took place in September 1959, when Denny, Rumney and Smith collaborated in 'Place'. Coleman arranged for it to be held at the ICA, where he was Exhibitions Secretary.[127] 'Place' emerged from loosely linked ideas about the interaction between people and their environment under controlled conditions. An essential contributory factor was a perception of the artwork as an enclosing nexus, rather than a portable object. One of the ideas that stimulated 'Place' is said to have been a proposal devised by Alloway and Rumney for a 'Hiss-chamber', to study behaviour in a maze-like environment.[128]

The predecessor to 'Place', only two years earlier, was 'An Exhibit', an installation shown first at the Hatton Gallery in Newcastle and then at the ICA, on which Alloway collaborated with Pasmore and Richard Hamilton. It consisted of perspex panels of different degrees of opacity, arranged to form an abstract environment which was structured by the activities of visitors, who wandered as if through a maze. Their random progress through the space confronted the ordered plan of the installation in a way that was comparable to the use of a public building. The organisers considered 'An Exhibit' to be a structured game which presented a high number of variables, while avoiding the illogicality of pure chance: 'Play is a form of order, an order that contains both standards and free improvisation'.[129]

While 'An Exhibit' may have suggested possibilities for constructive art unsuspected except by its practitioners, for Denny at least, 'Place' went further, to act as a model for public art. The intention was to turn the inert space occupied by the installation into an 'animated place'[130] and thus to stimulate the visitor to an interpretative or physical response. 'Place' was as much an event as an exhibition, occupying a notional space between the murals that Denny made for public places in 1959[131] and Rumney's assertion that the life of an artist is in itself a creative statement.

'Place' drew on sources which ranged from Abstract Expressionism to the Situationist International, the Independent Group, game theory and semiotics. The participants decided to limit the paintings to combinations of red with green and black with white, and to make them in uniform sizes of seven by six feet and seven by four feet. Twenty-four paintings were fixed back to back and set at a forty-five degrees angle to the walls, while ten more projected obliquely into the gallery space from the end walls.[132] Most important, they stood directly on the floor, anticipating by a few months Anthony Caro's revolutionary abandonment of the plinth for his new welded steel sculpture. The 'Place' canvases acted like marks on a plan, to formulate the space they occupied. The way in which that space was used and the meaning to be construed from it could, however, be determined only by those who walked through it, as they might wander along streets and in and out of buildings.

The arrangement of the canvases meant that they partially concealed one another, permitting glimpses of different combinations of colour and image. Rumney's paintings were variations on a rudimentary head, a notation for the whole body, while Denny's were connected with paintings like *Home from Home* (1959), where an irregular black band frames an indeterminate blue area above a black horizontal barrier that acts as a conceptual threshold.

Many critics treated 'Place' as an exhibition of individual works, singling out Smith's paintings for approval since they most closely resembled the contemporary art seen in commercial galleries. Eric Newton's comment that 'To ignore it would be unforgivable. To praise it would be impossible',[133] summarised the rearguard action still being fought by centrist critics. As so often, Alloway provided the most searching response. In one of the very few serious reviews of 'Place' he singled out the cinematic wide screen as a focus, dismissing the impact of American painting in his determination to situate popular culture at the creative centre.[134]

The grid, ostensibly a formal device for ordering a surface, has a wider significance as a parallel to the *dérive*, a means of plotting the progress of a body through a given space, whether a city or a canvas. The faint rectangular network on the surface of *The Change* may thus be understood as a mental mapping, the purpose of which was to assert the priority of the artist in the creative process.

A useful analogy is the explanation given by Tim Ingold of the task of the surveyor, who is required 'to take instrumental measurements from a considerable number of places, and to combine these data to produce a single picture [i.e.

a map] which is *independent* of any point of observation.' The significant locus on the map is the internally determined position of the individual body: 'we use our bodies as the surveyor uses his instruments, to register a sensory input from multiple points of observation, which is then processed by our intelligence into an image which we carry around with us, like a map in our heads, wherever we go.'[135]

The painted grid, as flexible and indeterminate as the Situationist *dérive*, may be extended into a metaphoric perception of the artist's relationship with the canvas. This in turn signifies a wider relationship with the city and its chance encounters, as they are processed and notated by the individual. The grid may thus also denote a temporal location, significant only in relation to a specific, temporally bounded activity. Such was the visitor's experience of 'An Exhibit' and 'Place', three-dimensional equivalents of the painted grid. In an analogy with the situation of the surveyor/cartographer, 'independent of any point of observation', neither installation offered a predetermined route through it, nor fixed points of entry and exit. Each was activated and rendered significant only by the haphazard progress of the viewer/participant, whose task was to establish an individual location within the installation, one that was necessarily physical but primarily visual and psychological.

Whereas 'Place' and 'An Exhibit' had been experimental, almost playful investigations into the interactions of chance with given data, another temporary installation, albeit on a much larger scale, provided the opportunity for collaborative work on a public art and architecture project. The complex that Theo Crosby designed for the International Union of Architects Congress, which took place in London from 3 to 7 July 1961 was built hurriedly on the grassed-over, circular site of the Festival of Britain's Dome of Discovery, after arrangements to use the Royal Festival Hall had collapsed.[136] Many of the artists whom Crosby invited to work with him had taken part in 'This is Tomorrow'; the South Bank initiative was an opportunity, especially for constructive artists, to install in a public environment what they had, in a broad sense, sketched in maquette form in the 1957 exhibition.

The axial IUA complex was defined at the river end by a tower, forty-two feet high, designed by John Ernest, and at the Belvedere Road end by the headquarters building, in front of which stood Anthony Caro's bright orange steel sculpture, *Capital* (1960). This axis was crossed by a rectangular exhibition hall with a long enclosed court at each end, which served as outdoor exhibition spaces.

To fulfil the theme of the Congress: 'The influence of materials and techniques on architecture', artists and architects collaborated from the design stage, using materials, principally asbestos, aluminium and glass, produced by the sponsors.[137] While Crosby saw the courts as 'spaces to house a collection', he conceived the headquarters building as 'a kind of visual opera'. Wishing to use it to achieve a more resolved synthesis of art and architecture, he called on the Constructionists to collaborate with him.[138] Three dramatic works, on a scale far larger than anything that the artists had previously undertaken, dominated the main hall, where Kenneth Martin's paired mobiles, *Twin Screw* were flanked by forty-eight-feet long panels constructed across each end wall by Mary Martin and Anthony Hill. The three pieces engaged in a mute but eloquent dialogue concerning stasis and motion, colour and monochrome, matt and reflective surfaces, structure and space.

Hill took the opportunity of the unprecedented scale to make a screen of glass and aluminium panels, modulated by protruding sections, which appeared to float in front of the wall plane.[139] Practically, its purpose was to unite two disparate roof levels, but the *Screen*, constantly modified by the play of light across its surface, can also be seen as the culmination of the project initiated by Pasmore's early glass reliefs: the creation of a convincingly ambiguous relationship between wall plane and interior space.

Mary Martin's relief was a counterpoint to Hill's structure in that it was 'based on an opposition to the roof and a destruction and reassertion of the wall's surface'.[140] It was constructed as a series of red and white panels arranged in permutations of squares. Although the maquette had incorporated tilts, in the finished relief these became projections from the base plane, also in a system of permutations.

As well as his dramatic tower, John Ernest designed some of the building's interior partitions. They took the form of colour mosaics in twelve-inch squares and triangles, perhaps a prelude to the five *Mosaic Reliefs* that he was to make a few years later, which exploited relationships between colour and shape, and relief and planar surfaces.[141] Turnbull devised an alternative model for partitions by combining groups of standard colours sequentially in flat planes, in acknowledgement of Rothko's paintings, which he had seen on a visit to New York in 1957.[142]

The West Court, which Crosby designed in collaboration with Alloway, contained murals by Bernard Cohen, Peter Stroud and John Plumb, multipartite works on panels which suggested a modular construction. Crosby himself, Paolozzi and Turnbull contributed sculptures which stood in the central space, where their organic forms acted as counterpoints to the geometry of the panels. The East Court was intended to explore the 'relationship of man/machine' in order to convey an affinity with the Congress exhibition, 'The Architecture of Technology',[143] but the effect was incoherent since every artist took an intensely individual line. Richard Hamilton made a large collage, *Glorious Techniculture* which, like the series of paintings initiated by *Hommage à Chrysler Corp.* (1957), combined a complex imagery of machine parts, domestic appliances and cars, with film stills and magazine photographs.[144] It stood in front of the half-finished Shell building, making, as Crosby noted, 'an apt comment on the Shell tower rising behind it'.[145]

Unresolved though this East Court seemed to Crosby,[146] its diversity underlined the scope of the collaborative project. The main hall, at the heart of the complex, was a triumphant vindication of constructionist principles which coincided with the artists' recognition by critics[147] and institutional patrons[148] to mark the culmination of their first, hermetic phase. Yet Alloway found himself finally unable to accept the principal of a subsuming art form. As a result of his belief that collaboration with architects might compromise an artist's individuality, he expressed a preference for the model of the temporary festival, in which individual works might be prominent, over long-term collaboration.[149]

By 1961 Alloway had come to understand Constructionism as 'architectural play'; the artists' early focus on rigorous process had developed into a richer synthesis where the organic and the intuitive might determine the final form of a work. The screens and mobiles in the main hall of the IUA complex confirm the interrelationship of play and rationality: the effects of shifting light on their reflective surfaces could no more be predicted or controlled than could the slow motion of the mobiles. Process is, as Kenneth Martin had remarked, constantly reinvented.

The IUA complex confirmed that both the strands of process-dominant art discussed here had fulfilled their aspirations to achieve an environmental art. The unprecedentedly large paintings of the previous year's 'Situation' exhibition were a prelude to the murals of the West Court and Turnbull's interior screens. The crowds of people who flocked to the Congress brought about the essential interaction that had been theoretically plotted in 'Place' and 'An Exhibit'. Moving in space, recreating it in relation to artworks, they enacted the principle of 'chance and order'[150] that was the defining paradox of the process-dominant art of the early 1960s.

7

THE CITY

People and objects in motion and change are both the stuff and the decoration of the urban scene.

Alison & Peter Smithson, 1970[1]

Cities should generate, reflect and activate life, their structure organised to precipitate life and movement.

Warren Chalk, 1963[2]

Reviewing the Young Contemporaries exhibition of 1952,[3] John Berger made his often-quoted comment that 'Slowly but quite certainly something is happening to British painting.' He singled out Derrick Greaves and Edward Middleditch who, he found, shared a 'common attitude' with other, now less well-remembered names.[4] That this attitude was the product of 'a deliberate acceptance of the importance of the everyday and the ordinary' could no doubt be deduced from the artists' work, but Berger added the more startling observation that their 'pictures imply an acceptance of the revolutionary theories of the last forty years'. He hoped, therefore, that these artists might 'help to re-form a European tradition', that is, a realist tradition. However, in his enthusiasm to promote a conscious and combative art of the Left, he was over-optimistic about the painters' commitment to a politicised art and failed to take into account that they were still students, whose work was likely to change rapidly and fundamentally.

Unlike most of his fellow critics, Berger deliberately focussed on young artists, women and those from the old colonial territories. Retrospectively he has been most closely linked with the Beaux Arts Quartet: John Bratby and Jack Smith, with Middleditch and Greaves, an association which has somewhat obscured his extraordinarily wide knowledge of contemporary art. It remains true, though, that he singled out the Quartet for special support and felt that his loyalty to them had been betrayed when their work diverged from his aspirations, just as the artists themselves felt shackled by the political tag which Berger attached to them.[5]

Named for Helen Lessore's Beaux Arts Gallery where the artists received their first solo shows,[6] the group is associated with images of the city, of streets and

50. Jack Smith, *After the Meal*, 1952. Oil on canvas, 44 × 47 in. Arts Council Collection, Hayward Gallery, London.

rain-washed buildings and the impoverished domestic life that they sheltered. The stark black industrial buildings in Greaves's *Sheffield Landscape* (1953), the grey emptiness of Middleditch's *Pigeons in Trafalgar Square* (1954), the comfortless clutter of Smith's and Bratby's interiors (figs 50, 52) have become visual notations for the privations of the years of austerity. Yet Ceri Richards painted Trafalgar Square *en fête*, in brilliant colour (fig. 10); the *Bicyclists against a Blue Background* (1951) (fig. 51) that Robert Medley entered for '60 Paintings for '51' proposed an urban life in which physical and social mobility were unquestioned, while popular figurative painters like the neo-Impressionist Ruskin Spear and the young Mary Fedden demonstrated that urban streets and interiors were not necessarily drab places of confinement.

Though Berger optimistically saw the London of his young protegés as the possible seedbed of socialist realism, for many people the early postwar city was a microcosm of a country in decline, unsure of its status or future, turned in on the minutiae of daily life as it is revealed in Bratby's *Still Life with Chip Frier* (1954) (fig. 52). The painting suggests a prosperous, if chaotic material culture, which is depicted not in the drab tones of the ration book often imputed to the Beaux Arts Quartet,[7] but in vivid colours and with a luxurious impasto that unequivocally signalled Bratby's allegiance to van Gogh. There is a sense of contemporaneity, a consciousness of a great tradition, even a certain optimism in Bratby's still lifes, which suggest that the artist had an independent agenda which complied neither with Berger's political aspirations nor with a perceptible, widespread sense of depressed insecurity. Focussing on his family and domestic life,[8] he set himself

51. Robert Medley, *Bicyclists against a Blue Background*, 1951. Oil on canvas, 61 × 53½ in. York City Art Gallery.

within a European lineage of modernity, rather than one of ideologically aligned realism.

Bratby's interiors present an aspect of vernacular culture – the daily experience of millions of people – very different from the popular culture disseminated through film, advertising and other aspects of the mass media, that was analysed and celebrated by members of the Independent Group. Bratby's vernacular was distinct also from the high culture of the fine arts, music and literature. Production and dissemination of this culture was predominantly associated with the city, though its imagery was more closely aligned with a mythologised pastoral. Berger's hopes had no doubt depended on the emergence, within an urban context, of a public for the new realism, whose allegiance would be cemented by class identification. Such a public would also embrace the strand of urban worker imagery which stands as a counterpoint to the inhumanity of Greaves's urban landscapes.

THE WORKERS' CITY

In the 1930s the Artists' International Association provided an ideological locus and exhibiting context for artists on the Left, who were as much concerned with the plight of workers at home during the Depression as with the Association's more publicised activities in support of the Spanish Republic. Cartoons in *Left Review*[9] extended a tradition of acerbic political satire, while the photographs of Edith Tudor-Hart and the paintings of Percy Horton provided shocking revelations of the pathos of the unemployed and life in urban slums.

52. John Bratby, *Still Life with Chip Frier*, 1954. Oil on board, $51\frac{3}{4} \times 36\frac{1}{4}$ in. Tate Gallery, London.

A decade later, satire gave way to a sense of achievement when the workers who had won the war returned to rebuild shattered cities and homes. Yet memories of the Depression were still vivid, bringing a politicised edge to the popular theme of the worker, which sharply differentiates it from Bratby's genre scenes. At a time when urban and industrial reconstruction came second only to agriculture as the national priority, the worker theme became ever more closely linked to the city. Representations of the worker ranged from Joseph Herman's monumental peasant farmers to the no less heroic labourers to be seen in Peter Peri's concrete reliefs.[10] His *Building Job* (1937)[11] is a characteristic scene of construction workers in an anonymous public space, whereas women, like the *Mother Looking Through her Window* (1950–65) watch from a more clearly defined domestic arena. Peri's reliefs, made in an intractable industrial medium with simplified forms and a limited colour range, are blueprints for socialist realism: his workers are idealised signifiers whose individuality is subsumed into work quotas and statistics.

A more humanised and individualised perception of the worker is to be found in Prunella Clough's fishermen, drivers and artesans. In her various series of worker paintings, made during the fifteen years after the war, Clough associated herself with an enclave of hitherto male-dominated practice in which she side-stepped both heroicisation and genre by her negotiation of a territory between modernism and realism.[12] In the *Lorry Driver* series of 1950–2 we can still recognise the severity of the cubist-related imagery introduced to London-based artists during the war by Jankel Adler.[13] Only two years later, in Clough's *Printer Cleaning Press* (1953) (fig. 53) this had been absorbed into a more humanised perception of the worker.

53. Prunella Clough,
Printer Cleaning Press,
1953. Oil on canvas,
36 × 22 in. Private
Collection.

The printer is an altogether subtler figure than the driver, whose sharply facetted face replicates the shape and colour of his cab. A lighter and less limited range of colour binds the simplified figure of the printer into a cramped, contradictory space that evokes the complexity and physical demands of his craft. The accumulated details of the painting establish a reciprocity between the realism of the figure and modernist pictorial autonomy, in which the man and his task are dominant. Purely formal devices underline the worker's pre-eminence: his head repeats the shape of the arched opening through which he leans, while the curves of his arms and his cleaning rag are set against the rigid geometry of the press; a startling acid-mauve half circle is echoed in the tone of an ink pot; even the healthy pink of his face recurs in a slab of colour across the work table, serving to identify the printer with his workplace and his craft.

Clough's workers are simultaneously defined by and define their work, but they are not reduced to mechanical cyphers. Their absorption is the opposite of alienation; her worker paintings reflect the dignity and value of labour, while her artesans appear to us as men complete in their consciousness of being also fathers, husbands and pigeon-fanciers.

THE ARCHITECTS' CITY

When Richard Hoggart published his seminal study of working-class culture, *The Uses of Literacy*, in 1957 he vividly characterised its distinctive nature at the moment when it was beginning to lose its singularity. Not long after the publication of his book, the hierarchy of class cultures merged in the hybrids of the youth and drug cultures of the 1960s. These in turn stimulated distinctive images of urbanity in the cities which had at last buried the scars of bomb damage deep beneath a new and still untarnished fabric of towers, highways and glittering commercial opportunity.

High art, a selective version of popular culture and a quest, led by architects, for a vernacular synthesis of the two, were the preoccupations of the first session of the Independent Group. In recent historiography the Group has been exhaustively discussed and analysed, at the expense of the ICA. It functioned within and as a part of the ICA; as an experimental microcosm within a parent structure it stood in the same relationship to the Institute as did the Institute itself to the Arts Council. In order to justify its existence, members of the Group developed a highly individual approach which has come to be seen as adversarial to the approach established by Herbert Read and Roland Penrose. Between its inception in 1952 and the end of its first session sometime in 1954, the Independent Group was to a considerable extent led by the architects Alison and Peter Smithson, with Reyner Banham, the architectural historian who acted as convenor for the first session. Working within a sociological framework, members sought to transform the role of art and the way it was defined, since they believed that it should actively construct meaning. The architects' contribution ensured that the Independent Group would be concerned with environment, rather than painting, sculpture or buildings. Many of the perceptions that emerged in Alloway's writing in the middle of the decade can be traced back to the earliest stages of the Independent Group, where communication was a prime objective and culture was understood as people's consciousness of themselves. The members were intensely interested in communication theory; they believed that art was an aspect of everyday culture and that artists might use any materials, however unconventional or mundane.

Equally significantly, they were as hostile to modernist concepts of art's purity and autonomy as to the academies.

While the Independent Group was being formulated, the Smithsons, two of its most active early members, were developing a theory of urbanism which drew on anthropology and avant-garde art, as well as earlier Corbusian models.[14] They presented it to the architectural community at CIAM 9, held at Aix-en-Provence in 1953. It was a younger generation's response to the Corbusian principles enshrined in the Athens Charter of 1933, which had hypothesised a city predicated on the docility of its inhabitants, whose lives were required to conform to rationality, order and acceptance of a geographical urbanism that would inescapably mould their lives.

The principal of the ideal city of the Athens Charter was a rigid distinction, which would determine the city's physical appearance, between dwelling, work, recreation and circulation. Formulated in a period obsessed by grand schemes, it represented the pinnacle of modern international planning at its most idealistic and a stark contrast to the reality of the degradation shared by many large cities and recorded by Edith Tudor-Hart in London. The city of the Athens Charter was implicitly hierarchical; it allowed for technological development while its inhabitants were offered only the possibility of satiation, since it afforded no space, physical or conceptual, for social change.

At CIAM 7 in 1950, in the context of a wide range of urban analysis,[15] Le Corbusier had posed the central question 'new city, reconstructed city, or transformed city'?[16] While his own, metaphysical response was contained within the concept of the Modulor, the Smithsons sought solutions to planning the built environment which were intimately linked to the living society, the detailed fabric and the material culture of small, specific areas. They were able to draw on the work and expertise of their close friends Nigel Henderson and his wife, Judith, an anthropologist. When Nigel went to the Slade in 1945 on an ex-serviceman's grant, Judith was working on a sociological project based in Bethnal Green, where they lived. Called 'Discover your Neighbour', it was an attempt to use the methodology of anthropology to convey the experience of working-class East End culture to professionals like doctors and the clergy.[17]

In 1949 Henderson began to photograph the shops, houses and street life of Bethnal Green, sometimes combining documentary images with his newly developed technique of drawing on unexposed film. Strangely hybrid images like *Boy in Window, East London* (1949–52), a vernacular subject[18] converted into a modernist icon, were forerunners of much of the work of the Independent Group, which was devoted to dissolving categorisations of high/low, fine art/documentation or, most important, art/not-art.

Henderson's photographs of Bethnal Green were his contribution to the Smithsons' *CIAM Grille* (1953), which they made as a visual aid to their presentation at Aix-en-Provence. In a radical reinterpretation of the Corbusian 'four-function model',[19] they proposed 'human association', rather than mechanistic function, as the basic dynamic of the city and the primary determinant of urban planning.[20] Association was fashioned by and in response to the built environment: 'The basic group is obviously the family, traditionally the next grouping is the street (or square or green, any word that by definition implies enclosure or belonging; thus "in our street" but "on the road"), the next the district, and finally the city.'[21] The Smithsons' analysis of the relationship between the individual and the social group: 'the street implies a physical contact community; the district an acquaintance community; and the city an intellectual contact community',[22] im-plied a hierarchy of economic and intellectual mobility that indicated both their debt to the Athens Charter and an unidealised perception of the semiotic richness of an urban street.

In the Smithson's grid, the street is the pivot between individual privacy and the wider experience of the city. The street may be an extension of home; its messages, conveyed by traffic signals, information in shop windows or advertising hoard-ings are both personal and generalised. Advertising was an acknowledged pas-sion among members of the Independent Group, particularly during the second session in 1955. For the Smithsons, advertisements were paradigms of contempo-rary culture: they demonstrated that within advanced capitalism commodities had displaced fine art both as a social signifier and a source of pleasing and complex images.[23] Apart from the desire that they stimulated, advertisements were aesthetically satisfying. The ubiquity of advertising, the mass appeal inher-ent in its promotion of mass-produced objects, appeared to be a powerful signal of the end of the fine art tradition and the herald of a new attitude to design and living. The Smithsons' confessedly symbolic *House of the Future*, displayed at the Ideal Home Exhibition of March 1956,[24] was a moulded plastic structure divided into cells, in which virtually the only moveable objects were chairs. Itself a proto-type for mass-production, it signified the fast-moving life-style of an upwardly mobile mass-consumer in a newly prosperous, American-oriented, not far-distant future.

During the earlier part of the decade, various members of the Independent Group organised exhibitions, all but one of which took place in the ICA gallery.[25] 'Parallel of Life and Art', a collaboration between the Smithsons, Henderson and Eduardo Paolozzi,[26] exposed the creative and serendipitous possibilities of asso-ciation. An investigation into the extended signification to be found in juxtaposi-tions of unlike images and objects normally disassociated from fine art, it consisted largely of photographs,[27] hung unframed, some from the ceiling, others projecting from the walls or propped against them. The images, which were grouped under such headings as 'Art', 'Date 1910', 'Landscape', 'Structure' and 'Football', ranged from art (a Dubuffet *Corps de Dame*) to radiography and microphotography ('Chest of a rat embryo, showing heart'); from a Klee etching to shoreline mud patterns, from a news picture of George VI's funeral to Hans Namuth's famous photographs of Jackson Pollock at work. Just as 'Parallel' built on 'Growth and Form', so was it the most important precursor of 'This is Tomor-row'. The ironic, opportunistic wit that contributed as much to 'Parallel' as its investigative approach re-emerged, albeit less prominently, in the 1956 exhibition, as did the startling and bewildering concept of the exhibition as total environment, which had been pioneered by Richard Hamilton with 'Growth and Form'.

While the decision to arrange the exhibits in 'Parallel' as a walk-through mon-tage may well have echoed, as Whitham remarks, the Independent Group's dissat-isfaction with linear thinking,[28] the exhibition was far from random and should not be seen as a late surrealist enterprise concerned with chance encounters.[29] The near total exclusion of fine art images and the emphasis on scientific and ethnographic sources, together with the neatness of the installation, and the careful alignment of the exhibits suggest that it was meticulously planned and researched in order to enable the Smithsons to explore the intellectual potential of the as-found principle.

This had a dual identity: on the one hand it was the theoretical foundation of association, that is, the casual, unplanned encounters that structure daily life.

Conversely, as-found was concerned with a generally unnoticed category of material human traces: 'all those marks that constitute remembrancers in a place and that are to be read through finding out how the existing built fabric of the place had come to be as it was.' Crucially 'as-found' involved 'a new seeing of the ordinary, an openness as to how prosaic "things" could re-energise our inventive activity.'[30] This way of seeing, probed in 'Parallel', was to be the impetus behind the collaboration of the same four artists when they made *Patio and Pavilion* for 'This is Tomorrow'.

Both exhibitions assumed that the relationship between art and life was as intimate and self-evident as that between science and life or science and art. 'Parallel' set out to demonstrate the interdependence of science and art by establishing analogies, visual and physical equivalences and affinities within an organic rather than an intellectually linear pattern. 'This is Tomorrow' was to focus on cultural synthesis and fluidity within micro-environments.

The second session of the Independent Group, in 1955, convened by Lawrence Alloway and John McHale, was tailored to Alloway's perception of cultural diversity as a continuum from high to low, in which Duke Ellington might be appraised in similar terms to Beethoven or prefabs compared with a Palladian mansion. Overlap and integration were recognised and exploited in opposition to older perceptions of hierarchic distinctions between media and practices. In its exploration of Alloway's 'long front of culture',[31] the Group's discussions covered advertising, information theory, popular music, fashion magazines and sociology. Members saw communication as their primary purpose; art in general was a means of imparting ideas, while the individual work was a contribution towards the elucidation of an idea and ideally part of an environment.

Outrageous fantasy, Constructionism, Tachisme and a sweep of architectural theories came together with surrealist panache in the melting pot that was 'This is Tomorrow', the exhibition held at the Whitechapel Art Gallery in August 1956,[32] just over a year after the Independent Group had ceased to meet formally.[33] While it is the event most regularly associated with the Group and the one which most fully represented the members' pursuit of lateral thinking and diversification, most of the participants were in fact not members of the Group.

The exhibition's origins were, unsurprisingly, complicated. They are important not least because they underline the prominence of its constructive and modernist strands as a corrective to later perceptions of an exhibition dominated by Pop Art and the New Brutalism. Anne Massey notes that a proposal for inter-disciplinary collaboration first came from J. M. Richards, editor of *The Architectural Review* from 1937 to 1971, as early as 1950.[34] A few years later, a similar idea was put forward by Paule Vézelay, the English representative of the French-based Groupe Espace, which had been founded to promote collaborative work 'between architects and abstract painters and sculptors'.[35] A committee was formed, involving some members of the constructionist core group, with the architects Erno Goldfinger and John Weeks. At least one meeting took place with Vézelay, but negotiations broke down because, in Alloway's account, 'The English artists and architects would not submit to the dogmatic ideas of synthesis held by *La Groupe Espace*.'[36]

At this stage Theo Crosby emerged as the principal organiser, setting up a meeting in Adrian Heath's studio between artists and architects.[37] Crosby devised the structure of twelve discrete groups, which he co-ordinated, each of which, notionally at least, consisted of an architect, a painter and a sculptor. As press officer, Alloway generated an astonishing volume of publicity for a show which proved as enticing as it was bewildering. Though critics tried conscientiously, if not with overwhelming enthusiasm, to come to terms with it,[38] it was only in the architectural journals that any attempt was made to elucidate 'the competing messages of the dozen exhibits'.[39]

Yet if 'This is Tomorrow' was confusing, it was so in part by design. Alloway elevated its apparent incoherence to a principle when he articulated the misgivings over synthesis that had led to the split with Groupe Espace: 'The independent competing groups do not agree on any universal design principles. This is the aesthetic difficulty about the idea of integration of the arts. It is continually opposed by the variety of human aims and performances . . . the universal has to compete on equal terms with other principles.'[40] His statement is significant in that it amounts to a summation of Independent Group thinking, inflected as much by the Smithsons' construction of association as by Alloway's own rejection of the notion of an intellectually dominant vanguard in favour of a cultural continuum.

There can be little doubt that 'This is Tomorrow' reflected Alloway's 'variety of human aims' with considerable panache, and effectively countered any universalising notions that might have persisted among artists from the constructionist core group. Alloway compared its spatial effects and 'play with signs' with the experience of the urban street.[41] He implied that 'This is Tomorrow' might best be understood as a metaphoric microcosm of the city, albeit one which ranged from fairground fantasy to rational architectural planning.[42]

The first section[43] through which all visitors were obliged to pass, presented a schematic juxtaposition of mechanical and organic structure,[44] which established the exhibition's inherent dialectic between irrationality and the 'mechanical environment'.[45] Irrationality made a spectacular claim for dominance in the fun-palace installation for which the exhibition is most famous, designed by Hamilton with McHale and John Voelcker.[46] Incomparably colourful, vulgar and large, it dazzled the eye, confounded sensory expectation and defied any possibility of logical interpretation. Mystifying and entertaining though it was, it emerged from a meticulously planned programme drawn up by Hamilton, under the two main headings of 'Imagery' and 'Perception'. Recalling the groupings of *Parallel of Life and Art*, the first included 'Advertising', 'Randomisation', 'Audience participation' and 'Photographic image'; the second, besides the obvious 'Colour' and 'Light', noted 'Psychological shock' and 'Visual illusions'.[47]

Despite the prominence in memory and literature of Hamilton's installation, 'This is Tomorrow' remains primarily an architects' project since, as the organisers of the space, they effectively controlled circulation and the conceptual links between sections. Stepping out of the fun palace, the visitor would have confronted the Group 3 installation, a long curved space defined on the left by a dramatic painted mural by James Hull and on the right by John Catleugh's rough plaster paintings on board, through which he had punched holes, in order to demonstrate 'the interpenetration of spaces'.[48] The installation terminated with a screen, made by Leslie Thornton, of plaster-coated wire in which small found objects were embedded.

From here the visitor passed into the body of the gallery, which was arranged with a dominant constructionist axis. The two central installations, Groups 7 and 9, were set up by members of the core group to emphasise the reciprocity of art and architecture. Acting effectively as life-size maquettes, which demonstrated the viability of the artists' belief in aesthetic synthesis, Groups 7 and 9 suggest that

54. Nigel Henderson, *Head of a Man*, 1956. Photograph on board, $62\frac{7}{8} \times 47\frac{7}{8}$ in. Tate Gallery, London.

the immediate tomorrow of the exhibition was to be Theo Crosby's IUA building of 1961.[49]

At the far end of the gallery stood the legendary *Patio and Pavilion* designed by the Smithsons, working with Paolozzi and Henderson: 'Patio and Pavilion represents the fundamental necessities of the human habitat in a series of symbols The first necessity is for a piece of the world the Patio The second necessity is for an enclosed space the Pavilion These two spaces are furnished with symbols for all human needs.'[50] The installation was a poetic demonstration of the as found principle[51] in which the debris of an old garden shed formed a rudimentary shelter.[52] In the sand-covered patio was a small, roughly cast bronze figure made by Paolozzi, with Henderson's photocollage, *Head of a Man* (1956) (fig. 54), constructed from scraps of graffiti, torn paper, photographs of cell structures and foliage. Strewn around them were tiles, stones and plaster sculpture assembled to represent the kind of possessions that confirm a sense of human identity.[53]

Georges Matoré's analysis of existential space casts some light on the metaphoric significance of the two areas within *Patio and Pavilion*: 'modern man lives in two spaces – a geographical space (the place of habitation) and a social space – the one in which he pursues his economic and technical activities.'[54] *Patio and Pavilion* metaphorically encompassed both these spaces, and while it may have seemed closer to the implications of the geometry of fear than to the stimulating city suggested by the Group 2 installation, it can be seen to have conveyed Matoré's further perception that 'we not only apprehend space . . . through our senses . . . we live in it, we project onto it our personality. We are bound to it by affective ties.'[55]

Largely unintelligible, litter-strewn and tacked together, *Patio and Pavilion* remains ambiguous, in the manner of Paolozzi's lost-wax bronze figures. The remnants of the garden shed shared their battered but jaunty nature, recalling the opportunism of the *bricoleur*, the finely balanced blend of existential *angst* and black humour that sustained Vladimir and Estragon.

Hamilton's collage, *Just What is it that Makes Today's Homes so Different, so Appealing?* (fig. 55), made as the poster for 'This is Tomorrow'[56] and best known in its mass-produced form, has entered legend as the initiatory signal of Pop Art. Before making it, Hamilton drew up a much-quoted list of visual, textual and aural information,[57] employing domestic and industrial terms drawn from the multifarious activities and images to be found in a large city.

The imagery of *Just What is it?* was drawn from urban vernacular – or popular – culture. It made transparent the link between sexuality and advertising, the theme that Hamilton was to take up in his paintings of the late 1950s, which were daringly to draw advertising into a fine art context. Although there is a discreet reference to traditional painting in the form of a portrait of Ruskin over the television set, Hamilton defined his intellectual distance from this tradition by

55. Richard Hamilton, *Just What is it that Makes Today's Homes so Different, so Appealing?*, 1956. Collage, $10\frac{1}{4} \times 9\frac{3}{4}$ in. Kunsthalle, Tübingen, Sammlung G. F. Zundel.

his use of collage. To have painted *Just What is it?* would have diminished the impact of the banality of its constituent images and demanded that they be read like a painting, that is, separated from reality by a frame. The collage, however, functioned like advertising, announcing complicity for those who wished to participate. In the context of 'This is Tomorrow', it proclaimed the viewer to be a collaborator and echoed Reyner Banham's introduction to the catalogue: 'the supremacy of you/entered observer without/whom/the most complex structure /is no environment with/ whom/ even a hole in the ground is/ for you.'[58] By subsuming Banham's invocation, the formal qualities of Hamilton's poster metaphorised not only 'This is Tomorrow' but all the exhibitions associated with the Independent Group. None was complete without the active, interpretative participation of the visitor; equally, each was presented as a totality, an environment which demanded the rejection of old perceptions of a rural-centred, hierarchical fine-art tradition in favour of a dynamic, unpredictable, fast-changing urban vernacular art.

THE ARTISTS' CITY

While 'This is Tomorrow' was being formulated, a group of post-graduate students at the Royal College were immersing themselves in American popular culture in parallel with Independent Group members. Robyn Denny, Richard Smith and Roger Coleman, students in the Royal College Painting School from 1954 to 1957, were *habitués* of the ICA and though not members of the Independent Group, which they recall as being of no particular interest to them,[59] they adopted Alloway as their mentor.

Coleman's editorial policy brought *ARK* into a unique position as a medium for the analysis of cultural cross-currents. Text and images, always of equal importance, testified, if not always very coherently, to inter-departmental connections within the College, to relationships with the ICA and the Independent Group as well as an obsessive fascination with American-inflected street culture.[60] The attraction of the pursuit of popular culture within the ICA was, according to Richard Smith, that it involved all 'the ordinary things you really enjoyed, and you didn't have to take up attitudes . . . You could enjoy Piccadilly Circus and Charing X Road and the popular films'.[61] Denny recalls a further, unsought benefit in that the disdain of Royal College tutors, particularly in the Painting Department, for Americana and mass culture meant that students interested in them were left to their own devices.

In his first solo exhibition, at Gallery One in January 1958, Denny showed a group of mosaic images made during the previous two years. Each has a central cluster of tesserae piled thickly together in an equivalence of impasto or dense colour, while at the edges they tumble down the plaster surface like the dripped pigment of an action painting.[62] Looking unmistakeably like abstracted human heads, Denny's mosaics can be situated within the wave of enthusiasm for this subject which followed the ICA's exhibition, 'Wonder and Horror of the Human Head' in 1953. Denny recognised a potential in mosaic for image-making outside the painting tradition. Mosaic might, he wrote, 'contribute to the reconciliation between architecture and the fine arts'; it was a way for the artist to contribute to the expression of modernity in contemporary architecture.[63]

The mosaics rapidly gave way to images like *Painting, March 1957* (fig. 48) with its patch of scorched, collaged newsprint and scratched inscription. By the middle

of 1957 boldly collaged letters and numerals dominated Denny's images. They were inseparable from his profoundly urban sense of identity, which led him, like Alloway, to oppose the conventions of timelessness and tradition attached to landscape painting.[64] Denny's raw material was street scenery, advertisement hoardings, signage, the casual encounters and the shifting, unfocussed glimpses particular to the pace and mobility of the urban experience. In this culture of the city, the enduring, the simple and the natural were rejected for the transient, the style-conscious and the manufactured. This shift in aesthetic values corresponded to the growth of a consumer-led economy in which profit depended on the rapid, artificial wastage promoted by advertising.

If *Patio and Pavilion* had resonances of survival in the aftermath of a disaster scenario, Denny's collages moved a stage further, to comment obliquely on the postwar transition from austerity to plenty. His letters, numerals and coloured papers were densely overlaid, jostling for space, repeating messages like the beat of pop music, to reveal abundance, wealth and the security of surplus. Denny's celebration of the city as a site of exuberant plenitude culminated with the mural that he painted for the Austin Reed shop in Regent's Street in the Spring of 1959 (fig. 56). Wishing to attract newly prosperous younger customers,[65] the firm commissioned an artist who had already been featured in the press because of his exotic habit of listening to pop music on the radio while he worked.[66]

Adopting a typographic format related to *ARK*'s witty advertisements, Denny expanded it to mural dimensions and, using black and white with primary colours, made a collage-like, partly ideographic image,[67] which proclaimed 'great/big/biggest/wide/London'. The man who dressed at Austin Reed had the entrée to the culture of a city that was big in spirit, proclaiming the modernity and

56. Robyn Denny, *Austin Reed Mural*, 1959. Oil on board, 77 × 119 in. Austin Reed Ltd, London.

confidence suggested by the mural's hard-edged clarity. Curiously, Denny's mural was placed in the men's shoe department in the basement and was therefore invisible from the street. Clearly it was popular, since it remained in place for nearly twenty-five years, but its semi-secret location is a reminder of the exoticism of the modern at a time when bomb-sites still abounded, tower blocks were not yet a reality and outside the creative efflorescence of a few sites in central London, the city was a drab, dirty, worn-out place.

Invited by the London County Council to make a mural for Abbey Wood Primary School in Wood Green later in 1959, Denny took a similar approach, setting letters and numerals in red, black and white mosaic. Less legible than the Regent Street mural – it spells out 1,2,3,4 and 'IDEA' backwards – it wittily converted the basic data of primary school education into a cheerful sign that denotes both school and play. Its complexity can be read on different levels and, unlike the Austin Reed mural, it is skilfully integrated into the architecture. Placed in the angle of a walkway opposite the glass entrance door to the school, it signals the nature of the building and invites participation. Denny understood participation, as Smith wrote, as 'a function of environment',[68] which would be stimulated by the challenge posed by the textual element of the murals.

In August 1959, only a few months after the Austin Reed mural was installed, Gustav Metzger held his first solo exhibition.[69] It consisted of three paintings, two on steel and one on hardboard.[70] He followed it, in November, with a show of twenty-one cardboard pieces, sections of packaging for a television set which he had found lying in the Fulham Road and hung on the wall like paintings, without modification. The cardboards formed the setting for a public reading of Metzger's first manifesto of Auto-Destructive Art, which took place during the opening of the exhibition,[71] in which he announced a new ideology for the artist in an industrial environment.

Metzger, who had arrived in London from Germany as a stateless Jewish immigrant in 1939, had been a devoted student of David Bomberg, particularly during the Borough Bottega period of 1950 to 1953. There are echoes of Bomberg's teaching on the morality of politics and society in the idealism and high ethical tone of Metzger's manifestos, just as his early practice as a painter of the human body echoed Bomberg's.[72]

His three brief manifestos, issued between November 1959 and June 1961, take the form of aphorisms: 'Auto-destructive art is primarily a form of public art for industrial societies';[73] 'Man in Regent Street is auto-destructive. Rockets, nuclear weapons, are auto-destructive';[74] 'Auto creative art is art of change, growth movement.'[75] In formal terms, auto-destructive art was, as the phrase suggests, art that, through organic disintegration, corrosion or more violent processes such as the use of explosives, would either be obliterated or so altered that it took on a different nature. Its ideological implications are profound; Andrew Wilson has emphasised that 'He does not destroy art but instead constructs a situation where destructive forces can be turned in on themselves and revealed also as being creative and so help to stimulate a wider moral and actual change.'[76] Auto-destruction, like auto-creation implied metamorphosis as a continuous physical process inherent in the work. In this respect, though in no other way, Metzger's process was aligned with the self-reflexivity of high modernism.

Process and form were, however, only vehicles to convey the artist's passionate commitment to the anti-nuclear movement, the issue that dominated Left-wing politics at the turn of the decade. While the Monmouth Street exhibitions were bracketed, at least by the tabloid press, with William Green's more widely publicised activities,[77] Metzger's actions were to single him out as ideologically commit-ted outside a party apparatus.[78] His first action took place in June 1960 at King's Lynn in Norfolk, where he had had a studio for some years. According to his own account the event was as haphazard as the making of a burnt bitumen painting, since although he had arranged for a photographer to record the event, he had not decided what form it should take. Small-scale experiments indicated a dramatic reaction between acid and nylon so, for the first 'acid/nylon event', Metzger threw acid at an expanse of suspended nylon fabric which instantly dissolved into tatters.[79]

A year later, on 3 July 1961, he repeated the action on London's South Bank, assisted by a team of students from the Architectural Association, immediately outside the IUA complex and against the backdrop of St Paul's across the Thames.[80] This time the sheets of nylon were reputedly in red, black and white, the anarchist colours, while those performing the event wore white coveralls and masks. They looked both menacing and alien, militant and robotic, articulating, through their bodies and actions, a metaphorised version of the violent fate likely to overtake a nuclear world.

Metzger's work, of which virtually nothing survives except in the form of texts and photographs, is situated in a notional opposition of city and country, where the city, as the locus of industry, concentrated capitalist endeavour and political power represents all that Metzger opposes. The country, in which he envisaged placing auto-destructive or auto-creative works to fulfil their ordained processes, was perhaps never more than a notional territory to be designated not city, an unattainable ideal as conceptual as his art.

The two visions of the city proposed by Denny and Metzger are irreconcilably opposed. Whereas the London of the Austin Reed mural had progressed into a period beyond austerity, where the war had faded into memory, Metzger's city remained a site of threat, a place that might all too easily succumb to another devastating war.[81]

The 'Young Contemporaries' exhibition of 1962 saw the emergence of Pop Art from the Royal College. Its affinities, like those of Denny's Austin Reed mural, were with popular music, an American-oriented consumer culture and a genera-tion for whom the war had not been the primary experience. If the Pop Art city was a place of colour, noise and movement, filled with fashionable and vital people, with desirable objects, a tangible, experiential place, Metzger's city was scarcely more than a concept, a signifier of nuclear apocalypse. It is hardly surpris-ing that while Pop Art has inspired a huge literature and many exhibitions, Metzger's evanescent and ill-recorded work has until recently been almost forgot-ten. That this has not been the fate of his colleague John Latham suggests that Metzger has been bypassed because of the political content of his work rather than for its intellectual obscurity.[82] Latham's esoteric theorisation of his own work, grounded in an idiosyncratic reading of certain aspects of physics and couched in the mystificatory coding of an invented terminology has, on the other hand, passed into the mainstream of art history.

In the mid-sixties Latham undertook a number of well-publicised events, several of which Metzger attended, which consisted of burning towers of books (*Skoobtowers*) outside such cultural landmarks as the British Museum. Prior to this he had made bookworks in the form of reliefs, one of the earliest being the celebrated *Burial of Count Orgaz* (1958) (fig. 57). This matt black assemblage of twenty-odd volumes, together with a spoon, a bottle, bits of wire and miscellane-ous discarded ironmongery is attached to a 'miniature "bar-billiards" table'[83] in a

57. John Latham, *Burial of Count Orgaz*, 1958. Mixed media relief, 48 × 36 × $8\frac{1}{2}$ in. Tate Gallery, London.

way that recalls the general conformation of El Greco's eponymous canvas.[84] Latham's adaptation of El Greco's painting signals a wish that his work be seen as a radical extension of the western tradition,[85] rather than a rupture from it. His intellectual enterprise, still nascent in 1958, was no less than the development of a single, unified cosmology, which would override and subsume the different categories of knowledge and thought. Latham deplores the codification of knowledge into the fixed categories implied by books, while he respects the information and power that they embody.

Latham's work, like Metzger's, may be seen as a profound revision of the Keynesian construction of the artist as solitary creator,[86] where the auto-destructive artist is a contributor not so much to the culture of mankind as to its survival. The highly politicised nature of the 'acid/nylon' events and Latham's ceremonial book burnings was, however, entirely unKeynesian. The loss of innocence that they proclaimed marked their distance from the notions of tradition and aesthetic propriety that were the context for Keynes's perception of the artist's social role. For Metzger and Latham the city was predominantly political, a locus of power to be resisted rather than celebrated, yet it was this rebarbative city that enabled them to challenge the Keynesian paradigm. Keynes had not envisaged the possibility of a contemporary parallel to agitprop art. When he made his broadcast in 1945, art was one of the few props that remained to shore up the residue of civilisation: it was too precious to be wasted in ephemeral political action. Only in the plenitude of reconstructed societies, rebuilt cities and the security of high capitalism was it possible – and necessary – for another kind of agitprop to be devised.

THE CITY OF DREAMS

One of the contributors to the International Union of Artists Congress site was Richard Hamilton. His eight-foot high, billboard-like painting, *Glorious Techniculture* (1961), stood in the east courtyard of Crosby's complex, where its 'dream New York cityscape'[87] engaged in a dialectic with the still incomplete Shell building directly behind the site. Hamilton's purpose was to reflect on the theme of the Congress exhibition, 'The Architecture of Technology', with his habitual transformatory combination of high technology and commodified banality. His imagery included a multiple exposure photograph of New York at night, 'the three-ring pump agitator of the Frigidaire washing machine' and 'Charlton Heston as Moses'.[88] Hamilton felt that *Glorious Techniculture* was a failure in the context of Crosby's design[89] yet, divorced from the specificity of its original site, his painted tower signifies a desired city, constituted in dreams. The long-term future of London was plain to see in the massive, uninspiring bulk of the Shell Tower, but though the actual city was not to attain the glamour and prosperity of Hamilton's fantasy, his painting has a place in the context of spontaneity, transience and psycho-sexual liberation so prominent in sixties vanguard culture.

The principle of expendability, with the deep cultural implications that the Smithsons had acknowledged in 'But today we collect ads',[90] was to be exuberantly developed by the members of Archigram in the early 1960s. These young architects were to extend the Smithsons' concept of personal living spaces 'mass-produced like a consumer commodity'.[91] The Capsule Home and the Living Pod were the transformable, mobile, individual cells that would become elements in the totality of Archigram's Living City.

This was the title of their exhibition at the ICA in 1963. As Peter Cook acknowledged in his introduction, it was directly indebted to 'This is Tomorrow'.[92] 'The Living City' was a reassessment of the nature of the city within a culture dominated by technology, mobility and the availability of expendable commodities:

> 'Fashion' is a dirty word, so is the word 'Temporary', so is 'Flashy'. Yet it is the creation of those things that are necessarily fashionable, temporary or flashy that has more to do with the vitality of cities than 'monument building'. The pulsation of city life is fast, so why not that of its environment? It reflects rise and fall, coming and going . . . change, so why not build for this?[93]

Cook argued for the desired city as one infinitely responsive to contemporaneity, to novelty and mutability and, 'While we shall not bulldoze Westminster Abbey',[94] its purpose was to take the present into the future, rather than to struggle to retain the past.

While Archigram's architecture was to have a real impact on building design later in the decade, 'The Living City' of 1963 was a wonderfully imaginative projection. It suggested that in the years since 1945 perceptions of the symbolism and cultural significance of the city had been overturned. At the end of the war the city had represented labour, survival and devastating destruction; by the early 1960s Archigram's vision proposed it as a signifier of individual liberty, prosperity and cultural renewal. Yet Metzger's darker vision suggests that this was as much a myth as was the idyllic, unchanging, pastoral landscape that was the counterpart of the older city of the 1950s.

8

LANDSCAPE

Landscapes are formed by landscape tastes.

Lowenthal and Prince, 1965[1]

Landscapes are culture before they are nature: constructs of the imagination projected onto wood and water and rock.

Simon Schama, 1995[2]

Early in 1956 Andrew Forge organised an exhibition for the ICA called '10 years of English landscape painting 1945–1955'. At this time the status of landscape painting appeared to have declined, since the focus of advanced practice had shifted to the urban and technological.[3] Forge explained that he had conceived the exhibition as 'some landscapes since the war' rather than as a comprehensive survey, since that would 'suggest that landscape has been a prime mover, which it has not'.[4] It took place at the end of a decade overshadowed by Picasso and Matisse, just before the impact of American painting became evident. In these ten years the forms of landscape painting had changed as much as its symbolic significance; from being a practice respected as a marker of national identity, it had become transformed into one that was valued and justified as evidence of individual experience. Forge noted this focus in his introduction to the catalogue,[5] implicitly disclaiming group activity or symbolic content, consistent with current critical thinking.

Writing to Lawrence Alloway about his selection, Forge described all but one of the artists as 'more or less naturalistic. Some will be very'. He concluded that the proposed exhibition was 'Not awfully ICA I'm afraid'.[6] The artists ranged from Patrick George and John Bratby, surely in the very category, to William Gear, Patrick Heron and Peter Lanyon, whose painting strongly evoked nature without making any claim to reproduce it. While Forge's dismissal of landscape as a currently significant genre indicates that he saw it as neither fulfilling an ideological role nor offering an arena for the development of process, his comments on potential panellists for an ICA discussion suggest that he nevertheless considered it complex and problematic. He suggested Basil Taylor on the grounds that he was 'anti genius loci and all that', with John Berger, who had 'a good landscape-is-impossible-in-modern-life line'.[7]

The exhibition, with Forge's comments, raised issues that are discussed in this chapter. Prominent among them is the status of landscape painting in 1956. Arcadian myths of purity and redemption no longer carried the compulsion of the war years: in 1956 landscape might convey both social modernity and artistic innovation, as well as reworked readings of the rural. To locate the essence of Englishness within the rural was clearly anachronistic in the context of an economy geared to industrial revival, which suggests that landscape painting urgently needed to change if it were to retain its privileged position. As Forge sensed, it became a means of assimilating modernism to the tradition, which encouraged painters to develop fresh interpretations of landscape, while modernism provided the mechanism which enabled landscape painting to retain its centrality in an updated traditional hierarchy.

The inclusive nature of landscape, as a category of discourse or representation, has been obscured by a dual emphasis on formalism and literal interpretation. The difference between the objective Slade rendering of George's *Landscape at Hickbush* (1956) and the personalised, synechdochic representation of a place in Lanyon's *Boulder Coast* (1952), both of which were shown in the ICA exhibition,[8] prompts questions as to how an individual construction of landscape produces or is produced from a particular material practice; what that construction reveals of an attitude to locality and, in more general terms, what it reveals of an ideology which may underpin the wider significance of landscape representation.

Similarly, the gulf between the careful clarity of Edward Bawden's representations of an Essex village and the clotted impasto of Sheila Fell's paintings of a Cumbrian hill farm conveys more than a preference for one medium over another. Both artists were concerned with terrain, weather, buildings and crops but whereas Bawden displayed them neatly, as under human control, Fell embedded them in turbulent swirls of pigment, as if subject to forces beyond human agency.

These artists differ less in their perceptions of nature than in their interpretations of place – as physical location, metaphor, historical construction or personal emotional focus – and their readings of the relationship between places and 'social attitudes and relations'.[9] A year after the ICA exhibition Forge recorded a discussion between Lanyon and Anthony Fry which illuminates the range of perceptions of place.[10] Discussing Bakewell in Derbyshire, Lanyon, who later made a painting called *Highlow* as a memory of Great Rocks Dale, emphasised the visceral, physical and unrepresentational nature of his reactions,[11] whereas Fry maintained that landscape painting was exclusively a visual process, that the mood of a painting was imposed by the place depicted.

Given the historical prominence of the landscape genre and its significance in the ideology of nationalism, the relationship between conceptual constructions of the countryside and its appearance, between theorised space and visual perception, between contemporary and historical readings of landscape remain central to any discussion of its development within modernism. The physical variety of landscape allows it to be simultaneously the locus of distinctive cultures of work and economy; an idealised construction of wild, untamed nature inhabited by primitive, innocent people, and a repository of the pure and peaceful, to be set against the clamour and grime of the city.

Arguing that landscape is a metaphor for the social order, J. A. Walter has suggested that the attraction of the primitive landscape lies in its implicit rejection, which everyone desires to some extent, of order and conformity.[12] His interpretation renders landscape painting, with its emphasis on the individual creator, a practice almost as threatening to the social fabric as the use of explosives in auto-destructive art.

Postwar representations of landscape are polarised between the wildness of Cornwall and the grim mundanity of the city revealed in Derrick Greaves's paintings of Sheffield. The dichotomy has been most perceptively explored by Raymond Williams,[13] though half a century earlier a crop of books already denounced the ruin of the countryside by cars and suburban sprawl.[14] In 1955 W. G. Hoskins, a renowned local historian, published *The Making of the English Landscape*. It concludes with a famous tirade:

> . . . those long gentle lines of the dip-slope of the Cotswolds, those misty uplands of the sheep-grey oolite, how they have lent themselves to the villainous requirements of the new age! Over them drones, day after day, the obscene shape of the atom-bomber, laying a trail like a filthy slug upon Constable's and Gainsborough's sky. England of the Nissen hut, the 'pre-fab' . . . of the arterial by-pass, treeless and stinking of diesel oil, murderous with lorries . . . Barbaric England of the scientists, the military men, and the politicians: let us turn away and contemplate the past before all is lost to the vandals.[15]

Arcadia, Hoskins concluded, was too fragile to survive; only the past remained to be savoured. The desire to present landscape as it might be, rather than as it too often is, was a dilemma to which modernism offered a possible solution. The combination of realism, abstraction and knowing naivety that characterised the painting produced by modernists in St Ives was an attractive response to Hoskins's romantic nostalgia. Yet not long after the publication of his book, the profoundly urban culture of the Independent Group and the Royal College produced a strong counter-current and a challenge to the values attached to landscape painting.

Since Forge saw landscape painting as a practice outside the social nexus, we may ask what common threads bound it into the central tradition. He was certainly aware of the perception of place-as-construct expressed by the *genius loci* and of the centrality of this theme in English art and literature since Pope had famously commanded its acknowledgement. The thread that ran from Pope to Wordsworth and to Samuel Palmer and his Shoreham cronies was transformed by Constable and taken up again by twentieth-century modernists. Paul Nash in Dorset, Wiltshire and Oxfordshire, Ivon Hitchens in Sussex (fig. 68), Sutherland in Pembrokeshire (fig. 26) and Lanyon in Cornwall all produced numerous images that testify to the special relationship between artist and place. In addition, they extended their painting in written texts which contribute significantly to a theorisation of mid-twentieth-century landscape art.

Distinctions can be made between the intersecting categories of place, countryside and landscape, with place the least easily defined, in that in its most potent sense it is recognised by an individual and appropriated to that person's psychological make-up.[16] In practice, convention establishes the metonymic relationship between place and a component of landscape[17] that Paul Nash developed in *Nocturnal Landscape* (1938) (fig. 21) where pieces of flint are enlarged into prancing monsters. Nash created places by visually redefining them, filtering their history, mythology and lineaments through his sense of the mysterious and evocative.[18]

While all landscapes that have undergone human intervention have been accul-turated and carry symbolic meaning,[19] Nash has probably contributed more than any other artist to our contemporary emphasis on personal constructions of place, in contrast with readings of earlier representations of landscape symbolism as expressions of political and social values.

Very different from Nash's perceptions of place are those revealed by L. S. Lowry, Derrick Greaves, Sheila Fell and the group of artists based at Great Bardfield in Essex, who included Edward Bawden, John Aldridge, Michael Rothenstein and the weaver, Marianne Straub.[20] Their paintings focussed on human labour and landscape as a productive system rather than an aesthetic object. Their distinctive material practices indicate the range of social relations embedded in what the Marxist archaeologist Tim Ingold has described as the 'taskscape'. Rejecting symbolic or cultural readings, Ingold sees landscape as a 'process' constantly amended by the activities of those who live and work within it. Body and landscape are complementary in a constant process of incorporation, which is the generation of new forms. The taskscape is a temporal expression of the relationship between body and landscape, while particular places are its visible and always changing products.[21]

The creamy-grey, even tonality of Lowry's townscapes, broken only by restrained terracotta and red, suggests an urban infinity populated by the scurry-ing figures of workers too small to show individual features, whose anonymity measures their incorporation into the uniformity of industrial culture, just as they are absorbed by an unnatural, flat light. In Greaves's theatrical, monochrome *Sheffield Landscape* (1953), people are absent; the derelict industrial buildings con-stitute a reverie on the condition of workers. The painting may be read as a threnody for a rural culture displaced by factories, which are painted in a harsh, mechanical way that underlines the absence of organic life. In *Potato Pickers 1* (1960) (fig. 58) Fell characteristically set small bent figures against a lowering hill backed by a stormy sky. No rural idyll intrudes on her vision of Cumbria and it is clear that she understood landscape as a product of cultural values: 'I do not want to be thought of purely as a landscape painter. I hope that the nearby community is always implicit in my landscapes.'[22]

THE GREAT BARDFIELD ARTISTS

For Fell, a community was identified by its dependence on a shared form of labour: the sheep-rearing and small crops of a Cumbrian hill farm. A very dif-ferent agricultural community was recorded by the artists who settled in Great Bardfield and the flat Essex countryside around it. No less an artists' colony than the better known St Ives, with painters, printmakers, a weaver and theatre designers, who opened their studios in an annual summer exhibition, it was neither a centre of modernism nor a locus of romantic primitivism. The colony was founded in 1930, when Bawden and Eric Ravilious settled at the Brick House, a prominent building in the village that became one of Bawden's constant subjects. Ravilious was killed on active service as a war artist but Bawden remained in the house until 1971, a member of an active informal group.[23]

In his affectionate chronicle of the Great Bardfield artists, published in 1957, the critic Colin McInnes remarked that they had 'firmly based themselves in a robust English village, surrounded by a radiant, fruitful countryside . . . rooted in a place that is a microcosm of the older rural England.'[24] His text echoed a common

58. Sheila Fell, *Potato Pickers 1*, 1960. Oil on canvas, 50 × 40 in. Arts Council Collection, Hayward Gallery, London.

nostalgia for a calm and creative past even while it obscured the urgency of the labour that Bawden meticulously recorded. Although naturally unaware of the secret famine programme described by Peter Hennessy, the artist was certainly conscious of recent exhortations to 'Dig for Victory' and the need to sustain agricultural productivity in peacetime. By investing all his work, whether in print media or oil-paint, with the clarity of linocut, Bawden worked within the vernacular trope of Mass Observation and Recording Britain, to produce a chronicle of a georgic landscape where material facts dismiss the artifice of the Picturesque.

After the war he took Great Bardfield as the model for his lithographic illustrations in Noel Carrington's King Penguin, *Life in an English Village*, a gently propagandist text which optimistically proclaimed the renaissance of the village through the adoption of modern social measures.[25] Whereas the urgency of wartime agriculture had ignored the specificities of place, transforming parks and gardens into allotments, Bawden and Carrington identified a farming culture with its distinctive physical and social location and emphasised the singularities of the place within a wider ideology.

The landscape art of Great Bardfield stands on the periphery of modernist practice, portraying ancient country life and work in terms of prosperity and the satisfaction of material demands, rather than the interpretation of place. Less exotic than Cornwall, more mundane than Sussex and free from the disturbing undercurrents of Paul Nash's Dorset, Great Bardfield stands for social values, community and co-operation.

Its geographical context is perhaps best described as countryside; landscape is a subject for painting and poetry, but the countryside is where ordinary people live and work. It suffers the changes that Hoskins deplored: roads are driven through it and buildings interrupt its views; it is visited by tourists and can be defined in terms of acres, crop yields, mineral resources and real estate. While landscape may be viewed in these terms it is often also understood as a metaphor for national values, and taken to represent the elemental in human nature, the spontaneous, uncalculating person, filled with natural wisdom. The countryside, however, is the site of human activity and its values are often invoked in assessments of society,[26] whereas landscape is an abstract construction subject to rapid shifts of meaning. In practice, country and landscape are difficult to differentiate: Alfred Wallis's seascapes and fishing boats depict a dangerous, uncertain rural industry and at the same time introduce a mythology of innocence beyond material experience (fig. 59).

ST IVES

In contrast to Great Bardfield, St Ives is an artists' colony characterised by myths of purity and innocence the more poignant since they are allied to perceptions of a culture in decline. By the end of the war tourism and art had replaced fishing and mining as the area's principal industries. Those seeking authenticity or the primitive could no longer find them in a living culture but had to trace their remnants in carefully preserved landscapes, villages and harbours. Lanyon's references in his paintings to mining as a dangerous, exploitative industry reveal his rejection of the Cornwall of romantic legend.

Many artists have commented on the compelling beauty of the Cornish landscape, once admired for its remoteness and wildness and more recently appreciated as ideally unspoilt. Modern St Ives represents an untroubled haven, 'a return to stability, secure and untroubled after the confusion of war'[27] and a place

59. Alfred Wallis, *The Hold House Port Mear Square Island Portmear Beach*, (*c*?1932). Oil, 12 × 15¼ in. Tate Gallery, London.

untouched by the sophistication of the capital. A powerful contribution to this perception has been the construction of the primitive artist, embodied in Wallis, the former scrap-metal dealer turned painter. The opening ritual of modern St Ives took place in August 1928 when Ben Nicholson and Christopher Wood, on holiday near Truro, met Wallis. The encounter, often described as a discovery of the old man by the two London-based artists, has been combined with accounts of his religious fervour and domestic habits to establish a scenario in which he acquires the attributes of an unrecorded anthropological specimen.

His personality and paintings, the equivalent for St Ives modernists of tribal art for Cubism, demonstrated the survival of a simple fishing culture in its natural setting. Before his meeting with Wallis, Nicholson's paintings wandered between modernism and sophisticated naturalism; subsequently he made a knowing appropriation of Wallis's idiosyncratic naivety,[28] comparable to Henry Moore's assimilation of Mexican sculpture at about the same time. The distance between the two painters is apparent in their handling of paint: Wallis built up his ships and harbours with thick impasto into simulacra of material objects, whereas the light, fleeting marks of *1928 (Porthmeor Beach, St Ives)*, characteristic of Nicholson's early primitivising paintings, suggest that landscape is to be represented as an immaterial thought. It was Wood, though, who most presciently subsumed Wallis into modernism, through a pictorial device that he probably learnt from his close friend Winifred Nicholson. In Wood's *Cornish Window Scene* (1928) a distant Wallis-like steamer is set on a choppy blue sea, framed by a window embrasure with a generic cubist still life of pipe and ashtray on the sill.

In one of the first accounts of Wallis, written shortly after his death in 1942, Nicholson initiated the transformation of his poverty, near-illiteracy and crude self-taught technique into an account of a child-like[29] character whose innate talent must be shielded from corruption. The old sailor was like 'the first creative artist', rooted in the soil of Eden: '. . . his imagination is surely a lovely thing . . . it is something which has grown out of the Cornish earth and sea, and which will endure.'[30]

The perceived simplicity of the primitive offered a means of mediation between representation and modernism. In the large group of paintings represented by *November 11–44 (Mousehole)* (fig. 60). Nicholson found a way to overcome the disjunction between a *faux primitif* style and modernist sophistication by setting a cubist still life in front of a naive landscape as though framed by a window.

The importance of Wallis for the younger generation of artists was emphasised by the publication in 1948 of Sven Berlin's romantic biography. Berlin, a painter, sculptor, dancer and quondam odd-job man, has contributed as much, through his writing and life-style, to the exoticism of St Ives as to its art.[31] His account has served as a model for a convention in which artists are discussed biographically, in terms of their relationship with the place, while their work is subsumed under a heading of St Ives as a shorthand for a modernising landscape practice.

Postwar promotion of regional interests, both industrial and cultural, combined with grassroots sentiment to perpetuate the perception of St Ives as a desired, mythic location. The writer, broadcaster and playwrite Denys Val Baker founded a periodical, *Voices*, in 1946 to promote 'the contemporary revival of regional cultural activities [and] . . . protest against the growing imposition of centralised ideas and codes of behaviour'.[32] In his books on artists in Cornwall[33] Val Baker presented the Tamar as a frontier between a mythic place and the hard realism of cities, austerity and a strike-bound economy.

60. Ben Nicholson, *November 11–47 (Mousehole)*, 1947. Oil on canvas on wood, 18 × 23 in. British Council Collection.

Artists who flocked to St Ives during and after the war found a singular place in terms of aesthetic activity. The St Ives region, once described as 'that Barbizon of England',[34] covers, for aesthetic purposes, the area south of a line between Portreath and the Lizard and includes Newlyn, the centre of the Newlyn School in the 1880s, whose genre painters used as a subject the local fishing culture. St Ives, on the opposite side of the peninsula, has been known to painters since 1811, when Turner made a brief visit, but like Newlyn, it only became a popular centre of production after the railway was built in 1877. Between the wars West Cornwall remained important for Academicians and Sunday painters alike,[35] with a special train carrying paintings to London every year for the Royal Academy Summer Exhibition.

This was the situation when, in the late summer of 1939, Barbara Hepworth, Nicholson and their close friend, the pioneer of Russian Constructivism, Naum Gabo, moved to St Ives to escape the anticipated annihilation of London by bombing. It is difficult to exaggerate the sense of loss that they must have experienced. In the late 1930s London was second only to Paris as a centre for contemporary art and the Hampstead artists strenuously cultivated their contacts with the French avant garde, while they lived in an intense atmosphere of invention and rivalry that was extended by the presence of refugees from the Continent, who included Gabo.[36]

London implied Paris; it offered exhibitions, critical stimulus and Herbert Read's devoted support, as well as occasional sales and a wide circle of friends. Read, Eric Gregory, J. D. Bernal, the critic E. H. Ramsden and Cyril Connolly were among the visitors to wartime St Ives[37] who helped to sustain old allegiances in exile. St Ives had one or two small galleries, a single exhibiting group, the St Ives Society of Artists, founded in 1927, the idiosyncratic if hardly supportive criticism of *The St Ives Times* and the company of a circumscribed group of fellow immigrants. In the history of St Ives as an artists' colony artists have been seen as a social elite, set apart from the local people, and though social divisions diminished steadily, the wartime arrivals at first followed the same pattern, operating as an exclusive group and retaining closer ties with the capital than with Penzance or Plymouth.

Hepworth and Nicholson joined the critic and painter Adrian Stokes and his wife, Margaret Mellis, in an influx which definitively modified perceptions of the aesthetic balance of the town. Almost immediately, the leading edge of St Ives art was converted to a constructivist practice disseminated by Hepworth, Nicholson and Gabo. They offered distinctive formal models: Lanyon, who studied with Nicholson late in 1939, made a group of linear, abstract drawings related to prototypes like Nicholson's *1933–5 (still-life)* and he continued to reduce his paint to a thin, scraped-down skin until the late 1940s. Equally fecund sources for younger colleagues for a short, intensive period were Hepworth's linear drawings of 1940–2. Precise, linear evocations of pure abstract form, they were, as Alan Wilkinson has pointed out, deeply indebted to Gabo,[38] whose *Spiral Theme* (1941) (fig. 19) was to assume an almost talismanic status for Lanyon.[39] Unlike Nicholson, Gabo had a profound intellectual impact on the younger artists, who found in the 'constructive idea' expounded in *Circle* an ethical model sufficiently flexible to be relevant across a wide range of practice.

The conversion of St Ives from an avant-garde outpost to a prominent centre for the production of a modern art formulated in a cognitive relationship with landscape is inseparable from the development of its internal support system. Accounts of exhibitions in Downing's Bookshop and the crypt of the Mariners' Chapel, of artists' gatherings in the Zennor Arms portray an intense, isolated community of artists immersed in a romantic struggle for self-definition through engagement with a place. Such narratives have tended to conceal the extent to which the same artists were engaged, no less than their progressive counterparts in London, in the development of a consciously contemporary art. Like the Constructionists, they exploited available facilities to develop an *ad hoc* alternative exhibiting network while they worked to establish themselves in the London commercial system. The newcomers of 1939 imported a model for a structure, practice and theory from Hampstead, though any dreams they may have harboured of sustaining a strictly constructive practice in the long term were confounded by the fracturing of the group at the end of the war, a process precipitated by the departure of its theoretician, Gabo, for the United States in November 1946.

The constructivist refugees had shown in strength in 'New Movements in Art' in 1942, with new recruits like Margaret Mellis confirming the vitality of Gabo's 'constructive idea'. She showed a collage, one of a series made on Nicholson's suggestion, many of which incorporated geometric drawings. They led on to shallow wood reliefs, like *Construction in Wood* (1941) (fig. 61) which exploited

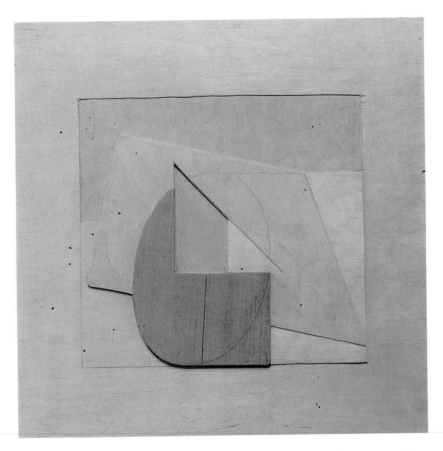

61. Margaret Mellis, *Construction in Wood*, 1941. Scottish National Gallery of Modern Art, Edinburgh.

variations in colour and grain.[40] Mellis's reliefs have affinities with those made by John Wells and Lanyon. In Wells's *Relief Construction 1* (1941) (fig. 62), which he showed at the London Museum, dark and light areas and forms are held together visually by convergent strings arranged in a way that echoes the stringing of a guitar and thus, perhaps, the cubist still life motif that Nicholson had appropriated with such enthusiasm in the early 1930s.

Lanyon made his first two constructions shortly before he joined the RAF in 1940. As he was to do later, he seems deliberately to have produced a complementary pair, with both parts related to aspects of Nicholson's work. Nicholson's static, Mondrian-like paintings may have informed the *Box Construction No. 1* (1939),[41] which was, Lanyon remarked, 'rather like a stage':[42] a closely defined area in which spatial relationships might be established. Andrew Causey has suggested a link between its counterpart, *White Track* (1939–40), a flat surface animated by a diagonal, and Nicholson's more dynamic works, such as *1933 (milk and plain chocolate)*.[43] Another pair of constructions, which Lanyon later destroyed, carried strong formal echoes, in one instance of Hepworth's Crystal drawings, and in the other, of the fluid, interlocked curves of Gabo's paintings and constructions.[44]

By the end of the war the 'New Movements in Art' group had dissolved and after Gabo's departure the interests of the younger artists rapidly diversified. While postwar St Ives has been overwhelmingly associated with a landscape-based practice, the process of conversion from a constructivist focus was not without tensions. In September 1946 Lanyon, Wells, Bryan Wynter, Berlin and the printer, Guido Morris held the first Crypt Group exhibition.[45] In that the four

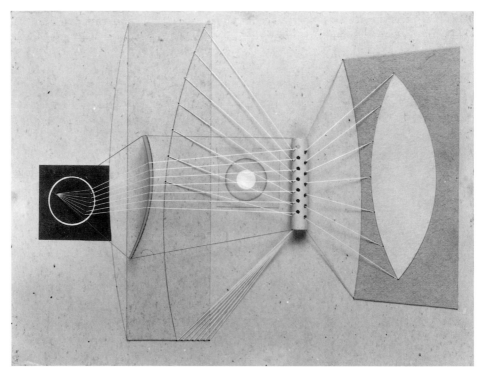

62. John Wells,
Relief Construction 1,
1941. Mixed media,
$12\frac{5}{8} \times 16\frac{5}{8} \times 1\frac{3}{8}$ in.
Tate Gallery,
London.

painters were members of the St Ives Society of Artists, whose academic creden-
tials were to be underlined by the election of Alfred Munnings as its president in
1948,[46] the show was a manifestation of their frustration and their declaration of
independence as modernists. Their invitation to Borlase Smart, Lanyon's first
teacher and president of the Society until his death in 1947 to open the first Crypt
show, signalled the younger artists' allegiance to a respected traditional painter,
and a more complex situation than a simple academic/modernist confrontation.

Though Lanyon and Wells both showed a few constructions in the 1946 exhibition, the focus of the Crypt artists was away from an increasingly alien
constructivist aesthetic towards a phenomenological approach mediated by modernism. Despite the departure from the *Circle* aesthetic evident in works like
Hepworth's *Pelagos* (1946) and Nicholson's *November 11–47 (Mousehole)* (fig. 60),
these artists were significantly absent from the Crypt shows. As if to underline the
increasingly conspicuous presence of a younger group with clearly divergent
interests,[47] the catalogue-folder for the third and final exhibition in August 1948
contained a resumé of the previous two events.

Lanyon vividly conveyed a dilemma that was probably not unique to him when
he wrote to Gabo early in 1949: 'I find a continual temptation to seduction by the
appearance painting of the scenic boys . . . Curiously enough my paintings are all
of landscape or in the sense of landscape. I don't know whether I can claim to be
a Constructivist any longer, because of this.'[48] Wells, his close friend, made a
comparable break with compelling precedents when he began to graft atmospheric colour onto geometric shapes.

The Crypt exhibitions may now be seen, as Matthew Rowe has pointed out, as
the prelude to the formation of the Penwith Society of Arts early in 1949.[49] They
mark a formative point in the definition of a non-constructive, perceptually
grounded aesthetic closely, though not exclusively related to landscape. The
Penwith Society has a prominent part in the history of postwar art in St Ives;

central to it is an account of the accomodation between landscape art and the purity of Constructionism. Also founded by dissidents, the Penwith Society[50] was formally constituted and planned to maximise its impact as a local institutional basis for modernism. Though the criteria for membership were elastic,[51] its weighting towards advanced practice was confirmed by the election of Read as the first president. Yet despite the strength of its links with the art establishment,[52] its claim to be an umbrella for all vanguard practice in the area was compromised by the bitter faction-fighting which began only a few months after its foundation.[53] In May 1949 Hepworth proposed that artists – and their work – should be classified by dividing entries for the Society's exhibitions into three categories broadly corresponding to 'Traditional/Figurative and Modern/Abstract',[54] with craft set firmly apart. Her system sought to sustain a rigid dichotomy and implied a value judgement which, while it was consistent with the metaphysical concepts of purity and the absolute central to the *Circle* group, failed to take into account the complex processes of transformation and mark-making that informed perceptual abstraction. The inadequacy of the scheme was immediately demonstrated by such images as Lanyon's *Porthleven* (1950) (fig. 72), and Terry Frost's *A Walk along the Quay* (1950) (fig. 63), all of which combined conceptual process with evocative colour and reference to real places.

The acceptance of the new system in November 1950 was taken by some members as a denial of the Society's former tolerance,[55] a perpetuation of the interests of the older constructive artists and, most damagingly, as a pre-emptive claim by them for dominance of the Society.[56] It brought to a head the tensions that had been growing since Nicholson had assumed Gabo's position as the doyen of progressive artists in St Ives[57] and resulted in the resignation of a group of founder members, who included Berlin, Lanyon and Morris. Despite the bitter divisions that this revealed, the benefits of possessing a nationally recognised local exhibiting system were considerable. Even for those artists who rejected the Society, the process of aesthetic definition required to bring it and the Crypt Group into existence had forced them to clarify the direction of their work and to elucidate its distance both from academic painting and what they considered to be the equally outdated work of an earlier avant garde.

At the end of the war Nicholson had considered returning permanently to London where he was busy establishing an active schedule of exhibitions in commercial galleries, as well as with the British Council.[58] During the war his dealers at the Lefevre Gallery had pressed him to increase his production of *faux-naif* landscapes since, unlike his 'pure abstract painting', they sold readily.[59] Nicholson, on the contrary, feared that the carefully calculated combination of modernism and naivety, which culminated in *November 11–47 (Mousehole)* would compromise his position as a leader of the avant garde. He therefore preferred to maintain a clear distinction in exhibitions between work made for income and that made to sustain a progressive position. He continued with this dual practice in the 1950s, when he diverted the landscape element into drawings and prints which he produced in parallel with a long series of monumental still lifes. Widely exhibited, these consolidated his international reputation.

The hint of abstracted landscape at the top of *February 28–53 (vertical seconds)* (fig. 64) is in startling contrast to the busy harbour scene of *November 11–47 (Mousehole)*. We may ask, then what is signified by Nicholson's transition between representational modes. Virginia Button has argued that though he never identified himself with a neo-Romantic culture, his landscape still lifes of the 1940s were

63. Terry Frost, *A Walk Along the Quay*, 1950. Oil on canvas, 60 × 22 in. Private Collection, on loan to Graves Art Gallery, Sheffield.

64. Ben Nicholson, *February 28–53 (vertical seconds)*, 1953. Oil on canvas, $29\frac{3}{4} \times 16\frac{1}{2}$ in. Tate Gallery, London.

congruent with a neo-Romantic insistence on personal identification with land-scape as a locus of Englishness and that they would have been understood in this context.[60] His own impetus, though, was to re-establish, as rapidly as possible after the war, the links with the French artists whom he had admired and emulated in the 1930s, especially Braque, though he almost programmatically differentiated his work from its primary source. Whereas the still lifes that Braque showed at the Tate in 1946 were portraits of his studio, located by details of wainscoting, wall-paper, windows and furniture, Nicholson's were pared down so as to deny any physical context.

February 28–53 (vertical seconds) represents his contribution to a new interna-tional modernism, appropriate for the Venice Biennale and the many other events in which he was a tireless participant. Such paintings proclaimed their allegiance to Cubism, and thus to the cause of twentieth-century modernism, while the artist's authorship and autonomy are signalled by the jars and jugs that he depicted. The repeated appearance in paint of these familiar objects that Nicholson kept in his studio converts his tabletops into metonymic renderings of his work place. In this way the anomaly of the still-life-in-landscape is rationalised, since the tabletop may be read as a metaphor for the structure that houses it.

In *February 28–53 (vertical seconds)* landscape is represented by a mnemonic: the patches of vivid blue and the greenish tinge at the top of the canvas.[61] In the monumental *1956 (boutique fantasque)* the blue more clearly denotes sky, abutting a horizon line and perhaps a building on the right. Minimal though they are, Nicholson's landscapes are open and unobstructed. While they lack specific geographical references, their persistent presence in many paintings suggests that they play a more integral role than compositional decor or setting. An extension of John Barrell's distinction between the ideal 'panoramic prospect' and 'representations of enclosed, occluded landscapes' in eighteenth-century painting and poetry may elucidate this role. Barrell argues that

> among the meanings attached to the panoramic view may be the notion of a wider society, and the notion of the ability to grasp objects in the form of their relations to each other; among the meanings attached to the occluded view, from a low viewpoint, are seclusion . . . and privacy as something opposed to the social . . . a tendency to see objects not in terms of their relations, or their common relation to a general, and representative term, but in and for themselves, as objects of consumption and possession.[62]

A taste for and ownership of a panoramic swathe of land is equated with fitness to exercise political authority, whereas the occluded landscape indicates membership of a lower social class and exclusion from a position of authority.

In mid-twentieth-century Britain, where rural landscape had recently functioned as a potent metaphor for the nation-state, the open landscape may be taken, as it was two centuries earlier, to represent an ideal: the good government of a free nation or, differently expressed, the benign macrocosm that subsumed the microcosms – or studios – of free individuals. The minimal landscapes of Nicholson's still lifes may thus be understood as signifiers of the cultural and political context in which the paintings were made, and of democratic liberalism.

For Nicholson, his grand tabletop still lifes no doubt simply marked a return to the kind of ambitious painting that he had made before the war. For other artists in St Ives they may have represented the exemplary accomodation between modernism and 'appearance painting'[63] that has been central to the construction of St Ives art. So successful was this accomodation, that by the end of the 1950s the leading artists of St Ives formed what amounted to an official avant garde, prominent in British Council exhibitions and international competitions; sought-after by American dealers and applauded by critics at home. Their perceptual abstraction had become established as an exemplary modern practice, so that by the mid-1950s the erstwhile fishing village was acknowledged as the centre of English landscape art. This new status of St Ives as centre implies a considerable degree of homogeneity between individual practices and suggests that each artist focussed on the communication of identifiable and unique characteristics of the place. Yet Nicholson's still lifes underline the extent to which a perception of St Ives art is not necessarily dependent on representations of landscape.

In the same period, Hepworth's most important works, following *Contrapuntal Forms* (1951) (fig. 103), commissioned for the Festival of Britain, were the first of a dozen monumental wooden sculptures, which included *Curved Form (Delphi)*

65. Barbara Hepworth, *Curved Form (Delphi)*, 1955. Scented guarea, string and paint, 42 in. high. Ulster Museum, Belfast.

(1955) (fig. 65).[64] Evocative in a general sense of sea, sky and caverns, their titles assert a primary association with the landscape of Greece rather than of Cornwall.[65] Moreover, the emphasis on a formal contrast between smooth, polished exterior surfaces and carefully roughened internal curves, and between the colour of natural wood and high, light paint suggests a deeper absorption in the *matière* of sculpture and painting than in the particularities of place.

Parallel dislocations are evident among the younger artists. Although he habitually spent holidays in Cornwall, Heron was based in London until 1955. Braque was a revered model for the still lifes and interiors which formed much of his early output,[66] though Heron's process of assimilation diverged sharply from Nicholson's[67] and arguably had a more intensively formalist focus.[68] Mel Gooding has commented that the artists whom Heron adopted as models were precisely those for whom 'subject matter was the pretext for formal invention and design: those painters whose work achieved an equilibrium of form and content . . . those caught between the impulse to abstraction and the requirement to keep an eye on the world.'[69] Heron's *Balcony Window with Green Table: St Ives: 1951* (fig. 8) reveals an intimate domestic space full of incident and rooted, by the view through the window, in its locality, but Heron has insisted that the picturesque view was primarily 'the pretext for formal invention'.[70] Though it is not necessary to accept the reductive reading of his interiors that this interpretation implies, it does indicate a certain lack of engagement with landscape as a subject.

Briefly overwhelmed by the 1952 de Staël exhibition, Heron produced a small number of paintings formed with thickly knifed, rectangular *taches* of pigment which may be read, if only with the artist's guidance, as still lifes.[71] With the long series of *Garden Paintings* of 1956, that followed his purchase of his house, Eagle's Nest near Zennor, he turned conclusively away from an identifiable subject towards a perceptual abstraction based initially on the paintings of Sam Francis, which he had seen in the ICA's 'Opposing Forces' exhibition in 1953.

This exemplary amalgamation of Ecole de Paris Tachisme with a personal and local imagery was followed by the stripe paintings, the largest of which, *Horizontal Stripe Painting: November 1957–January 1958* (fig. 3), had been commissioned for Eric Gregory's London offices. In its bands of colour, analogous to light, sky, sea and horizon, there are, perhaps, further echoes of de Staël and the semi-figurative landscapes he had shown at the Whitechapel Art Gallery in 1956.[72] Both tachiste and stripe paintings have been linked, not least by Heron himself, to the landscape in which he lived, but whereas it would be absurd to deny any perceptual content, the example of the majestic Lund Humphries canvas suggests that both series are fundamentally decorative. This is not to denigrate Heron's paintings; rather it is to set them in the lineage of earlier decorations by French modern masters. Like those made by Vuillard, Bonnard and Monet for specific interiors, Heron's non-figurative paintings create transformatory environments where, in his own words, 'the space is the light and the light is space'.[73]

Terry Frost was one of the more traditional of the St Ives modernists in that he was the most undeviatingly perceptual. Studying at Camberwell in the late 1940s on an ex-serviceman's grant, he came into contact with the nascent constructionist group through Adrian Heath. Victor Pasmore, who was then a visiting teacher at Camberwell, became Frost's mentor and provided formal models for his most ambitious early paintings, like the 1950 *A Walk along the Quay* (fig. 63).[74] The melon-slice arcs which punctuate the image were appropriated, with some modifications, from Pasmore, while the central area of small rectangles may be indebted to Kenneth Martin's *Composition 1949*.

In contrast to the static imagery of *A Walk along the Quay*, Frost simultaneously worked on a group of paintings which explored illusions of motion,[75] like *Movement, Green, Black and White* (1951) (fig. 43),[76] in which arcs drop rhythmically down the canvas, held within a sparse geometric framework, and *Movement, Green and Black*, (1952) where clusters of curved marks whirl around a central point.[77] This rendering of the sea wall of St Ives harbour, in which the clustered marks represent spray and waves, suggests that despite Frost's adoption of constructionist forms, he used them pictorially: his paintings are arranged intuitively and even at their most non-representational are grounded in visual experience. He confirmed this in his statement in *Nine Abstract Artists*, where he wrote of 'a synthesis of movement and counter-movement', where the subject was 'the sensation evoked by the movements and colour in the harbour'.[78]

Occasionally Frost's choice of format suggests that visual sensation is extended into an identification between canvas and place, where the artist's presence in both is implied by his marks on the canvas. Heath saw such an identification in Frost's 'choice of a long, narrow canvas to symbolise the strict limitations of his daily walk',[79] for *A Walk along the Quay*.

In 1954 Frost became the Gregory Fellow in Painting at Leeds University, where he responded to the very different landscape of the Yorkshire Dales. In *Winter 1956, Yorkshire* (fig. 66) it is again the format which is the most telling part of the total image. This tall, vertical painting, 97 inches high, echoes the expanse of the hills, their steepness evident in the bold parallel stripes, each one formed by a sweep of the painter's arm. Frost left Leeds in 1957 and his work changed again

66. Terry Frost,
Winter 1956,
Yorkshire. Oil on
board, $97\frac{1}{8} \times 49\frac{1}{8}$ in.
Tate Gallery,
London.

under a fresh stimulus, but it seems that his period as a Gregory Fellow strengthened his preference for perceptual painting and finally released him from any
lingering impulse to geometric imagery.

The examples of Heron and his colleagues suggest that St Ives painting is
heterodox and assimilative, by no means exclusively concerned with the locality,
despite the insistence of numerous commentators that the place has, almost
unaided, fostered the development of a school of romantic landscape art. The
area's reputation is grounded in the development of such a practice, though its
defining characteristics are far from clear. Wallis, Wells, Lanyon and Heron have
little in common, yet all are inscribed in the same location biographically,
historiographically and in the record of their work. In the diversity of postwar
landscape painting, the single recurrent factor is the relationship, which ranges
from a deep sense of physical and psychological identification to the disengagement of the passing visitor,[80] between the artist and a notion of place.[81]

A large literature produced principally by cultural geographers testifies to the hermeneutic problems posed by the term landscape. In an essay subtitled 'Ten versions of the same scene', David Meinig has indicated the diversity of theoretical models through which a single stretch of landscape may be analysed.[82] Most can be related, with varying degrees of frequency, to the work of postwar landscape artists, though only one model, namely 'place', has been identified by both artists and critics as consistently significant. The final section of this chapter is therefore devoted to the interpretation of place and, in one instance, its absence, in the work of four painters, Graham Sutherland, Ivon Hitchens, William Gear and Peter Lanyon.[83]

ARTISTS AND PLACE

Curiously, Forge and his contemporaries placed little emphasis on the relationship between landscape painting and place. The precedent of Constable in Suffolk was echoed more closely by the relatively traditional painters of Great Bardfield than by those in Cornwall, indicating that modernist concepts of place were quantifiably different from historical representations of great properties, the sublime or the invented landscape. Modernist place, as it has been depicted and described by Nash, Sutherland, Lanyon and Hitchens among others, is primarily experiential in that it focusses on the individual's unique relationship with a locality.

'Places', Edward Relph writes, 'are . . . incorporated into the intentional structures of all human consciousness and experience . . . The essence of place lies in the largely unselfconscious intentionality that defines places as profound centres of human existence.'[84] Any investigation of modernist depictions of place is complicated by the implications of formal aspects of painting: the apocalyptic colour and black ink marks of neo-Romantic images are as heavily inflected, historically and ideologically, as the bravura, arm-sweep marks associated with Abstract Expressionism. An assessment of the significance of place must also take into account an artist's textual exegesis, not so much in an endeavour to match image and text as to establish a datum point from which to initiate enquiries.

Graham Sutherland's *Red Landscape* (1942) (fig. 26), made during a rare trip to Wales in the intervals of work for the WAAC, exemplifies the way in which he depicted a generalised landscape with motifs reworked from both Palmer and Surrealism. He used apocalyptic colour, heightened with dramatic black marks which articulate rock formations, roads and vegetation so that they appear to be organic presences. In the same year Sutherland's 'Welsh Sketchbook' was published,[85] describing his first trip to Pembroke and its impact on his work. He wrote vividly of the 'foreignness' of the place, in which he was acutely aware of himself as an intense but alien observer. Uninterested in painting directly from nature, he found in Wales a wealth of material to stimulate the kind of transformation that resulted in *Gorse on Sea Wall* (1939) (fig. 27),[86] an image evolved through the conversion of a twisted plant into a hybrid that is part vegetable, part clawed animal.

What then, was Sutherland's relationship with places? Interviewed by Andrew Forge in 1962 he emphasised his attraction to 'the individual form, the form which interests me for its own sake' over a sense of place: the root that produced *Gorse on Sea Wall* was inspirational, its location in a familiar part of Wales irrelevant.[87] By

67. Graham Sutherland, *Standing Form against a Hedge*, 1950. Oil on canvas, 53 × 46 in. Arts Council Collection, Hayward Gallery, London.

1947, when Sutherland first visited the South of France, his last vestiges of landscape as topography were giving way to landscape as an animating presence, a process which culminated in the *Standing Forms* that he began in 1949. The active agent in *Standing Form against a Hedge* (1950) (fig. 67) is part root or tuber, part statue, derived from sculpture in the garden of an old house at Saint-Jean-Cap-Ferrat where Sutherland stayed for a time; more generally the image evolved from an animist approach shared by several of his contemporaries. It produced hybrids whose identity is unknowable, whose alien nature is accentuated by the precision with which they are depicted and which, like the *Standing Form against a Hedge*, repel rather than attract.

Sutherland's conversion of place into organic presence developed into a metamorphic process in which selected features of a landscape were transformed from anonymity to uniqueness. The hybrids, which he called 'personages', like the figure in *Standing Form against a Hedge*, also constitute extended metaphors for changing perceptions of landscape painting itself, or for a conceptual metamorphosis, in which landscape was on the one hand converted to country or town, as an unidealised site for work and on the other, released from the conventions of representation.

Ivon Hitchens, ten years older than Sutherland,[88] also became prominent soon after the war and, though he was never internationally famous in the same way as Sutherland,[89] he was extremely successful both commercially and critically[90] and was a frequent participant in British Council exhibitions. In terms of innovation he was considered almost Sutherland's peer in the early postwar period, a judgement overlooked in recent years when he has been more admired for atmospheric representational qualities.

In the 1930s Hitchens was associated with the Hampstead avant garde, where his work was closer to the 'Objective Abstractions' group than to Constructivism. In 1940, when his Hampstead studio was bombed, he moved with his family to Lavington Common in Sussex where he began to paint landscape, often working in series on a limited range of motifs related to the small area near his home. The Terwick Mill and Winter Walk series were Monet-like enterprises, 'trying different groupings and effects at different times of the day'.[91] Like most of Hitchens's landscapes, *Winter Walk No. 2* (1948) (fig. 68) was painted in a horizontal format, with the canvas roughly divided into near, middle and distant space, with progressions from warm to cool and light to dark.[92] There is also a roughly tripartite horizontal division where each section opens up an eponymous walk into deep space.

Hitchens was later to rationalise illusion through a musical analogy in which the mark was the equivalent of the note, allied to the Japanese concept of *notan*, or harmonic tonal relations within a scaled progression of colour.[93] In practical terms illusion involved a conversion of the impressionist *tache* to a larger mark, which represented natural colour and a single object in the landscape.[94] Hitchens's involved exegesis of *notan* has somewhat obscured the indebtedness to French painting that Heron emphasised in his Penguin Modern Painters monograph, where he saw the artist as a follower of Cézanne and the early Cubists.[95] Writing of *Winter Walk, No.3*, Heron vividly conveyed the literalness of response evoked by Hitchens's paintings:

> this space can be *felt* while we are still in the clearing . . . when we come back down the avenue we hover . . . then we go left, not right . . . From here we may escape up a rich passage of transparent pink or red . . . or we may try to push a way past those horizontal leaves – a single light flick of the brush defines each . . .[96]

Hitchens was, it seems, attracted by the possibility of narrative, which led him to the horizontal format, because 'There is no "progress", no time element in a square picture, which the eye sees all at once'.[97] More pressingly though, he sought a sense of illusion grounded in the viewer's physical identification with the

68. Ivon Hitchens, *Winter Walk no. 2*, 1948. Oil on canvas, 17 × 43 in. Government Art Collection.

image,[98] in which the horizontal format played an important part.[99] While his landscapes have been prized as evocations of nature and real space, they convey a perception of place very different from Sutherland's or from the looser relationship between artist and locality displayed by Hitchens's friend Patrick Heron.

'Simultaneous perception'[100] facilitates a multi-sensory awareness of the environment in which it is possible 'to divide our attention equally between ourselves and things outside ourselves' so that 'we look for ways in which we are connected to or are part of our surroundings'.[101] Hitchens's places were specific and named, part of the Sussex of waterways, valleys and rich woodlands,[102] a hidden, personalised landscape that constituted his refuge from the clamour of London and its art world. It represented both his personal space, a parallel to the privacy of the studio, and a desired landscape, an ideal beyond the city, the suburb or the motorway, which the viewer was invited to experience as real and accessible. It is rendered credible by the broad brush marks and bold slabs of colour which indicate that far from being nostalgic anachronisms, his places have a contemporary material existence.

These landscapes exclude people; human intervention is suggested only by an occasional sketched-in boat or building subsumed into the scene as part of its nature.[103] The human presence is provided by the viewer, who is invited to enter the painting down carefully delineated paths and offered a multi-sensory illusion. Our presence also is naturalised; we are granted a place within the painting and thus within a landscape both real and idyllic, where we are invited to replicate the artist's experience.

Whereas Hitchens's balance of formalism and illusion is characteristic of middle ground painting, William Gear was considered to be an arch-modernist very early in his career. After serving in Germany with the Monuments, Fine Arts and Archives section of the Control Commission, he moved to Paris, where he lived until 1950. His success in integrating himself into the Parisian – and international – art world can be measured by his association with the international COBRA group,[104] which was then virtually unknown in Britain.[105] By the time that Gear showed with COBRA in 1949, he had developed a highly identifiable imagery. Gear's use of heavy black outlines, or armatures, around patches of jewel-like colour were much closer to the work of young Ecole de Paris painters like Jean-Michel Atlan than to the COBRA artists, from whom Gear was also distanced by not sharing their immersion in myth and fantasy.

Gear's connection with COBRA did, however, ensure that when he returned to London he had a wider experience of the international avant garde than most of his contemporaries, though he remained somewhat isolated. In the early 1950s his work was recognised as advanced and formally in line with progressive French artists. A tireless exhibitor who understood and exploited the structures of the art world, Gear shot to prominence as a result of his entry for '60 Paintings for '51'. *Autumn Landscape* (1950) (fig. 69), a composition of taut, irregular forms in rich autumnal greys and russets, linked by a rudimentary black armature, won one of the Arts Council's five purchase prizes, an event which touched off a notorious art scandal, when a vituperative correspondence in *The Daily Telegraph* culminated in a Parliamentary question.[106] Far from harming Gear's career the furore confirmed his reputation as a leading radical,[107] whose fine balance between abstraction and representation[108] ensured the favourable attention of progressive critics.[109] *Autumn Landscape* marked the beginning of a successful long-term practice closely related

69. William Gear, *Autumn Landscape*, 1950. Oil on canvas, 72 × 50 in. Laing Art Gallery, Newcastle-upon-Tyne.

to the *paysagisme abstrait* of Bazaine and Manessier, with which Gear's work was often compared.[110]

Titles like *Spanish Landscape* (1948), *Gay Landscape* (1952) or *Summer Garden* (1951) often evoked a generalised landscape, though never a specific place. Gear gradually replaced his heavy black armatures with softer, more organic frameworks or fan-like pleats which unfurl across the canvas, providing a supporting structure for the small *taches* of vivid, sometimes acidic colour which may be read as literal transpositions of sunlight, trees and flowers.[111] Unlike Hitchens's deep perspectives, Gear's forms lie like cut-outs on the surface, fragments seen in intimate close-up, which act both as mnemonics and as metonymic references to the familiar. The economy of his landscape paintings is an essential element of his interpretation of landscape as a place universally available because it is non-specific.

In a review of the ICA's 'London–Paris' exhibition in 1950 the *Sunday Times* critic described the 'near-abstract essays in grey and grey-yellow' that Lanyon showed as 'recognisably Cornish'.[112] The comment implies both a degree of 'appearance painting' and a concept of landscape filtered, as Berger put it, through 'a sailor's knowledge of the coastline, a poacher's knowledge of the cover, a miner's knowledge of the seams, a surveyor's knowledge of the contours, a native's knowledge of the local ghosts, a painter's knowledge of the light.'[113] Even more consistently than being seen as a place painter, Lanyon was described as intuitive and spontaneous, though these qualities only became apparent after a decade of eclectic experiment. They mark his mature work and represent a hard-won intellectual position on landscape painting, where they were balanced by Gabo's constructivist ethos.

While Lanyon was stationed in Italy during the war he expressed his appreciation for the exchange of letters between Gabo and Read that was published in *Horizon*,[114] in which Gabo presented Constructivism as a liberal philosophy of creativity.[115] For Lanyon, Gabo was mentor, father-figure and model: he saw himself as a Constructivist well into the 1950s. To read his paintings after 1948, as nearly all critics did, exclusively as abstract, intuitive evocations of mood, weather and atmosphere, was to ignore Lanyon's strong streak of nonconformist idealism, that was encouraged by Gabo's philosophy. Critics also overlooked his understanding of place as an historical entity,[116] and his perception of the identity between place and body. This was revealed both in fortuitous, semi-hidden figures within what are ostensibly pure landscape paintings and in the multi-sensory implications of much of his later work, stimulated by his teaching experience at Corsham.

In the paintings called the Generation Series (1946–7),[117] most of which are formally indebted to Gabo, Lanyon first developed his polysemous landscape imagery. *The Yellow Runner* (1946) (fig. 70) simultaneously represents a real place, a personal narrative and private and communal mythologies. Three years later, in a linocut called *The Returned Seaman* (1949) (fig. 71), he brought together the themes that dominated his work through the first part of the 1950s: the body in landscape and a view of the landscape below the earth's surface, seen in cross-section, which served as a metaphor variously for social relationships, sexuality and organic, natural processes.

In the linocut, male and female figures frame a 'womb'-like subterranean cavern[118] in which a horse stands, a 'symbol of virility (or lust)'.[119] The group is set on a hilltop, surrounded on three sides by water. In Lanyon's personal mythology the sea represented the male, penetrative element, the land the female, a conjunction poignantly apparent in the Cornish mines, constantly under threat of flooding. The print represents a place in the mind that equates home-coming from the war, as did *The Yellow Runner*, to which it is closely related, with fecundity, marriage and the birth of children. Geographically non-specific,[120] this place is linked with Cornwall through the Wallis-like string of boats which climb up the left-hand side, recalling the economic fecundity of a local industry.

70. Peter Lanyon,
The Yellow Runner,
1946. Oil on board,
$18\frac{1}{2} \times 24$ in. Private
Collection.

Porthleven (1950) (fig. 72), the first of Lanyon's large-scale canvases, was painted in response to an invitation to participate in '60 paintings for '51'. The place of the title is a small fishing town set around a long, curving harbour with three basins, and a church near the seaward end. Lanyon's painting conflates the distinctive

71. Peter Lanyon,
*The Returned
Seaman*, 1949. Hand-
coloured linocut,
$20\frac{1}{2} \times 28$ in. Tate
Gallery, London.

72. Peter Lanyon, *Porthleven*, 1950. Oil on board, 96¼ × 48 in. Tate Gallery, London.

73. Peter Lanyon, *St Just*, 1952/3. Oil on canvas, 96 × 48 in. Private Collection.

lineaments of the place with a pair of rudimentary human figures. The church, topped with a cross, doubles as a lamp, held in the right hand of a tall, thin figure, while the semicircular shapes at the foot of the canvas indicate both the billowing skirts of the right-hand figure and the innermost of the three harbour basins.

If *Porthleven* is in part a tribute to Cornish fishing culture, *St Just* (1952–3) (fig. 73)[121] is a still more resolved elegy to the county's miners. It takes its name from a village near Land's End and alludes to the nearby Levant Mine, the site of a notorious disaster which killed thirty-one men in 1919, when a man-machine failed.[122] The mine, the richest in Cornwall, has become a symbol of the exploitation of Cornish labour and of the slow death of Cornish culture, following the demise of local industries. The imagery of *St Just* is complex: the central black core, seen in section, alludes to a mineshaft, as a route to the earth's regenerative core, with pithead machinery at the top. In a series of letters that Lanyon wrote to

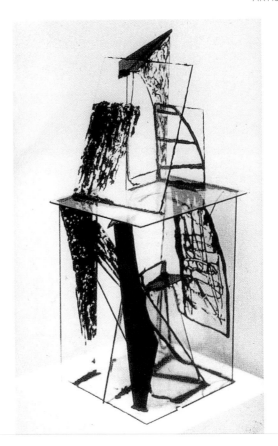

74. Peter Lanyon, *Construction for St Just*, c.1950. Glass, paint and Bostik, 23 × 10 × 9 in. Private Collection.

Roland Bowden in 1952–3, he repeatedly referred to his work-in-progress which, clearly alluding to *St Just*, he described as a Crucifixion.[123] Regeneration implies death, so that the black shaft is also to be read as a crucifix, topped by a crown of thorns, as a 'tree of life', or as a more generalised reference to war: 'all gossip and mocking and napalm burning . . . the charring of bones, Eisenhower's and Eden's'.[124] Round the edges of the canvas run rudimentary buildings and fields, seen in plan, while on each side of the shaft a rough human figure is half-buried in the thick paint. On the right a female figure is spread-eagled, scratched in thin outline; an etiolated man on the left can be identified by his rib-cage.[125]

In 1949–50 Lanyon had begun to make constructions of found objects and glass, often precariously assembled, to help him to transfer the multi-dimensional experience of a place onto a flat canvas.[126] The *Construction for St Just* (1952) (fig. 74) is a dramatic, house-of-cards arrangement of thin, clear glass, bearing dense black marks, some of which resemble the rib-cage in the painting. Emphatically vertical, the glass sheets are arranged to suggest that they surround an empty core, topped by a sheet of green glass.[127] Lanyon's letters to Gabo in the late 1940s reveal his extreme anxiety over his work, most graphically when he compared painting with 'climbing the ventilation shaft of a mine inch by inch away from a tomb'.[128] It seems likely that in *St Just* and its construction we see not only the well-attested dual imagery of mine and crucifixion, but also Lanyon's own shadowy presence, signalled in the construction, as in later works, by the self-inscription of dense black marks.

Lanyon developed the process of recording the trace of his own body on the landscape at Corsham, where he taught between 1950 and 1957. He would take his

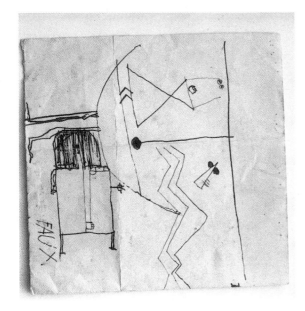

75. Marie-Christine
Treinen, letter
to Peter Lanyon,
c.1951. Private
Collection.

76. Peter Lanyon,
Two Place, 1962. Oil
on canvas, 72 ×
50 in. Private
Collection.

students into the countryside to immerse themselves in a multi-sensory experience which went as far as making paint marks on the ground. Eccentric as they
may seem, such activities had a serious purpose in questioning the nature of
representation and seeking to establish an understanding of place mediated by
individual experience.[129]

Events at Corsham were responsible also for an abrupt change in Lanyon's
concealed imagery of the body. In 1952 he wrote to Peter Gimpel, asking 'Have
you had a visit from Mlle. Treinen a student at Corsham? . . . She has already
influenced William Scott and myself.'[130] Marie-Christine Treinen was a French
student who arrived at the Bath Academy in 1950. She made drawings, apparently
closely related to Jean Dubuffet's imagery, in which the human body was reduced
to a square, shapeless sack without sexuality, grace or intellect (fig. 75). Small,
crude illustrations in the margins of letters to her tutor, Lanyon, are the only
surviving records of these images,[131] which must have been crucial to paintings
such as William Scott's *Reclining Red Nude* (1956)[132] and to Kenneth Armitage,
whose *Figure Lying on its Side* (1957) is a sculptural interpretation of Treinen's
imagery. Her work, which astonished her tutors and clearly made a considerable
impact on them, particularly on Lanyon, casts a revealing light on the creativity of
teaching and learning processes at Corsham and the interchange between
staff and students.

Lanyon's semi-concealed figures changed abruptly even while he was painting
St Just, presumably in reaction to Treinen. In future, he was often to represent
single or paired bodies as the sagging, rectangular shapes seen in *Two Place* (1962)
(fig. 76). The persistence of human imagery in his work, coupled with his insistent

identification of himself as a 'provincial landscape painter',[133] underline the complexity of his perception of the cultural significance of landscape. His emphasis, particularly in the postwar decade, on landscape as an historically formed locus of human labour recalls Ingold's 'taskscape', though Lanyon's perception is not of harmonious communal creativity but of communities destroyed by capitalist excess.

In 1956, after a year in which he produced very little work, Lanyon adopted a more gestural approach to paint handling and replaced his earlier cross-sections through landscapes with bird's-eye viewpoints, which were increasingly focussed on transient effects of light and weather, rather than the material properties of places. He was no doubt encouraged by seeing 'Modern Art in the United States' in 1956, and particularly by his visit to America the following year, for his first solo exhibition at the Catherine Viviano Gallery in New York.[134] The paintings of the late 1950s often contain map-like images and convey the sense of violent movement evident in *Offshore* (1959) (fig. 77), in contrast with earlier, more static canvases. In this 'weather painting',[135] Lanyon was concerned with conveying, without portraying himself directly, his physical sensations in a north-westerly gale. The image is the result of a dual process of transformation in which the visual features of a place were translated into marks which also record the artist's physical contact with the terrain: the 'process which, starting in an extreme awareness of oneself in a place, ends in an extreme awareness of oneself in painting'.[136]

As a measure of how far Lanyon had moved from a conventional understanding of landscape painting, *Offshore* may be compared with *Portreath* (1949), made a decade earlier as 'a direct portrait of a place'.[137] The elision of locality and body that distinguishes *Offshore* from *Portreath* corresponds to the sense of psychological identification with a place that Edward Relph describes as 'existential insideness'.[138] It was at the core of Lanyon's landscape paintings in the late 1950s. He explained: 'While I am moving about the country here with all this history underfoot I find the sky on my back as I climb the hills and the sea behind me, then at my side and it becomes the same thing in my painting, but is not remote because I have it up my side and in my belly.'[139] Body and canvas were similarly conflated: if a painting 'extended at a terrific rate up one side it is simply because I felt like that in my own side, in fact, I'm painting what's happened like my knee right up to my armpit . . . I have to project myself as it were with my feet where I am, and my head may be 50 miles away.'[140]

Late in 1959 Lanyon took up gliding and began to paint the sensations of a free-floating body in space. In *Soaring Flight* (1960) (fig. 78) we can identify the streak of red common to many of the gliding paintings, which records the path of the aircraft.[141] It is set among swathes of cloud which break to reveal what is perhaps a stretch of coast and a patch of green field. The gliding paintings often depict the surf along a beach, notional figures and infinite layers of clouds, but only rarely specific locations.[142] As their titles suggest, they record, in a manner analogous to *Offshore*, the techniques, sights and physical sensations of gliding.[143] These images exist outside place; their datum point is the ever-mobile aircraft, controlled by the artist's body and it is on this undepicted body, represented by his gestures in paint, that the painting is centred.

A further, metaphoric reading can be made of the gliding paintings. While they are centrally placed in the historical tradition and within the formal discourse of modernism, they also reveal the artist released from the restraints of culture and aesthetic convention, so that their prospects, or wide views, parallel his creative

77. Peter Lanyon, *Offshore*, 1959. Oil on canvas, 60 × 72 in. City Museum and Art Gallery, Birmingham.

autonomy. They are, then, images of the artist consistent with the construction developed by Keynes as appropriate to western liberal ideology and the role of the creative artist in a Cold War context.

The historical centrality of landscape painting ensured its prominence in the postwar period as well as its role as a conduit between tradition and modernism. Yet Forge had felt that its status was problematic and, taking a position that was to become increasingly popular among progressive writers, that it was only of marginal significance in terms of defining the new.

Recent changes, lamented by Hoskins, to the physical landscape, had their parallel in the modifications, made inevitable by modernism, to the ways in which landscape was represented. By 1956 there was good reason to question the viability of Forge's category of naturalistic painting: the spread of Subtopia threatened to complete the conversion, begun by enclosure and encouraged by nineteenth-century industry, of landscape from a polysemous material phenomenon to a romanticised mythic concept. The achievement of progressive landscape artists was to sidestep myth and to reinvest the materiality of landscape with contemporary ideology.

Place, diversely constructed and no longer enshrined as the *genius loci*, may be seen to be the unifying factor in mid-century landscape painting. It has arguably

become a metaphor for the uniqueness of the artist, who is in turn perceived in terms of an idealised landscape: one that is wild, unmediated, even primitive. So persuasive has this construction proved, that despite the compelling models offered by scholars of the eighteenth century, the possibility of reading twentieth-century landscape art in terms of ideology, production or gender has been largely ignored. An appropriate analytic model for postwar painting requires acknowledgement that the modern landscape is a diverse cultural construction as open to contextual readings as urban sculpture or formal portraiture. To persist in simplistic, romanticised readings is to deny the achievement and significance of modern landscape artists.

78. Peter Lanyon, *Soaring Flight*, 1960. Oil on canvas, 60 × 60 in. Arts Council Collection, Hayward Gallery, London.

9

IMAGES OF THE BODY

Picasso's operation of his subjects produces in the mind of men and women an imagination of the fantastic blended with metaphors and bizarre ideas resulting in mental phenomena incapable of logical interpretation.

Sidney Arnold, 1951[1]

One does not see oneself as one is seen by others, and this difference in perspective turns on the body.

Ann Jefferson, 1989[2]

Francis Bacon's *Three Studies for Figures at the Base of a Crucifixion* (1944) (fig. 79) went on public view for the first time just weeks before the end of the war. Few of those who saw it failed to acknowledge its power; nearly all saw it as an image of horror. An incomparable icon of the period, it encapsulated the recent past and appeared to prophesy the immediate future. Its title announced Bacon's position squarely within the European tradition and related it to an important body of contemporary work based on Christian, often specifically Catholic, imagery.[3] It contributed significantly to current aesthetic discourse and its ontological status is still widely discussed.

Unleashed on a society lulled by neo-Romantic nature symbolism, Bacon's triptych created a *tabula rasa* for representations of the human body. In the decade that followed the body became a metaphor rather than a mirror, appropriated in ways that called into question its integrity and its significance. That it could convey – literally embody – almost any theme, demonstrates its centrality for artists; their readiness to deform this image – to question and test its constancy – is a paradox which conceals, like a Chinese box, yet more and more complex dilemmas. Not the least of them is that critics, notably Herbert Read, wrote of images like Reg Butler's *Woman* (1949) (fig. 86) as though they responded directly to a general consciousness of human vulnerability. Without sharing Read's fondness for the *zeitgeist*, there was clearly widespread revulsion at the barbarities of the war and deep anxiety about the likelihood of another conflict, yet the visual art that expressed these emotions was unpopular, derided and misunderstood.

Butler's sculpture, like Bacon's triptych, was not generally held in high esteem; by 1955 the outstanding popular image for private homes was Pietro Annigoni's *Portrait of Queen Elizabeth II* (1954), exhibited in that year's Royal Academy summer exhibition. Its *succès fou*,[4] triggered by the sentimental appeal of the subject, was inseparable from its intense and anachronistic illusory quality. It was overtaken by Sir Gerald Kelly's *Saw Ohn Nyun* (fig. 80), a portrait of a Cambodian dancer at rest. A writer in *The Studio* ingenuously remarked that 'It has a serenity and relaxed Oriental mood which is at once mysterious and refreshing'.[5] Decorative and apparently open in content, both paintings also suggest something withheld, to be revealed only implicitly, unlike the popular photographic reportage of *Picture Post*, which operated under the convention that the camera cannot lie.

Oil paint, Norman Bryson has argued, has been used in the Western tradition 'primarily as an *erasive* medium',[6] which privileges the cool, reflective gaze,[7] so that

> the body (of the painter, of the viewer) is reduced to a single point, the *macula* of the retinal surface; and the moment of the Gaze (for the painter, for the viewer) is placed outside duration. Spatially and temporally, the act of viewing is constructed as the removal of the dimensions of space and time, as the disappearance of the body . . .[8]

Annigoni's impenetrable enamel surface, which restated the unifying, distancing, obliterative tendency of western painting,[9] more effectively concealed the humanity and sexuality of the young woman who was his subject than the heavy Garter robes that marked the portrait as a royal icon.

Kelly's stereotypical image of sexual subjugation was at its most popular when the dismantling of the empire was at its height, placing a time limit on the patriarchical and colonial assumptions that underlay the painting.[10] It implied a sexual availability not open to consumers of the royal portrait. Annigoni depicted the Queen posed above a traditional landscape – in that it was entirely without modern features – which transformed his subject into a timeless icon[11] while it also returned her to nature. Both images depended for their appeal largely on the sentiment aroused by vulnerability and sustained by a concealed sexuality. Modernist contemporaries of Kelly and Annigoni were to reverse their terms, stripping away the sentiment, bringing content to vulnerability and restoring sexuality.

79. Francis Bacon, *Three Studies for Figures at the Base of a Crucifixion*, 1944. Oil on board, each panel 37 × 29 in. Tate Gallery, London.

80. Gerald Kelly, *Saw Ohn Nyun, c.*1931.

The high-low divide is underpinned by the theory of 'self-other relations',[12] which maintains that the depicted body is a construct of the author, whether painter or writer, who has total control of the created being. Within this nexus of construction, it was acceptable in the postwar period, both within social convention and art historical tradition, that the Other exist as a (male) consumer of the available (female) body. The popularity of Kelly's *Saw Ohn Nyun*, like Meredith Frampton's images of docile, compliant society women and, not least, the conventions of advertising products as diverse as cigarettes, household appliances and women's underwear, support this contention. They also help to explain why the modernist body, so often overtly constructed as physically and intellectually powerless and evidently not 'free or self-determining . . . because it is subject to the grip and grasp of the Other',[13] constituted too great a threat to the equanimity of the preferred self-image and was thus set outside the discourse of normative representation.

Bacon's triptych raised the question of the limit of humanity: at what stage would it be destroyed, to be replaced by the bestiality of his vision? Shortly after the liberation of Belsen and Buchenwald in April 1945, photographs of the concentration camps were published in the press. These were images as potent as the Crucifixion for mediaeval believers, testifying to unimagineable cruelty, degradation and humiliation. While popular art evaded the convulsive emotions engendered by the war and continued to focus on sex and sentiment, modernists, so often accused of evading reality, were swept up by Picasso's wartime paintings as models for the body constructed through psychosis, abnormality or simply non-conformity.

In December 1945 the opening of the Picasso and Matisse exhibition at the Victoria and Albert Museum marked the beginning of the postwar era in the visual arts. Critics immediately recognised that the two modern masters demonstrated very different approaches. Matisse's paintings, which amounted to a retrospective, received less comment than Picasso's which, all made in Paris during the Occupation, aroused virulent criticism and controversy. Picasso's figures were presented in close-up, fractured, predatory and witty, while Matisse offered a vision of an idealised life: sensual, relaxed and elegant. Whereas Matisse's odalisques and sunlit Mediterranean vistas appealed to a longing for the exotic, Picasso's swollen, distorted bodies were considered shockingly ugly, a denial of the integrity of the body as the mirror of human nature. Picasso's impact had been evident during the war, transmitted by the Polish exile, Jankel Adler,[14] but after the revelations of the camps, his cubist dislocations were more acutely sensed; they were taken to reject both an accepted moral order and the belief that things were as they appeared to be.

To the horror of their conservative elders, Picasso took young artists by storm; Matisse's impact was no less profound and was central to the rejection of academic tonal painting. The alliance evident in both painters between a liberated representational tradition and an anarchic surrealist attitude provided a model for artists confronted with facts and concepts for which they had no visual language. Many writers have commented on the impossibility of continuing to replicate a prelapsarian imagery of the body,[15] which was replaced by recourse to the primitive, to metamorphosis and robotic mechanisation.

A REPRISE OF THE GRAND MANNER

In Churchillian vein, at the low point of the war, Read declared in *Horizon*, 'We shall rebuild, of course', though he had no clear vision of the shape of postwar art, assuming that it would retain 'the eternal harmonies of all great art; but it will be so original in its outward manifestations that its first impact must inevitably seem, and be, revolutionary.'[16] In his editorials for the magazine, Cyril Connolly hammered home the necessity for a reintegration of European culture with Britain as a leader in restoring 'liberty of expression, economic security and mental audacity to the world of art and ideas'.[17] The response of artists to the opening up of Europe in 1945 was to roll back the barriers of war as though they had never existed, to turn to Germany as well as France, Greece as well as renaissance Italy.

There was no close parallel to the *rappel à l'ordre* that had gathered the French avant garde in 1920. However, there was an unarticulated, *ad hoc* impetus away from the relics of Surrealism[18] and neo-Romanticism, towards a greater visual and thematic clarity; a stable, intellectually coherent image of a common European culture and history, which a postwar society might seek to reinterpret. Classicism, despite its recent connotations, represented exotic physical locations, a central cultural and historical concept and the prospect of personal escapism. Read continued to reject the academic tradition,[19] but many artists turned the conventions of classicism to account, finding in them opportunities for transgression which were most deeply explored in representations of the human body.

Henry Moore's *Madonna and Child*, completed for St Matthew's Church, Northampton in 1944, initiated an unproblematic, modernising classicism grounded, according to his own account, in Masaccio's *Virgin and Child* in the National Gallery. Graham Sutherland, like Moore, was intent on reinvesting the central theme of western culture with topicality, but when his *Crucifixion* was unveiled at St Matthew's in November 1946, in the transept opposite the *Madonna and Child*, it was seen to dismiss the classical tradition. Sutherland presented Christ as a war victim, in the pose of the fifteenth-century Isenheim altarpiece, which had been upheld by Worringer[20] as a visionary expression of the essential German spirit, to be set against 'sensual, empathic' French classicism.[21] He wrote a few years later to Robert Melville:

> the Buchenwald thing also was tremendously in my mind at the time. *The stains of blood on the walls after firing parties*: the reek: the rot: the patterns of the helpless dead body the '*dust drinks up the blood*' and '*the reek of human blood smiles out at me*' of Aeschylus: – the photographs in K-Z,[22] the publication of hangings in Minotaur, and the affidavit photographs from Russia.[23]

Moore's Dartington Hall *Memorial Figure* (1946), commissioned in memory of Christopher Martin, a friend of the artist and former Arts Director at the Hall, conflated the classicism of the *Madonna* with the theme of the body-as-landscape. The conjunction between nurturing body and rolling landscape, later a cliché of Moore criticism, was then an almost unexplored subject, though Philip Hendy had already identified it, writing of the 1930 *Reclining Figure*: 'I had likened this figure to a range of hills before I knew that it had been reproduced under the title of "Mountains".'[24]

With the *Madonna and Child* Moore initiated a new way of representing women. The image of motherhood in his reclining figures is usually the earth mother, or *genetrix*, which emphasises biological function, whereas the Northampton carving presents the *mater*, or social mother, whose role is cultural.[25] Postwar modernism tended to dwell on the primitivising *genetrix*, whereas the *mater* was often represented as an absent, desired Other by transgressive counter-images of violence and sexual aspiration. Moore was an exception to this with his abundant family groups, though their tenderness was shockingly countered by the 1953 *Mother and Child* where the voracious infant and rejecting mother present an unconventionally harsh image of maternity.[26]

As soon as it was possible to travel abroad artists flocked to the Continent, with former neo-Romantics prominent among them. John Craxton initiated a trail to southern Europe when he left for Greece in 1946. His elegiac *Pastorale for P.W.* (1948), dedicated to Peter Watson, his patron, restated an old arcadian theme in a modern idiom, setting a Virgilian goatherd on the faceted rocks of a post-Cubist landscape. This was classicising at its most straight-forward, a reworking of ancient literary themes stimulated by a visit to their source. Other artists adopted classical themes in order to sidestep convention, appropriating models accepted as authoritative symbols of a normative culture.

A familiar arcadian bather imagery enabled Keith Vaughan to paint beach parties attended by young homosexuals at a time when gay men were condemned to a furtive, criminalised existence. His sophisticated assimilation of Matisse's colour and composition and Cézanne's bather paintings, masks the impact of his own homoerotic imagery. Though these beach paintings were understood and were commercially successful in terms of a modernising classicism, Vaughan's dream of a Golden Age to emerge from the ashes of war found little visual expression beyond the edenic, pastoral imagery of his mural, *At the Beginning of Time* (1951), made for the Festival of Britain, where it was a poignant public statement of private distress.

John Minton's grand history painting, *The Death of Nelson* (1952), based on Daniel Maclise's House of Lords mural[27] and exhibited in the 1952 Royal Academy Summer Exhibition, signalled the artist's uncertainty about his career and a wider dilemma over the future of painting. His solution was a compromise between a traditional subject, a modern composition and the decorative gloss of figures symmetrically posed on the parallel lines of the deck planking.[28] For such an image to be truly popular it would have had to be painted in Annigoni's style, which Minton, who believed that 'No-one mirrors his age clearer than the artist',[29] would have found impossible. Yet he deplored and mocked abstract art[30] and in the history paintings that he made until his death a few years later, his purpose was to sustain the realist tradition of the Academy and the Royal College.

His portraits were more successful mirrors of his period than the strained patriotic sentiment of his Festival mural, allied to history painting.[31] His *Painter and Model* (1953) (fig. 81) a double portrait of the artist and his lover, Norman Bowler, was a formal set-piece, made for the exhibition 'Figures in Their Setting'. Bowler's pugnacity, the informality of his clothes and the emphasis on his genitals confirm the artist's disregard for convention. The image is, nevertheless, as class-ridden as any grand portrait, as is evident in the disparity between Minton's correct, middle-class attire and his sitter's tight, revealing garments, although Bowler's body language suggests that he relished the modernity conferred on him by his defiance of social rituals. The tension between Bowler's trangressions and Minton's conventions are poignantly underlined by the academic format of a portrait transformed by its revelation of sexual confrontation and exploitation.

If Lucian Freud is to be seen as a classicist it can only be through reworkings of the classical in ways that are almost programmatically transgressive. Freud, like Bacon, has drawn on the vast resources of the European realist tradition in ways not open to stricter modernists, but the apparent lucidity that this has brought to his work has been called into question by his almost constant refusal to speak of it. The mystification that this has created has reflected back onto the work so that studio props, family relationships and the identity of his models have become of disproportionate interest.

Much has been made of his roots in the northern renaissance tradition, evident in the flat, hyperreal close-up portrayal of his first wife, Kitty Garman, as the *Girl with Roses* (1947/8) (fig. 82). The stark face of the girl intent on lacerating her hands with a thorny stem was a conciously anachronistic image. Its immaculate surface recalls the opaque concealment of Annigoni's portrait, while the pose hints at a distressingly private content. Freud's thrust towards modernity inevitably led him to abandon the mannered historicism of the Garman portrait as conclusively as he avoided the academic conventions of life painting. What he was to retain from *Girl with Roses* was the sense of the body as an index of emotional frailty, of little significance beyond its ability to reveal psychological vulnerability through every pore and blemish.

There is a parallel to Freud's subsequent work in A. J. Ayer's elevation of 'the sensible world' of phenomenology. In one of the artist's few comments on his painting, he stressed the intensity of feeling and knowledge of his subjects that are essential to him: 'The subject must be kept under closest observation: if this is done, day and night, the subject – he, she or it – will eventually reveal the *all* without which selection itself is not possible.'[32] The intensity with which Freud has painted flesh since the late 1940s encourages a parallel reaction in the viewer, who

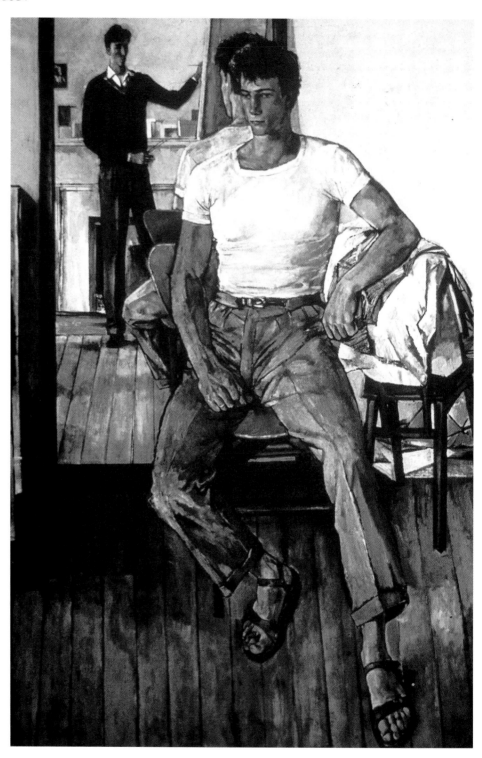

81. John Minton,
Painter and Model,
1953. Oil, 72 ×
48 in. Russell-
Cotes Art Gallery
and Museum,
Bournemouth.

is invited to become the artist's accomplice in holding the sitter under surveillance,
controlled and manipulated by paint.

Although it is apparently more straight-forwardly modern, the *Sleeping Nude*
(1950) (fig. 83) sits firmly within the European tradition of the reclining nude,
which Freud subverted as thoroughly as Manet. In Freud's painting convention is
assaulted by the grimy mattress with its rumpled grey coverings, his ubiquitous

studio props. They hint at a predilection for urban low-life assumed, it seems, in order to dismiss the conventions of high art so that he might more cogently define his reformulation of the body. Lying rigidly, with hunched shoulders, the model's physical discomfort appears to mirror her state of mind. It is this exposure of the body as mind that is Freud's particular transgression and rejection of the niceties of English painting.

82. Lucian Freud, *Girl with Roses*, 1947–8. Oil on canvas, 41 × 29 in. British Council Collection.

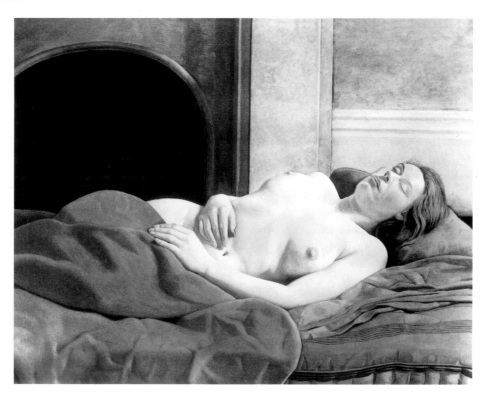

83. Lucian Freud,
Sleeping Nude, 1950.
Oil on canvas,
30 × 40 in. Private
Collection, Canada.

The extent of his subversion of studio paintings of the model can be demon-strated by comparison with William Coldstream's *Seated Nude* (1952/3) (fig. 84) – 'not a picture but a life painting of the strictest kind'.[33] Here the model is reduced to a still life object, depicted with cartographic accuracy[34] in an agony of self-effacement by the last and most committed of the Euston Road School painters.[35]

METAMORPHOSIS

Released by Surrealism from conventional categorisations of the subject, artists turned to the creation of hybrids, extensions of the surrealist investigation of the sub-conscious. Metamorphic imagery was the product of a surrealist sensibility, poetically expressed by Max Ernst as 'the pairing of two realities which apparently cannot be paired on a plane apparently not suited to them.'[36] Ernst's telling rationale for the suspension of reason implied by the coupling of incompatibles was published in 1937 and followed by his exhibition at the London Gallery early in 1939. It is likely that his example impelled Sutherland into his extended explo-ration of metamorphosis.[37]

Sutherland's *Gorse on Sea Wall* (1939) (fig. 27), conceived in the last months of peace, established a model for the mutant, a combination of creature and plant with disturbing human references.[38] Such images were often described as person-ages, in reference to an anthropomorphic quality accessible through primitivism, as well as to the identification between the human body and the machine, soon to be extended through the iconography of the robot.

After several years as a war artist, Sutherland seems to have turned to Julio Gonzalez, Picasso's Catalan colleague and fellow member of the Ecole de Paris, whose sculpture and drawings would have been known to British artists through

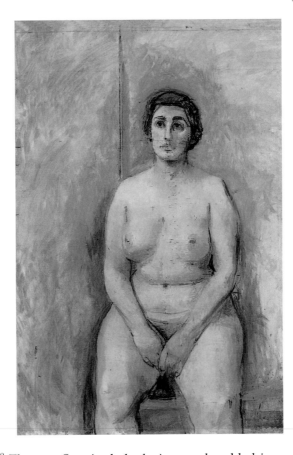

84. William Coldstream, *Seated Nude*, 1952–3. Oil on canvas, 42 × 27 in. Tate Gallery, London.

reproductions in *Cahiers d'Art*.[39] The two Spaniards had pioneered welded iron sculpture in the late 1920s,[40] and Gonzalez's first filiform sculptures, described as 'drawing in space', were made in 1930.[41]

Carefully hoarded by artists, *Cahiers d'Art* was an important source of ideas and information which Sutherland began to quarry as early as 1934.[42] Clearly he took a long time to develop the ideas he drew from the Spanish sculptor, since the *Thorn Heads* of 1945–7 were based on a drawing reproduced in 1935.[43] Following Gonzalez's death in 1942, a belated tribute apeared in the magazine in 1947, in the form of several pages of drawings ('Projets de sculptures') and photographs of sculpture.[44] The drawings convey the idea of complex organic forms conceived as sculpture. Their clarity and solid, three-dimensional nature, often their actual shapes, are echoed in the paintings that Sutherland made of palm trees in 1947/8.[45]

After the bombing of Hiroshima and Nagasaki in August 1945 the surrealist 'sleep of reason' was brutally transformed from creative liberation to an all-too concrete terror. A third world war seemed imminent, in which atomic weapons would cause not only unimagineable devastation but a reversion to bestiality as a result of genetic damage. While press reports dwelt enthusiastically on the destructive capacity of the new bomb,[46] fostering the impression that it differed 'from its predecessors only in degree and not in kind',[47] scientists were well aware of the dangers of exposure to radiation.[48]

Connections were quickly made with research into bacteriological weapons. A commission appointed by the British Council of Churches was one of several sources to raise the spectre of genetic mutation.[49] Rumour, prejudice and fear were inseparable: '. . . our cheerful military blockheads are talking of "the next war".

Only recently we have been told of a "spray" (most likely a radioactive gas or some other fission product) which can destroy every kind of life, whether animal or vegetable, over unlimited areas of territory.'[50]

Annihilation was discussed more often than the revolting and terrifying idea of metamorphosis into an alien species, but mutants became a science fiction staple, widely familiar from books and films like John Wyndham's *The Day of the Tryffids* and Nigel Kneale's *The Quatermass Experiment* (1953), from which they entered the stock of visual artists.[51] Though usually ominous, the mutant occasionally appeared as the witty product of punning double vision, as in Sutherland's *Turning Form* (1949), where a dried root becomes an insect-like figure, or Moore's *Leaf Figures* (1952), where leaves are transformed into slowly turning dancers. Here the loss of identity is rendered positive, to imply that categorisation is restrictive and a disavowal of natural organic development.

The publication of Sigmund Freud's *Totem and Taboo*[52] in a new translation in 1950 took place when the primitive was a subject of intense interest. It seemed to offer an alternative to surrealist interpretations. There is a striking, if coincidental congruence between Freud's presentation of psychic migration and animism, and metamorphic paintings, like Sutherland's *Gorse on Sea Wall*. 'Primitive races', Freud wrote, 'people the world with innumerable spiritual beings both benevolent and malignant; and these spirits and demons they regard as the causes of natural phenomena and they believe that not only animals and plants but all the inanimate objects in the world are animated by them.'[53] Primitive beliefs in psychic migration paralleled beliefs in sophisticated societies: '. . . primitive peoples believe that human individuals are inhabited by similar spirits. These souls which live in human beings can leave their habitations and migrate into other human beings; they are the vehicle of mental activities and are to a certain extent independent of their bodies.'[54]

Though it is very unlikely that Sutherland was aware of *Totem and Taboo* in 1939, its republication coincided both with a resurgence of interest in primitivism and with explorations of metamorphosis by writers, film-makers and visual artists. That Freud's text was long out-of-date as an anthropological text by 1950 did not diminish its poetic acuity for artists.[55] Indeed, it helped to create a sympathetic context for metaphorical readings of the work of Sutherland and some of his contemporaries. It is evident from his notes for Robert Melville's monograph that Sutherland exerted himself to ensure such readings. He suggested subheadings such as 'Metamorphosis' and 'Personification' and wrote of metaphor as 'a way of discovering one thing with the help of another and by their resemblance discovering and personifying the unknown'.[56]

While he was preparing the Northampton *Crucifixion*, Sutherland made a group of paintings which are effectively studies of the transformatory possibilities of thorns. His famous account of the links between them and the *Crucifixion* introduces the train of thought that sustained his more thoroughly metamorphic works a few years later:

> . . . I started to notice thorn bushes, and the structure of thorns as they pierced the air. I made some drawings, and as I made them, a curious change developed. As the thorns rearranged themselves, they became, whilst still retaining their own pricking, space-encompassing life, something else – a kind of "stand-in" for a Crucifixion and a crucified head.[57]

The *Thorn Heads* and *Thorn Trees*, made between 1945 and 1947 and elegant paradigms of what Heron was to designate the 'fruit and thorn' aesthetic, were metaphors for a Crucifixion without a body. The two paintings called *Chimère* (1946/7),[58] worked out in sketchbooks concurrently with the *Crucifixion*, show a mutant with both human and plant characteristics. Melville saw in it 'an elaborate, subtly comic attempt on the part of an inanimate form, vegetable in origin, to assume the human condition'.[59] Douglas Cooper placed its origins in a fallen tree trunk,[60] but while its face is indeed formed from a knot in the wood, the lilacs, pinks and oranges[61] of *Chimère II* (1946–7), as reproduced in Melville's monograph, are closer to Bacon's *Painting 1946* and *Study for Three Figures at the Base of a Crucifixion* than to anything in nature. The way the creature is placed on the canvas, behind a structure which underlines its separation from normality, together with the lines around its head, which suggest an unreadable interior space, also appear to have been appropriated from Bacon.

The two artists were close friends by the late 1940s,[62] when they shared a stock of images and both applied paint in long, thin, concealing streaks like curtains.[63] Six years before Bacon painted his *Van Gogh* series, Sutherland wrote of 'realising the mystery of the *presence*. (How wonderfully colour does that in Van Gogh's *"The artist on the road to Tarascon"*!)'[64] More striking than shared images was their sense of the interchangeability of organic forms: the dissolving of barriers between plant, human and animal. Both used similar phrases about the effect of these paintings: Sutherland wrote that 'One should bare the nerves; so that one is ready to react to something in objects that makes them hold more than their original meaning.'[65] In his interviews with David Sylvester, Bacon repeatedly insisted that his goal was to work directly from his 'nervous system', rather than from his intellect.[66] Sutherland's metamorphic paintings make no such affective claims; instead they present curious, even shocking objects with aloof detachment, for cool scrutiny.

His metamorphic theme reached a peak of ambiguity with the *Standing Forms* of the early 1950s. He called them presences, to indicate images that were in some way extra-human. *Standing Form against a Hedge* (1950) (fig. 67) crudely echoed his *Crucifixion*, with a limbless torso, wrapped like a leaf or bulb, swollen and gashed and sprouting uncontrollable growths, posed against a cruciform support. Three similar objects dominated his Festival of Britain mural, *The Origins of the Land* (1951). Part plant, part animal or human, they are arrested in a state of constant physical transformation, which can be read in terms of Freud's 'spiritual beings', as an elision of living and inorganic matter into another order.[67]

The *Standing Forms* were among Sutherland's most sculptural paintings, with close formal and thematic equivalents in Moore's *Upright Motives* (1955/6), which were conceived a few years later in response to a proposal that he make a sculpture to decorate Olivetti's Milan headquarters.[68] Moore began them shortly after some unfruitful, preliminary work on a Crucifixion theme, which was perhaps in his mind when, ten years later, he remarked that the first three *Upright Motives* 'assumed the aspect of a crucifixion scene'.[69] It seems that in these sculptures Moore drew on his earlier scheme to produce a set of variations on natural forms that were congruent with Christian imagery in a manner comparable to Sutherland's *Standing Forms*.

The roughly cruciform *Upright Motive No. 1: Glenkiln Cross* is the most dramatic of the *Upright Motives*, with its allusions to a human torso, with truncated limbs and facial features that are reduced to a gaping orifice. Susan Compton has suggested that the presence of Bacon's *Three Studies for Figures at the Base of a*

Crucifixion in the Tate had a formative impact on the *Upright Motifs*.[70] Certainly the painting and sculptures share an unfettered transformatory impulse. Yet Moore's work, like Sutherland's, can more convincingly be located within a pastoral and holistic reading of nature than in the existentially oriented context of Bacon's painting. Sutherland was concerned with a poetic, atmospheric evocation of nature in which landscape and the body overlapped, without situating either with philosophical precision, while Bacon restricted his concern to the human and principally the male, condition in tightly confined physical settings. As Berger commented, 'Other things in his paintings (chairs, shoes, blinds, lamp switches, newspapers) are merely illustrated.'[71]

When the *Three Studies for Figures at the Base of a Crucifixion* was first shown, it amounted to an account of the agony of war as vivid as Picasso's *Guernica* (1937).[72] Though Bacon denied that his triptych was an icon of war and Michael Peppiatt has argued convincingly for an enigmatic and guilt-ridden private stimulus to Bacon's obsession with the imagery of the Crucifixion,[73] the triptych had a greater moral authority than any contemporaneous work of art produced in this country. Bacon was conscious of its importance and referred to it as his first work as a 'serious artist'.[74] The cultural continuity of its theme was underlined by his insistence on identifying the figures as the Eumenides,[75] the Greek Furies.

Not the least curious aspect of these three biomorphic creatures is that they have been consistently described as human. Eyeless and almost limbless, the left-hand one even lacks the mouth that gapes from the central figure and on the right is open in a full-throated scream. The only continuity between the three panels is the implication of sound, or rather a progression from silence to a screamed assault on the viewer, while the scream is the creature's only claim to humanity.

In *Head VI* (1949) (fig. 85), the first in the series that Roland Penrose described as 'Bacon's bellowing Popes',[76] the scream, 'the operation through which the entire body escapes through the mouth',[77] is uttered by an unequivocal human being, though it is no more eloquent than the creatures in the triptych. What then, is the status of this man? Ernst van Alphen has written of 'the loss of self' in Bacon's paintings, comparing it with an aspect of schizophrenia in which 'bodily sensations are experienced as having their original locus in another version of one's body'.[78] He suggests that in *Head VI* the subject is screaming because he is being revealed by the artist, as a prelude to death.[79] If this is so, Bacon's screaming heads speak for the impotence of authority, as well as for a generation that questioned all authority. His man/Pope, isolated inside a spaceframe, may stand for both subject and author, whether expressive or dumb, articulate or impotent.

The spaceframe has been one of the most discussed aspects of Bacon's work, explained by the artist prosaically as a way to emphasise an image,[80] but by others as an isolating device, which also suggests surveillance.[81] Paintings like *Pope* (1955) or *Self-portrait* (1956), where the frame has an important formal function, to focus attention on a specific area of the canvas, support Bacon's explanation, whereas the role of the frame in, for instance, *Head I* (1948) is more problematic, suggesting, perhaps, impalement.

The frame has also been taken as a link with Alberto Giacometti, raising the issue of Bacon's relationship with Existentialism.[82] Sylvester referred to him in terms compatible with existential thinking, notably in the short essay that he wrote for the artist's Venice Biennale exhibition in 1954, where he conclusively detached Bacon's 'creatures faced with their tragic destiny' from the still powerful residue of English romanticism, 'painters in name but illustrators in effect'. The

85. Francis Bacon, *Head VI*, 1949. Oil on canvas, 36 × 30 in. Arts Council Collection, Hayward Gallery, London.

reference, underlined by Sutherland having occupied a large part of the British Pavilion at the previous Biennale, could hardly have been clearer; Bacon was presented as the authoritative painter for the future, who communicated not in illusion but *'in the paint'*.[83] Much has been written about Bacon's so called accidents on the paint surface: marks that vary from flecks of paint to great impasted lumps, cherished by the artist as a means to bypass narrative and representation, though their perfect placing and form seriously weaken the case for a fully fortuitous origin. They have been seen to act on the canvas as smears or visceral traces, 'the disintegration of the form', as Sylvester wrote.[84] The Biennale essay indicates that Sylvester's perception of Bacon was at least inflected by Existentialism, suggesting that there is a critically convincing case for situating his work, as David Mellor does, within the category of 'existentialist related' art.[85] However, the relationship is a matter of congruence rather than a demonstrable historical connection between Bacon and Existentialism.

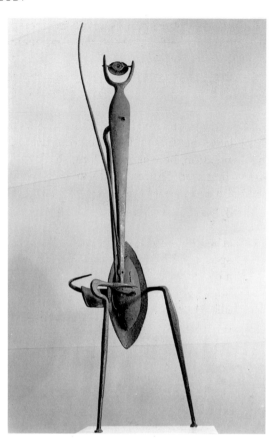

86. Reg Butler,
Woman, 1949. Iron,
87 × 28 × 19 in.
Tate Gallery,
London.

John Russell saw in the *Three Studies* 'a mindless voracity . . . a ravening undif-ferentiated capacity for hatred',[86] implying that the power of Bacon's creatures lies in their tormented and deformed residue of humanity. John Berger was to extend Russell's perception of mindlessness. 'Bacon', he wrote, 'is the opposite of an apocalyptic painter who envisages the worst is likely. For Bacon the worst has already happened. The worst that has happened has nothing to do with the blood, the stains, the viscera. The worst is that man has come to be seen as mindless.'[87] While some of Bacon's portraits – of Michel Leiris, Muriel Belcher, Isabel Rawsthorne – are notable exceptions to Berger's reading, when he turned from portraiture to the use of the model to explore events and human conditions which represent psychological and physical extremes, there was, as Berger understood, no metamorphosis or redemptive construction of an identity to follow the loss of humanity. It was this perception of loss that echoed so poignantly among younger artists in the early 1950s.

'HOLLOW MEN'[88]

The 'loss of self' is a theme that can be recognised in a number of artists, though none explored it as thoroughly as Bacon. His impact is nowhere more obvious than on Reg Butler, the most prominent of the group of young sculptors who showed at the 1952 Venice Biennale. Butler's direct formal appropriations from Bacon began after the Biennale, though there is a loose thematic parallel between Bacon's mindless figures and the literally empty-headed wire people like *Woman* (1949) (fig. 86), that Butler showed in Venice. While Bacon probed painfully for the limits of human endurance, Butler's wire sculpture punned, with mannered artifice, on metamorphic links between humanity and insects. A more poignant parallel is in both artists' concentration on a single sensory organ: whereas Bacon had given priority to sound, presenting the scream as the final degradation of reasoned speech, Butler and Lynn Chadwick both emphasised vision, interpreting it as a control mechanism.

A group of small lead sculptures made at the start of Butler's career, which includes a *Reclining Figure* (1946) and a *Mother and Child* (1946), demonstrate the extent to which, like other artists of his generation, he was in the long shadow of Moore's dominance.[89] Yet when Butler's first iron figures, made in 1948, were shown a year later at the Hanover Gallery,[90] they revealed a perception of the body startlingly at odds with Moore's, especially in their disregard for gender and the capacity for regeneration.

In the late 1940s, sculptures like *Woman* were considered less clearly human than they are today. In his essay 'New aspects of British sculpture' Read interpreted Butler's iron and wire aesthetic as a condition of barrenness, analogous to the non-being of the war victim.[91] The head of *Woman* is a forked terminal supporting a single eye, an evocation of surveillance which inevitably recalls George Orwell's novel, *1984*, in which the all-seeing eye is itself unseen, concealed in the form of a vast television screen. The voice that issued from the loudspeaker in Winston's room was disembodied, while Butler's *Woman* has a physical presence but, like Bacon's degraded figures, no intellect. She is reduced to an eye housed in a skeleton and trapped in a process of metamorphosis which has already produced an insect's waving antenna and carapace-like torso. Melville, who described the rather similar *Boy* as 'based on a cocky schoolboy with his hands in his pockets',[92] also recognised a punning aspect in the flickering shift between human and insect.

Melville drew attention to the farm machinery which Butler had repaired as a blacksmith during the war,[93] which resonates faintly through the early wire figures with a hint of nostalgia for the rural.[94] For Butler, an engineer before he was a blacksmith, machinery offered a route to modernity, if the problem of its transformation into art could be solved. In fact, the aesthetic dilemma was only resolved when he adopted Bacon as a model some years later. The relationship between Butler's linear sculpture and the precedents provided by Gonzalez is unclear: there are few close equivalences between the work of the two artists, except in the two versions of Butler's *Head*, which is very close to a photograph in *Cahiers d'Art*.[95] However, Gonzalez did offer a general model for sculpture defined by line, as opposed to Moore's mass. Comparison of Sutherland's *Thorn Heads* with the forked terminals and antenna-like wires that identify many of Butler's personages suggest that the general resemblances of his work to Gonzalez's may have come through Sutherland.

Chadwick's *Inner Eye* (1952) (fig. 87), neither human nor animal, has generally been interpreted as menacing and predatory.[96] Its forged framework, which protects a hollow core, is set on attenuated supports and inclined inwards, so that it appears to be precariously balanced. Its focus, and the sole rationale for the structure, is a lump of glass set on a pivoting bar, which acts both as eye and head. It embodies the creature's sentience and intelligence, which are directed through the malevolent eye, engaged a constant act of surveillance.

Butler's *Birdcage* (1950) and his maquette for the 'Unknown Political Prisoner' competition replaced the ambiguity of the earlier personages with an image of the

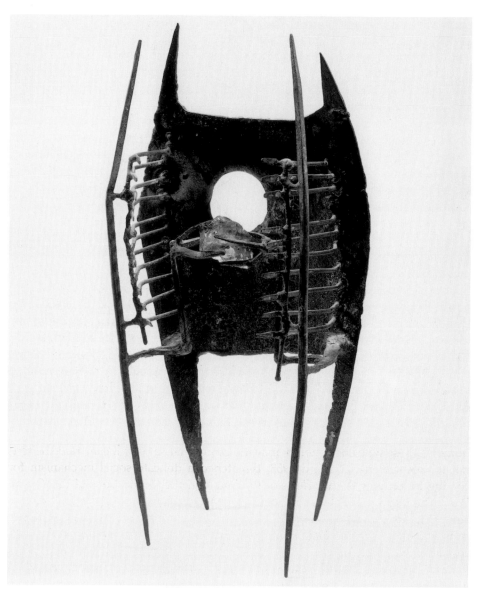

87. Lynn Chadwick,
*Maquette for the
Inner Eye*, 1952. Iron
and glass, 11 in. high.
Artist's collection.

body as its own, self-sufficient, isolating container. Like Chadwick's *Inner Eye*, the structure of the *Birdcage*, like that of the maquette, is both a skeleton and an isolating frame, analogous to Bacon's spaceframes. Butler's iron frames combined existential solitude, imposed by the imprisoning structure of mind or cage, with a fortress for protection and survival. Eduardo Paolozzi produced a more elemental version of the same idea in his wire and plaster *The Cage* (1950) (fig. 88). Commissioned, like *Birdcage*, for the South Bank Exhibition, it has a comic, precarious aspect lacking in Butler's sculpture and is to be situated within the Smithsons' developing as-found aesthetic, rather than the 'geometry of fear'.

Read's essay for the 1952 Venice Biennale is famous principally for the phrase that has become common currency: 'the geometry of fear'. It applied not only to an ill-defined sculptural aesthetic but also to the culture of the early phase of the Cold War, when fear was overlaid with such statements of confidence as the Festival of Britain and the Coronation. Fear was more often signalled by conformity than directly expressed. As in the Blitz, it was displaced by sarcasm and gallows

88. Eduardo Paolozzi, *The Cage*, 1951. Bronze, 58 × 29 × 29 in. Arts Council Collection, Hayward Gallery, London.

humour; those who chose not to obey the communal rules of the air-raid shelters, not to celebrate in 1951 and 1953, threatened a delicate social mechanism for coming to terms with the effects of the Blitz and the implications of the Korean War. The young sculptors of 1952[97] were not to be grouped by anything as superficial as style, but, in Read's words, through 'some general extension of consciousness' that articulated emotional currents buried by the day-to-day process of national recovery.

Read's essay evoked the chaos of post-disaster scenarios, denied individual accountability and resoundingly dismissed classicism, either as a component of the modern or as an appropriate means of evaluation:

> These new images belong to the iconography of despair, or of defiance; and the more innocent the artist, the more effectively he transmits the collective guilt. Here are images of flight, of ragged claws 'scuttling across the floors of silent seas', of excoriated flesh, frustrated sex, the geometry of fear. Gone for ever is the serenity, the monumental calm, that a Winckelmann had imposed on the formal imagination of Europe.[98]

Butler's *Woman* and Moore's *Double Standing Figure* (1950) confronted one another at the entrance to the British pavilion in Venice. Although Moore's figure was developed from drawings made many years earlier,[99] its open linearity was new in his sculpture and may to some extent be seen as a riposte to Butler's radical reinterpretation of the body as a void where intelligence is reduced to the bare retention of life: *Woman* and her fellows are neither *genetrix* nor *mater*. To compare Moore's *Standing Figure* with his *Three Standing Figures* (1948) (fig. 98) is to see a reversal of the terms of either piece; void replaces mass, emptiness plenitude, barrenness fecundity and despair, optimism.

Thematically and formally the works shown at Venice in 1952 announced a departure from the conventional concerns of sculpture with mass, volume, classical serenity and the clearly formulated gender roles that this implied. The 1952 exhibition has assumed a retrospective significance much enhanced by Read's poetic essay, but the high point of sculpture prior to the explosion of the New Generation in the early 1960s was arguably Butler's maquette for the 'Unknown Political Prisoner' competition rather than the Biennale.

In 1950 he began three years as the Gregory Fellow in Sculpture at Leeds, where he produced his most controversial work, acquired an international reputation and abandoned welded iron for modelling and casting in light, shell bronze,[100] a change in technique which contributed to a richer, less style-conscious imagery. The *Box* and its maquette (1951), made during preparations for the 'Unknown Political Prisoner' competition, testify to Butler's continuing obsession with the body-as-machine, which culminated in the 1953 maquette.[101] The structure of the maquette alludes both to the human body and to an external system of control which is open to reading as watch-tower-television-screen-cage, embodying a mechanical and totalitarian intelligence.[102] Butler is reported to have introduced the three 'watchers' at the foot of the tower as women 'in whose minds the unknown prisoner is remembered'.[103] As the only fully human presences in a structure that was to be several hundred feet high, they would themselves have been poignant reminders of human frailty.

Butler's *Oracle*, commissioned for Hatfield Technical College, was unveiled in December 1952 and defaced with paint the following March, shortly after the destruction of the 'Unknown Political Prisoner' maquette at the Tate by a political refugee. The incidents underline Butler's prominence, for the 'Unknown Political Prisoner' exhibition at the Tate was one of very few to elicit widespread lay comment, almost unanimously unfavourable. Butler's imagery was controversial and was to become, if anything, more shocking as the decade progressed. In the *Oracle*, he replaced the eye-teasing quality of the earlier metamorphic figures by a primitive organism with an arched head on a grotesquely extended neck, appropriated from Bacon's *Three Studies for Figures at the Base of a Crucifixion*.[104]

Although Butler had minimised gender differentiation in his early linear works, it defined the character of the shell bronzes that followed the *Oracle*. These were usually female and often mutilated, while his complete figures were posed to maximise their sexuality or portrayed, like *Girl* (1953–4), in the act of removing their clothes. They indicate sexual or natural and essentially passive roles, in contrast to the *Manipulator* (1954), one of Butler's few male figures. These are active agents, 'usually shown holding rods or operating machinery of some kind'[105] and, in keeping with their dominant, cultural, interventionist function, possess undamaged bodies.

In 1950, Butler, Bacon and the French sculptor Germaine Richier showed together in 'London–Paris' at the ICA.[106] When, a few years later, he made the *Figure in Space* (1957/8) (fig. 89) he combined Richier's image of a body tensed against strings with Bacon's pictorial use of a frame to emphasise physical and psychological extremity, as it does in *Fragment of a Crucifixion* (1950). Two of Richier's *Diabolo* sculptures, where human figures strain, painfully taut, against the strings to which they are attached, were reproduced in *Cahiers d'Art* in 1953,[107] along with *L'Ouragane* (1948–9), a dramatic bronze figure with a heavily pitted,

89. Reg Butler, *Figure in Space*, 1957–8. Bronze, 36 × 36 × 21 in. Edn 8. Private Collection.

expressive surface which displayed the same disregard for finish as the *Oracle*. At the same time, there was a wide thematic divergence between the two artists: whereas Richier, like Bacon, explored the boundaries of human identity under stress,[108] Butler's sculptures proclaim a strong sado-masochistic content.[109]

They show female bodies manipulated, attached to wire frames, to be stretched, pulled and flayed. Their shape and their actions are determined by a technological device, though, as Richard Calvocoressi suggests, these are primarily psychological portrayals.[110] Like Bacon, Butler was concerned less with the retention of humanity than with its loss, through degradation and cruelty, to mindlessness. His dismemberment of the body and his denial of intellect and gender recall the inevitable concomitant of human existence that Sartre called 'nausea', since 'All our contact with the world, whether in perception, emotion or action, is contact through the medium of our own awareness of our bodies.'[111]

ROBOTS

In the late 1950s the robot replaced the organic hybrid as the Other of popular fantasy. The robot possessed immense strength and could be programmed to reason beyond the capacity of the human brain even while it exhibited endearing human quirks. Reassuringly, the robot was controllable, a fantasy designed to exhibit unquestioning, even self-destructive loyalty.[112]

If Robbie, the MGM prop that opened 'This is Tomorrow' in 1956, is the most familiar robot of the period, it had many fellows in the collective imagination of the Independent Group. A definitive marker in the development of the robot was the exhibition, 'Man, Machine and Motion' that Richard Hamilton organised with students in Newcastle.[113] He devised it as a parallel to 'Growth and Form', which had focussed on the natural,[114] whereas 'Man, Machine and Motion' surveyed the ways in which people use machines, from diving-bells to space-ships, to overcome limitations on their mobility. In photographs and reproductions, astronauts and divers in their transformatory suits, even swimmers wearing flippers were revealed as so radically adapted to their machines and equipment that their humanity was compromised. Individuality was subsumed into the attributes of motion,[115] yet it was only by allowing the machines to redefine the parameters of human nature that they could fulfil the functions required of them. The unarticulated text of the exhibition was not so much man *and* machine as man *as* machine.

A drawing by Paolozzi, annotated 'Man with a camera', (1955) shows a crude, child-like head with a clockface for an eye. A precisely drawn camera is an integral part of its face. The image indicates man *as* a camera, the all-seeing eye of the man-machine and a prelude to the bronze figures, like *The Philosopher* (1957) (fig. 12), that Paolozzi began to make in 1956. Their appearance suggests not only robots, derived from science fiction and announcing the impending realities of space travel,[116] but the heroic wartime image of the fighter pilot, with heavy boots, body-suit and helmet.

The lost wax process allowed Paolozzi to incorporate insignificant, discarded objects like machine parts and toys into his bronzes, turning them into three-dimensional collages. Robert Melville grasped their complexity when they were shown at the Hanover Gallery in 1958, describing them as 'disused robots which have turned into active fetishes, with a hint of the kind of charred figure which many of us visualised when some of the victims of naphtha bombs were rumoured to be still standing upright on the battlefields of Korea.'[117]

Touched with the *bricoleur's* 'imaginative power of transformation'[118] these quasi-existential images of the machine-man evoked unresolved and intensely emotional issues, while they retained an unfaltering attitude of ironic detachment. Despite their battered appearance, they are untouched by the loss that defines Bacon's and Butler's vision of humanity.

The eclecticism of Paolozzi's sources, from *Esquire*[119] to the Musée de l'Homme, from Giacometti, Dubuffet and Duchamp to the Pitt Rivers Museum,[120] from *Documents* and *Minotaure* to *Science Fantasy*, was as fundamental to the activities of the Independent Group as to his bronze figures. His attitude to the constituents of his imagery was illuminated by 'Lost Magic Kingdoms', the exhibition that he

90. John McHale,
First Contact, 1958.
Collage, 48 × 72 in.
Albright-Knox Art
Gallery, Buffalo.

arranged in 1985, drawing on the ethnographic collections of the Museum of Mankind. Introducing the exhibition, Malcolm McLeod wrote of the 'dismember-ment' in Paolozzi's material and methods, 'of parts from the whole and a disloca-tion of those parts from their contexts'.[121] This denial of context to establish a new identity is, McLeod considers, central to Paolozzi's process.[122] He concluded that 'Meaning is suggested both by the previous existence of the partial images he uses, and their original context, and by the new relationship the artist has established between these.'[123]

If Paolozzi challenged the fine art tradition and questioned the stability of its subject matter, he simultaneously and ironically claimed a place for his figures, through their titles, in the European high cultural lineage. They combine ancient tradition with a brash new culture of obsolence; dignity with absurdity; humour with pathos. They are both conquering heroes and anti-heroes in retreat from conflict, with an affective range 'between the intimate (it is like you or me) and the monstrous (it has been made and is *other*)'.[124]

Alloway might have described as monstrous the collage-paintings made by John McHale. His source material was a legendary trunkful of magazines which he brought from the United States in 1956, from which he made collages of fragments of machinery, buildings, print and natural organisms, which transformed the human body into equivalents of Paolozzi's bronze figures. *First Contact* (1958) (fig. 90) shows a family of machine-people confronting a similar creature, whose head is a television screen, a preview, Jacquelynn Baas suggests, of the viewer's own future.[125] McHale's collages stand midway between the triumphalist cybernetic art of the 1960s,[126] and the Orwellian notion of the all-seeing, controlling eye.

By the late 1950s it was no longer remarkable to own a television set and domestic appliances and it may have seemed, especially to those who saw the Smithsons' automated *House of the Future* in 1956, that the robot would soon be a familiar household item. Beside such intimations of the space-age, McHale's and Paolozzi's figures remain closer to the postwar ethos of fear and attrition than to the confidence paraded by American culture.

TOWARDS THE EROTIC ABSTRACT

For women, the 'loss of self' was an issue to be confronted daily. The title of Myrdal and Klein's book, *Women's Two Roles*, written to justify married women's claims to equality in working opportunities and conditions, suggests a conflict of loyalties and a consequent problem of identity. The vernacular imagery of advertising, the cinema and magazines constantly juxtaposed conflicting ideals of womanhood: the natural, perfect wife and mother and the culturally constructed sex-goddess. Popular taste responded to *Saw Ohn Nyun* (fig. 80), while high art and critical convention sought refuge in formalism rather than address the sigificance of such images of the female body. Eroticism was displaced into vulgar postcards or, conversely, fashion and society photographs, with the pin-up as the vernacular equivalent of the classical nude so much appreciated by late Victorians. No modern classicising images took their place in the 1950s, though several artists produced erotic images barely concealed by the pictorial and verbal rhetoric of modernism.

The still lifes that William Scott began to paint after a visit to Paris in 1946[127] have a dual imagery which operates through witty visual punning. He constantly redeployed a small repertoire of domestic objects: a frying-pan, fish, eggs, lemons and a rudimentary range of kitchen utensils set down in clear, flat colour on uptilted tabletops. Alan Bowness has pointed out that between 1949 and 1951 the objects in Scott's still life paintings were often arranged to disclose a second identity as male or female sexual organs, a dualism which the artist acknowledged as 'another image – it's a private one, ambiguous, and can perhaps be sensed rather than seen'.[128]

During the early 1950s Scott and Roger Hilton were caught up in a way of painting that led them to produce a number of images of the body as radical as Butler's waifs. This would not have been possible without the example of Nicolas de Staël and the notion of an image inherent in the paint, to be elicited rather than willed by the artist, and thus always sensed rather than seen. Hilton's earliest work to contain implicit bodies was a series of paintings which he called, non-committally, 'Composition' or 'Untitled'. At the beginning of the 1950s Hilton adapted the gridded structures developed by French artists like Jean-Michel Atlan which had already proved inspirational to Hilton's friend William Gear. He painted several *Compositions* that resemble groups of skeletal standing figures (fig. 91).[129] The structure, filled with *taches*, offered either a route into non-figurative painting, where, as we have seen with Gear, the grid, or armature, provided an internally rational composition; or a way of introducing a generalised, allusive imagery, referring to still life, landscape or the human body[130] with additional implications of cages and robots.

With the *Compositions* Hilton's faltering career began to gather impetus, with a well-received solo show at Gimpel Fils in June 1952[131] and invitations to take part in group exhibitions. His painting was considered an apt reflection on his world, where the existential individual was becoming a familiar concept. It was sadly appropriate to Hilton himself, wracked by the anxiety manifest in a mass of often incoherent texts, of which the best known is his statement in *Nine Abstract Artists*.[132] It is perhaps appropriate to see in the voids of Hilton's incorporeal bodies a resonance of the existential nothingness described by Mary Warnock:

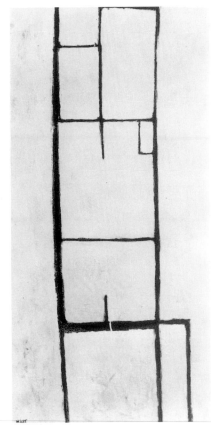

Authenticity consists in a realization of one's position in the world, one's isolation, and one's inevitable orientation towards one's own death. Before this realization can be complete, one has to experience oneself as something suspended over a void. Things in the world must lose their solidity . . . and one must feel deep alarm at the vacancy which surounds one.[133]

Scott and Hilton, both participants in the final Fitzroy Street weekend exhibition and contributors to *Nine Abstract Artists*, shared an intense interest in the structural properties of non-figurative imagery divorced from mathematical process. Their common mindset sometimes resulted in paintings in which they seem to have tracked one another's thoughts. Hilton's *October 1953–March 1954* is very close to Scott's *Seated Figure No.1* (1953) (fig. 92), though the former is bowed like a living body whereas Scott's image is as straight as a wooden chair. Both artists were deeply indebted to de Staël's luscious, thick paint, a striking formal innovation which concealed and metaphorised the heavily gendered content of their work.

Early in 1953 Hilton renewed his acquaintance with Constant van Nieuwenhuys, a Dutch painter and, like Stephen Gilbert who introduced them, a former member of COBRA,[134] though both artists had moved away from COBRA's expressive focus to explore their interest in colour through three-dimensional constructions. Constant introduced Hilton to Mondrian's paintings in the Stedelijk Museum in Amsterdam,[135] after which he almost immediately began the abstract paintings, like *July 1953* (fig. 45), that he hoped would function as painted equivalents of constructions. In *Nine Abstract Artists*, where *July 1953* was reproduced,

91. Roger Hilton, *Composition*, 1950–2. Oil on canvas, 26 × 22 in. Private Collection.

92. William Scott, *Seated Figure No.1*, 1953. Oil on canvas, $60\frac{1}{4}$ × 30 in. Private Collection.

93. William Scott,
The Harbour, 1952.
Oil on canvas,
24 × 36 in. William
Scott Foundation.

Hilton wrote optimistically that 'The effect is to be felt outside rather than inside the picture: the picture is to be not primarily an image, but a space-creating mechanism.'[136]

August 1953 (fig. 44) is built up from thick, tactile slabs of paint. Hilton described such paintings in formal terms as 'space-stops', but his manuscript notes show that he attributed an overriding metaphoric quality to them which measured their validity as communications: 'I believe they tie up with the advance of mankind into the unknown in other spheres of activity.'[137] Although Heron wrote, with reference to Hilton's paintings, of 'a set of forms so powerful that they appear to be projecting themselves bodily out from the surface of the picture into the *actual* space of the room',[138] thus contributing authoritatively to the construction of the artist as a pure formalist, it is impossible to see *August 1953* as other than a rudimentary female torso, an 'inescapably human aesthetic remainder'.[139] Such images are too small, too richly worked and too complex to function like de Stijl colour planes.

In *Still Life: Coffee Pot I: Black Composition* (1952/3) (fig. 47) Scott transformed a table top into a rectangle of heavily scumbled colour, broken by a few indistinct objects: the pot is placed between two cups, flanked by a pair of dark vertical bands that transform the table into a woman's body, where the pot is the head and the cups breasts. This is not so much metamorphic imagery, indicating alienation from the human species, as a punning reversal, which can be constantly switched back and forth. *Figure into Landscape* (1953) (fig. 46) was the culmination of this process, a painting in which Scott reduced his imagery to a linear grid, conflating body, landscape and still life.

His *The Harbour* (1952) (fig. 93), in which a long linear shape protrudes into a mass of grey-white paint sparsely broken by a loose framework, preceded a group of paintings by Hilton where abstract shapes intrude from one edge of the canvas. Scott's *Harbour* and *Seated Figure* can be read as notional pendants: if *Seated Figure* is female, her gender barely indicated by a single rectangular breast, *The Harbour* represents her male counterpart, expressed metonymically as a penis.

That Hilton felt compelled constantly to justify his constructivist-related painting is revealed in the manuscript notes where he argued the case back and forth to himself, from his determination that 'The tyranny of the image must be overcome', in order 'to create a picture which shall have an impact on the spectator solely as a result of the plastic means employed', to a position where figuration might be validated through recourse to a kind of automatism. Hilton presumably saw Jean Dubuffet's exhibition at the ICA in March 1955; certainly it would be difficult to exclude the impact of Dubuffet from a consideration of his painting after the middle of 1956. In his catalogue essay, Georges Limbour wrote of the centrality of *matière* (rather inadequately translated as 'material') in Dubuffet's paintings: '. . . the perpetual and essential theme is not the object represented but the material used . . . the materials used have imposed their own demands on him, even going so far as to change his mood and intention when he is actually working.'[140] In a section of his copious unpublished notes, Hilton explored the implications of something very close to *matière* painting for a return to figuration, which he increasingly felt to be desirable: 'Very often in the course of working your medium will say something you hadn't thought of . . . in the term medium I include subject matter . . . figuration or non-figuration is an element in the medium . . . The central problem at the moment is to reintroduce figuration without making it descriptive.' He continued: 'the picture must be geared to something outside itself. Let us have untidy but alive pictures, let us not have the too complete, the too aesthetic, the too tidy, the too gestalt.'[141]

Late in 1955 he wrote to Terry Frost that he had resolved his dilemma: 'I am going in future to introduce if possible a more markedly human element in my pictures while endeavouring at the same time to dispose their forms in a space creating manner. I already feel much happier . . .'[142] The new paintings were crude but complicated images like *October 1956*,[143] which has the charcoal hemispheres that were Hilton's signs both for breasts and boats scrawled over shapes that resemble the domestic containers in Scott's paintings, set out on a rough tabletop. Charcoal lines connect the objects and suggest that this is in reality a body on a table, for whereas Scott converted the table into a sign for a woman, Hilton allowed it to retain its identity, painting a 'figure into still life'.

With *October 1956 (Brown, Black and White)* (fig. 94), however, Hilton transformed Scott's theme. A brown rectangle indicates a tabletop; roughly scratched into it are a neck, an arm and a buttock, bearing the dense circular scribble with which Hilton indicated female genitalia.[144] Arranged non-anatomically to connect a rudimentary head with the black strips that stand for legs at the lower edge of the canvas, these disparate signs for the body are further metaphorised by the tabletop into which they are inscribed.

These images are cruel representations of women obliterated, marked and violated through paint. Neither *mater* nor *genetrix*, they are emptied of all but a residual, worn-out sexuality. Clearly aware of their effect, which differentiated them from fully abstract paintings, Hilton wrote to Frost:

> It is disconcerting not knowing whether my next show will be of chaste abstracts or violent figuration . . . if abstracts they will be chaste, spiritual, calm. If figurative they will be fulgurant, demonic, tragic, expressionistic, violent, wanton and destructive . . .[145]

The overt sexuality of Hilton's 'violent figuration' was glossed over when the paintings were first exhibited and, though it was obvious that he could no longer

94. Roger Hilton,
*October 1956 (Brown,
Black and White)*.
Oil on canvas, 55 ×
50 in. British Council
Collection.

be dismissed as 'a purely formal composer and agreeable colourist',[146] few were prepared to go as far as Patrick Heron in acknowledging 'a sort of nostalgic eroticism'.[147] Since convention precluded discussion of the erotic or the sexually transgressive, Hilton was acknowledged as one of the most competent exponents of a kind of painting that was recognised as difficult to interpret and linked with Abstract Expressionism,[148] while the content of his work was alluded to only briefly.

Scott's interpretation of the elemental woman differed considerably from Hilton's though, as we have seen, both drew on Dubuffet. In the catalogue of Scott's retrospective at the Tate Gallery in 1972 is a small, uncaptioned reproduction of the *Venus of Laussel*,[149] a little prehistoric relief of a woman's body with a featureless face, swollen belly and pendulous breasts. For Scott, primitivism meant prehistory rather than tribal art and, it seems, the notion of the *genetrix* reflected both in the *Venus* and his own paintings of the female nude. The bodies of Scott's nudes are often truncated, their hands and feet cut off by the edge of the canvas to concentrate attention on the torso as a sexual and reproductive zone. Their worn, misshapen bodies suggest that they have been used and set aside; they become the equivalents of tables, objects for exploitation.

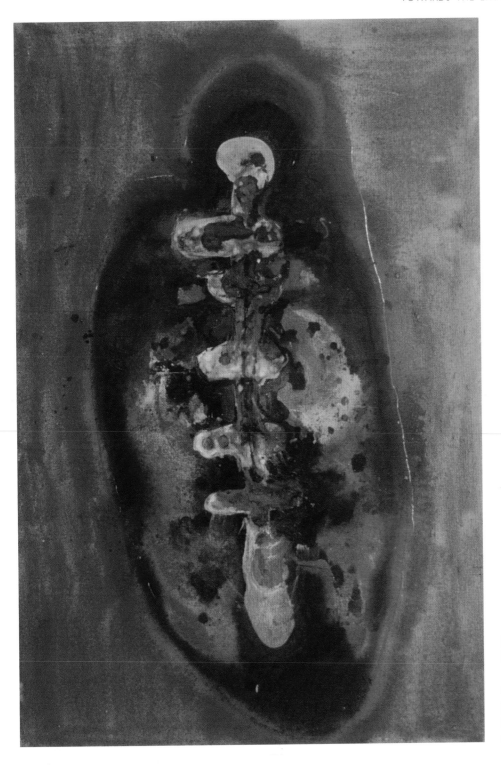

95. Magda Cordell McHale, *Presences*, 1959–60. Pigment, coloured ink and polymer on canvas, 60 × 40 in. Artist's collection.

We may compare them with the paintings and prints made by Magda Cordell between 1954 and 1960. Some, like *Presences* (1959–60) (fig. 95), have hints of X-ray images and others compare with prehistoric Venus figures, but all are triumphantly female. Despite the rawness of their colour and the suggestions of skeletal structure, they are the opposite of Butler's skeletal survivors; Cordell's frequent emphasis on swelling breasts and bellies transforms her women into confident progenitors and modern icons of fertility.[150]

The ubiquity of the erotic abstract as a theme for artists in London, Cornwall, Corsham and beyond confirms that it is inadequate to seek to explain it simply as a set of disparate reactions to Dubuffet. As we have seen, it interacted with and expanded still life and landscape themes, but retrospectively it is most powerful as a counterweight to the concealments of social convention. Hilton and Scott confronted raw, undisguised sexuality in the Other and sought to destroy it in paint, whereas in Cordell's paintings it was a focus for celebration. Other artists in the Independent Group approached the erotic abstract through the social codes that constructed woman and her social role in a way that domesticated the sexuality of the Other. For them, collage was to be a central medium.

CONSUMERS

The image of the vamp, ubiquitous in Paolozzi's collages, was associated principally with the cinema, where she was at once unattainable, implausible, titillating and an idealised girl next door. The otherness of the vamp resided in physique and glamour, in a sexuality that presented a class challenge to the aloof aristocrats whose portraits adorned the Royal Academy Summer Exhibition and were imitated by *Vogue* models. Composed with minute care for verbal felicities and visual puns, Paolozzi's collages identify women, objects of sexual consumption, with the consumer goods that surround them. Images like *Real Gold* (*c.* 1950) (fig. 96) lie within the ethos of the American dream presented by films and food parcels from a land which offered an abundance of flesh, food and music. They mediate the gap between the dream and the political reality of ecomomic dependence, a condition which rendered the object of desire, America itself, literally inaccessible.

Richard Hamilton's *Just What is it that Makes Today's Homes so Different, so Appealing*? (1956) (fig. 55) brings together complex strands of imagery, combining consumer and hero figures in a setting that is a lexicon of themes in contemporary culture. The remote realms of science and space exploration, signalled by a moon map on the ceiling, confront the populism revealed by a carpet which is in fact a photograph of a crowded beach; high and low culture clash in the juxtaposition of a portrait of Ruskin and a page from a popular comic; class divisions are summarised by the contiguity of the respectable girl on the television screen and the stripper on the sofa.

The divergence between the representation of the central couple as mannequins and the small, unglamourised woman on the stairs identifies gender relations as the pivot of the relationship between the three figures. While the couple are the bearers of a multiplicity of signs, the lone woman is a signifier of herself as commodity, her personality subsumed into the vacuum cleaner to which she is attached, so that her naturalness is identified as the use of the domestic equipment with which she is identified.

Hamilton explored the relationship of woman, commodity and image in his paintings of the late 1950s, questioning the implications of American consumer culture in defiance of his colleagues' obsession with Abstract Expressionism. In 'An exposition of *$he*' he wrote:

> The worst thing that can happen to a girl, according to the ads, is that she should fail to be exquisitely at ease in her appliance setting – the setting that now does

96. Eduardo Paolozzi, *Real Gold*, c.1950. Collage on paper, 14 × 9¼ in. Tate Gallery, London.

much to establish our attitude to woman in the way that her clothes alone used to.[151]

A year later, in 1963, Betty Friedan published *The Feminine Mystique*, one of the principal catalysts to the women's movement of the 1960s and 1970s in which, commenting on the role of women within capitalist societies, she asked sardonically 'why is it never said that . . . the really important role that women serve as housewives is *to buy more things for the home*'.[152]

$he (1958–61) (fig. 97) combines a well-stocked refrigerator, vacuum cleaner, toaster and an air-brushed woman, naked except for her apron. Airbrushing provides a mechanical, perfect, implicitly inviolate image to set against the aproned whore, who offers herself in the personification of her refrigerator. Hamilton's fantasy woman was constructed in an acute awareness of the

97. Richard Hamilton, *$he*, 1958–61. Oil and mixed media on board, 48 × 32 in. Tate Gallery, London.

subservient economic and social status of most women in the 1950s. The culmina-tion of these paintings is *AAH!* (1962), from a series in which woman and car are identified.[153] Here the woman is identified with the interior of the car and a sexual act as explicit as anything painted by Hilton, in which the car-as-woman is driven by the alien, male hand on the gear lever. In a further twist, characteristic of Hamilton's image-building, this painting may be inverted, as a homoerotic image, through the (male) finger on the gear lever-as-penis, mocking and undermining the sexual power structure built on the identification of car with woman.

Hamilton disclaimed irony in $he and, implicitly, the paintings related to it, preferring to see 'a search for what is epic in everyday objects and everyday attitudes'[154] and aligning the irony of advertising with modernism in order to conceal content. In that the subversive quality of paintings like $he and AAH! depends on irony to distinguish them from tasteless exercises in male chauvinism, this is hardly convincing. The 'feminine mystique', identified by Friedan as the myth which kept women subservient to male requirements for reproduction and the domestic routine, succeeded by denying their identity. The achievement of Hamilton's exposition of woman-as-consumer was to deconstruct the sexist methods of the advertising industry[155] and demonstrate the importance of women's ironic subversion of the natural male order of social relations in order to establish their identity.

'Cultural order includes both the rule and the transgression'.[156] If modernism was a component of the dominant cultural order of the 1950s, it was a double-edged weapon, a trickster as well as an enabler, allowing elisions and connections between object and subject, object and idea not previously possible. Bearing both the rule and the means to subvert it, it allowed the entrance of irony.

In a period dominated by formalist criticism, which accepted abstraction as unreadable, the diversity of representations of the human body is remarkable. Coldstream's minutely annotated models stand at one pole of an axis, where the body is secondary to its notation, a cultural artefact and a means of professional gratification for the artist. At the other extreme are Hilton, conventionally described as an abstract artist and the figurative Bacon. Both grasped the opportunities offered by random marks, accidents with paint and their disregard for the conventions of *facture* in order to conceal violence and degradation.

More than any other artists of the 1950s, painters of the human body appropriated models which transgressed the conventions of their genre, seizing on Dubuffet, prehistoric and tribal imagery, Picasso and Gonzalez. For Scott and Hilton, still life played an unlikely, central role in enabling them to paint with an ambiguity which has, almost until today, concealed the underlying matter of their work. Similarly, the formal constraints of modernism – its denial of narrative and tradition, its emphasis on technique and material – made it possible to devise an imagery of anti-heroes: pathetic, broken, almost de-gendered in their likeness to the ever-subservient robot. It is hardly coincidental that the formulation of this imagery narrowly preceded the revival of the women's movement after its postwar dormancy.

10

PUBLIC ART

Generally speaking, modern art is a personalist art, subjective in its origins and arbitrary in its conventions. It has never, hitherto, aspired to be a monumental art, a public art used in public rituals. It must necessarily undergo certain modifications if it is to become a functional art in this sense.

Herbert Read, 1951[1]

In May 1948 the London County Council's first open-air sculpture exhibition opened in Battersea Park. It brought together works by many of the leading twentieth-century sculptors, from Rodin and Maillol to Matisse and Zadkine, in an unprecedented format that allowed people to explore works of art at leisure in a relaxed atmosphere very different from the intimidating formality of the gallery. The exhibition proved immensely popular and was widely imitated. For London-ers and other town-dwellers it had particular resonances, as its centre-piece, the most widely discussed of all the works that it contained, was Henry Moore's new group, *Three Standing Figures* (1948) (fig. 98), in which many people saw references to the endurance of the civilian population in wartime. Moore's sculpture was taken as a prototype for a new kind of public art for the postwar world: one that would complement the reconstructed cities and, most importantly, proclaim the values of the New Britain. *Three Standing Figures* initiated a debate on the content and purpose of public art which continued for more than a decade.

Public art is primarily an art of shared urban spaces; it excludes the private domains of gallery, home or corporate patron. Between the wars it overwhelm-ingly took the form of war memorials,[2] which denote their sites as places of communal significance and ritual, or 'sites of memory' for 'communities of the bereaved'.[3] After the vast losses of the Great War, when many communities saw a whole generation of young men annihilated, rituals and memorials provided some sense of cathartic relief and of meaning.[4] After 1945, after the death-camps and the atom bomb, meaning, which implies an element of justification, was no longer to be found. No common form of memorial could be devised, like the cross

98. Henry Moore, *Three Standing Figures*, 1948. Darley Dale stone, 84 in. high.

on the village green that served so many communities after 1918, to encompass the Second World War. So names were added to old memorials, while human imagination failed, unsurprisingly, to find any adequate memorial form for such 'sites of mourning' as Auschwitz.[5]

If public art was to be viable in the aftermath of 1945 it would have to develop new forms, functions and meanings; it would have to turn its back on the cataclysm of the previous six years in order to celebrate the future. In a society overcome, as Victor Pasmore said, 'by the spirit of reconstruction', the desire to forget was accomodated, though the process of forgetting offered no solution to the thematic and formal *tabula rasa* facing the potential public artist. It was, rather, the process of physical reconstruction that was to suggest ways in which a secular and non-commemorative public art might assume some communal significance. With the rebuilding of huge areas of London and other towns such as Coventry and Plymouth, a new form of city came into existence; planned, ordered and uniform, it was psychologically impossible that they should be immediately accepted as adequate substitutes for the old local places – pubs, shops, street-corners – around which communities had been structured. In replacing slums with decent housing, the new cities had also swept away the complex, informal networks that bind a society into something more than a number of households. One of the functions of postwar public art was to be the visual, symbolic reinstatement of a sense of community.

If a city is to convey the sense of history and community that prevents it being no more than a placeless nonentity,[6] it must have a clear visual structure. The

99. Henry Moore, *Family Group*, 1954– 5. Hadene stone, $64\frac{1}{2}$ in. high. Formerly in Harlow New Town.

quality that Kevin Lynch described as imageability implies an imaginative mental mosaic embracing not a basic street plan but the sense of a city's history and its relationship with the flux of present activity.[7] The contemporary city is a complex, shifting environment, sometimes threatening and often confusing; coherent structure and a recognisable identity are essential signs for those who enter it.[8] At the same time, the city is home to innumerable small groups who identify themselves in large part through their relationship with a locality, which may be restricted to a housing estate or a few streets. Both on the level of the abstract macrocosm of the greater city and the concrete microcosm of the local community, public art may contribute significantly to a sense of real place and personal identity within it.

The development of the new public art was accompanied by a long-drawn-out discussion of its role in a democracy. Inconclusive though this debate was, it involved a wider range of lay and expert opinion than almost any other aesthetic issue of the period. It was complicated by the diversity of public art, which ranged from small, secluded, decorative pieces, like the sculpture called *Faun and Goose* (1959–60) made by George Ehrlich for an old people's home in Bethnal Green, to such authoritative statements of collective values as Moore's *Family Group* (1954) (fig. 99) in Harlow. Unfortunately discussion of the social significance of public art and of the forms that it might most appropriately take was all too often hindered by the formalist conventions of early postwar criticism.

The old controversy over Jacob Epstein's carvings for the London Underground Headquarters, made in the 1920s,[9] opened a long-running debate on the account-ability of artists working in the public domain and whether concessions should be made to a hypothetical normative taste. The debate called into question the less prominent but fundamental relationship between artist and architect. Moore, whose *West Wind* (1928–9) on the London Underground head quarters building was his first commission, later complained of architects who 'only thought of sculpture as a surface decoration, and ordered a relief as a matter of course'.[10]

After 1945 issues of accountability were complicated both by the ideology of artistic autonomy and the distaste for abstract art that was projected by many critics onto an amorphous public. The role of public art as a social phenomenon became conflated with the question of an appropriate style. Inevitably, the status of abstraction became a problem, particularly for constructionist artists, whose work was often considered fit only for architectural decoration, that is, as an adjunct, rather than an integral part of a building.[11] A stage beyond architectural decoration, which acknowledged the status of a work as art, was the adoption of public sculpture to signpost buildings by symbolizing their function, in the way that Siegfried Charoux's *The Cellist* (1958) signals the meaning of the Royal Festival Hall. Resistance to these simplistic functions for public art were among the issues that divided modernist artists from the majority of civic patrons and from tradi-tionalists. The latter included the academic sculptors Charles Wheeler, President of the Royal Academy from 1956 to 1966, and Gilbert Ledward, who designed the fountain in Sloane Square, completed in 1953 and widely acknowledged as extremely successful. It is one of the paradoxes of postwar public art that though it was largely determined by modernity and the spirit of a renewed society, it represented the prime meeting ground for modernism and tradition.

The public art debate focussed initially on a new civic art to express the aspira-tions of postwar society. From the beginning there was an anomaly at its core, since those who conducted it, in terms of high art and high principles, persistently overlooked the identity of the public, that 'monstrous abstraction'[12] in whose name the discussion took place. Only within the London County Council was this identity, so often assumed to be homogeneous and simple, despite clear evidence that it was fractured and complex, recognised as inseparable from the question of the purpose of public art.

Discussion was predicated on the old-fashioned terms of the monument, since there was a sense that only monumental sculpture, ratified by public approval, was capable of reconciling 'modern art . . . with the civilisation that brought it into being'.[13] For critics in sympathy with modernism, public art had a crucial role to play in bridging the gulf between the contemporary artist and the general public. Writers on Moore's *Three Standing Figures* proposed a new type of monument[14] which was neither overtly celebratory nor a memorial, yet retained a symbolic content. Even the ponderous humour of the LCC representative who described the group to a party of official foreign visitors as 'sort of members of the Civil Defence in atomic armour expecting an air-raid',[15] hints that the figures were to be read as emblems of a wider population.

The 1948 Battersea exhibition, with an assemblage of works by the leading sculptors of the European tradition, provided an ideal opportunity to isolate the essential qualities of the modern monument. Robert Melville,[16] a strong and per-ceptive protagonist of Moore's work, attempted to analyse the problem, calling for an approach that would retain the conventional distance and anonymity of the public monument. In subject matter and style it should avoid the depiction of specific events and emulate the dignified serenity of Wilhelm Lehmbruck or Aristide Maillol, rather than adopt an idiosyncratic style from outside the 'European canon', such as the 'Negro sculpture' which he saw reflected in the work of Jacques Lipchitz.[17]

Melville also touched on function, and though his assertion that Moore's figures were 'modifiers of landscape . . . intended to exert a peculiar influence upon their environment'[18] was inevitable in view of the parkland setting, it implied that a specific purpose should be a concomitant of public art. His remark also suggested a role for public art in the articulation and identification of urban spaces, an issue that became prominent in connection with the South Bank exhibition in 1951.

The debate which began so vigorously trailed on inconclusively into the 1960s, when it focussed increasingly on subject matter. By this time public art was seen as a status symbol for industry, leading the *Times* critic to comment breathlessly: 'Public bodies, industrialists, and architects are vying with one another to acquire the latest works by the best known names to decorate and advertise the new premises that are going up all over the country.'[19] This comment, made when the postwar spirit of reconstruction was all but forgotten, swept away by the fantastic promises of new building technologies, symbolised the inconclusive end of the debate on public art. With neither a satisfactory role nor form having emerged, by the early 1960s public art was held by those who commissioned and wrote about it to be generally beneficial, while artists were glad to be employed to make it. Those few critics who questioned its *raison d'être* and efficacy failed to direct the debate onto a more sophisticated theoretical level where either a new social role for public art or its unacknowledged place in urban planning might be discussed.

Given the large number of disparate works that constitute the corpus of public art, the issues are best clarified by focussing on a few cases, most of which involved prominent patrons. In the 1951 South Bank exhibition for the Festival of Britain the Arts Council promoted modernist art as an autonomous, value-free receptacle of meaning, apt for adoption by corporate sponsors seeking a public image. Two years later, the 'Unknown Political Prisoner' competition was an attempt to create a monument with the scale and import of the Statue of Liberty, while simultaneously and less transparently enlisting art in the service of Cold War politics. In 1956 the London County Council, advised by the Arts Council, embarked on a programme to embellish its many properties with works of art, an ambitious scheme which made a prominent contribution to the public art debate.

Among the hundreds of artists who made works for public places, Moore occupied a unique position, despite his reluctance to undertake commissions[20] which generally obliged public patrons to select from what was available in the studio. His relationship with the British Council, which began in earnest shortly after the end of the war, was closer and more complex than with any other patron, institutional or private. The Council supported Moore loyally and, because of the humanist themes of his work and his international stature – for which he was much indebted to the Council – was able to reap indirect diplomatic benefits from promoting his work, discreetly accomplishing what the 'Unknown Political Prisoner' competition notoriously failed to achieve.

Other organisations and individuals naturally contributed to the corpus of public art in the early postwar years, with constructionist artists providing some of the most aesthetically successful examples. They were committed to working closely with architects, and Pasmore took the opportunity to put ideals into practice when he took up the post of Consulting Director of Urban Design for the south-west area of Peterlee New Town in 1955.

He was invited by A. V. Williams, general manager of the New Town, to collaborate with two young architects on a 300-acre site, with a brief to raise the aesthetic quality of design.[21] Pasmore's principal contribution was to reinstate the relationship between landscape and architecture, through informal planning which incorporated curving roads and distinctive groupings of flat-roofed houses with facades strongly reminiscent of his reliefs.[22] He also designed the Pavilion, a walk-through construction of masses and voids set across a small lake, a public building for pleasure, play and visual delight, now in sad disrepair. On its pale rectilinear surfaces Pasmore painted flowing abstract shapes appropriated from his easel paintings, which fused organic and geometric forms and painting and architecture in a delicate balance where they remained distinct but mutually enhancing.

This goal was shared by Mary Martin, whose *Waterfall* (1957), a relief in plaster and gleaming matt steel at the entrance to Musgrave Park Hospital in Belfast, was one of the earliest constructionist public commissions. It is a reticent and compelling piece which marks the route into the building and is also visible from the wards. Martin wrote with insight of 'that tenuous border between art and architecture where the abstract artist and the architect speak a common language . . . the work becomes a comprehensible symbol of the building itself, a part of the architecture but not architecture.'[23]

Kenneth Martin's *Fountain*, made for the courtyard of the Brixton College of Further Education in 1961 reveals a similarly intimate relationship with building design. A cluster of bright steel pipes, springing from a central stem, complements the severely orthogonal architecture. The Martins were among the artists who contributed to the temporary complex designed by Theo Crosby for the International Union of Architects London congress in July 1961. Though not strictly speaking a public building, it was the most fully resolved collaboration between artist and architect of all the constructionist endeavours.

THE SOUTH BANK EXHIBITION

The South Bank Exhibition, a purpose-built, temporary city within a city, offered the first opportunity to test the theoretical issues so enthusiastically discussed since 1948. Like the rest of the nationwide Festival, it was organised by a hierarchy of committees set up under a Festival Executive[24] chaired by Gerald Barry, editor of the *News Chronicle*. It is Barry's phrase, 'The People's Show' that most evocatively sums up the South Bank Exhibition. Accounts of the crowds that flocked to the site around the Royal Festival Hall, to dance in the rain, delight in the floodlighting and learn from the displays, all agree on the populist appeal of this heavily symbolic event, which promised an end to wartime austerity, if not immediately.

Murals and sculpture were abundant, skilfully incorporated into individual thematic displays and the overall site plan. Visitors who marvelled at the abundance of art and colour and contemporary design were unaware of the acrimonious haggling between the two principal patrons, the Festival authorities and the Arts Council, that had preceded the opening of the exhibition.

Early in the planning process, members of the Arts Council expressed a wish to be involved in the Festival, seeing an unparalleled opportunity for the young

100. Victor Pasmore at work on his mural outside the Regatta Restaurant at the South Bank Exhibition, 1951.

organisation to emerge as a creative and innovative patron.[25] In 1949, as the need to finalise arrangements became pressing, Sir Edward Pooley, Chairman of the Arts Council, proposed that the Council organise a Festival of the Arts, acting independently of the Festival authorities,[26] with extra staff and funding. His proposal was strenuously opposed by Lord Ismay, representing the Festival Council, since Pooley insisted on disengagement from the South Bank exhibition and consequently a diffusion of effort and emphasis. Yet a month later he accepted Pooley's limited contribution, perhaps recognising that by refusing to play a full part in the South Bank commissions, the Arts Council would be the chief loser; indeed, the confusion over who commissioned what and under what terms persists to this day.

The Arts Council commissioned some important sculptures for the South Bank and advised on the appointment of mural artists, but its main Festival exhibitions took place elsewhere. Other works of art were commissioned by the Festival authorities and the architects who designed the pavilions. The differences between the Arts Council and Barry and his colleagues emerged, it seems, from radically opposed readings of the Festival. For Barry it was a popular celebration with an educational subtext, so it was appropriate for the Festival Executive to commission numerous works as decorative or illustrative aids to didactic displays, while the Arts Council took it as an opportunity to promote high art, its cultural exclusivity underlined by sculptures set prominently apart on raised plinths.

Mural painting was widely seen as the popular art form of the future, a view boosted by wartime decorations in workplaces and British restaurants. This alone would have ensured their prominence on the South Bank, although the Arts Council declined to commission murals and would only advise on artists who might paint them. Most murals were integrated into displays and while some were necessarily technical or diagrammatic, there was considerable latitude for artists to assert their individuality, even when the subject matter was prescribed.

John Minton and Keith Vaughan made murals for the Dome of Discovery, on the themes of Exploration and Discovery respectively,[27] which were extensions of their current private work. Minton, who was preoccupied with history painting, produced a panoramic view of renaissance explorers and their ships. Vaughan's fifty-foot long mural, *At the Beginning of Time* (1951), was an arcadian classicising scene of male nudes on a beach.

Graham Sutherland's commission to paint *The Origins of the Land* (1951) for the Land of Britain pavilion may have been an unexpected opportunity to extend his imaginative practice; he saw it as an important work and, as was his habit, showed fifty of the preliminary studies late in 1952 at the Redfern Gallery.[28] While Sutherland's mural was a gloss on a heavily metaphorical display, the sheet of painted tiles that Victor Pasmore extended across the south wall of the Regatta Restaurant was, as befitted a constructionist artist, indivisible from the architecture (fig. 100). His mural elegantly complemented the building and provided a memorable marker not only for the restaurant, but for the stairs which flanked it and provided access to the Festival site from Hungerford Bridge.[29]

The creators of the People's Show had no misgivings about contemporary art. In the courtyard garden of the same restaurant, Lynn Chadwick's *Cypress* (1951), a tall chrysalis-like form in sheet metal, acted as another prominent sign for the building. Clearly visible from the river, Reg Butler's *Birdcage* (1951), an attenuated humanoid form on a tripod base, towered over the Regatta Restaurant, proclaiming its presence and that of the entire South Bank Exhibition.

To assign a purpose to any of the works of art on the South Bank is a reductive exercise; they were simultaneously embellishments, symbols and markers. Many of the most prominent pieces served as landmarks,[30] visual features that enabled visitors to orient themselves in a confusing situation. Since they also conveyed strong, if conflicting messages of unease, strength and modernity, the sculpture and murals made a considerable contribution to the imageability of the South Bank.

The most highly acclaimed and compelling image of the entire Festival was Powell and Moya's *Skylon*, which was immediately converted into a symbol of discovery and an image of interplanetary travel. Its position beside the Dome of Discovery meant, as magazine editors quickly realised, that the two most prominent landmarks of the South Bank together formed a compelling image of its futuristic architecture (fig. 101).[31]

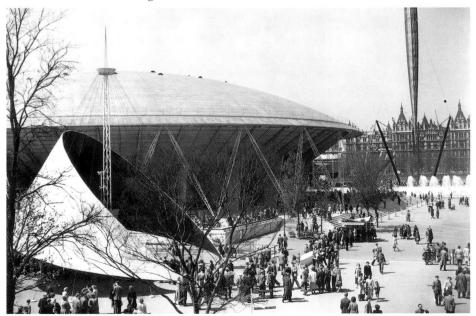

101. The South Bank Exhibition from the York Road entrance showing the Dome of Discovery and the lower part of the Skylon.

102. Laszlo (Peter) Peri, *Maquette for Sunbathers*, 1951. Concrete. Leeds City Art Gallery.

On the whole, however, symbolic content, dramatic scale and advanced style were unusual on the South Bank and most sculptors conformed to an unstated convention of easily read, familiar subject matter, like the high-relief, *Sunbathers* (1951) (fig. 102), by the Hungarian Marxist and protegé of John Berger, Peter Peri. Vertiginously perched high on a wall at the main entrance to the site, it wittily suggested an appropriately relaxed mood and offered the artist a rare opportunity to fulfil his desire to make art for the people. Whether or not patrons accepted his ideology, Peri's narrative art was the kind favoured by borough councils, from which he later received numerous commissions.

The Arts Council's commissions were arranged on a two-tier system based on current market prices, which perpetuated the established hierarchy of major and minor, or young, artists. Moore, Barbara Hepworth, Epstein and Frank Dobson were offered a choice of the most appealing sites and worthwhile financial contracts to work in stone or bronze on agreed subjects, while eight younger artists were asked to address any theme in 'fairly permanent materials'.

Moore and Epstein received the most valuable commissions[32] and had priority in the choice of sites,[33] but the notoriously slow progress of construction on the South Bank[34] made it impossible to undertake site-specific works. Writing to the two artists in May 1949 in virtually identical terms, Mary Glasgow directed their attention to the most appropriate subjects for their sculptures, while leaving them free to demur: 'While no restriction is placed on the subject of your group the Festival Committee themselves have suggested a Family Group and a subject symbolizing "Discovery" as a suitable theme for the Festival.'[35]

We may speculate as to why, after Moore had opted for the Family Group, he then set aside the terms of his commission and produced a tense, angular *Reclining Figure* (1951). He had made a life-size *Family Group* for the Barclay School at Stevenage (1948–9) and would make another for the Civic Square of Harlow New Town. Both these sites are embedded in the day to day fabric of society; the values proclaimed by the two groups are those which cement communities together. On the other hand, the Festival of Britain was a national celebration, an event far removed from the daily realities of local government and education. The South Bank exhibition was, as far as was possible in 1951, a reversal of normality: it was the product of an austerity culture given over to carnival. For this context, an elemental female symbol of energy and vitality was surely more appropriate than a reiteration of civic virtues in the form of another family group.

Epstein chose to represent Discovery or Adventure. His golden bronze figure, *Youth Advancing* (1949–50), was placed on the edge of a landscaped pool behind the Homes and Garden Pavilion. The life-size nude, in bright metal, striding forward with outstretched hands, has intimations of the Risen Christ or at least a being of much greater import than simply a sculpture over a garden pool. In its rather incongruous situation it was incorporated into the picturesque planning of the South Bank[36] which was laid out, in contrast with the Beaux Arts symmetry and grand vistas of nineteenth-century international exhibitions, in small, semi-enclosed areas with deliberately broken sightlines, so that each work of art acted as a local focus, rather than a distant climax.

Hepworth's stone group, *Contrapuntal Forms* (1951) (fig. 103), was her first public commission. After the muted reception of her Venice Biennale exhibition in 1950, it was an important vindication of her work by an official agency. Her contract made no stipulations as to subject matter or site, though the caveat that the sculpture would be placed in the nearby LCC exhibition in Battersea Park if it proved unsuitable for the South Bank reads as a warning not to revert to the severely abstract mode of her pre-war work, on which her reputation was founded. The massive, over life-size monoliths make slight concessions to the human form but not enough to have placed the group in the category of popular artworks.

Hepworth was at first determined to make a site-specific work[37] and, on accepting a position near the Dome of Discovery, previously rejected by Moore and Epstein, indicated that while she had a very clear concept of the work from which she was unwilling to depart, the site would necessitate doubling its size to ten feet high. Although she later reduced this to eight feet, six inches, the cost of an assistant, tools, scaffolding and the decision to use Irish Bluestone rather than Hoptonwood stone considerably increased the value of the commission. The finished work, now in Harlow New Town, remains a tribute to the extraordinary patience of Philip James, as revealed in their almost daily correspondence.

Frank Dobson's *Woman with Fish* (1951), an uncontroversial sculpture in the manner of Maillol, shown in the Battersea Park exhibition, completed the major commissions. The Arts Council's minor commissions were divided between artists like Karin Jonzen, whose work was in the classical tradition of Maillol and Dobson, and those who would soon be associated with the 'geometry of fear' aesthetic. The distinction is exemplified by Jonzen's *A Dance Begins* (1951) (fig. 104) and Eduardo Paolozzi's *The Cage* (fig. 88), a rough, open construction in plaster-coated wire mesh which proclaimed its allegiance to the *art brut* aesthetic.[38] In its disdain both for the conventions of the gallery and any possible formulation of public art it testified to the Arts Council's determined eclecticism. The Council

103. Barbara Hepworth, *Contrapuntal Forms*, 1951. Irish blue limestone, 102 in. high. Harlow New Town.

104. Karin Jonzen, *A Dance Begins*, 1950–1. Walker Art Gallery, Liverpool.

insisted that these sculptures should only be exhibited as a group, effectively denying them a function as public art, although the Festival authorities wished to place some of them on the South Bank. As a result they were shown in the RBA Galleries, thus sustaining the Council's determination that art demonstrate its separation from the themes of the exhibition.

The proliferation of contemporary art on the South Bank and in Battersea Park prompted critics to reassess the relationship between art and the built environment.[39] David Sylvester's comments in *The Studio* anticipated some of the ephemeral, light-hearted public art of the 1980s. He found little to praise in the most prominent works, such as Moore's and Epstein's,[40] where the demands of public art had taken second place to the artists' preferences, although the occasion called for work made for specific sites and stated purposes.[41] Dwelling on the purpose of the commissions, Sylvester, like many of his colleagues, singled out the Skylon and Richard Huws's elegant bucket fountain near the Sea and Ships pavilion as models for public art. The principal requirement of public art, he concluded, was accessibility, achieved in these instances by adapting high art forms[42] and favouring wit and imagination over originality to produce objects not for contemplation but for impact.

David Baxandall reached a similar conclusion when he reviewed '60 Paintings for '51', a touring exhibition devised by Philip James for the nationwide Festival. He recognised a rare opportunity for the Arts Council to support the leading edge of contemporary art and suggested that it might encourage corporate patrons to purchase works of art for their buildings.[43] James attributed the success of '60 Paintings' partly to the Council's insistence on a minumum size of forty by sixty inches, then an unusually large scale. No less important was the awareness of artists of the opportunity to make a new type of painting to hang 'in a new church, a modern liner, the offices of the National Coal Board, the hotel lounges of British Railways, the waiting-rooms of airports, the foyers of cinemas'.[44]

James was not in a position to admit that some painters failed to come to terms with the demands of an unfamiliar scale. In his *Aquarian Nativity – Child of the Age* (1951) (fig. 105), the largest painting in the exhibition, Hitchens enthusiastically expanded the format which he habitually used for landscape painting. Applied to an involved mythological programme,[45] it produced an incoherent composition, though the painting was among the five prizewinners. Baxandall, enthusiastic, like most commentators, about the creativity of the event, considered its implications for painting in public spaces. Like Sylvester, he felt that accessibility was paramount, that a public site must preclude the kind of 'private fantasy' that lay behind Hitchens's canvas.[46]

Sadly the Festival did little to encourage commissions for modern public art. It offered models from reworkings of the monument to cheerful frivolity, which could be read literally or as highly-charged metaphors. Content apart, the South Bank site provided an unmatched opportunity to explore the potential of art to define and limit open spaces, to identify buildings and assist the flow of crowds. The opportunity, though, was missed; the issues were skirted, while majority taste and influential architects continued to prefer traditional swags and garlands to controversial contemporary art and its demands on building design. Indeed, it proved difficult to give away some of the pieces made for the South Bank[47] and many works were destroyed, along with the buildings that had housed them, after the exhibition closed, in what now appears to have been an act of vindictive vandalism by the incoming Tory government.[48] The only building to survive, other than the Royal Festival Hall, was Jane Drew's Riverside Restaurant, which remained in place for another ten years. Free-standing sculpture fared best and many of the commissioned pieces can be tracked down in museums and, occasionally, public spaces, around the country. Very few of the reliefs and murals escaped the demolition gangs, though rare survivals, such as John Piper's vast external mural for the Homes and Gardens pavilion, are still in storage.

105. Ivon Hitchens, *Aquarian Nativity – Child of the Age*, 1951. Oil and wax on canvas, 83 × 223 in. University College, London.

THE 'UNKNOWN POLITICAL PRISONER' COMPETITION

Public art, brought to prominence by the Festival, remained an issue of compelling theoretical interest, despite the reluctance of corporate patrons to come to terms with modernism. The terms of the debate were complicated by the 'Unknown Political Prisoner' competition of 1953. As so often, it was John Berger who provided the most penetrating commentary on the event. Attacking the idealism which demanded art's disengagement from daily life, he contended that 'All works of art, within their immediate context, are bound directly or indirectly to be weapons: only after a considerable passage of time, when the context has changed, can they be viewed objectively as *objets d'art*. Also any artist who treated this subject purely aesthetically would obviously betray it . . .'[49] Berger equated ideological neutrality with fashionable abstract art, a synthesis which he condemned as morally bankrupt, dismissing it as 'the "official" modern art of the West'. The commitment to abstraction of most of the artists who entered for the competition was one of Berger's principal reasons for considering it to have been a 'total failure'.[50]

The detailed organisation of the competition was undertaken within the ICA by Anthony Kloman, an American who had joined the Institute as Director of Planning in May 1951,[51] with a brief to render it financially viable. He returned from a trip to the United States to take up the post with the suggestion that the Institute organise an international sculpture competition for a monument on the theme of the Unknown Political Prisoner, to be financed by American industrialists.[52] The immediate response was to reject the scheme, which seemed over-ambitious and difficult to organise. More ominous were the threat to the Institute's treasured independence and the mystery surrounding the financial arrangements: only Herbert Read, Roland Penrose and Eric Gregory[53] were allowed to know the identity of the backers. The decision, taken with considerable misgivings on Read's part, to become involved in the competition can only have been made in the hope of alleviating the chronic underfunding which recurrently threatened the Institute's existence. A rare opportunity to stage a major international exhibition, with the promise of widespread publicity, was a strong additional attraction for a small and exclusive organisation.

Nominally under the control of a sub-committee chaired by Kloman,[54] the competition was in effect conceived and organised independently of the Institute. Kloman, working in separate, adjacent premises, formed the sole link between sponsors and participants. It is not possible to uncover every link in the chain of funding for the competition, but it has been established that the immediate source of money for prizes and expenses was John Hay Whitney, later US Ambassador to Britain.[55] This would be unremarkable were there not circumstantial evidence that suggests a complicity between Whitney and the administrators of CIA funds clandestinely used to promote cultural undertakings. In 1967 Whitney's family trust was revealed to be one of several used as conduits by the CIA to channel these funds.[56] It is not clear to what extent the originators of trusts were aware of the use that was made of their money, but Whitney's affiliations suggest that there would have been no clash between his intentions and those of the CIA over the 'Unknown Political Prisoner' competition. Robert Burstow, who had access to Whitney's private papers, has found convincing evidence that Whitney was more closely involved with the competition than had previously been supposed. Nevertheless, the evidence for direct CIA involvement remains circumstantial.[57]

The years of denial, prevarication and mystification over the source of the funds and the disinclination of historians to acknowledge the competition as first and foremost a generator of 'political art' are not the least curious aspects of an event which is still not fully clarified. The entire undertaking may well have been an ingenious exercise in Cold War propaganda, an area in which culture was frequently invoked, as officers of the British Council were acutely aware. Among the major European powers, only Britain offered the ideal conditions for staging the competition, since only the British refused to countenance the idea of political art and insisted on inviolate artistic autonomy as a precondition of creativity.

Everywhere but in Britain, where it was presented as a humanitarian gesture of homage,[58] the competition was understood to be a politically motivated enterprise which sought to rewrite the history of the Second World War as an East–West confrontation: the monument, never built, was to have been sited on a hill in West Berlin. The rules of the competition, which required entries to be submitted by country rather than by individuals, enforced a strong undercurrent of nationalism. Acknowledging the event's unspoken premises, no eastern bloc country took part.

The announcement of the competition in January 1952 produced an astonishingly wide response, with an entry of 2,000 maquettes, rather than the forecast 400–500.[59] As a result, preliminary contests were held in each participating country with local judges. Thirty-three maquettes selected from the total British entry, together with the twelve chosen to enter the final stage of the International Competition,[60] were exhibited at the New Burlington Galleries in January 1953; the final International Exhibition opened at the Tate Gallery in March.

The first prize of £3,500, then a very substantial sum, was won by Reg Butler (fig. 106). Hepworth, Naum Gabo, Antoine Pevsner and Mirko Baldasella were awarded equal second prizes. In the final tally, Britain and the United States each claimed three major prizes, France and Italy two and Switzerland and Australia/New Zealand one each. No practising sculptors or architects sat on the International Jury, which was made up of four gallery directors, five writers on art, including Read, and the wife of the Australian Minister for External Affairs, who is said to have been appointed at Kloman's request and to have asked for a reconsideration of the judging at a late stage.[61] It appears that the jury was appointed with a view to diplomatic balance and that the allocation of prizes was also a diplomatic exercise, though the accusations of horse-trading over second places, even if confirmed, would hardly be unusual among international juries.[62]

The most surprising episode in the drama was the destruction of Butler's maquette by Lazlo Szilvassy, a Hungarian refugee, in full view of visitors and the Tate's officials the day after the exhibition opened to the public. Szilvassy proclaimed his motive in a prepared statement: 'Those unknown political prisoners have been and still are human beings. To reduce them – the memory of the dead and the suffering of the living – into scrap metal is just as much a crime as it was to reduce them into ashes or scrap. It is an absolute lack of humanism.'[63]

Not only had a self-declared victim of political oppression denounced the winning work, but his status clarified the competition's essentially ideological nature. As a result, most commentators immediately condemned it as a promotion of political art. The *Daily Worker* provided the most accurate assessment: 'The Unknown Political Prisoner competition resolved itself into an American attempt to embroil sculptors in the Cold War. It has been greeted with coolness by the public partly for that reason and partly because the style of the sculpture favoured has no meaning for the public.'[64]

106. Reg Butler, *Working Model for the Unknown Political Prisoner*, 1955–6. Bronze, iron and plaster, $87\frac{5}{8} \times 34\frac{5}{8} \times 33\frac{5}{8}$ in. Tate Gallery, London.

The entries were seen collectively as 'a triumph for abstraction',[65] though it was left to a French writer to spell out the cause of British distaste for the affair. With the comment: 'l'art abstrait en Angleterre étant consideré comme l'émanation d'esprits socialisants or même communisants',[66] the equation of abstract art with

Left-wing politics was made explicit. Local press reports, which concentrated on the art rather than the event, were uniformly unenthusiastic, ranging from the extreme, if popular view that 'modern art, like the atomic bomb, is a dangerous innovation'[67] to the more measured conclusion that 'It is beyond question that the majority of people in this country see little to admire in this work. Quite a number are actively irritated that such a production can be taken seriously and that it can bring its originator substantial economic reward.'[68]

Butler's maquette was generally understood to be abstract and was therefore considered inappropriate as a monument to the virtues of western liberal human- ism. This facile interpretation ignored the rich symbolism of the maquette, which has been exhaustively analysed by Robert Burstow. The tower carried connota- tions of a trap or enclosure; the watchtower so familiar to former prisoners of war, perhaps evoked instruments of torture; it has, additionally, been interpreted as a metaphor for the Crucifixion.[69] In contrast, the soaring antenna at the apex of the maquette recalled the Skylon, with its promise of flight into the freedom of space. The horizontal platform, tripod legs and lateral extensions of the tower resembled another South Bank sculpture, Butler's own *Birdcage*. Both made unmistakeable references to the human body, transformed in the tower into a dual image, a metaphor simultaneously for dominance and surveillance and for the endurance and aspiration of the observed.

At the tower's base stand three tiny watchers, whose fragility poignantly paralleled the situation of ordinary people caught between the political colossi of the Cold War. Their straining, upturned heads and extended necks were indebted to the anguished creatures in Bacon's *Three Studies for Figures at the Base of a Crucifixion* (1944) (fig. 79).[70] Neither maquette nor painting referred directly to war, politics or religion, yet, against the grain of convention, both were read in these terms by contemporaries. Such readings are scarcely acknowl- edged except by implication, yet paradoxically the works to which they were attached are now considered to be among the most eloquent icons of the period.

The divergence between the verdict of the International Jury and the virtually unanimous rejection of the maquette by the public is a measure of the gulf between popular taste and innovatory art. By combining the unfamiliar technique of welded iron with an image of mute, defenceless women overshadowed by a towering symbol of technological power, Butler produced a distinctively modern work, which was open to a quasi-literal reading and was considerably less radical than some of the maquettes which were awarded second prizes. The jury was thus able to compromise, to avoid proclaiming either an overtly figurative work, which would have been a popular verdict, but would have carried uneasy overtones of socialist realism; or a completely non-figurative piece which would have been even more roundly derided than Butler's entry and would have elicited references to the left-wing associations of abstraction.

The ICA, which had hoped to gain so much from the competition, at least emerged untouched by the chicanery of the promoters, who exploited its idealism and financial weakness. The promoters' first and irreversible mistake was to misjudge the ICA's status; far from adding lustre to the competition, it was unknown outside a very small section of the art world and was almost totally ignored by both public and critics. The competition and exhibition were accounted failures[71] and Butler's maquette was never erected in its intended monumental form.

THE LONDON COUNTY COUNCIL

The Council's role as art patron originated indirectly in plans developed after the Blitz for the reconstruction of London. The need to replace the Victorian slums that disfigured the East End had long been recognised, though it was bomb damage that stimulated Lord Reith, the wartime Minister of Works, to commission Abercrombie and Forshaw's 1943 *County of London Plan*, on which the rebuilding of the capital was based. Priority was naturally given to rehousing the hundreds of thousands of people whose homes had been destroyed or damaged. Here the LCC shared responsibility with local borough councils, with an inevitable concentration on the East End, though the Alton estate at Roehampton in west London was its flagship estate.

Schools were the second most pressing need. The Council's new primary schools were initially based on a model devised by the Hertfordshire county architects to cope with the demands of the 1944 Education Act for radically improved premises and greatly increased numbers. It produced elegant, light buildings, appropriate symbols of postwar planning, in stark contrast to the forbidding Victorian structures that they replaced.[72] The schools were central to community planning, since Abercrombie and Forshaw took the population estimated to support a primary school, between 6,000 and 10,000 people, as a basic social unit. Each one would constitute a neighbourhood, with its own school, pubs, churches, shopping centre and open space, all separated by zoning from industrial areas.[73] A cluster of such neighbourhoods would make up a larger community. Acknowledging the strength of old networks of extended family and neighbours, the planners of the 1940s were committed to sustaining the ethos of old communities in new building complexes.

Lansbury Estate in Poplar, part of which formed the Festival of Britain's 'Live Architecture' exhibit, was one of the first to be built and remains as evidence of how radically the new architecture of the East End differed from what had preceded it. Blocks of flats spaced to allow light and air in wide streets, houses with small gardens, pedestrian areas and the spacious market square surrounded with shops were admirable social architecture, but they could not replicate the sense of identity established by old patterns of behaviour.

By the mid-1950s the most urgent reconstruction work was complete and resources could be allocated to embellishment. The success of the LCC's first two open-air sculpture exhibitions[74] indicated at least a certain level of grass-roots support for art in public places. The siting of sculpture in the South Bank Exhibition to identify buildings and punctuate open spaces may also have stimulated consideration of a long-term role for art in community architecture. Encouragingly, a successful example of a public art programme already existed in the form of the pioneering 'per cent for art' scheme, under which a percentage of total building costs was allocated to art. It operated in Hertfordshire's primary schools between 1949 and 1953.[75]

In 1956 a scheme was initiated within the LCC to provide works of art for its buildings and public spaces which, by the time the Council was abolished in 1965, had provided approximately seventy works. Its weakness was that most members of the LCC had only a rudimentary knowledge of art and were obliged to rely heavily on Philip James and Gabriel White for advice on artists, cost and the appropriate type of art for a given site. Inevitably, lay and expert taste clashed and compromises had to be sought, since the Arts Council advisors, however tactful, were felt to dominate the commission programme, which resulted in confrontations with councillors who considered themselves to be the true representatives of working-class interests and tastes.

In practice this meant that although LCC members acknowledged that a Moore sculpture would bring lustre to any site, they tended to be antagonistic to modernist works by less famous artists. For their part, the Arts Council advisors, whose preference was to promote modernist-oriented art of high aesthetic quality, seem to have taken little or no account of the tastes of local residents. Formal public consultation on the siting of works of art was not even a consideration in the late 1950s, and would in any case have been at odds with the Arts Council's educational principles,[76] but it is clear that strong local preferences did exist and could be compatible with the Council's aesthetic standards. Ten years after the disappearance of a bronze group of swans commissioned from Gertrude Hermes for a pond at Ashburton Estate in Wandsworth, residents recalled it with appreciative regret.

It is much more difficult, given the controversy that had already arisen in connection with the LCC's exhibitions,[77] to understand why the question of style was not addressed until it had become a problem. From one point of view, style might be determined by site and function: the neo-classical reclining female figure commissioned by the LCC from Karel Vogel in the late 1950s was startlingly anachronistic, but chimed perfectly with the Greek Revival church of St Peter's in Hammersmith, in front of which it still stands. The sculpture is a prominent feature of the north side of the Cromwell Road extension and its awkward stance, with arms and upper torso partly raised from the plinth, is explicable as a visual link to the road, leading the eye round the slight bend on which it is placed.

Many LCC commissions were not controversial; there was a tendency to favour younger Academicians like Siegfried Charoux, whose chunky, simplified figures were acceptable across a wide spectrum of opinion. His unproblematically realist group of two men in animated conversation seated on a bench, *The Neighbours* (1959), is set among blocks of flats on the Quadrant Estate in Highbury, where it presents a model for good community relations. In a similar vein, Franta Belsky's *The Lesson* (1956) (fig. 107), a mother supporting a toddler, stands at a road junction on the Avebury Estate in Stepney, where it marks out a small garden area as a meeting place for women and children. On the new estates, with their neat street patterns and clearly designated communal areas, art could contribute to a sense of locale and create a visual focus in repetitive surroundings. In these circumstances, certain stylistic conditions recur and seem to have been considered essential: the works in question are easily identifiable, close to lifesize and show people engaged in conventional activities.[78]

Despite an elaborate process of selection and vetting of maquettes and sketches by the LCC, no soundings were taken among the inhabitants of the estates. Consequently, works of art often seem to have been allocated with an eye to outsiders as much as to the local people. The Stifford Estate in Stepney and the Brandon Estate in Kennington replaced areas of acute urban blight and enabled large numbers of people to be rehoused in immeasurably improved conditions. In order to register the importance of the estates, to signal the Council's regard for their inhabitants and, perhaps, to enhance its own prestige, each estate was allocated a Moore sculpture. In Stepney the monumental *Draped Seated Woman* (1957–8) (fig. 108) rests forlornly on a hummock in a wind-swept plot of grass.[79] The *Two*

107. Franta Belsky, *The Lesson*, 1956 in London County Council Open Air Exhibition, Holland Park London 1957. Metal-coated concrete, 64 in. high.

108. Henry Moore, *Draped Seated Woman*, 1957–8. Bronze, 73 in. high. Edn. 6.

Piece Reclining Figure No. 3 (1961) in Kennington is more successfully sited as the visual focus of a semicircle of buildings. A third Moore sculpture, the *Two Piece Reclining Figure No. 1* (1959), was placed by the Council in front of the Manresa Road site of Chelsea School of Art, where it related closely to the building, both symbolically and in terms of scale.

Moore was asked to sell a cast of *The Falling Warrior* (1956–7) to the Council for the Alton Estate at Roehampton, but refused, possibly because he disliked the site. After several abortive attempts to commission sculpture for the estate, two bronzes were purchased. Lynn Chadwick's *The Watchers* (1960) (fig. 109) stands at the head of a long grassy slope, overlooking Richmond Park, demarcating a viewpoint and emphasising the coherence of the site plan. In contrast a great chunky *Bull* (1961) by Robert Clatworthy stands beside a block of flats, a witty reminder that Roehampton is in London and that in the city, nature is a matter of artifice.

The demarcation of prestigious buildings is an obvious function for public art, so that when the National Recreation Centre was completed at Crystal Palace in 1962, the Council allocated £10,000 beyond the annual commission budget to acquire a work by Reg Butler. The artist produced a maquette,[80] an armless female nude with shoulders hunched forward and head bent into her chest. It was unexceptional in Butler's oeuvre but lacked any obvious connection with sport or the purpose of the building. It met with such opposition from members of the LCC that the commission was cancelled and the money used to purchase a life-like black marble gorilla from David Wynne. Placed near the entrance to Crystal Palace Zoo, which it unequivocally signposts, it is reputed to be enormously popular.

Objections to Butler's maquette arose because, far from signalling the site, it had not even a symbolic connection with it. In general, the most sustained opposition to the Arts Council's proposals for commissions came from the Education Department of the LCC, whose chairperson expressed a deep antagonism to abstract art. A cement relief, *Descending Forms* (1957), made by Robert Adams for Eltham Green Secondary School, became a focus of controversy. The sculpture distinguishes an otherwise undecorated theatre block at a prestigious school, but was considered to be drab and unappealing to children. Oddly, no objections were raised to Oliffe Richmond's *Striding Man* (1962) (fig. 110), a great headless bronze figure in the courtyard of Dulwich High School for Boys (formerly William Penn Secondary School), that might well have been considered disturbing.

Murals were the favoured form of art for primary schools, where colour and decorative qualities outweighed questions of style. As with sculpture commissions, no general guide lines were laid down and artists were left free to work as they chose. There were no common features between John Verney's bright Miró-like mural at Lewisham Primary, the complicated tactile panel constructed by Francis Carr at Holman Hunt Primary or the abstract mosaic of fragments of letters and numbers designed by Robyn Denny for Abbey Wood Primary, though all of them proved popular with the recipients.

As an undertaking which sought to employ contemporary, often young, artists to provide art for places and buildings not previously considered worthy of it, the LCC's commission programme was undoubtedly successful. It was an undertaking in accordance with the Council's committment to raising the living standards of Londoners within the Welfare State. Despite the LCC's inexperience in the visual arts and the Arts Council's lack of sociological insight, the programme

109. Lynn Chadwick, *The Watchers*, 1960. Bronze, 92 in. high. Edn. 3.

110. Oliffe Richmond, *Striding Man*, 1961. Bronze, 72 in. high. Dulwich High School for Boys, London.

overall was a bold attempt to provide public art with new social and architectural roles, where it could function both as a symbolic and a physical marker of places.

It is evident that the programme worked best when it adopted the aesthetic middle ground and placed works of art where they were most obviously needed for visual reasons. Verney's and Denny's murals, lightening and embellishing the entrances to the schools for which they were made, are obvious cases in point. It is extremely revealing that probably no other commission received as much enthusiastic press coverage as the play sculpture made by Trevor Tennant for a site in Limehouse. A cement reclining figure, derived closely from Moore's work, was placed in a sandpit for children to climb on. Here the sculpture married practical function with modish aesthetics and, emptied of esoteric content, appeared to confirm that high art had no more value than a children's climbing frame.

HENRY MOORE

To focus on Moore as an exemplary public artist is clearly to do a gross injustice to other sculptors, like Wheeler, Dobson and, especially, Epstein. As a foreigner and a Jew, as well as one of the most fearless and versatile modernists of the century, Epstein attracted extraordinary hostility which he deflected from younger colleagues like Moore. There can be no doubt that Epstein suffered greatly from the ignorance and prejudice that were directed against his public works until the last few years of his life. After the controversies over *Rima* and the sculptures for the London Underground Headquarters in the 1920s, he was not offered another public commission until 1949, when he was invited to take part in the South Bank Exhibition.[81]

This was followed by a flurry of prestigious commissions which together reveal a sensitivity to the demands of architecture perhaps unsurpassed in the twentieth century. The *Madonna and Child* (1950–2) (fig. 111) on the facade of the Convent of the Holy Child Jesus in Cavendish Square was the most widely acclaimed. A sensitive articulation of the bridge which links the two blocks of the facade, it is at the same time a discreet but unequivocal announcement of the nature and function of the convent building. Much more dramatically, Epstein's *St Michael and the Devil* (1955–8) fulfils a similar role for Coventry Cathedral, where the group is posed on the wall flanking the entrance to the building. Though the relationship between the two figures is not entirely satisfactory the triumphant pose of the saint proclaims the symbolic role of the Cathedral as a marker of a resurgent society. Sadly, Epstein, aware of advancing age and frailty, wrote to his daughter in 1956 that 'it is all coming too late'.[82] He died three years later, after a brief and belated period of acclaim and recognition.

During this time Moore had risen to prominence as an artist extraordinarily attuned to the nuances of social discourse. It is this, together with his unparalleled institutional career, especially with the British Council, that sets Moore apart as the leading public artist of the postwar period. Moore presents a paradoxical case of an artist deeply reluctant to undertake commissions, though best pleased when his work was placed out of doors and thus usually in the public domain. The 1940s was a crucial decade, when he emerged from an esoteric avant garde to become an articulator of national aspiration. During these years he began to address generalised social themes through monumental figure sculptures. His work became more representational and more accessible to the non-specialist viewer.

The bronze *Family Group* at Barclay School, Stevenage (1948–9) was followed by the reclining figure for the Festival, the Time-Life *Screen* (1953) and the *Draped Reclining Figure* (1952–3), the *King and Queen* (1952–3), the *Upright Motives* (1955–6), the *Warrior with Shield* (1953–4) (fig. 112) and *Falling Warrior* (1956–7) and, in 1958, the *UNESCO Reclining Figure*. Some were started with no client in mind and later purchased for public sites but all were images apt for public appropriation.

Julian Stallabras has demonstrated the significance of certain important aspects of Moore's work for the postwar ideology of the family, which was itself the foundation of the Welfare State. There was, as he puts it, a 'congruence of Moore's work with social policy'.[83] With the return of ex-servicemen to the labour market and, for childless women, the end of industrial conscription, women, particularly those who were married, were encouraged to stand aside, to return to hearth and home. Many were glad to do so, an inclination much encouraged towards the end of the decade by a government anxious to boost a birthrate in sharp decline following the end of the wartime baby boom. This reversal of women's employment prospects was facilitated by the abrupt closure of many local authority nurseries shortly after the end of the war, by the provisions of the 1947 National Insurance Act, which militated against married women working[84] and by the perception that whereas men were considered antisocial if they did not work, women were held to be more respectable if they were exclusively devoted to the home.[85]

In this context Moore's *Family Groups* assume a new cogency. They originated before the war in a suggestion by the architect, Walter Gropius, that Moore make a sculpture for a Village College that Gropius was to design at Impington near

111. Jacob Epstein, *Madonna and Child*, 1950–2. Lead, 153 in. high. Convent of the Holy Child Jesus, Cavendish Square, London.

112. Henry Moore,
Warrior with Shield,
1953–4. Bronze,
60 in. high. Edn. 5.

Cambridge. The artist proposed a family group[86] and though the scheme foundered for lack of finance, it was revived in 1944 when Moore produced a series of drawings and maquettes of family groups. However, these were rejected by the Education Authority and it was the New Towns, with their emphasis on the family as the kernel of the community, that were finally to provide sites for Moore's *Family Groups*.

Under the Hertfordshire 'per cent for art' scheme, Moore was invited in 1947 to make a sculpture for the Barclay Secondary School, designed by F. R. Yorke and Partners. He took the opportunity to make a large scale bronze group, thus fulfilling a long held ambition.[87] The bronze stands against a baffle wall, in a logical and prominent position which nevertheless failed to satisfy Moore since he felt that it prevented the work being seen as fully free-standing.

An opportunity for a fully independent work occurred when the newly formed Harlow Arts Trust offered its first commission to Moore in 1954.[88] One of the 1944 Impington maquettes was chosen as a model for the massive *Family Group* in pale grey Hadene stone (fig. 98).[89] It was unveiled two years later by Sir Kenneth Clark in a landscape setting, but unfortunately fell victim to vandalism and was moved onto a high plinth in the Civic Square, a more fitting symbolic site at the heart of the town, but one where it all too easily merged into its grey surroundings.[90]

Moore's position as the leading public artist of a socially conscious society was paralleled in the international arena through the dissemination of his ideologically sensitive works by the British Council. The exhibitions that first brought him to the attention of a wide foreign public, a show of drawings at the Buchholz Gallery in New York in May 1943 and a retrospective at the Museum of Modern Art three years later, did not involve the Council, though in 1947, in an effort to promote British interests in Australia it sent a reduced version of the Museum of Modern Art exhibition on a tour of state galleries.

It was as the winner of the Grand Prize for Sculpture at the first postwar Venice Biennale in 1948 that Moore was acclaimed as an artist of international stature, Britain's riposte to Picasso. The Biennale exhibition, a retrospective of thirty-six sculptures and thirty-three drawings, dwelt particularly on Moore's depiction of the nurturing female body and culminated with a large group of maquettes for the Northampton *Madonna and Child* and the *Family Group*. The emphasis was in keeping with the Biennale's spirit of reconciliation, expressed by the Secretary General, Rodolfo Pallucchini, who wrote with a sincerity not entirely concealed by rhetoric: 'Art invites all people, beyond national frontiers, beyond ideological barriers in a language which must invite them into a humanist understanding and universal family.'[91]

Moore's exhibition received enormous and enthusiastic publicity, in contrast with the British ambassador's tepid comment in a letter to a colleague that 'the Henry Moore sculpture is a matter of individual taste and, although I am too old to enjoy it, I was glad to notice that all the many people who like or profess to like modern art were wildly enthusiastic.'[92] It was a not uncommon response to contemporary art by a member of the Foreign Office, tempered by a pragmatic recognition that Moore's work was a diplomatic asset that amounted to a statement of national achievement and cultural continuity, a point underlined by the rapturously acclaimed Turner exhibition which accompanied it. Seeking to capitalise on this success, Lilian Somerville set in train a more extensive Moore retrospective which toured Europe in 1949–50.

It differed from the Venice exhibition in that it included large scale works and casts such as the *Three Standing Figures* and the Stevenage *Family Group*. Photographs of the Northampton *Madonna* and the Dartington Hall *Memorial Figure* filled inevitable lacunae and provided additional evidence of Moore's popularity at home. Reception in Brussels was deeply divided,[93] though in Paris, 'the contemporary art capital of the world', Frank McEwen felt that Moore's exhibition had significantly weakened a long-standing resistance to foreign art.[94] In Hamburg the exhibition opened when Anglo-German relations were particularly strained[95] and a member of the Control Commission reported that the exhibition was badly attended, though two artists walked from Berlin to see it.[96] Local critics examined it eagerly for the insights it might hold into German culture and society.[97]

Late in 1948, in the course of a visit to Britain sponsored by the Council, Angelos Procopiou, Professor of Art History at the University of Athens, had proposed a Moore exhibition in the city. It finally took place in 1951. The schedule allowed only a modest assemblage, though it included maquettes for the *Family Groups* and the by now ubiquitous cast of the *Three Standing Figures*, as well as drawings and photographs. The exhibition was received with vast enthusiasm, matched by 'a torrent of indiscriminate abuse' from nationalist publications,[98] once again suggesting that, like the Unknown Political Prisoner competition, it was only in Britain that Moore's work was understood to occupy a notional space outside ideology. The Athens exhibition was particularly significant for Moore as it enabled him to visit Greece where, relatively late in his career, he came to terms for the first time with ancient Greek sculpture, having previously always been more attracted by archaic or tribal art.

Later the same year, the British Council took a group of drawings and maquettes[99] to the Haus am Waldsee in the American sector of Berlin as the official British contribution to the Berlin Festival, in a politically significant gesture of reconciliation. The exhibition travelled on to the Albertina in Vienna, where the comments of the Director, Dr Benesch, vividly indicate the significance of western European art and Moore's humanism in Cold War cultural politics: 'We are really a long way east. It is vital that we keep open our relations with the great art centres of the west. If our museums are to lose this contact, then that is one more position that we surrender to the Powers of Darkness.'[100]

While this extraordinary sequence of solo exhibitions travelled the world, a less formal type of regular outdoor sculpture show, modelled on the 1948 Battersea event, was growing in popularity. The first was held in 1949 at Sonsbeek, near Arnhem and was considered so important, not least as a signal of international harmony at the site of a bloody battle not many years earlier, that the Fine Art Committee gave it a very high priority. The four sculptures that constituted the British section[101] included Moore's 1937 *Sculpture* and the cast of *Three Standing Figures*.

A biennial was initiated at Middelheim, near Antwerp, shortly after Sonsbeek, while others were established at Varese and Hamburg. Generally they were organised in international sections and held in public parks. They proved extremely popular with the public and with artists, who welcomed the opportunities to show abroad and the sales that resulted.[102] Politically the exhibitions symbolised aspirations towards western European unity and reconciliation with former enemies. The Fine Art Department vigorously encouraged them, not least as it was required to make only a minimal financial contribution,[103] though reception was, as always, minutely scrutinised.

Moore was the only British artist invited to participate in the Ruhr Miners' Festival at Recklinghausen in 1952, in an exhibition entitled 'Mankind and design in the modern world today'.[104] Held at the heart of the major German industrial area, the festival was a celebration both of the worker and of the foundation of the new European economy. Following reports of an overwhelming success,[105] Moore continued to take part in the festival and two years later, in 1954, contributed the Barclay School *Family Group*, with a *Warrior* maquette, to an exhibition called 'Testimonies to European Unity'. We may ask why Moore enjoyed such a uniquely privileged position, ubiquitous in exhibitions for which he was always the principal selector of his own work. The answer does not lie entirely in his international reputation.

German critics of Moore's 1949–50 European exhibition understood the skeletal *Standing Figure* (1950) and the 1950 *Reclining Figure* as signifiers of the dehumanisation of a machine-obsessed culture intent on producing ever more powerful weapons of destruction.[106] The *Three Standing Figures*,[107] the two large *Family Groups*,[108] the *King and Queen*[109] and the *Draped Reclining Figure*,[110] also repeatedly exhibited throughout Europe and beyond in the 1950s, are, in contrast, affirmative images, reassuring in their static monumentality. The values that they proclaim: the centrality of the family, women's dignity, the respect due to benign authority, the survival of tradition and, especially in the *Warrior* sculptures, the heroism of suffering, are those of western European culture, in whose defence the war had been fought and the Cold War sustained.

That no ideological claims were made for these works underlines their import; the most effective propaganda, as the British Council had long been aware,[111] is not recognised as such and Moore's sculpture was exhibited simply as the recent work of a major artist, which took its place in a prolific and varied practice. It is clear however, as German critics quickly recognised, that his work was uniquely apposite to postwar Europe, not least because the artist was so demonstrably independent, mistrustful of the demands of commissions and active in the arrangement of his own exhibitions.

The mutual benefits to Moore and the Council of their collaboration were immense; his career was given every possible assistance, while the Council gained an unofficial ambassador in the form of a popular and internationally respected figure willing to travel extensively in the service of cultural relations. Perhaps the most telling testimony to the ideological centrality of Moore's work in the culture of the Cold War years is that it was for so long unacknowledged, a now you see it, now you don't situation, in which the freedom to ignore the proffered symbols was the most powerful aspect of the message.

Moore's case serves as a reminder that, while there is no need to justify public art, its flowering in the early postwar years resulted from something more than an access of aesthetic sensibility. Not least among the impulses that stimulated it was the compulsion to reconstruct both buildings and society:

> both the Britain that the Hun has destroyed and the slum and shoddy Britain that we have got to destroy and rebuild because, candidly it's a disgrace to us. The new Britain must be our War Memorial . . . in rebuilding the fine old chuches and halls that have been destroyed, don't let us be too much enslaved by the idea of restoration. It is so much more important to encourage creation by living artists.[112]

War damage, postwar politics, a sense of social justice and a fierce desire for cultural renewal lay behind the reformulation of public art, yet the movement proved inconclusive. Instead, the LCC's solutions of compromised modernism or recourse to a great name were widely adopted. The dilemmas of function and style, brought into prominence by the South Bank exhibition and the 'Unknown Political Prisoner' competition, proved insoluble in the complex pluralism of postwar British society. Berger called for an engaged art, made in response to common feeling for a specific site[113] but, always idealistic, failed to acknowledge the lack of what Lawrence Alloway defined as 'a community of interest'.[114] Had such a communal sense existed on a larger than street-corner level, Alloway felt that it would demand a public art on the model of the fountains by Richard Huws and Paolozzi that he had admired in the South Bank Exhibition. They would constitute a neutral but psychologically sensitive environment for human social activities.

This was, of course, very close to constructionist theories of public art. Pasmore's work at Peterlee, together with the temporary buildings designed for the International Union of Architects Congress in 1961 are justifications of Alloway's somewhat restrictive reading of public art. Despite the widespread prejudice against it, constructionist art admirably fulfilled the often overlooked role of public art as street language, in which it signals and identifies locations and provides easily recognised images for orientation. In a secular society unable to agree on the appropriate form for a modern monument, which arguably had '*no* need of public painting and sculpture',[115] constructionist art, discreetly elegant and unencumbered with symbolic values, has strong claims to have provided some of the most successful examples of all public art in the early postwar period.

NOTES

ABBREVIATIONS

Abbreviations used in the text and the notes are as follows:

AIA Artists International Association
CAS Contemporary Art Society
CEMA Council for the Encouragement of Music and the Arts
COI Central Office of Information
GLC Greater London Council
ICA Institute of Contemporary Arts
LCC London County Council
RAI Royal Anthropological Institute
RBA/RSBA Royal Society of British Artists
TGA Tate Gallery Archive
USIA United States Information Agency
USIS United States Information Service
PRO Public Record Office

NOTES TO INTRODUCTION

1. T. Crosby, 'Experiment in integration', *Architectural Design* November 1961, pp. 480–1.
2. '. . . which is not represented in the statement but which is the acknowledgement of its discursive embeddedness and address, its cultural positionality, its reference to a present time and a specific space' (H. K. Bhabha, *The Location of Culture* London and New York 1994, p. 36). I am grateful to Professor Anthony Chennells for alerting me to Homi Bhabha's book.
3. *Ibid.* p. 36.
4. *Ibid.* p. 1.
5. *Ibid.* p. 37.
6. *Ibid.* p. 36.

NOTES TO CHAPTER I

1. H. Read, 'Foreword', *Wonder and Horror of the Human Head* London 1953, p. 5.
2. R. A. Butler, *The Art of the Possible* London 1971, p. 172.
3. While acknowledging that the high/low distinction is, more often than not, untenable, I have retained it in order to emphasise a difference of intentionality between self-conciously intellectualising practices and those which are equally deliberately populist. However, frequent and diverse examples, from the portraits of Pietro Annigoni to the work of the Independent Group, serve as reminders that the fluidity of high/low boundaries can hardly be over-stressed.
4. P. Hennessy, *Never Again: Britain 1945–51* London 1992, p. 296.
5. 'If we permit, as in the last war, inequality of sacrifice so that at the end the gulf between rich and poor is greater than ever, we shall have failed in our task. If we really wish to build a new world wherein justice, mercy and truth shall replace brute force, wherein equality and good neighbourliness shall take the place of violence, aggression and domination, we must also build a new Britain worthy to lead the world away from anarchy and strife into the paths of peace.' (Clement Attlee, speech to Labour Party Conference, 1939, broadcast early 1940, quoted in Attlee, *As It Happened* London 1954, pp. 106–10).
6. K. Harris, *Attlee* London 1982, p. 180.
7. P. Addison, *Now the War is Over: a Social History of Britain 1945–51* London 1985, p. 56.
8. W. Beveridge, *The Pillars of Security* London 1943, p. 81.
9. '. . . unemployment did not exceed 2 per cent for 20 years after 1945' (M. Pugh, *Women and the Women's Movement in Britain 1914–59* London and Basingstoke 1992, p. 289).
10. C. Barnett, *The Audit of War: the Illusion and Reality of Britain as a Great Nation* London and Basingstoke 1986, p. 264.
11. The winter of 1946–7, the convertibility crisis and, especially, the Korean War and the concomitant rearmament programme (P. Calvocoressi, *The British Experience 1945–75* Harmondsworth 1979, pp. 17–18, 22).
12. At the beginning of 1945 it was expected that the war against Japan would continue into 1946 which, assisted by Roosevelt's goodwill, would have ensured a continuation of Lend-Lease (C. J. Bartlett, *A History of Postwar Britain, 1945–74* London 1977, p. 23).
13. '. . . planted in British public opinion those seeds of anti-Americanism which in spite of the Marshall Plan and the Berlin Airlift bore unwelcome fruit during the Korean War' (Harris, *Attlee* 1982, p. 271).
14. $3,750m. at 2 per cent, with the start of repayment deferred to 1951; there was also an agreement to write off the wartime cost of Lend-Lease; in return the UK consented to end trade discrimination which had favoured the Dominions and to introduce convertibility for the pound by July 1946.
15. The spring of 1946 saw a world grain shortage; Britain had to feed not only her own population but India and the British zone of occupied Germany (Harris, *Attlee* 1982, p. 327).
16. Addison, *Now the War is Over* 1985, p. 55.
17. Harris, *Attlee* 1982, p. 336.
18. 'By the Marshall Plan the USA took upon itself to finance for four years and as an emergency measure the dollar gap created by the incapacity of Europeans to grow or make exportable surpluses to pay for essential imports of food, timber (for housing), fertilisers and other raw materials.' (Calvocoressi, *The British Experience* 1979, p. 17).
19. Hennessy, *Never Again* 1992, p. 294 et seq.
20. *Ibid.* pp. 299–302.
21. *Ibid.* p. 292.
22. By 1959 over 70 per cent of the population possessed television sets; hire purchase debts 'increased by 75 per cent between 1955 and 1959' (Bartlett, *A History of Postwar Britain* 1977, p. 147). Private car ownership doubled between 1955 and 1958 (C. Booker, *The Neophiliacs: a Study of the Revolution in English Life in the Fifties and Sixties* London 1969, p. 132).
23. B. Friedan, *The Feminine Mystique* London 1963.
24. A. Myrdal & V. Klein, *Women's Two Roles: Home and Work* London 1956. That the authors were strongly in favour of the proposition does not modify the attitudes that made the book necessary.
25. Pugh concludes that 'Women's position in the labour force did remain very extensive and, indeed, actually strengthened, during the decade after the war' (*Women and the Women's Movement* 1992, p. 286).
26. J. Stallabras, 'The mother and child theme in the work of Henry Moore' in *Henry Moore, Mother and Child* exh. cat. Henry Moore Foundation and Käthe Kollwitz Museum, Cologne 1992, pp. 13–39.

27. Bartlett, *A History of Postwar Britain* 1977, p. 148.

28. I. Nairn, 'Outrage', *The Architectural Review*, special issue, June 1955.

29. T. Fyvel, 'The stones of Harlow', *Encounter* 6, June 1956, pp. 11–17.

30. Pugh, *Women and the Women's Movement* 1992, pp. 288, 290.

31. J. Morgan, ed., *The Backbench Diaries of Richard Crossman* London 1981, p. 507.

32. David Pryce-Jones describes Eliot's *The Cocktail Party*, first produced for the 1949 Edinburgh Festival and revived in May 1950 in London, as 'a play defending minority culture at a time when the barbarian nomads appeared to have got the upper hand, even to have elected a government of their choice' ('Towards the Cocktail Party – the conservatism of post-war British writing' in M. Sissons & P. French, eds, *The Age of Austerity, 1945–51* London 1963, p. 228).

NOTES TO CHAPTER 2

1. J. Boswell, 'The Artist's Dilemma', *Our Time* 7, 1, August 1947, pp. 4–5.

2. Generally artists were beneficiaries of the art establishment rather than active within it, though Sutherland was a Trustee of the Tate 1948–54; Moore was a Trustee of the Tate 1941–6 and 1949–56 and of the National Gallery 1955–63 and 1964–74; he was a member of CEMA's first art panel and of the Arts Council Visual Arts Panel 1942–9 and 1955–9 and a member of the Arts Council itself from 1963–7 (R. Berthoud, *The Life of Henry Moore* London 1987, p. 202).

3. J. Hayes, *Portraits by Graham Sutherland* exh. cat. National Portrait Gallery, London 1977, no. 76, p. 74.

4. M. Secrest, *Kenneth Clark, a Biography* London 1984, pp. 103–4.

5. '. . . a way out of the virtuous fog of Bloomsbury art' (K. Clark, *Another Part of the Wood, a Self-Portrait* London 1974, p. 254).

6. K. Clark, *The Other Half, a Self-Portrait* London 1977, p. 22.

7. H. Read, 'A nest of gentle artists', *Apollo* September 1962, pp. 536–40.

8. J. L. Martin, B. Nicholson, N. Gabo eds, *Circle: International Survey of Constructive Art* London 1937, p. 6.

9. *Ibid.* p. 8.

10. He was previously Director of Leeds City Art Gallery and the Ruskin Museum in Sheffield. He retired in 1964.

11. J. Rothenstein, *Brave Day, Hideous Night, Autobiography 1939–1965* London 1966, pp. 21–2. Though the Treasury grant of £2,000 trebled within eight years, it remained 'a joke' given the Tate's responsibilities (*Ibid.*, p. 179). Early records of the ICA reveal its hostility to the Tate: a preliminary, unpublished draft of the Institute's Policy Statement issued in 1946 commented that the gallery 'has so far shown no inclination to honour any but octogenarians. The need is simply for an *unofficial* organisation which will make the British public visually and aurally accustomed to the modern idiom.'

12. *Ibid.* pp. 20–1.

13. Organised by the British Council and accompanied by exhibitions of Cézanne watercolours (originated by the Arts Council), with the Massey collection of Modern British painting assembled for the National Gallery of Canada (*Ibid.* p. 176).

14. The Paul Nash memorial exhibition (1948), Moore (1951), Epstein (1952), the Ethel Walker, Frances Hodgkins and Gwen John joint memorial exhibition (1952), Charles Ginner (1953), Sutherland (1953) were all organised with or entirely by the Arts Council.

15. M. Parkin, Obituary, *The Independent* 28 February 1992.

16. J. Rothenstein, *British Art since 1900* London 1962, p. 24.

17. 'I fail, beyond a certain point, to respond to the uncommunicative forms and relationships which constitute at the same time the language and message of abstract art.' (J. Rothenstein, *Modern English Painters* II: *Lewis to Moore* London 1956, 1976, p. 261).

18. *Ibid.* pp. 271–8.

19. H. Read, *A Coat of Many Colours* London 1947, pp. 79–87. In place of Read's Platonic account of abstraction Rothenstein proposed a theory of physical empathy derived from Geoffrey Scott's *The Architecture of Humanism*: 'It is a reasonable account of the matter which certainly cannot be refuted . . . You will look in vain for metaphysical revelations of the structure of reality from Ben Nicholson.' (Rothenstein, *Modern English Painters* II, p. 277).

20. *Ibid.* p. 275.

21. Rothenstein, *Modern English Painters* I: *Sickert to Smith* London 1976, p. 19.

22. M. Yule, '"A place for living art": the Whitechapel Art Gallery, 1952–1968', unpublished MA Report, Courtauld Institute, University of London, 1991. I am indebted to this Report, which is the best source of information on Bryan Robertson's period at the Whitechapel Art Gallery.

23. Pollock's retrospective was held November – December 1958, selected by Frank O'Hara and originated by the International Circulating Exhibitions programme (ICE) at the Museum of Modern Art, New York, based on the 1957 retrospective at the São Paulo Bienal. It toured to Amsterdam, Brussels, Paris and Berlin (S. Tenenbaum, '"A dialectical pretzel", the New American Painting, the Museum of Modern Art and American cultural diplomacy, 1952–1959: revisionism revised', unpublished MA Report, Courtauld Institute, University of London, 1992, App. 1, p. 64).

24. T. Marlow, 'The marketing and impact of New Generation sculpture', unpublished MA Report, Courtauld Institute, University of London, 1988.

25. Eric Gregory (1887–1959) endowed the Gregory Fellowships at Leeds University, was Chairman of Ganymede Prints, a director of *The Burlington Magazine*, Chairman of the Design Research Unit, a committee member of the Contemporary Art Society and governor of Chelsea Polytechnic, St Martin's School of Art and the Bath Academy of Art at Corsham.

26. M. Shelden, *Friends of Promise: Cyril Connolly and the World of Horizon* London 1989, p. 80.

27. *Ibid.* p. 39.

28. Neither magazine concentrated on neo-Romanticism, as is frequently claimed; their illustrations were eclectic, including war art as often as theatre design. See *ibid.* p. 80, for the artists published in *Horizon*.

29. He was a member of the Arts Council Art Panel 1946–52; Chairman of the CAS 1956–60; Vice-Chairman of the Trustees of the Tate 1953–9; Chairman of the Royal College of Art 1952–6; Trustee of the National Gallery representing the Tate 1963–7 and a member of the Royal Fine Art Commission 1959–76.

30. V. Sekules, 'The ship-owner as art patron: Sir Colin Anderson and the Orient Line 1930–1960', *Journal of the Decorative Arts Society* 10, 1986, pp. 22–33.

31. Sekules lists the artists and designers commissioned for each ship; they included several members of the Great Bardfield group, Ceri Richards, John Piper, John Tunnard and Ernest Race (*Ibid.*).

32. S. Scott, 'The Commonwealth and group exhibitions of Australian painting in London, 1953–1963', unpublished

MA Report, Courtauld Institute, University of London, 1996, n. 21, p. 7.

33. '17 Collectors. An Exhibition of Painting and Sculpture from the Private Collections of Members of the Executive Committee of the Contemporary Art Society', Tate Gallery, London 21 March – 27 April 1952.

34. J. Darracott, 'British artists and patrons 1940–1960', in The Contemporary Art Society, *British Contemporary Art 1910–1990* London 1991, p. 73.

35. L. Alloway, 'Introduction. The challenge of post-war painting' in *New Trends in Painting* exh. cat. Arts Council 1956, p. 5.

36. Most of them were car manufacturers who recognised that trade agreements with foreign competitors would be more psychologically binding if underpinned with the courtesy of cultural *douceurs* in the form of exhibitions, concerts and theatrical tours. The Council also took over an increasingly prominent educational function from a series of short-lived organisations that had preceded it, aware that language teaching and libraries would be effective conduits for soft propaganda.

37. In 1936 Keynes saw no role for the state as a patron of the visual arts ('Art and the State – 1', *The Listener* 26 August 1936, pp. 371–4). It seems that he was persuaded to change his mind partly by CEMA's successful diversification.

38. L. Alloway, *The Venice Biennale 1895–1968, from Salon to Goldfish Bowl* Greenwich, Connecticut 1969, p. 114.

39. Sir John Troutbeck to Ernest Davies, Under Secretary for Foreign Affairs, 27 January 1951, quoted in F. Donaldson, *The British Council: the First Fifty Years* London 1984, p. 169.

40. He commented: 'a distinction may have to be drawn between exhibitions of Old Masters which have a sort of prestige value and appeal to the wider public, and the exhibitions of contemporary British painting or Theatrical Design' (PRO/FO 924/615, 19 April 1948).

41. The Director General of the Council, Sir Robert Adam, always supportive of the Fine Art Department, pointed out that expenditure on the visual arts had been so far reduced that the proposals had effectively already been implemented (*Ibid.*).

42. R. Hutchison, *The Politics of the Arts Council* London 1982, p. 31. Somerville joined the Department in 1941 and became Deputy Director in 1947. Mary Glasgow, First Secretary General of the Arts Council, devoted to its educational role, was eased out after a few years to make way for W. E. Williams and a less idealistic attitude.

43. Interview, 11 February 1991.

44. Interview, 24 November 1984.

45. Membership was remarkably constant, with no fixed term; nine people, including Read, Rothenstein and Philip James, (Director, Arts Council Visual Arts Department) were members throughout the postwar decade and provided an inner core of expertise. Other members, whose interests lay outside contemporary art, like Leigh Ashton, an expert on Chinese and decorative art, and the anthropologist, T. S. Boase, were less active.

46. H. Read, 'Scultura recente' exh. cat. XXVI Biennale di Venezia, 1952; translated as 'New aspects of British sculpture' exh. cat. British Council, XXVI Venice Biennale, 1952.

47. The phrase originated in an exhibition title: 'Four Middle Generation Painters: Heron, Frost, Wynter, Hilton', Waddington Galleries, London May 1959.

48. Gestural painting was officially sanctioned at the 1958 Venice Biennale, when Sandra Blow and Alan Davie showed in the Central Pavilion, entirely given over to artists under the age of forty. Constructivist art reached

49. As did Paul Nash, who died in 1946 and whose late works were much exhibited by the Council at the end of the 1940s.

50. Hepworth, who showed at Venice in 1950, was the least successful; her work was not well received, being considered cold and derivative in the inevitable comparisons with Moore. Somerville later felt that she should have waited longer before exposing Hepworth at the Venice Biennale (Interview, 24 November 1984).

51. Report by Michael Middleton on an exhibition sent to Sweden in 1948 (British Council/Fine Art Advisory Committee minutes, 26 May 1948).

52. Recommended in the Drogheda Report (*Survey of the Report of the Independent Committee of Enquiry into the Overseas Information Service*, Cmd.9138, April 1954, Part V, Para. F).

53. British Council/Fine Art Advisory Committee minutes, 31 January 1956.

54. The Hill Report, published in July 1957, recommended a modest increase in the arts budget.

55. F. Donaldson, *The British Council* 1984, p. 199.

56. A. Wilson, *Hemlock and After* London 1952, p. 25.

57. E. Ardizzone, *Diary of a War Artist 1943–1945* London 1974, p. 187.

58. See P. Wyndham Lewis, 'Contemporary art at the Tate', *The Listener*, 6 April 1950, pp. 610–11. For a discussion of the implications of this situation, where ' "Public" power and authority have been made "private" ', see N. Pearson, 'The Quango and the gentlemanly tradition: British state intervention in the visual arts', *The Oxford Art Journal* 5, 1, 1982, pp. 56–60.

59. The Art Department was the smallest and least prestigious of the original three specialist departments. Since its foundation the Council has favoured the 'flagship' national theatre companies to the detriment of other art forms (Hutchison, *The Politics of the Arts Council* 1982, pp. 62–5).

60. R. Hoggart, *The Uses of Literacy* Harmondsworth 1957, 1958, p. 143.

61. M. Keynes, 'The Arts Council: its policy and hopes', *The Listener* 12 July 1945, pp. 31–2.

62. Arts Council minutes, 5 May 1948.

63. It was the Arts Council's major visual arts client throughout the 1950s.

64. For many years Read had wanted to establish a contemporary arts foundation: in 1932 he had tried to set up a 'laboratory for "experimental art" ' in Edinburgh, modelled on the Dessau Bauhaus (D. Thistlewood, *Herbert Read, Formlessness and Form: an Approach to his Aesthetics* London 1984, p. 16); another scheme involved a Museum of Living Art devoted to abstraction which was discussed by a committee drawn from the *Circle* group (Minutes of First Meeting, 'Museum of Modern Art Group' 30 January 1946, TGA/ICA Archive); a third scheme involved plans for a collection to be selected by himself and Peggy Guggenheim (*Ibid.* and J. King, *The Last Modern: a Life of Herbert Read* London 1990, p. 178).

65. In order to avoid too close an identification with the London Gallery, offices were rented at 15 Soho Square from December 1947 to December 1950, when the Dover Street rooms opened.

66. The model was the Museum of Modern Art, New York but when Read visited it in 1946 he was dismayed by the power of wealthy individual patrons and abandoned the idea of a privately funded museum ('Modern Art Centre Scheme', minutes 21 May 1946, TGA/ICA Archive). Minutes of the first two meetings of what became the ICA Management Committee were headed

67. 'Museum of Modern Art scheme', but at the third meeting on 6 March 1946, this was amended to 'Modern Art Centre Scheme'.
68. 'Museum of Modern Art scheme', TGA/ICA Archive, 30 January 1946. 'Read pointed out that a Museum run by the state can never afford to be adventurous' (*Ibid.*).
68. Cooper, letter to Read, October 1946, TGA/ICA Archive.
69. 'The ICA', Arts Council paper No.298, 19 February 1951. Read in turn desired a liaison with the Arts Council because he was aware that it was prepared to support schemes 'without attempting to interfere with their policy' (TGA/ICA Archive, minutes, 29 April 1947).
70. He was made a life member in December 1948 as a gesture of thanks for the Arts Council's support for the ICA's first two exhibitions, each of which received a £500 grant, though the organisers had asked for £1,000 for '40,000 Years of Modern Art'. Clark 'had seemed ready to go to the limit and give them a guarantee of £1,000' (Arts Council/ICA files, 18 November 1948). The Institute first received a regular annual grant from the Council in 1951/2.
71. Thistlewood, *Formlessness and Form* 1984, p. 117.
72. Two early discussions entitled 'The relationship between primitive and modern art' were chaired by Philip James, opened by Read and Fagg and included as panellists the anthropologist E. R. Leach and Leon Underwood, sculptor and author of several books on West African art.
73. In the first five months of 1951 Siegfried Giedion spoke on 'Art and the continuity of human experience', Anton Ehrenzweig on 'A psychoanalytical evaluation of abstract art', Matila Ghyka lectured twice on art and mathematics and J. P. Hodin gave a course of lectures on contemporary art. 'Public View' discussions of exhibitions were devoted to Pasmore, Bernard Buffet, Jean Hélion, Sutherland and the Royal Academy's exhibition, 'L'Ecole de Paris 1900–50'.
74. Brunius complained that 'It took no risks and contained nothing controversial' (Minutes, 19 November 1947, TGA/ICA Archive). Douglas Cooper, having refused an invitation to write the catalogue, (*Ibid.*) was subsequently reported to have attempted to sabotage the exhibition by persuading collectors to refuse requests for loans (*Ibid.*, 9 December 1947).
75. See photograph in R. Penrose, *Scrap Book 1900–81* London 1981, p. 142. The makeshift entrance looked remarkably similar to the prophetic ruined buildings painted in the 1930s by the English Surrealist, John Banting.
76. Minutes, 4 April 1949, TGA/ICA Archive. An unnamed commentator felt that it had 'established the name and reputation of the Institute as an active and influential factor in the artistic life of London' (Memo, 8 February 1949, TGA/ICA Archive).
77. Penrose was also an old friend of Picasso, from whom he tried to borrow 'trois ou quatre de vos poteries que j'ai vu reproduit dans les C[ahiers].d'A[rt]' (Letter, Penrose to Picasso, 11 October 1948, TGA/ICA Archive). Picasso appears to have been unresponsive. Through his second marriage to the American photographer Lee Miller, Penrose also had close links with the USA, which were to prove invaluable in promoting the ICA abroad.
78. With the considerable exception of the Unknown Political Prisoner competition, they lacked the sinister implications suggested by King (*The Last Modern* 1990, pp. 256–8). Only one exhibition, 'Eight American artists' (1957) was funded by the USIS. Lincoln Kirstein paid his own costs in 1950, as in later years did Fahr el Nissa Zeid and Georges Mathieu. Other exhibitions were funded by

La Voce degli Italiani and *Ambassador* magazines and the Galerie Rive Gauche. Many made a loss or minimal profit.
79. Devised as a comparison of young French and British artists, to replace a proposed exhibition of Picasso's ceramics, it took place at the New Burlington Galleries, London 7 March – 4 April 1950. The participating artists were Jean Bazaine, Hans Hartung, Jacques Hérold, Pierre Pallut, Raoul Ubac, Henri-Georges Adam, André Bloc, Germaine Richier, Francis Bacon, John Craxton, Lucian Freud, Isabel Lambert, Peter Lanyon, Robert Adams, Reg Butler, F. E. McWilliam.
80. ICA Gallery, London 29 January – late February 1953. The participating artists were Sam Francis, Georges Mathieu, Henri Michaux, Alfonso Ossorio, Jackson Pollock, Jean-Paul Riopelle, Jaroslav Serpan.
81. Minutes of exhibitions sub-committee, 12 October 1952, TGA/ICA Archive. He suggested the Nigerian artist Ben Enwonwu; an Indonesian, Affendi; Russkowski and Josef Herman, originally from Poland and an unnamed Australian.
82. Letter to Penrose, 29 January 1953 (Exhibitions sub-committee correspondence, TGA/ICA Archive).
83. Mathieu's exhibition, arranged at his own request, was only accepted on condition that he pay all expenses (Exhibitions sub-committee minutes, 14 December 1955). For its first few years the ICA operated a strict no-solo shows rule, which was gradually relaxed under economic pressure.
84. The Wols exhibition was proposed by Mme de Broglie and came largely from her collection (*ibid.* 8 May 1957).
85. Only a handful of commercial galleries had remained open during the war, among them the Redfern, Oliver Brown's Leicester Galleries and Alex Reid and Lefevre, which functioned on a part-time basis from 1940 to 1944, when it reopened fully.
86. Founded in 1913, with the Camden Town painter, Harold Gilman, as President. See D. Farr & A. Bowness, 'Historical note', *London Group Jubilee Exhibition Catalogue, 1914–64* Tate Gallery, 1964.
87. R. Radford, *Art for a Purpose: the Artists International Association 1933–1953* Winchester 1987, p. 51.
88. R. Marvell, 'The London Group', *New Statesman & Nation* 7 June 1947, pp. 412–13.
89. Radford, *Art for a Purpose* 1987, pp. 156–7.
90. *Ibid.* p. 166.
91. L. Morris & R. Radford, *The Story of the Artists' International Association 1933–1953* Oxford 1983, p. 91.
92. A. Brighton, 'Consensus painting and the Royal Academy since 1945', *Studio Int.* November 1974, pp. 174–6.
93. Reprinted in *Munnings v. the Moderns* exh. cat. Manchester City Art Gallery 1987, pp. 11–15.
94. *Ibid.* p. 6.
95. *Ibid.* p. 9.
96. February 1952. 'For the artist himself it was his most important exhibition to date, and the first of any consequence outside France' (A. Bowness, 'Introduction', *Nicholas de Staël* exh. cat. Tate Gallery 1981, p. 5).
97. A second, posthumous show at the Whitechapel Art Gallery in 1956 was less rapturously received by critics who disapproved of de Staël's partial reversion to figuration.
98. Bazaine and Manessier, both associated with lyrical abstraction, first showed in London in 1950, in 'London-Paris' (ICA) and 'Paris Now' (Leicester Galleries, April – May 1950). (A. Lewis, *Roger Hilton: The Early Years 1911–55* exh. cat. Leicester Polytechnic Gallery 1984, p. 10, n. 6.)
99. 'Young Painters' was a reduced version of an exhibition selected for the Scottish Arts Council by Frank McEwen.

Only seven artists were in both exhibitions: Dominguez, Estève, Gischia, Hartung, Le Moal, Marchand, Pignon.

100. 'Objective Abstractions', held at Zwemmer's Gallery, London in 1934, was a rare predecessor.

101. 'TNAP' was organised by Dorothy Miller, Curator of Museum Collections, for the International Programme of Museum of Modern Art, New York, at the request of Arnold Rüdlinger of the Basel Kunsthalle, Robert Giron of the Palais des Beaux Arts, Brussels and Wilhelm Sandberg of the Stedelijk in Amsterdam. (Tenenbaum, 'A dialectical pretzel', pp. 36–40)

102. The Redfern was founded in 1923 by Rex Nan Kivell; Gimpel Fils opened in 1946 and Rowland, Browse and Delbanco and the St George's Gallery, centre for Robert Erskine's promotion of prints in the 1950s, in April 1945.

103. The British Council, art colleges and businesses provided a steady market for prints (M. Leavitt-Bourne, 'Some aspects of commercial patronage 1950–1959: four London galleries', unpublished MA Report, Courtauld Institute, University of London, 1990, p. 20).

104. The gallery organised an exchange exhibition with the Parisian Galerie de France in October 1953. English participants were Adams, Clarke, Hull, Armitage, Fairley, Lanyon, Le Brocquy, Gear, Williams, Chadwick, Hilton, Scottie Wilson; French artists included Arnould, Bercot, Dominguez, Gischia, Tal Coat, La Grange, Manessier, Pignon, Prassinas, Singier, Ravel (*Ibid.* p. 37).

105. The Young Contemporaries exhibitions started in 1949. 600 works were selected by a committee of established artists from *c.* 2,000 submitted by art schools. From this exhibition the Gimpel Fils committee, which consisted generally of a critic, an artist, a collector and a member of the family, selected ten students to make six paintings each. For the final show, six artists were chosen on condition that they were under thirty and that none had exhibited in the West End except as a student (*Ibid.* p. 38 and n. 28, p. 67).

106. B. Taylor, 'In the bazaar', *The Spectator* 16 August 1957, p. 231.

107. In 1949 restrictions were relaxed for museums importing works of art for permanent retention; national museums were allowed to spend up to £5,000 annually and municipal museums up to £1,000, both excluding US dollars (*The Times* 8 April 1949). The Board of Trade lifted restrictions on imports from the USA in 1953.

108. When Duncan MacDonald reopened the Lefevre Gallery he concentrated on an impressive list of British artists; his successor Gerald Corcoran was only able to reactivate the gallery's long-standing French connections in the early 1950s (D. Cooper, 'A Franco-Scottish link with the past' in *Alex Reid & Lefevre 1926–76* London 1976, pp. 3–26).

109. '... the role of the Leicester Galleries may be judged by the number of artists who compete for the honour of being represented in their summer shows' (G. S. Whittet, 'London commentary', *The Studio* November 1955, p. 159).

110. B. Robertson, J. Russell, Snowdon, *Private View* London 1965, p. 182.

111. A notable exception was Francis Bacon, who showed at the gallery in 1953. Lessore received consistent support from Rodrigo Moynihan and William Coldstream, Professors of Painting respectively at the Royal College and the Slade. Through Frank Auerbach and Leon Kossoff, who between them had no less than eleven shows at the gallery, there was a connection also with Bomberg's Borough Group, where both had studied (A. Forge, 'Helen Lessore and the Beaux Arts Gallery, in *Helen*

Lessore and the Beaux Arts Gallery exh. cat. Marlborough Fine Art, London 1968, pp. 5–12).

112. Albert Irvin, Bridget Riley, Robyn Denny, Philip King and Gillian Ayres were among those who held their first solo shows here.

113. *The Observer* 6 August 1961.

114. *The Guardian* 25 May 1961.

115. Baj was an important forerunner of International Situationism. The first Manifesto of Nuclear Painting was published in Milan in 1952.

116. Musgrave's most spectacular undertaking was the 'Festival of Misfits' in 1962, which included the work of many Fluxus artists, selected by Daniel Spoerri. Gustav Metzger and Robin Page were among those who took part in the two-week event, during which Ben Vautier lived in the gallery window, 'offering himself for sale as a "living sculpture"' (A. Glew, J. Hendricks, *Fluxbritannica, Aspects of the Fluxus Movement, 1962–73* 1994, pamphlet for Tate Gallery Archive display, unpaginated).

117. *The Guardian* 2 December 1957.

118. The gallery grew out of the New Vision Group. Initiated in 1951 by Bowen when he was teaching at Hammersmith College of Art, it was confined to non-figurative artists. The Group held several exhibitions at the Stockpot Coffee Bar in Notting Hill Gate and the Coffee House in Northumberland Avenue. The third and last show took place in 1956 and included Gillian Ayres and Maurice Jadot, founder of the Free Painters' Group, an offshoot of the ICA. Nalecz opened the Drian Gallery in 1957, although she remained a partner in the NVCG until 1962. Avray Wilson resigned in 1960 and in 1964 the critic Kenneth Coutts-Smith became a co-director with Bowen (M. Garlake, *New Vision 56–66* exh. cat. Bede Gallery, Jarrow 1984, p. 3).

119. D. Val Baker, *Little Reviews 1914–43* London 1943, p. 48.

120. Launched in 1936 'to bring together ... middle-class and working-class writers and encourage the latter to come forward' (*Ibid.* p. 34). In 1940 Allen Lane took over its publication as a monthly under the Penguin imprint and the name changed to *Penguin New Writing*; it sold for 6d. and was 'reputed to have a print order of 100,000' (*Ibid.*, p. 35). It closed in 1950 because of costs.

121. 'The principal purpose of the Review was to list all, and review many of the exhibitions current in Britain.' (D. Fraser Jenkins & S. Fox-Pitt, *Portrait of the Artist* London 1989, p. 11). The magazine became *The Arts Review* in April 1961.

122. Produced by the critic and painter, Kenneth Coutts-Smith, who intended to follow the tradition of the 'subversive broadsheet'. There were five issues between December 1954 and June 1955.

123. *Other Voices* was published in 1955. *Voices* (1946–7), edited by Denys Val Baker, was intended as a quarterly but only two issues were published. Its platform was the support of individual initiative against bureaucracy and it made a strong plea for an emphasis on regional culture, subsequently carried over to Val Baker's *Cornish Review* (published at Hayle, 1949–52).

124. 1958–63.

125. The print revival had a marked effect on magazine production, resulting in publications like *Image* (1949–52) and *Typographica*. *Image* was concerned principally with graphics; *Typographica*, which began publication in 1950, was noted for the quality of its printing and its specially commissioned lithographs.

126. A. Calder, *The People's War: Britain 1939–1945* London 1969, 1971, pp. 590–3.

127. S. Hare ed., *Penguin Portrait. Allen Lane and the Penguin Editors 1935–1970* Harmondsworth 1995, p. 35.

128. They sold for 2/6d: the equivalent of roughly 12 pence.
129. Awarded until 1950 under the Further Education and Training Scheme for the study of almost any subject.
130. Interview, 18 January 1990.
131. N. Lynton, 'Painting: situation and extensions', in *British Art Today 1960–76* exh. cat. British Council 1976, p. 23. Lynton was referring to art schools in the 1960s.
132. Gowing was a former Euston Road School student, who taught at Camberwell until he went to Durham as Professor of Fine Art in 1948. The three joined an earlier intake of mostly surrealist and neo-Romantic oriented artist-teachers who included F. E. McWilliam, Toni del Renzio, John Minton, Michael Ayrton, Keith Vaughan, Kenneth Martin and Pasmore.
133. B. Laughton, *The Euston Road School* Aldershot 1986, p. 299.
134. These resulted in 'measurements of proportions, or ratios'. (*Ibid.* p. 147.)
135. *Ibid.* pp. 188–9.
136. *Ibid.* p. 113.
137. Jay Hambidge, *The Elements of Dynamic Symmetry* New Haven 1919, 1920, 1948; *Dynamic Symmetry in Composition* New Haven 1923, 1948; Matila Ghyka, *The Geometry of Art and Life* New York 1946; J. W. Power, *Les Eléments de la Construction Picturale* Paris 1933 (A. Grieve, *New Beginnings: Postwar British Art from the Collection of Ken Powell* exh. cat. Scottish National Gallery of Modern Art, Edinburgh 1992, p. 64).
138. Quoted in N. Lynton, 'Introduction', *Adrian Heath* exh. cat. Graves Art Gallery, Sheffield 1971, unpaginated.
139. J. Morgan, 'Basic Design: pedagogy or aesthetic?', unpublished MA Report, Courtauld Institute, University of London 1992, n. 19, p. 37 & conversation with June George, a student at the Slade in the early 1950s.
140. 1949–75. His successors, Lawrence Gowing, Patrick George and Bernard Cohen were all his former students.
141. Painted when Medley was visiting teacher in the Department of Theatrical Design.
142. The 'only art school in London, with the possible exception of Camberwell, which could provide teachers informed and enthusiastic about abstract art and Bauhaus design'. (A. Grieve, *Anthony Hill a Retrospective Exhibition* exh. cat. Arts Council 1983, p. 6). Morgan maintains that the Painting School remained firmly academic and separate from the design departments ('Basic Design' 1992, p. 7) though Plumb saw the painters as 'the leaven in the dough' in a school of applied art. He states that Johnstone told him that he did not approve of painters (Interview, 18 January 1990).
143. 'Most of the subsequent basic design courses in British art schools owe something of their character to work done at the Central.' (R. Coleman in *The Developing Process* exh. cat. ICA 1959, p. 1).
144. Morgan remarks that by August 1955 all the leading members of the IG were teaching at the Central School ('Basic Design' 1992, n. 24, p. 45). By this time the architects, Alison and Peter Smithson, were less active in the Group than at its formation in 1952; Peter Smithson had taught at the School 1951–2.
145. These were in categories of 'Point; Line; Plane; Area; Space; Volume; Tone; Colour; Drawing from Nature; Technique' (Thistlewood, 'The new creativity in British art education 1955–65' in *A Continuing Process* exh. cat. ICA 1981, p. 28).
146. *Ibid.* pp. 6, 8. Thistlewood understands this approach to be distinct from that of Harry Thubron, Maurice de Sausmarez and Anton Ehrenzweig.
147. In a report on the postwar development of Camberwell W. Johnstone wrote: 'Just before the war classes were started at Camberwell in "Industrial Design" . . . These

experiments had in the beginning no functional or practical importance, but were meant to provide new kinds of experience for the student.' (GLC records, S.O.124, 5 April, 1946). However, Thistlewood maintains that the earliest basic design course was 'shaped by Olive Sullivan at Manchester School of Art: this was inspired by an understanding of the Bauhaus, gained from such sources as Herbert Read's *Art Now*' ('The new creativity' 1981, pp. 4, 6).
148. W. Johnstone, *Points in Time: an Autobiography* London 1980, p. 205.
149. R. Hamilton, *Collected Words 1953–1982* London 1982, p. 177.
150. J. Morgan, 'Basic Design' 1992, p. 28.
151. *Ibid.* p. 27.
152. For a detailed analysis see H. Griffiths, 'The Bath Academy, Corsham Court, Wiltshire, 1946–*c*.1955', unpublished MA Report, Courtauld Institute, University of London, 1979.
153. This approach was not confined to Corsham; it was, for instance, the basis of the teacher training course at Bretton Hall in the early 1950s (Conversation with Joy Burke, a student at Bretton Hall in the 1950s).
154. P. Lanyon, 'The Nature of Painting', *Athene* April 1957, pp. 11–12.
155. P. Lanyon, 'Offshore in Progress', *Artscribe* 34, March 1982, pp. 58–61.

NOTES TO CHAPTER 3

1. D. Sylvester, 'Round the London galleries', *The Listener* 24 July 1952, p. 150.
2. D. Thistlewood, 'Herbert Read's paradigm' in *Herbert Read: a British Vision of World Art* exh. cat. Leeds City Art Galleries 1994, p. 76.
3. Symposium at Camden Arts Centre, London, 15 October 1994.
4. Obviously this usage is extremely problematic. I have retained it only because it describes a particular discourse not covered by less loaded phrases such as tribal art. 'Primitivism' is also especially apposite to a moment in that discourse in the late 1940s/early 1950s, on which I focus later in this chapter. For further discussion of terminology, see M. Torgovnik, *Gone Primitive: Savage Intellects, Modern Lives* Chicago and London 1990, 1991, p. 21.
5. 'I certainly feel, when productions like "Unknown Political Prisoner" by Mr. Butler are given the prize in an important international competition, by those who are supposed to be able to guide us to what is best in art, that I am being "got at". . .' (J. S. M. Jack, 'Trouble at the Tate', letter to *The Spectator* 27 March 1953, p. 378).
6. H. Hopkins, *The New Look: a Social History of the Forties and Fifties in Britain* London 1963, p. 222.
7. *The Observer* 4 March 1951.
8. *The Times* 17 October 1949.
9. *The Observer* 14 January 1951.
10. L. Alloway, 'The limits of abstract painting', *Art News & Review* 5 September 1953, p. 4.
11. Both reproduced in *Broadsheet No.1 Devoted to Abstract Art* 1951, unpaginated.
12. H. Read, 'Barbara Hepworth: a new phase', *The Listener* 8 April 1948, p. 592.
13. Whereas 'Figure paintings and landscapes will be said to have been abstracted from figures and landscapes' (L. Alloway ed., *Nine Abstract Artists* London 1954, note 1, p. 17).
14. K. Martin, 'Abstract Art', *Broadsheet 1* 1951, unpaginated.

15. 22 May–11 June at the AIA Gallery in Lisle Street.
16. *Broadsheet* carried articles on architecture (Anon., 'New Architecture and Abstract Art, the Regatta Restaurant South Bank'; John Weeks, 'Mondrian and Mies van der Rohe'); on Alexander Calder (Anthony Hill, 'Mobiles and Alexander Calder') and illustrations of sculpture and painting respectively by Barbara Hepworth and Ben Nicholson.
17. Alloway used this phrase as 'an inclusive term for the whole field [of abstract art]' (*Nine Abstract Artists* note 1, p. 17) though he had previously written: 'what distinguishes non-figurative painting from other kinds of painting is that the paint is itself and does not stand for abstracted natural forms'; that is, it was synonymous with concrete art ('The limits of abstract painting' 1953).
18. E. Newton, 'Round the London Galleries', *The Listener* 28 August 1958, p. 310.
19. *The Times* 20 October 1956.
20. Awarded to Ben Nicholson for *August 1956 (Val d'Orcia)* (*Ben Nicholson 1894–1982* exh. cat. Tate Gallery, London 1993, p. 247).
21. Literally a blot or patch.
22. S. Wilson, 'Paris sans fin, 1945–1975' in *Paris After the War* exh. cat. Sainsbury Centre, University of East Anglia, Norwich 1989, unpaginated.
23. Harold Rosenberg, quoted by John Golding, 'Into Action', *New Statesman & Nation* 2 February 1957, p. 131. Berger was probably closer to the general feeling of critics when he wrote: 'Action Painting, Tachism or Abstract Expressionism (the terms are very roughly interchangeable) . . .' ('The Art of Assassination', *New Statesman & Nation* 18 January 1958, pp. 69–70).
24. R. Coleman, 'Comment', *ARK* 19, 1957, p. 3.
25. L. Alloway, 'Foreword' *Magda Cordell, Paintings* exh. cat. Hanover Gallery, London 1956, unpaginated.
26. Alloway, 'The siting of sculpture', 1, *The Listener* 17 June 1954, pp. 1044–6.
27. M. Keynes, 'The Arts Council: its policy and hopes', *The Listener* 12 July 1945, pp. 31–2.
28. See, for example, P. Rouve, 'Regimented Forms', *Art News & Review* 22 January 1955, p. 4.
29. Eric Newton noted the ambiguity of 'modern' which, instead of meaning chronologically up-to-date had acquired a frozen sense referring to style (*European Painting and Sculpture* Harmondsworth 1941, p. 234).
30. P. Carpenter, 'Artists and critics', letter to *New Statesman & Nation* 4 April 1953, p. 400.
31. See 'Picasso and other abstract artists', *The Times* 13 October 1948.
32. Leader, *The Times* 17 October 1949. See also an unsigned editorial in the ultra-conservative *Art and Reason*: 'Deformity and the abnormal and abortive representations of latter-day theorists do not convey meanings better worth knowing or more easily grasped than do truthful representations' ('Our creed', 140, August 1946, unpaginated).
33. The fear of the *un*restricted is evident in Sidney Arnold's remark that 'One thing ought to be quite certain to intelligent people, namely: art cannot have any connection with abstract ideas, for art is not art if it is ambiguous.' ('Picasso and the ethics of art', *The Arts and Philosophy* 2, Autumn 1951, pp. 4–12).
34. T. Bodkin, 'Modern Art', *New English Review* June 1945, pp. 117–25.
35. 'Our creed', August 1946.
36. J. Maiden, 'Art. Left Bank, Right Bank', *New English Review* August 1948, pp. 189–92.
37. 'In Russia the state imposes a painfully dull political photogravure. Our freedoms give us other arms against the coteries as well as the liberty to enjoy a great deal of

38. See Thistlewood, 'Herbert Read's paradigm' 1994, p. 82 and note 27, p. 92.
39. 'Peter Thoene was the pseudonym of Hans Feibusch.
40. '. . . we accept in contemporary art the ready-made values associated with Latin culture, and ignore the art of a people more akin to us in race and temperament' (P. Thoene, *Modern German Art* Harmondsworth 1938, p. 8).
41. *Ibid*. p. 108.
42. Thistlewood suggests that Read, aware by 1936 that 'Soviet Communism had also stamped on the avant-garde', concluded that 'contemporary art had to become active rather than contemplative' and thus aligned himself with its most militant wing, Surrealism ('Herbert Read's paradigm' 1994, p. 82).
43. This term was routinely used, especially of Moore's work, in the 1940s to indicate empathy, warmth and tenderness. Writers did not intend connections to be made with renaissance usage.
44. Anti-modernist attacks were restricted to Moore's holes, the stock-in-trade of a generation of cartoonists (See G. Melly & J. Glaves-Smith, *A Child of Six Could Do It* London 1973, pp. 70–3).
45. *The Observer* 26 April 1953.
46. S. Bone, *The Guardian* 13 April 1953.
47. Described as 'bathroom fittings' by Berger ('Victor Pasmore', *New Statesman & Nation* 17 May 1952, p. 586); 'grubby carpentry' by Middleton ('Art', *The Spectator* 16 May 1952, p. 641) and compared with 'furnishing' (*The Observer* 11 May 1952).
48. *The Observer* 26 April 1953.
49. *The Guardian* 29 July 1950.
50. 'Abstract painting in England', *The Listener* 9 August 1951, p. 230.
51. 'Abstract painting in England', letters to *The Listener* 16 August 1951, p. 265; 30 August 1951, p. 343; 6 September 1951, p. 383; 20 September 1951, p. 471.
52. 'Abstract painting in England', letters to *The Listener* by Michael Rothenstein, 23 August 1951, p. 308; Louis le Brocquy, 30 August 1951, p. 343 & 13 September 1951, p. 427; Victor Pasmore, 13 September 1951, p. 427 & 27 September 1951, p. 509. See also Charles & Peter Gimpel, 23 August 1951, p. 308 and Douglas Cooper, 6 September 1951, p. 383.
53. P. Heron, 'Three exhibitions', *New Statesman & Nation* 7 March 1953, pp. 260–1.
54. J. Berger, 'A return to Realism?', letter in *ibid.* 14 March 1953, p. 297.
55. P. Heron, 'Return to Realism', letter in *ibid.* 21 March 1953, pp. 341–2.
56. J. Berger, *Permanent Red* London 1960, 1969, pp. 8–9.
57. G. Dyer, *Ways of Telling: the Work of John Berger* London 1986, p. 14.
58. Berger, *Permanent Red* 1960, p. 16.
59. J. Berger, 'Peter Lanyon, at Gimpel Fils', *New Statesman & Nation* 15 March 1952, p. 303.
60. J. Berger, 'The Unknown Political Prisoner', in *ibid.* 21 March 1953, pp. 337–8.
61. With William Green, John Barnicoat, Peter Blake, Peter Coviello and Richard Smith; ICA Gallery, London, January 1958.
62. J. Berger, 'The art of assassination', *New Statesman & Nation* 18 January 1958, pp. 69–70.
63. M. Ayrton, 'The re-opening of the Tate', *The Spectator* 19 April 1946, p. 400.
64. Heron wrote eleven articles for *The New English Weekly* between October 1945 and July 1947.
65. 'When France disappeared into silence in 1940 we knew

that somewhere or other nine men lived on whose artistic achievement already ensured a position in history for each and all of them. The glory of permanent achievement rested, in 1939, on Picasso, Matisse, Bonnard, Vuillard, Braque, Rouault, Derain, Utrillo and Maillol . . .' (P. Heron, 'Braque', *The New English Weekly* 4 July 1946, pp. 118–19).

66. P. Heron, 'Art. Ben Nicholson', *ibid*. 18 October 1945, pp. 6–7.

67. P. Heron, 'Art is autonomous' in *The Colour of Colour*, E. William Doty Lectures in Fine Arts, The University of Texas at Austin, 1978, pp. 41–59.

68. Heron, 'Braque' 1946.

69. V. Knight, 'The Pursuit of Colour' in *Patrick Heron*, exh. cat. Barbican Art Gallery, London 1985, pp. 5–12.

70. Heron named Hepworth, Nicholson, Lanyon and Wells ('The School of London', *New Statesman & Nation* 9 April 1949, p. 351).

71. P. Heron, 'Ivon Hitchens; Ben Nicholson', *ibid*. 20 November 1948, p. 438.

72. In *Contemporary British Art* Harmondsworth 1951, Read quoted a letter from Hitchens: 'The essence of my theory . . . is that colour is space and space is colour . . .' (Footnote, p. 27).

73. P. Heron, *The Changing Forms of Art* London 1955, plate 13.

74. *Ibid*. p. 41.

75. P. Heron, *Space in Colour* exh. cat. Hanover Gallery 1953.

76. The former were in this instance, Hitchens, Vaughan, William Johnstone, Lanyon and Heron; the latter Hilton, Pasmore and Frost, while Scott and Davie were considered to alternate between the two modes (*Ibid*).

77. He showed *Winter Walk* II and III (nos 23 and 24).

78. See chapter eight. Lanyon understood landscape painting as part of the physical process of coming to terms with a landscape. Painting was preceded by intense multi-sensory physical involvement in the landscape: walking, driving, seeing, smelling and hearing it.

79. Lanyon showed seven paintings, including *St Just*, named as 'St Just–Penwith: 1953' (no. 34).

80. All titled *Black and white motif* (nos 42–4). See A. Bowness & L. Lambertini, *Victor Pasmore, with a Catalogue Raisonné of the Paintings, Constructions and Graphics 1926–1979* London 1980, no. 179 *Abstract in Black, White and Umber* (1953) and *Victor Pasmore, Retrospective Exhibition 1925–65* exh. cat. Tate Gallery, London 1965, no. 110.

81. Heron, *The Changing Forms of Art* 1955, p. 9.

82. '[Painting] is exclusively concerned with *the seen*, as distinct from *the known*.' (P. Heron, 'Colour in my paintings', *Studio Int*. December 1969, pp. 204–5).

83. Letter to Terry Frost, Tate Gallery Archive, February 1953.

84. '. . . the vital communication: air, light, space. And the space is the light and the light is space'. (P. Heron, 'The abstract Pasmore', *New Statesman & Nation* 12 November 1949, pp. 547–8).

85. P. Heron, 'English and French in 1950', *ibid*. 7 January 1950, pp. 9–10.

86. G. Whittet, 'London commentary', *The Studio* June 1956, pp. 188–90.

87. Nevile Wallis summed up the goodwill generated by Richards's work when he wrote ' "Abstractions" is a dispiriting word and "transfigurations" more happily defines.' (*The Observer* 2 September 1951).

88. The elision is clear in Wallis's dismissive comment on 'formal decorations which only rarely impart an illusion of spatial recession' (*Ibid*. 19 October 1952).

89. D. Mellor, 'Existentialism and post-war British art' in *Paris Postwar: Art and Existentialism 1945–55* exh. cat. Tate Gallery 1993, pp. 53–62.

90. S. Wilson, 'Cosmopolitan patternings: the painting of William Gear' in *William Gear 75th Birthday Exhibition* exh. cat. Redfern Gallery London 1990, pp. 5–12.

91. *Uppercase* 4, 1961, unpaginated.

92. D. Sylvester, 'In Giacometti's studio', *The Weekend Independent* 10 July 1993.

93. It was reprinted in *The Tiger's Eye* 4, June 1948, pp. 76–8.

94. Mellor describes the excitement with which Turnbull read Sartre's 'Is Existentialism a humanism?', with its 'electrifying . . . example of a painter freed from *a priori* rules as an allegory of existentialism' ('Existentialism and post-war British art').

95. 'Auguries of Experience' *The Tiger's Eye* 6 December 1948, pp. 48–51.

96. 'In a late Klee, every point of arrival at once becomes a point of departure. The journey is unending.' (D. Sylvester, 'Auguries').

97. D. Sylvester, 'Eduardo Paolozzi and William Turnbull' in *Kenneth King, Eduardo Paolozzi, William Turnbull* exh. cat. Hanover Gallery 1950, unpaginated.

98. D. Sylvester, 'The paintings of Francis Bacon', *The Listener* 3 January 1952, pp. 28–9.

99. L. Alloway, ed., *Nine Abstract Artists* 1954, p. 30.

100. Undated (but 1957) MS; collection Rose Hilton.

101. C. Wilson, *The Outsider* London 1956, p. 202.

102. Robert Hewison has connected Wilson with Alexander Trocchi and the counter culture of the *Sigma Portfolio*, albeit as a member of an 'older generation' (*Too Much: Art and Society in the Sixties 1960–1975* London 1986, 1988, p. 107).

103. First published in 1936; reprinted in 1946.

104. C. Wilson, 'Beyond the Outsider', in T. Maschler, ed., *Declaration* London 1957, 1959, p. 31–59. Ten years earlier Ayer had been characterised as an 'English critic who calls existentialism "very largely an exercise in misusing the verb 'to be' " ' (R. McLaughlin, in 'To be or not: 5 opinions', *The Tiger's Eye* 1, October 1947, p. 45).

105. B. Morrison, *The Movement: English Poetry and Fiction of the 1950s* Oxford 1980, p. 9.

106. *Ibid*. pp. 58–98, *passim*.

107. *Ibid*. p. 98 and R. Hewison, *In Anger: Culture and the Cold War 1945–60* London 1981, pp. 113–22.

108. The point was implied by a reviewer of the 1947 Tate Gallery exhibition of Hogarth, Turner and Constable: 'The exhibition is for those who go to the great painters for purely aesthetic reasons; it is also for those who still hold to the more old-fashioned approach which sees in every art "a criticism of life".' (*The Times* 21 August 1947).

109. The phrase tribal art was popularised by William Fagg in the 1970s.

110. 1942; quoted in *The Daily Graphic* 2 November 1948.

111. 1936; quoted in *The Daily Mail* 19 February 1949.

112. D. Goldsworthy, *Colonial Issues in British Politics 1945–61* Oxford 1971, p. 12.

113. Under-Secretary of State for the Colonies in 1945, Secretary of State in 1946 and Minister from 1948 to 1950.

114. Goldsworthy, *Colonial Issues* 1971, p. 140.

115. R. Hinden, ed., *Fabian Colonial Essays* London 1945, with an introduction by Arthur Creech-Jones.

116. '[The Colonial Office] and the Foreign Office have been considerably disturbed by the volume of criticism of Britain in foreign countries on account of British colonial policy – criticism which came to a head at the last session of the United Nations in New York . . .' (Sir Charles Jeffries, Colonial Office, draft letter to Sir James Crombie, Treasury, PRO CO875/55/6, 1950).

117. Goldsworthy, *Colonial Issues* 1971, p. 173.

118. 'Public knowledge about the British Colonies', PRO 00875/72/2.

119. The source, through the Benin Raid of 1897, of some of the British Museum's most spectacular holdings and the location of regular archaeological research since 1910.

120. The exhibits included photographs of the Lascaux paintings; copies of southern African rock paintings from the Frobenius Institute; ancient Greek carvings; African, Oceanic and Native American masks and carvings. Many of the leading twentieth-century artists were represented; Moore, Nicholson, Hepworth, Sutherland and McWilliam were the British contributors.

121. D. Thistlewood, *Herbert Read: an Introduction to his Aesthetics Formlessness and Form* London 1984, p. 118.

122. H. Read, 'Preface' *40,000 Years of Modern Art* exh. cat. ICA 1948, pp. 6–7.

123. William Fagg was listed as one of 'The More Important Members' of the Institute in 1951 ('List of Committee of Management, Advisory Council and more important members', TGA/ICA Archive).

124. 'Postscript to *Image*' Autumn 1949.

125. 'The Wonder and Horror of the Human Head', 5 March–19 April 1953; 'Lost Wax: Metal Casting on the Guinea Coast', 1–21 March 1957.

126. His first debate was 'The relationship between primitive and modern art', in March 1949, when his principal discussant was Read. An earlier discussion with the same title took place at the School of Hygiene and Tropical Medicine on 26 January 1949. The panellists were the anthropologist E. R. Leach, the sculptor Leon Underwood, John Rickman, a psychiatrist and Frederick Laws, an art critic.

127. He reviewed '40,000 years' twice: see Fagg, 'Ancient arts and modern parodies', *Nature* 163, 22 January 1949, pp. 146–7; 'Primitive and modern art in London', *Man* January 1949, p. 9.

128. Records suggest that these were relatively insignificant though there were no doubt individual contacts, such as Fagg's own, that were valuable both to ethnographers and artists.

129. June 21–July 20 at the Royal Anthropological Institute, London; the exhibition was supported by the Arts Council.

130. The Zwemmer Gallery's 'Masks and Headdresses of Nigeria', June 21–July 23 1949 was also a constituent of Colonial Month. This exhibition consisted of pieces collected by Keith Murray, Surveyor of Antiquities for Nigeria, for the proposed Nigerian Museum in Lagos.

131. 'Public knowledge about the British Colonies', PRO 00875/72/2.

132. Visual art was hardly represented; the only contemporary art exhibition featured in the official brochure was held at the Berkeley Galleries, where Kofi Antubam and Dennis Williams showed paintings and drawings.

133. Street directories give no indication of such a building, which may have been a tented structure in Hyde Park.

134. *The Times* 21 June 1949.

135. 'Londoners made conscious of colonial empire', *The Crown Colonist* August 1949, pp. 467–70.

136. M. Brown, 'An African at the Colonial Exhibition', *Daily Worker* 29 June 1949.

137. W. Fagg, 'New discoveries from Ife on exhibition at the Royal Anthropological Institute', *Man* June 1949, pp. 61–2.

138. 'How [then] can the West African natives, to whom distortion and stylization come naturally, have arrived at this humanistic conception?' (W. Fagg, 'The antiquities of Ife', *Image* 2, Autumn 1949, pp. 19–30).

139. Leo Frobenius, the German scholar who first made the art of Ife known in Europe, 'was satisfied that Ife and Yoruba culture must be the last relics of Atlantis, the islands of Poseidon, lost in the oceans beyond the Pillars of Hercules' (P. Garlake, *The Kingdoms of Africa* Oxford 1978, p. 40). Subsequent research has yielded radiocarbon dates asssociated with the Ife sculpture 'clustered between the late 10th century and the 14th century' (*Ibid.*, p. 128).

140. W. Fagg, 'Introduction', *Traditional Art of the British Colonies* exh. cat. Royal Anthropological Institute, London 1949, pp. i–iv. Fagg vigorously defended the continued use of the term 'primitive': 'it is precisely the "primitiveness" of primitive art which they admire ... an utter misconception ... to represent "primitive" in this sense as meaning "crude", or anything like it'.

141. W. Fagg, 'The antiquities of Ife' 1949.

142. L. Underwood, *Figures in Wood of West Africa* 1947; *Masks of West Africa* 1948; *Bronzes of West Africa* London 1949.

143. European art 'has turned gradually from the classical precedent towards the primitive' (Underwood, *Figures in Wood* 1947, p. ix).

144. 'The child, the romantic and the ancient or pre-classical artist, see things not in proportion to their measurement but in proportion to their subjective meaning.' (Underwood, *Bronzes* 1949, pp. 9–10). 'The adult negro preserves the child's initial impulse for self-expression.' (Underwood, *Figures in Wood* 1947, p. xix).

145. The primitive artist 'regarded himself and the animals as children of a great universal mother (EARTH).' (Underwood, *Masks* 1948, p. 5).

146. Underwood, *Figures in Wood* 1947, p. xii.

147. Underwood, *Bronzes* 1949, p. 1.

148. Fagg, 'The antiquities of Ife' 1949. Formalism was the natural result of Fry's continued prominence and was no doubt encouraged by J. J. Sweeney's important *African Negro Art* (Museum of Modern Art, New York 1935, 1966). He wrote: 'it is not the tribal characteristics of negro art nor its strangeness that are interesting. It is its plastic qualities ... the consistent, three-dimensional organisation of structural planes in architectonic sequences, the uncompromising truth to material with a seemingly intuitive adaptation of it, and the tension achieved between the idea or emotion to be expressed through representation and the abstract principles of sculpture' (p. 21).

149. See Rosalind Krauss' distinction between 'soft', or formally derivative primitivism and the use of 'the "primitive" in an expanded sense (although with close attention to ethnographic detail) to embed art in a network that, in its philosophical dimension, is violently anti-idealist and anti-humanist' (Krauss, 'Giacometti' in *'Primitivism' in 20th Century Art* exh. cat. Museum of Modern Art, New York 1984, pp. 503–33).

150. The prehistorian Miles Burkitt felt, like his ethnographic colleagues, that 'the art-critic investigator', as well as artists, would benefit from the study of prehistoric art ('Art in the Old Stone Age', *Eidos* 1, May–June 1950, pp. 3–10).

151. 'Prehistory from the air', *Axis* 8, early winter 1937, pp. 4–8.

152. 'How reminiscent it was of an earlier Germanic onslaught, when the warlike and pagan Anglo-Saxons swept down on eastern Britain and unhappy Celts fled before them to seek safety among the Western hills.' (C. & J. Hawkes, *Prehistoric Britain* Harmondsworth 1944, p. 11).

153. G. Grigson, *The Painted Caves* London 1957, p. 138.

154. Reviewed by Berger, 'Ancient and modern', *New Statesman & Nation* 30 October 1954, pp. 534–35.

155. H. Breuil, 'Altamira-Lascaux', *Eidos* 2, September–October 1950, pp. 4–10.

156. See Tate Gallery, *Illustrated Catalogue of Acquisitions 1986–8*, pp. 494–8, and R. Hobbs, 'Haydn Stubbing –

School of Altamira' in *Rituals: N. H. (Tony) Stubbing* exh. cat. England and Co., London 1990, pp. 7–8.

157. P.O'Conor & E. Thaw, *Jackson Pollock, a Catalogue Raisonné of Paintings, Drawings and other Works, Vol. 2, Paintings 1945–55* New Haven and London 1978, no. 283; this is misdated in the 'Opposing Forces' catalogue to 1949. An installation shot is reproduced in Melville, 'Exhibitions', *The Architectural Review* April 1953, pp. 272–3.

158. Tobey, Pollock, Pousette-Dart, Rothko, Still, Kline, de Kooning, Motherwell, Gorky, Guston, Baziotes, Glarner, Hartigan, Pereira, Salemme, Stamos and Tomlin. With over 200 works, the exhibition also contained nineteen sculptures and eighty-two prints, none of which aroused any noticeable interest.

159. London 1954. Four of the nine artists: Victor Pasmore, Kenneth and Mary Martin and Anthony Hill were strict Constructionists; Terry Frost, Roger Hilton and William Scott were non-geometric painters; their work involved 'irrational expression by *malerisch* means' (*Nine Abstract Artists*, p. 3). Robert Adams was a sculptor of whom Alloway wrote 'the human figure haunted his work, as in the series of vertical constructions of 1948–9. After that the physical identity of his materials asserted their autonomy.' (*Ibid.*)

160. 'Nine Abstract Artists', Redfern Gallery, January 1955. The works shown differed in many instances from those illustrated in the book, though the two were organised as linked events (See A. Grieve, 'Towards an art of environment: exhibitions and publications by a group of avant-garde abstract artists in London 1951–55', *The Burlington Magazine* November 1990, pp. 773–81).

161. Alloway, ed., *Nine Abstract Artists* 1954, p. 4.

162. *Ibid.* p. 5.

163. *Orthogonal Painting*, 1953. Reproduced in *ibid.* pl.20, p. 29 and subsequently destroyed.

164. 16 January–16 February 1957.

165. *Statements. A review of British Abstract Art in 1956* exh. cat. ICA 1957, unpaginated.

166. 'Their work must function on a domestic scale' ('Introductory Notes', *ibid.*).

167. L. Alloway, 'Background to Action, 1, Ancestors and Revaluations', *Art News & Review* 12 October 1957, pp. 1–2.

168. O'Hana Gallery, London December 1957. The organisers (Alloway with Toni del Renzio) hoped that it would be the first of 'an annual show reviewing the development of abstract art in Britain' (Note in catalogue, unpaginated).

169. *The Sunday Times* 8 December 1957.

170. 'New Trends in Painting', Arts Council touring exhibitions, 1956 and 1957, for which Alloway wrote variants of the same essay; 'Some Paintings from the E. J. Power collection' ICA, 13 March–19 April 1958; 'The Exploration of Paint', Arthur Tooth & Sons, London 1957; 'The Exploration of Form', Arthur Tooth & Sons, 21 January–15 February 1958.

171. Turnbull showed with Guiette, Hantai, Jorn and Tàpies in 'The Exploration of Form', Arthur Tooth & Sons, 1958, the only British artist in this group of exhibitions.

172. Alloway, 'Background to Action, Ancestors and revaluations', *Art News & Review* 12 October 1957; 'The marks', *ibid.* 26 October 1957; 'Paris in the 1940s', *ibid.* 9 November 1957; 'The shifted centre', *ibid.* 7 December 1957; 'Cobra notes', *ibid.* 4 January 1958; 'The words', *ibid.* 18 January 1958.

173. Alloway, 'Introduction', *The Exploration of Paint* exh. cat. Arthur Tooth & Sons 1957, unpaginated.

174. Alloway, 'The Marks' 1957.

175. Alloway, 'Ancestors and revaluations' 1957 and 'The marks' 1957.

176. 'Later impressionist landscapes are often on the verge of turning into paint; conversely in abstract impressionist pictures the free, sensual paint, liberated by action painting, turns into landscape all the time.' (Alloway, 'Some Notes on Abstract Impressionism' in *Abstract Impressionism* exh. cat. Arts Council Gallery, London 1958, unpaginated).

177. Committee members were Bernard Cohen, Roger Coleman, Gordon House, Henry Mundy, William Turnbull, Robyn Denny (Secretary) and Hugh Shaw (Arts Council).

178. Intended as an annual event, the idea was appropriated first by the Marlborough New London Gallery in 1961 and then by the Arts Council, which toured a similar exhibition in 1962/3.

179. For information on the 'Situation' exhibitions I am indebted to Caryl Meaker, 'The Situation Exhibitions 1960–1963', unpublished M. Phil. thesis, Courtauld Institute, University of London, 1981 and Sally Bulgin, 'Situation and New Generation: Abstract Art in the 1960s', unpublished Ph.D. thesis, Courtauld Institute, University of London, 1991.

180. Tate Gallery, 24 February–22 March 1959.

181. Unpublished letter to Robyn Denny, quoted by D. Mellor, *The Sixties Art Scene in London* London 1993, p. 75.

NOTES TO CHAPTER 4

1. C. Rosen, 'The scandal of the classics', *The New York Review of Books* 9 May 1996, pp. 27–31.

2. S. Daniels, *Fields of Vision: Landscape Imagery and National Identity in England and the United States* Cambridge 1993, p. 204.

3. N. Gabo, 'On constructive realism', the Trowbridge Lecture at Yale University 1948 (K. Dreier, J. Sweeney, N. Gabo, *Three Lectures on Modern Art* New York 1949, reprinted in S. Bann, ed., *The Tradition of Constructivism* London 1974, pp. 234–48).

4. R. Williams, 'Base and superstructure in Marxist cultural theory' 1973 in Williams, *Problems in Materialism and Culture* London 1980, pp. 31–49. But, 'under certain social conditions alternative and even antagonistic traditions can be generated within the same society . . . alternative examples of admirable or desirable precedents and continuities are practically presented' (R. Williams, *Culture* London 1981, pp. 188).

5. '. . . it is inherent in the concept of a culture that it is capable of being reproduced'; 'any language or system of non-verbal communication, exists only to the degree that it is capable of reproduction'. 'A tradition is the process of reproduction in action' (*Ibid* p. 184).

6. J. Berger, 'British abstract art, at Gimpel Fils', *New Statesman & Nation* 11 August 1951, p. 155.

7. A. Brighton, 'Consensus painting and the Royal Academy since 1945', *Studio Int.* November 1974, pp. 174–6.

8. Reproduced in *Munnings v. the Moderns*, exh. cat., Manchester City Art Gallery, 1987, pp. 11–15.

9. *The Observer* 6 May 1951.

10. A. Brighton, '"Where are the boys of the Old Brigade?": the post-war decline of British traditionalist painting', *The Oxford Art Journal* 1, 4, July 1981, pp. 35–41.

11. Brighton, 'Consensus painting' 1974.

12. Brighton, '"Where are the boys of the Old Brigade?"' 1981.

13. P. Wright, *On Living in an Old Country: the Nationalist Past in Contemporary Britain* London 1985, p. 142.

14. See e.g. W. Gaunt, *British Painting from Hogarth's Day to Ours* London 1946.

15. E. Newton, *European Painting and Sculpture* Harmondsworth 1941, p. 211.

16. '. . . stocky little man, with plain features . . . prejudiced against foreigners' (Gaunt, *British Painting* 1946, p. 6).

17. *Ibid.* p. 9.

18. *Ibid.* p. 14; Read described a 'native linear genius' (*Contemporary British Art* Harmondsworth 1951, p. 22); Ayrton an 'indigenous gift for linear illustration . . . backbone of the British tradition since the "Winchester Bible"' ('The heritage of British painting, 11, Inferiority complex', *The Studio* September 1946, pp. 65–72).

19. A. Bertram, *A Century of British Painting 1851–1951* London and New York 1951, p. 100. '. . . our natural talent . . . romantic by nature . . . the general trend of contemporary art may be interpreted as a return to our romantic tradition' (Read, *Contemporary British Art* 1951, p. 39).

20. Gaunt, *British Painting* 1946, p. 26.

21. '. . . turning his native linear genius into the channels of satire and caricature' (Read, *Contemporary British Art* 1951, p. 22).

22. *Journal of the Warburg and Courtauld Institutes*, 15, 1952, pp. 166–97. I am grateful to James Hyman for bringing this article to my attention.

23. F. Antal, 'The moral purpose' 1952.

24. '. . . the most significant landscape painter of the [eighteenth] century . . . the "English Claude"' (A. Bermingham, *Landscape and Ideology: the English Rustic Tradition, 1740–1860* London 1987, p. 58).

25. 'What is common to Constable and Turner is a conscious rejection of the classical ideals which obscured whatever native genius there was in Romney and Reynolds.' (Read, *Contemporary British Art* 1951, p. 23).

26. Grigson commented of Palmer, a lynch-pin of the English tradition: 'Palmer's light, moonlight, twilight, or the flush on the summit, the light of Constable or Cotman, or the light of Caspar David Friedrich, was the northern light to which they were habituated . . . Italian light and colour . . . was alien and fatal to Palmer' ('Samuel Palmer: the politics of an artist', *Horizon*, November 1941, pp. 314–328). See also D. Cosgrove, *Social Formation and Symbolic Landscape* London 1984, pp. 225–6.

27. For an equation of liberty with romanticism and repression with classicism, see Read, *The Philosophy of Modern Art* London 1964, p. 109.

28. J. Piper, *English Romantic Artists* London 1942, p. 21.

29. T. D. Lander, ed., Uvedale Price, *An Essay on the Picturesque as Compared with the Sublime and the Beautiful, and on the Use of Studying Pictures, for the Purpose of Improving Ideal Landscape* Edinburgh and London 1794, 1842.

30. '. . . the manifest desolation of the [picturesque] landscape could work as a justification for transforming it to a more efficient, vital one' (Bermingham, *Landscape and Ideology* 1987, p. 69).

31. See Cosgrove, *Social Formation* 1984, pp. 199–206.

32. *Ibid.* p. 203.

33. *Ibid.* p. 205.

34. Read, quoted in D. Mellor, G. Saunders, P. Wright, *Recording Britain: a Pictorial Domesday of pre-war Britain* Newton Abbot and London 1990, p. 7.

35. J. Turner, *The Politics of Landscape* Oxford 1979, p. 43.

36. J. Barrell, 'The public prospect and the private view: the politics of taste in eighteenth-century Britain', in S. Pugh, ed., *Reading Landscape, Country–City–Capital* Manchester 1990, pp. 19–40.

37. J. Barrell, *The Idea of Landscape and the Sense of Place* Cambridge 1972, p. 144.

38. In 1941 Grigson wrote of Palmer: 'he came to understand landscape, especially landscape looking into infinity from a high ridge of hills, as a symbol of the promise of futurity – of eternal life' ('Samuel Palmer').

39. Turner, *The Politics of Landscape* 1979, p. 101.

40. See R. Williams, *The Country and the City* London 1973, *passim*.

41. 'English art, historically and thoroughly, is a romantic art, an art of individuals.' (Grigson, 'Samuel Palmer' 1941).

42. 'Epistle IV', *Moral Essays* 1735. The text continues 'That tells the Waters or to rise, or fall,/Or helps th'ambitious Hill the heav'ns to scale,/Or scoops in circling theatres the Vale;/Calls in the Country, catches op'ning glades,/Joins willing woods, and varies shades from shades;/Now breaks, or now directs, th'intending Lines,/Paints as you plant, and as you work, designs.'

43. W. Wordsworth, *Guide to the Lakes* 1810, Oxford 1977, p. 83.

44. Statement in H. Read, ed., *Unit One: the Modern Movement in English Architecture Painting and Sculpture* London 1934, pp. 79–81.

45. Michael Rothenstein updated the concept in 1947: 'A special sensibility to the radiations which so many localities and buildings seem mysteriously to emit' ('Notes on the new romanticism in art', *The Listener* 9 January 1947, pp. 58–9).

46. Barrell, *The Idea of Landscape* 1972, p. 7.

47. P. Heron, *Ivon Hitchens* Harmondsworth 1955, p. 11.

48. Statement in Read, ed., *Unit One* 1934, pp. 79–81.

49. '. . . perceived among many things the hidden significance of the land he always called Albion. For him, Albion possessed great spiritual personality and he constantly inveighed against Nature, the appearance of which he mistrusted as a false reality.' (Nash, statement in *Ibid.*).

50. Bermingham, *Landscape and Ideology* 1987, p. 41.

51. 'The goal is not localism but specificity; each place is assumed to be unique. Individuality is valued for its own sake.' (D. Lowenthal & H. Prince, 'English landscape tastes', *The Geographical Review* April 1965, pp. 186–222).

52. E. Relph, *Place and Placelessness* London 1976, *passim*.

53. J. Appleton, *The Experience of Landscape* London 1975, *passim*.

54. Cosgrove, *Social Formation* 1984, *passim*.

55. 'Gainsborough's . . . landscapes celebrate a sylvan idyll, exotically remote and far from the noise and bustle of the city' (Bermingham, *Landscape and Ideology* 1987, p. 40).

56. E. W. Martin, 'The necessity of regionalism', *Voices* 2, Winter 1946, pp. 13–20.

57. Turner, *The Politics of Landscape* 1979, p. 48, referring to landscape poetry, particularly during the Civil War.

58. Wright, *On Living in an Old Country* 1985, p. 179.

59. Turner, *The Politics of Landscape* 1979, pp. 38–9.

60. M. Ayrton, 'Young painters of today', *The Listener* 12 July 1945, p. 46.

61. Ayrton, 'The heritage of British painting, IV. Resurrection', *The Studio* November 1946, pp. 144–9.

62. '. . . the striving for originality had gradually become the motive force of painting. Black magic superseded white . . . black magic is the cult of supernatural power for evil . . . The final expression of this change is contained in the work of one great man, Pablo Picasso.' ('Fifty years of change in art, II – The "Black Magic" of Picasso', *The Listener* 5 April 1945, pp. 382–3).

63. '. . . his art is a vampire art . . . instead of standing upon the rock of tradition, and building on it, Picasso has devoured and destroyed that very tradition . . .' (*Ibid.*).

64. 'He has left the painters of my own generation no standards but those of his single and original genius.' (*Ibid.*).

65. These qualities were 'linear, poetic, vital, rhythmic in design and shrewd in perception of individual character' ('The heritage of British painting, I. Continuity', *The Studio* August 1946, pp. 33–41).

66. 'The heritage of British painting, II. Inferiority complex', *The Studio* September 1946, pp. 65–72.

67. 'The heritage of British painting, III. Cosmopolitanism', *The Studio* October 1946, pp. 102–10.

68. 'Gainsborough, Constable, and Turner . . . our greatest poetic or lyrical romantics . . . the tradition continues today'; 'Pictorial satire . . . an esssential part of our visual expression . . . The power of Wyndham Lewis is as a satirist, so later is that of Spencer, of Burra and of Leslie Hurry . . .' ('The heritage of British painting, IV. Resurgence' 1946).

69. 'Nothing would do our young painters more good than to set out, like apprentices of old, to study, imitate and emulate those modern masters they most admire – Matisse, Bonnard, Picasso, Braque, Rouault, Utrillo, Sutherland or Matthew Smith – they should take their pick, and to Hell with Originality!' (P. Heron, 'At the Mayor Gallery', *New Statesman & Nation* 11 October 1947, pp. 288–9).

70. 'Paris: summer, 1949', *Ibid.* 16 July 1949, pp. 67–8.

71. 'The School of London', *Ibid.* 9 April 1949, p. 351.

72. In 1951 only one household in fifteen owned a television set; by 1960 ownership had risen to ten in fifteen (M. Pugh, *Women and the Women's Movement in Britain 1914–1959* Basingstoke and London 1992, p. 290).

73. R. Murphy, 'Rank's attempt on the American market', in J. Curran & V. Porter, eds, *British Cinema History* London 1983, p. 171.

74. P. Addison, *Now the War is Over* London 1985, p. 130.

75. Board of Trade, *Tendencies to Monopoly in the Cinematograph Industry*, HMSO, 1944, para. 7, quoted by M. Dickinson, 'The state and the consolidation of monopoly', in Curran & Porter, eds, *British Cinema History* 1983, p. 82.

76. The vast presence of American troops prior to D-Day, better paid, fed and clothed than their British counterparts, and the inevitable appointment of Eisenhower as Supreme Commander of the allied armies later in the year, thus relegating to second place Montgomery, the hero of Alamein, contributed to equivocal attitudes to America even before the onset of postwar political manoeuvring (See A. Horne, *The Lonely Leader, Monty 1944–1945* London 1994, p. 76).

77. F. Pohl, 'An American in Venice: Ben Shahn and United States foreign policy at the 1954 Venice Biennale', *Art History* 4, 1, March 1981, pp. 80–113.

78. M. Vetrocq, 'National styles and the agenda for abstract painting in postwar Italy', *Art History* 12, 4, December 1989, pp. 448–71.

79. Editorial, 'We want to be Un-American', *Our Time* 7, 3, November 1947, p. 51.

80. M. Frank, 'Inside the Iron Curtain, the witch-hunt and the writer in America', *Ibid.* pp. 52–5.

81. S. Aaronovitch, 'The American threat to British culture', *Arena* 2, 8, special issue, 'The USA threat to British culture', June/July 1951, pp. 3–22.

82. L. Crombeke, 'American Paintings at the Tate', *Our Time* 6, 1, August 1946, pp. 12–13.

83. J. T. Soby, *Ben Shahn* Harmondsworth 1947.

84. Pohl, 'An American in Venice' 1981.

85. Soby, *Ben Shahn* 1947, pp. 3 & 5.

86. *Ibid.* p. 16.

87. 'Shahn and Graves belong, respectively and in essence, to two of the oldest and most continuous American traditions in art: the realism which produced Copley, Eakins and Homer; and the romanticism which claimed Washington Allston, the Hudson River School, Albert Pinkham Ryder and Robert Newman.' (Soby, 'Ben Shahn and Morris Graves', *Horizon* October 1947, pp. 48–57).

88. 'America, in two or three big cities, is being rapidly divested of its provincialism, but the cosmopolitanism replacing it is the product of a levelling out and rationalization of culture, which we now import or imitate the way we do French wines and British cloth.' (C. Greenberg, 'The present prospects of American painting and sculpture', *ibid.* pp. 20–30).

89. *Ibid.*

90. '. . . Smith and Pollock, both products of a completed assimilation of French art . . .'; 'Originally from Munich . . . Hofmann lived in Paris for a time and felt the point of School of Paris painting as only an outsider could – and as no one else in our time has.' (*Ibid.*).

91. S. Tenenbaum, '"A dialectical pretzel": the New American Painting, the Museum of Modern Art and American cultural diplomacy, 1952–59: revisionism revised', unpublished MA Report, Courtauld Institute, University of London, 1992, *passim*.

92. It was first proposed by the Royal Society of Arts (A. Forty, 'Festival Politics', in M. Banham & B. Hillier, eds, *A Tonic to the Nation: the Festival of Britain 1951* London 1976, p. 26).

93. Ramsden Committee Report, 1945, quoted in DoT, E & F, 6236/46 (Greater London Records Office, CL/GP/2/64, Festival of Britain 1951, General Papers May 1946–May 1949).

94. R. Banham, 'The Style: "Flimsy . . . Effeminate"?', in Banham & Hillier, eds, *Tonic* 1976, pp. 190–3.

95. Members of the Group were Ralph Tubbs, Misha Black, James Holland and James Gardner, under Casson as Director of Architecture for the South Bank (*Ibid.* pp. 76–8).

96. See I. Cox, *The South Bank Exhibition. A Guide to the Story it Tells* London 1951, pp.lviii–lix.

97. I am indebted to Clare Preston's analysis of this theme in her 'Robots, heroes and covergirls: the language of the body in a mechanized world', unpublished MA Report, Courtauld Institute, University of London, 1993.

98. J. Hawkes, *A Land* London 1951.

99. Sutherland, quoted in R. Alley, *Graham Sutherland* exh. cat. Tate Gallery, London 1982, p. 130. The mural, painted in oil on canvas, survived the demolition of the pavilions and is now in the Tate Gallery.

100. *Ibid.* no. 165, p. 128.

101. *Ibid.* no. 169, pp. 129–30.

102. For a more detailed analysis of the thematic consistency of architecture and geological metaphor in the South Bank exhibition, see M. Garlake, 'The construction of national identity at the 1951 Festival of Britain', *AICARC, Bulletin of the Archives and Documentation Centers for Modern and Contemporary Art* 1 & 2, 1991, pp. 16–20. Berger's painting is in the Arts Council collection.

103. This theme was more closely investigated by Richard Hamilton's exhibition 'Growth and Form', ICA Gallery London 3 July–31 August 1951.

104. Hawkes, *A Land* 1951, p. 142.

105. R. Cork, 'An art of the open air: Moore's major public sculpture' in *Henry Moore* exh. cat. Royal Academy, London 1988, p. 20.

106. A. D. B. Sylvester, 'Festival sculpture', *The Studio* September 1951, pp. 72–7.

107. N. Pevsner, *The Englishness of English Art* Harmondsworth 1956, 1964, p. 25.

108. *Ibid*. p. 193.
109. *Ibid*. p. 15.
110. A. Hartley, *A State of England* London 1963, p. 15.
111. *Ibid*. p. 145.
112. *Ibid*. p. 76.
113. See I. Nairn, 'Outrage' *The Architectural Review*, special issue, June 1955, *passim*.
114. It also divided the government and Commonwealth, while 'there was never a popular majority' for the use of force (P. Calvocoressi, *World Politics Since 1945* London and New York 1968, p. 215).
115. '. . . both left and right can combine in attacking America, and anti-Americanism is one of the meaner and more sinister symptoms which have recurred in the crisis of post-war England' (Hartley, *State* 1963, pp. 79–80).
116. *Ibid*. p. 80.
117. *Ibid*. p. 81.
118. *Ibid*. pp. 82–3.
119. 'There is a an intellectual tariff in Elizabethan England on American culture . . . the general feeling about American painting and sculpture is one of resistance' ('U.S. modern: paintings', *Art News & Review* 21 January 1956, pp. 1, 9).
120. T. del Renzio, in *Mathieu* exh. cat. ICA; the exhibition took place 4 July–11 August 1956.
121. R. Hewison, *Too Much: Art and Society in the Sixties, 1960–75* London 1986, 1988, p. 7.
122. H. Cahill, 'American painting and sculpture in the twentieth century' in *Modern Art in the United States* exh. cat. Tate Gallery 1956, pp. 11–28.
123. '. . . there have emerged some abstract expressionists who have excited curiosity here, principally . . . Pollock and de Kooning . . . Their works wear already an air of impermanence' (N. Wallis, *The Observer* 8 January 1956); Abstract Expressionism 'should certainly not shock or surprise anyone familiar with abstract or non-figurative painting in Europe since the early abstract pictures of Kandinsky' (B. Taylor, 'Modern American painting', *The Spectator* 20 January 1956, p. 80); 'the greatest . . . is Jackson Pollock, for whom no praise can, in certain quarters, be too high' (*The Sunday Times* 8 January 1956).
124. *The Times* 5 January 1956.
125. 'US modern: painting', *Art News & Review* 21 January 1956.
126. M. Schapiro, 'The younger American painters of today', *The Listener* 26 February 1956, pp. 146–7.
127. P. Heron, 'The Americans at the Tate Gallery', *Arts*, (New York) 30, 6, March 1956, pp. 15–17. See also R. Melville, 'Exhibitions', *The Architectural Review* May 1956, p. 267.
128. Seminar at the Courtauld Institute, University of London, November 1993.
129. Pevsner, *Englishness* 1964, pp. 134, 136.
130. 4 April–4 May 1957. The title was devised by Delia Heron. It subsequently travelled to Liège under the title 'Peinture Anglaise Contemporaine' (O. Barker, 'Art from France in Britain, *c*.1948–1959. Influence and reception', unpublished MA Report, Courtauld Institute, Unversity of London, 1993, n. 22, p. 67).
131. D. Sutton, 'Preface' *Metavisual, Tachiste, Abstract* exh. cat. Redfern Gallery, London 1957, unpaginated.
132. 'He asks of the spectator that he must enter a "Jardin d'Amour" in which the conventions established are those provided by his own imagination' (*Ibid*.).
133. Roger Barr was American.
134. Sutton, 'Preface' 1957.
135. Davie, Holden and Frost showed in Scandinavia and Germany in 1956 (British Council); Henry Cliffe took part in a print exhibition in Scandinavia in 1956; Ayres

136. had a solo show in Oslo in 1957; Avray Wilson had studied in Norway. German links were also becoming established: Gear had had a solo show in Hamburg in 1947; John Coplans one in Munich in 1957; Derek Middleton had studied in pre-war Munich.
136. Rothko 1961; Tobey 1962; Guston 1963; Rauschenberg, Kline, Johns 1964; Louis, Krasner 1965; Motherwell 1966; Betty Parsons 1968; Frankenthaler 1969 (M. Yule, '"A place for living art": the Whitechapel Art Gallery 1952–1968', unpublished MA Report, Courtauld Institute, University of London, 1991, Appendix 1, pp. 69–76).
137. March to April, 1960; organised by the ICA in conjunction with the USIS and Stefan Munsing. The exhibition was arranged by Jules Langsner and first shown at the Los Angeles County Museum and San Francisco Museum of Art in 1959.
138. Some were organised by the International Council of MoMA, such as 'Abstract watercolours by 14 Americans', 7 June–12 July 1963. A note in the catalogue stated that in 1962 more than eleven such exhibitions were circulated worldwide.
139. Interview, 12 March 1993.
140. R. Coleman, 'Reinforcements', *Art News & Review* 22 November 1958, p. 6. The artists were all under forty-five and the exhibition had come from the American Pavilion at the 1958 Brussels Expo.
141. Listed in *Art News & Review* 3 January 1959, as currently on view.
142. 26 May–10 June 1961. A note in the catalogue states that B. Collingwood Stevenson, curator of the Laing Art Gallery, Newcastle-upon-Tyne, had asked the USIS to organise the exhibition but that there had not been sufficient time to assemble it from American sources (*Modern American Painting* exh. cat. USIS Gallery, London 1961, unpaginated).
143. L. Alloway, 'Introduction', *Modern American Painting* 1961.
144. In 1956 Cahill had stressed the diversity of American abstract art: 'The insistence upon the spontaneous and uncalculated . . . has been modified by reflection, and with a number of young artists by specific subject matter and humanistic references. These are irreconcilables . . .' ('American painting and sculpture' 1956).
145. Francis showed *Big Red* (1953) 119 × 76"; *Blue and Black* (1954) 77 × 511/2"; Newman showed *Concord* (1949) 90 × 54"; *Abraham* (1949) 84 × 351/2" and *Adam* (1951/2) 95 × 79".
146. 'New American Painting', *The Guardian* 27 February 1959.
147. *The Sunday Times* 8 March 1959.
148. Alloway, 'Sic, sic, sic', *Art News & Review* 11 April 1959, pp. 5, 8.
149. Alloway, 'Paintings from the Big Country', *Ibid*. 14 March 1959, pp. 3 & 17.
150. 'He destroys the function of books as records of verbal information. This is a loaded gesture in a culture like ours in which libraries are repositories of "the wisdom of the ages".' (Alloway, *Theo Crosby, Sculpture; Peter Blake, Objects; John Latham, Libraries* exh. cat. ICA 1960, unpaginated).
151. Alloway, 'Sic, sic, sic' 1959.
152. Coleman, in *Situation* exh. cat. RBA Galleries, London 1960.
153. *Thornton Maximus* (1960) 192 × 144"; *Palomino* (1960) 108 × 144".
154. A. Bowness, 'The American invasion and the British response', *Studio Int.* June 1967, pp. 286–93.
155. D. Thompson, 'Introduction', in *New Generation 1964* exh. cat. Whitechapel Art Gallery, London 1964, pp. 7–8.

NOTES TO CHAPTER 5

1. R. Mortimer, 'Notes on shows', *New Statesman & Nation* 11 May 1940, p. 613.
2. RIBA, *Towards a New Britain* 1943, p. 142.
3. 18 March–9 May, 1942.
4. E. H. Ramsden, 'Foreword' in *New Movements in Art: Contemporary Work in England* exh. cat. London Museum 1942, p. 1.
5. Mortimer first used the term in 1935, referring to Nash's photographs (D. Mellor, ed., *A Paradise Lost, the Neo-Romantic Imagination in Britain: 1935–55* exh. cat. Barbican Art Gallery, London 1987, p. 11). It was only widely adopted in the 1970s when dealers and collectors became aware of a large body of conveniently sized, decorative works which had been virtually absent from the art market since the 1940s.
6. Moore was 'akin to them as a visionary' (R. Mortimer, 'Painting and humanism', *New Statesman & Nation* 28 March 1942, p. 208).
7. 'Their shock tactics, their ardent pursuit of the macabre, their meticulous elaboration of the unexpected were all very well in a world devoted to sanity. But today life has beaten them at their own game and they limp painfully behind it.' (E. Newton, 'Contemporary art at the London Museum', *The Listener* 19 March 1942, p. 376).
8. H. Read, 'Vulgarity and impotence', *Horizon* April 1942, pp. 267–276. See also Newton, 'Contemporary art at the London Museum' 1942.
9. Read, 'Vulgarity and impotence' 1942. Gabo showed four constructions, the one to which Read referred is *Spiral Theme*, no. 52.3 in Sanderson & Lodder's catalogue raisonné, in S. Nash & J. Merkert, eds, *Naum Gabo, 60 Years of Constructivism* Dallas and Munich 1985.
10. D. Stanford, *Inside the Forties* London 1977, p. 103.
11. Sutherland used the phrase to describe forms in his paintings derived from landscape ('Art and life', V. S. Pritchett, G. Sutherland, K. Clark, H. Moore in discussion, *The Listener* 13 November 1941, pp. 657–9).
12. D. Mellor, ed., *A Paradise Lost* 1987; M. Yorke, *The Spirit of Place: Nine Neo-Romantic Artists and Their Times* London 1988; V. Button, 'The Aesthetic of Decline: English neo-Romanticism *c.*1935–1956', unpublished Ph.D. thesis, Courtauld Institute, University of London, 1991.
13. Stanford, *Inside the Forties* 1977, p. 91.
14. J. F. Hendry, ed., *The New Apocalypse* London 1940; Hendry & H. Treece, eds, *The White Horseman* London 1941; Hendry & Treece, eds, *The Crown and the Sickle* London 1944.
15. G. J. Fraser, 'Apocalypse in poetry' in Hendry and Treece, eds, *The White Horseman* 1941, p. 3.
16. Fraser, 'Apocalypse in poetry' 1941, p. 30. Robert Melville saw a close link between 'Apocalyptic painting', Surrealism and automatism ('Apocalypse in painting' in Hendry, ed., *The New Apocalypse* 1940, pp. 135–52).
17. J. F. Hendry, 'The reflex of history' in Hendry, *The Bombed Happiness* London 1942, p. 32.
18. '. . . that had its roots in the Anarchist movement, and which provided a philosophical justification for Neo-Romanticism' (R. Hewison, *In Anger: Culture in the Cold War 1945–60* London 1981, p. 132).
19. See Hewison, *Under Siege: Literary Life in London 1939–45* London 1977, pp. 130–1.
20. D. S. Savage, *The Personal Principle* London 1944, pp. 1–58. Savage's scheme was closely related to Read's idealistic notion of a society of creative individuals within small, autonomous communities. See Read, *The Politics of the Unpolitical* London 1943.
21. Yorke has written about neo-Romanticism as a group phenomenon (*The Spirit of Place* 1988, *passim*); Mellor sees it as a broad cultural movement (*A Paradise Lost* 1987); Virginia Button has analysed it as 'an aesthetic of decline' identified with a patrician class elite whose own decline it mirrored ('The Aesthetic of Decline' 1991). I am much indebted to all these accounts and in proposing a different emphasis I do not intend to question the validity of their interpretations. I am concerned with a smaller group of artists during a few years of the much longer period that they all cover.
22. G. Grigson, *Samuel Palmer: the Visionary Years* London 1947. Publication was delayed by the war.
23. *Ibid.* p. 18.
24. Grigson, *The Crest on the Silver: an Autobiography* London 1951, p. 100.
25. Grigson, *Samuel Palmer: the Visionary Years* London 1947, pp. 103–4.
26. See R. Alley, *Graham Sutherland* exh. cat. Tate Gallery, London 1982, pp. 58–61.
27. Ayrton and Minton experienced this at first-hand when they lived in France in 1938–9. J. T. Soby's *After Picasso* (Hartford 1935) was the key contemporary source of information. For a general account of French neo-Romanticism, see Yorke, *The Spirit of Place* 1988, pp. 170–3.
28. Lucian Freud, Prunella Clough, Robert Colquhoun and Robert MacBryde are among those most consistently described in this way. Freud and Clough both produced a few works which are formally consistent with neo-Romanticism but in general they were associated with it through the social life of Fitzrovia rather than a common aesthetic or ideology.
29. Published by *Poetry London* in 1943 (Button, 'The Aesthetic of Decline' 1991, p. 195).
30. Sutherland designed the sets for Ashton's ballet, *The Wanderer*, in 1941. Ayrton taught theatre design at Camberwell between 1942 and 1944 and, like Minton, Colquhoun and Craxton, was involved with ballet design. Piper designed no less than twelve opera and ballet productions between 1942 and 1951 (M. Imms, 'British Neo-Romantic book illustration and theatre design', unpublished MA Report, Courtauld Institute, University of London, 1991).
31. Mortimer, 'Notes on shows', *New Statesman & Nation* 11 May 1940, p. 613.
32. 'Art and life', V. S. Pritchett, G. Sutherland, K. Clark, H. Moore in discussion, *The Listener* 13 November 1941, pp. 657–9.
33. First shown in 'Recent paintings by Graham Sutherland' at the Leicester Galleries, London May 1940.
34. Also exhibited in May 1940; (Reproduced in Alley, *Sutherland* 1982, p. 83).
35. P. Cannon-Brookes, *The British Neo-Romantics* exh. cat. Fischer Fine Art, London 1983, p. 21.
36. H. Treece, *How I See Apocalypse* London 1946, p. 86.
37. Encouraged, informally, by Sutherland, who regularly invited his younger colleagues for sketching holidays in Wales.
38. Alley, *Sutherland* 1982, pp. 92–5.
39. *Ibid.* no. 90, pp. 93–4.
40. Craxton painted his *Entrance to a Lane* (1944–5) on exactly the same spot that Sutherland had chosen, though his abstracted, linear painting is much simpler than Sutherland's (Yorke, *The Spirit of Place* 1988, p. 310).
41. Button, 'The Aesthetic of Decline' 1991, p. 193. Ayrton also appropriated the 'skewer-like forms' of Sutherland's *Thorn Head* paintings (Yorke, *The Spirit of Place* 1988, p. 203).
42. Yorke, *The Spirit of Place* 1988, p. 309.
43. Letter to the author, 20 October 1997.

44. Quoted from an interview with Virginia Button, in Mellor, *A Paradise Lost* 1987, p. 111. More recently he has cited Picasso's etching *Minotauromachy* (1935) of which Peter Watson owned a copy, as a source (Letter to the author, 20 October 1997).

45. F. Spalding, 'John Minton: an artist in his time' in *John Minton 1917–1957: a Selective Retrospective* exh. cat. Oriel 31, Newtown, Powys 1994, p. 10. *The House* is related to the set designs made by Minton and Ayrton for *Macbeth*, which they exhibited at the Leicester Galleries, London in October 1942 (*Ibid.*).

46. During 1941 Minton and Ayrton were designing sets and costumes for John Gielgud's production of *Macbeth*. See F. Spalding, *Dance till the Stars Come Down: a Biography of John Minton* London 1991, pp. 43–6. Similarly theatrical effects, with sharply recessive perspective, can be seen in Sutherland's *Devastation 1941: an East End Street* (1941) and a lithograph by William Scott in *Soldier's Verse* (selected by P. Dickinson London 1945, opposite p. 89).

47. Grigson, 'Authentic and false in the new "Romanticism"', *Horizon* March 1948, pp. 203–213.

48. For an account of the genesis of the tapestry, see R. Berthoud, *Sutherland, a Biography* London 1982, pp. 201–22.

49. He also contributed three of the ten stained glass windows in the nave, which were made at the Royal College of Art (see P. Black, *Geoffrey Clarke, Symbols for Man, Sculpture and Graphic Work 1949–94* exh. cat. Ipswich Borough Council Museums and Galleries 1994).

50. B. Spence, *Phoenix at Coventry* London 1962, p. 14.

51. 'I saw the old Cathedral as standing clearly for the Sacrifice, one side of the Christian Faith, and I knew my task was to design a new one which should stand for the Triumph of the Resurrection.' (*Ibid.* p. 18).

52. Read, *The Philosophy of Modern Art* London 1964, pp. 108–9.

53. Surrealist artists took place in an exhibition organised by the AIA at the Whitechapel Gallery in February/March 1939 and in the AIA's 'Travelling Exhibition of Contemporary Painting', which started in March 1939. 'By welcoming avant-garde artists who were not necessarily surrealists, the English surrealist group became a kind of guarantee of the struggle against any form of totalitarianism.' (M. Rémy, 'Surrealism's Vertiginous Descent on Britain' in *Surrealism in Britain in the Thirties* exh. cat. Leeds City Art Galleries 1986, p. 32).

54. Eileen Agar, Ithell Colquhoun, Grace Pailethorpe and Reuben Mednikoff sided with Read; Agar was reinstated later (Rémy, 'British Surrealism in the picture' in *British Surrealism Fifty Years On* exh. cat. Mayor Gallery, London 1986, pp. 13–21).

55. *The Daily Sketch* 14 June 1940, quoted in N. Halliday, *More than a Bookshop: Zwemmer's and Art in the 20th Century* London 1991, pp. 159–60.

56. *The Times* 14 June 1940, quoted in Halliday, *More than a Bookshop* 1991, p. 161. For a full account of this exhibition, see *ibid.* pp. 158–64.

57. See S. Wilson, 'L'oeil surréaliste en Angleterre' in *La Planète Affolée* exh. cat. Centre de la Vieille Charité, Marseilles 1986, pp. 159–69.

58. Rémy, 'British Surrealism' 1986.

59. D. Mellor, '"Recording Britain": a history and outline' in D. Mellor, G. Saunders, P. Wright, *Recording Britain: a Pictorial Domesday of Pre-war Britain* Newton Abbot and London 1990, pp. 9–24.

60. Read, 'English watercolours and continental oils', *The Listener* 24 July 1941, pp. 121–2.

61. P. Wright, 'Revival or ruin? The "Recording Britain"

62. 'Scheme for Recording Changing Aspects of England', Pilgrim Trust Archive, quoted in Mellor 'Recording Britain' 1990.

63. Wright, 'Revival or ruin?' 1990.

64. *Ibid.*

65. E. Newton, 'Recording Britain', *The Listener* 2 July 1942, p. 7.

66. B. Foss, 'Message and medium: government patronage, national identity and national culture in Britain, 1939–45', *The Oxford Art Journal* 14, 2, 1991, pp. 52–72.

67. *Ibid.*

68. For a full account see M. and S. Harries, *The War Artists: British Official War Art of the Twentieth Century* London 1983.

69. Foss, 'Message and medium' 1991.

70. That is, propaganda that is consistent but unprogrammatic and unobvious. See Lord Lloyd's comments to Sir John Reith with reference to the British Council: 'It is a fundamental paradox that the political effect of cultural propaganda increases in proportion to its detachment from political propaganda' (quoted in F. Donaldson, *The British Council: the First Fifty Years* London 1984, p. 74).

71. Foss, 'Message and medium' 1991.

72. '. . . the usual cohorts of over-life-sized chunky airmen by Mr Kennington still stare down at one, gaining by contrast with Mr Eves' muddy military notables, but not by contrast with anything else' (O. Lancaster, 'Art. War paintings at the National Gallery', *The Spectator* 28 March 1941, p. 343).

73. Representations of the Blitz exclude 'pictures of looting or riots, of the mass trekking away from the bombed areas, or of the displays of anti-Semitism not uncommon in the shelters . . . Corpses are occasionally apparent, but no shock cases' (M. and S. Harries, *The War Artists* 1983, p. 186).

74. Calder comments that Moore's Shelter drawings transformed the 'infamous' Tilbury shelter in Stepney, designated for 3,000 people but used by up to 16,000 or 17,000, into 'a phantasmagoric landscape reminiscent of Magnasco' (A. Calder, *The People's War: Britain 1939–1945* London 1969, 1971, pp. 210–11, 589).

75. Fraser, 'Apocalypse in poetry' 1941, p. 9.

76. Quoted in M. and S. Harries, *The War Artists* 1983, p. 161.

77. Newton, 'Democracy and the artist', *The Listener* 20 February 1941, p. 265.

78. W. J. Turner, 'Art. Three British artists, Henry Moore, John Piper, Graham Sutherland exhibition, City Literary Institute, Holborn', *The Spectator* 27 February 1942, p. 203.

79. A. C. Sewter, 'Round the art exhibitions', *The Listener* 16 May 1940, p. 980.

80. For the mythologisation of the Shelter drawings, see A. Lewis, 'Henry Moore's "Shelter drawings": memory and myth', in P. Kirkham & D. Thomas, eds, *War Culture* London 1995, pp. 113–27.

81. M. and S. Harries, *The War Artists* 1983, pp. 180–1.

82. 'Never does a full-grown human being appear so ignoble as when he is asleep in an uncomfortable position . . . The sight of sleepers in a shelter is not edifying . . .' (J. B. Morton, 'Introduction', *War Pictures by British Artists, No. 2, Blitz* London 1942, p. 6).

83. In *Blitz*, one of eight popular books reproducing various aspects of war art, twelve of the forty-eight images were devoted to shelters. Seven were by Ardizzone, one by Topolski and four by Moore.

84. Foss, 'Medium and message' 1991.

85. John Barrell, *The Dark Side of the Landscape. The Rural Poor in English Painting 1730–1840* Cambridge 1980, p. 52.

scheme fifty years after' in Mellor *et al.*, *Recording Britain* 1990, pp. 25–36.

86. 'In the art of the later eighteenth century . . . the shepherdess is often replaced by . . . the milkmaid; her appearance in the imagery of Pastoral is part of the process by which that imagery was adapted during that century to be able to depict more of what was thought to be the actuality of rural life.' *Ibid.* p. 51).

87. M. and S. Harries, *The War Artists* 1983, p. 194.

88. For a full account, see *Stanley Spencer RA* exh. cat. Royal Academy, London 1980, nos 216–30, pp. 181–93.

89. M. and S. Harries, *The War Artists* 1983, pp. 205–6.

90. However, they were apparently unsatisfactory to Sir James Lithgow, the Director of Merchant Shipbuilding, since at his request Henry Rushbury was commissioned and produced three anodyne drawings of Clydeside shipbuilding (*Ibid.* p. 208).

91. Grigson, 'The vitality of abstract art', *The Listener* 12 September 1940, pp. 373–4.

92. 'It seems to me that the wish to return to the imitation of nature in art has been given no more justification than the desire of certain partisans of abstract art to legislate it into permanency.' (C. Greenberg, 'Towards a new Laocoon', quoted in Read, 'The vitality of abstract art', *The Listener* 19 September 1940, pp. 407–8).

93. The AIA was active in the Central Institute for Art & Design, established in 1939 and housed in the National Gallery with the purpose of co-ordinating, for the benefit of individual members, 'some 40 different organisations concerned with art and design' (R. Radford, *Art for a Purpose, the Artists' International Association 1933–1953* Winchester 1987, p. 118). One such organisation was to be the Recording Britain scheme.

94. For the AIA's Everyman print scheme, see *Ibid.* pp. 119–21.

95. Radford cites 'around 150,000 in just three weeks', that is, 16 September–9 October 1941 (*Ibid.* p. 124).

96. *Ibid.* p. 136; the text as printed was headed 'Foreword by A. I. A.' and unattributed.

97. 'Foreword by A. I. A.', *For Liberty* exh. cat. AIA, London 1943, p. 3.

98. *Ibid.*

99. '. . . to show that artists can formulate and express *ideas* as well as illustrate and interpret *fact*' (*For Liberty*).

100. Radford, *Art for a Purpose* 1987, p. 137.

101. The 'Freedom of speech, freedom to worship, freedom from want, freedom from fear' (*Ibid.*).

102. Kokoschka contributed *What We are Fighting For*, unnumbered in the catalogue, now in the Kunsthaus, Zurich. *Ibid.* pp. 140–1.

103. Mortimer, 'Painting and humanism' 1943.

104. This is not to overlook the many occasions when the avant garde showed in AIA exhibitions in support of Left-wing political causes in the 1930s.

105. They showed together in a much-discussed exhibition at Temple Newsam Gallery, Leeds, then directed by Philip Hendy, 25 July–28 September 1941.

106. Clark, a friend of Drew, offered the National Gallery when she told him of her plans for the exhibition (interview with Jane Drew, 20 May 1995).

107. 'We are fighting for something a great deal bigger than freedom from Hitler – for freedom from Squalor, Idleness, Disease, Ignorance and Want, whose fantastic offspring Hitlerism is. And the machines are there to make victory a certainty provided we ourselves have the will.' (RIBA, *Towards a New Britain* London, British Library accession date May 1943, p. 139). The book was one of an Architectural Press series 'of special interest to all who are studying the problems of Reconstruction'. The author may have been Anthony Hippisley-Cox. Jane Drew stated in an interview with the author (20 May 1995) that he wrote the exhibition catalogue/book

RIBA, *Rebuilding Britain* London 1943, also published anonymously.

108. *Ibid.* p. 5.

109. Planning was to begin with 'good conditions in our homes and places of work, convenient transport between them, and good accomodation for education, for health services, and for our leisure occupations and entertainments' (*Ibid.* p. 12).

110. Drew, later a great admirer of the New Towns project and of Frederick Gibberd's achievement at Harlow, designed housing for the Tanys Dell area of Harlow.

111. RIBA, *Rebuilding Britain* 1943, p. 29.

112. *Ibid.* pp. 39, 40–1. As a possible solution a linear plan was proposed in which industry, the port, the cultural and administrative centre and the remaining historic area would be grouped together along a central spine, with residential areas to either side of it.

113. *Rebuilding Britain* carried a prescient warning: 'we can be sure that any plan that does not raise a certain amount of hostility, and disturb a number of sentimentalists, will be recognised as the timid, fiddling thing it is by the future generations who will have to suffer from it' (p. 24).

NOTES TO CHAPTER 6

1. A. Heath, statement in L. Alloway, ed., *Nine Abstract Artists* London 1954, p. 26.

2. H. Read, *Ben Nicholson: Paintings, Reliefs, Drawings* London 1948, 1955, vol 1, p. 20.

3. T. Hudson, 'Space and construction', *Athene* April 1957, pp. 28–30.

4. 'The most complete demonstration of the new conception of space is to be seen in construction, when the painter turns away from the illusion of space in two-dimensions to working in actual space . . . other developments of varying aspects of space and reality are apparent – from the extension of a classical neo-plasticism from Mondrian, to the safe enveloping light of the Tachistes . . .' *ibid.*).

5. '. . . a spontaneous abstract expressionism and a meticulous constructivism seem unrelated if not fundamentally opposed; and yet they possessed one common essential principle which in effect unified them. They were process-dominant.' (Thistlewood, *Herbert Read, Formlessness and Form: an Introduction to his Aesthetics* London 1984, p. 129).

6. H. Read, *The Philosophy of Modern Art* London 1964, p. 97.

7. The term 'constructionist' derives from Charles Biederman's *Art as the Evolution of Visual Knowledge* Red Wing, Minnesota 1948. Following Biederman, British artists used it to differentiate their work from Soviet and earlier international constructive movements (see A. Grieve, 'Charles Biederman and the English Constructionists 1: Biederman and Victor Pasmore', *The Burlington Magazine* September 1982, pp. 540–51).

8. The terms were, confusingly, often used interchangeably with no regard for their implications of different origins in recent French and American painting respectively.

9. K. Martin, 'Abstract Art', *Broadsheet No. 1 Devoted to Abstract Art* May/June 1951, unpaginated.

10. Probably no. 137 in A. Bowness & L. Lambertini, *Victor Pasmore, with a Catalogue Raisonné of the Paintings, Constructions and Graphics 1926–1979* London 1980; it is very similar to another collage with the same title (B&L 136). It was reproduced in *Broadsheet* as 'Rectangular motif (paper)'. See also *Victor Pasmore, Retrospective*

Exhibition 1925–65 exh. cat. Tate Gallery, London 1965, no. 75, unpaginated.

11. K. Martin, 'Abstract Art' 1951.

12. K. Martin, 'Extracts from notes for a *Screw Mobile* for *Nova Tendencija*' 1965, reprinted in *Kenneth Martin* exh. cat. Tate Gallery 1975, pp. 38–9.

13. It was shown at the Redfern Gallery in 1953, in Heath's first solo exhibition in London, following one at the Musée des Beaux-Arts, Carcassonne in 1948. The painting was reproduced in *Nine Abstract Artists* 1954, pl.18.

14. Both these formats are described and geometrically demonstrated in Jay Hambidge's *The Elements of Dynamic Symmetry* New Haven 1919, 1948. Within the root-two rectangle the picture surface is divided into a major square and a minor rectangle which is itself further subdivided into ever smaller proportional units.

15. Poliakoff had solo exhibitions in 1948, 1950 and 1951 at the Galerie Denise René, which Heath habitually visited on his regular trips to Paris; in 1951 he took part in the Royal Academy's 'Ecole de Paris 1900–50'.

16. A. Seago, *Burning the Box of Beautiful Things: the Development of a Postmodern Sensibility* Oxford 1995, p. 125. Green did not, apparently, visit 'Modern Art in the United States', though he had seen reproductions of Pollock's paintings in *L'Art d'Aujourd'hui* and was 'staggered' by the 1958 Pollock retrospective at the Whitechapel Art Gallery (conversation with the author, 12 March 1993). See also J. England, 'Chronology' in *William Green* exh. cat. England & Co., London 1993, pp. 6–10.

17. Referring to this event Robert Melville differentiated between Pollock and Mathieu on the grounds that when 'the American action painters ... "activate" their picture surfaces they do so to create an illusion of light and space' whereas Mathieu 'most certainly considers that any gesticulating upon a surface made by Georges Mathieu is its own justification' ('Action Painting, New York, Paris, London', *ARK* 18, 1956, pp. 30–2).

18. I. Sandler, 'Abstract Expressionism: the noise of traffic on the way to Walden Pond' in *American Art in the Twentieth Century* exh. cat. Royal Academy, London 1993, pp. 77–83.

19. England, 'Chronology' 1993 and Seago, *Burning the Box* 1995, pp. 125–6.

20. Pasmore's introductory talk was published as 'The artist speaks', *Art News & Review* 24 February 1951, p. 3. Panel members for the debate, which also covered Orneore Metelli's exhibition at the Hanover Gallery, included David Sylvester (chair), Bernard Denvir, Patrick Heron, Robert Melville, Eric Newton, Marvyn Wright and Pasmore himself (John Sharkey, 'Chronology', TGA/ICA Archive).

21. Together with *Abstract in Blue, Gold, Pink and Crimson: the Eclipse* (1950) and an unidentified canvas, possibly *Abstract in Grey and Ochre* (1950; Bowness & Lambertini *Victor Pasmore* 1980, no. 150). A transcript of the debate ('Public View' No. 1, 9 January 1951, TGA/ICA Archive) identifies the third canvas both as 'Abstract' and 'Palette Motif', which is consistent with the imagery of no. 150 in Bowness & Lambertini, *Victor Pasmore* 1980.

22. Pasmore, 'The Artist Speaks' 1951. However, Adrian Heath recalled Pasmore saying that the spiral imagery was inspired by a postcard showing the spreading ripples made by a group of women washing clothes in the river at Arles (conversation with the author, 14 January 1984).

23. 'Public View' no. 1, 1951.

24. Pasmore explained: 'The coast of the inland sea is ... a sea coast of subconscious experience. It does not refer to any coast known or seen by the artist.' (statement dated April 1954, quoted in *Victor Pasmore* exh. cat. Tate Gallery 1965, no. 89).

25. '... this little book remains the most important published on contemporary British art since the Second World War' (A. Grieve, 'Towards an art of environment: exhibitions and publications by a group of avant-garde abstract artists in London 1951–55', *The Burlington Magazine* November 1990, pp. 773–81).

26. D. Thistlewood, *Formlessness and Form* 1984, pp. 126–31.

27. D. Wentworth Thompson, *On Growth and Form* Cambridge 1917, 1942, pp. 127.

28. See also Hamilton's *Microscosmos (arbor type)*, *Microscosmos (plant cycle)* and *Structure*, (all etchings, 1950) and *Chromatic Spiral*, 1950, oil on panel. Hamilton distinguished these biologically inspired images from his *Reaper* series of etchings made in 1949 under the impact of Siegfried Giedion's *Mechanization Takes Command*. Published in New York in 1948, this immediately became 'a primary source book' for Hamilton and a complement to *On Growth and Form* (R. Hamilton, *Collected Words 1953–82* London 1982, p. 12; see also pp. 84–5).

29. Thistlewood, *Formlessness and Form* 1984, n.11, pp. 196–7.

30. A summary of the Giedion lecture on 18 August 1948 and the discussion two weeks later at the Victoria and Albert Museum is in the ICA Archive; the text has apparently not survived.

31. N. Gabo, 'On Constructive Realism', the Trowbridge Lecture at Yale University, 1948, in K. Dreier, J. Sweeney, N. Gabo, eds, *Three Lectures on Modern Art* 1949, reprinted in S. Bann, ed., *The Tradition of Constructivism* London 1974, pp. 234–48.

32. R. Wittkower, 'The artist and the liberal arts', *Eidos* 1, 1950, pp. 11–17.

33. J. Bronowski, 'The shape of science in the arts', lecture given at the ICA, 2 August 1951; typescript in TGA/ICA Archive.

34. A. Grieve, *New Beginnings: Postwar British Art from the Collection of Ken Powell* exh. cat. Scottish National Gallery of Modern Art, Edinburgh 1992, no. 53, p. 52.

35. Thistlewood, *Formlessness and Form* 1984, n.34, p. 198.

36. *Ibid.* p. 132.

37. Retrospectively, Hamilton has seen it as belonging within a lineage of avant-garde exhibitions: 'By the turn of the century the "exhibition" was beginning to be understood as a form in its own right with unique properties.' (*Collected Words* 1982, p. 10).

38. *Ibid.* See illustration p. 11.

39. On behalf of Routledge and Kegan Paul. Michael Fordham was the general editor (J. King, *The Last Modern: a Life of Herbert Read* London 1990, p. 229).

40. King cites Read's essay, 'Psycho-analysis and the critic' (*Criterion* 3, 1924–5) as among the earliest evidence of his interest in Jung (*Ibid.* p. 81) which culminated in *The Forms of Things Unknown: Essays Towards an Aesthetic Philosophy* London 1960.

41. Paraphrase of C. J. Jung to Read, 2 September 1960 (Thistlewood, 'Herbert Read's paradigm: a British vision of Modernism' in *Herbert Read: A British Vision of World Art* exh. cat. Leeds City Art Galleries 1993, p. 87).

42. 'We shall find their parallels in our myths and fairy tales, even in popular fiction and pictorial art.' (Read, 'Jung at mid-century', *The Hudson Review* IV, 1951, pp. 259–68).

43. 'It may be that the unconscious will "automatically" rely on certain symbols – the mother, the horse, the phallus, etc.; or that its dramatic constructions (our dreams) will follow the formulas we find embedded in ancient mythology.' (*Ibid.*).

44. D. T. Suzuki's *Essays in Zen Buddhism* and Herrigel's *Zen in the Art of Archery* were published in London in 1950 and 1953 respectively. There is some evidence that certain artists, including Davie, read them (F. Gaskin, 'Aspects of British Tachisme 1946–57', unpublished MA Report, Courtauld Institute, University of London, 1996, p. 34 and note 3, p. 34. I am indebted to this thesis for information on Zen in Britain in the 1950s).

45. W. Barrett, ed., *Zen Buddhism, selected writings of D. T. Suzuki* New York 1956, p. 84.

46. '. . . a Universe that cannot be accurately defined, that cannot be seized and fixed and categorized, cherished as these actions may be by rational thinking, is a Universe of endless becoming, a Universe dynamic and alive, incomplete, ceaseless, and one should see that, in the long run, it is this view which is extensive, and the static view demanded by reason which is limiting' (Avray Wilson, *Art as Understanding: a Painter's Account of the Last Revolution in Art and its Bearing on Human Existence as a Whole* London 1963, p. 30).

47. '. . . the theories of relativity imply the abandonment of fixed invariable references, and . . . space-time becomes the dynamic substitute . . . Relativism is incompatible with a static, precisely analysable and immutable view of things . . . this conclusion amounts to a profound cultural shock, for our entire culture has been based, since the Renaissance, on a confidence in material finality and reliability.' (*Ibid*. pp. 27–8).

48. *Ibid*. p. 79.

49. 'This type of painting, which has been given the name of *tachism* (French tache = stain, blot, spot) is the only face that the atomic age presents to the world – a face of blank despair, of shame and confusion.' (Read, 'A blot on the scutcheon', *Encounter* 1, July 1955, pp. 54–7).

50. K. Coutts-Smith, *London Broadsheet* 1, 15 December 1954.

51. P. Rylands, E. di Martino, *Flying the Flag for Art: the United States and the Venice Biennale 1895–1991* Richmond, Virginia 1993, p. 91. 'It was not just the first showing of her collection but the first official acceptance of her in Europe . . .' (ibid).

52. She bought *Music of the Autumn Landscape (British Art in the Twentieth Century* exh. cat. Royal Academy 1987, p. 425).

53. *The Peggy Guggenheim Collection* exh. cat. Arts Council 1964, p. 73.

54. Bowness notes the relevance of Davie's knowledge of Pollock's 'pre-drip' paintings such as *She-Wolf* and quotes him as saying: 'there is no question of the activity expressing the activity of its production or even the emotions of the artist at the time' (*Alan Davie* London 1967, p. 170). 'For Davie all these shapes are . . . symbolic (and in this he is not an abstract artist) but the use of symbols is always intuitive.' (*Ibid*. p. 171).

55. A. C. Sewter wrote in response to his exhibition at the City Art Gallery, Wakefield two years later that Davie was '. . . already of international reputation . . .' and that it was 'obvious that Davie is the most significant phenomenon which has irrupted in British painting since the war' (*The Guardian*, 3 March 1958).

56. 'Sometimes I think I paint simply to find enlightenment and revelation.' ('Notes by the Artist', *Alan Davie, Paintings and Drawings 1936–58* exh. cat. Whitechapel Art Gallery, London 1958, p. 7).

57. Mary Martin, 'Notes on Biederman', *Studio Int.* September 1969, p. 60.

58. See A. Grieve, 'Towards an art of environment', *The Burlington Magazine* November 1990.

59. Anon., 'New architecture and abstract art', *Broadsheet 1* 1951, unpaginated.

60. Pasmore first showed abstract paintings with the London Group in May 1948. In November 1948 he exhibited eight abstract canvases at the Redfern Gallery (A. Grieve, *Victor Pasmore* exh. cat. Arts Council 1980, p. 8 and no. 16, p. 37). Bowness & Lambertini list three works shown with the London Group in 1948: nos 128, 131 and 132 (*Victor Pasmore* 1980).

61. Pasmore was born in 1908, Kenneth Martin in 1905, Mary Martin in 1907. Of their closest associates, none of whom began to exhibit until the late 1940s, Robert Adams was born in 1917, Heath in 1920 and Anthony Hill in 1930.

62. The core constructivist group had close practical associations with modernist architects: John Weeks contributed an article to *Broadsheet No. 1*, designed the third group exhibition in Heath's studio in May 1953 and took part, with Heath, in 'This is Tomorrow' in 1956. Trevor Dannatt arranged and took part in the first studio exhibition and probably the second (Grieve, 'Towards an art of environment', *The Burlington Magazine* November 1990).

63. Grieve, *Victor Pasmore* exh. cat. Arts Council 1980, p. 10.

64. For a detailed account of reactions to Biederman's book, see Grieve, 'Charles Biederman and the English Constructivists 1: Biederman and Victor Pasmore', *The Burlington Magazine* September 1982, pp. 540–51. and '2: an exchange of theories about abstract art during the 1950s', *ibid.*, February 1984, pp. 67–76.

65. Wittenborn, Schultz Inc. publications cited by Heath are Mondrian's *Plastic Art and Pure Plastic Art* (1947), Vantongerloo's *Problems of Contemporary Art* (1948) and Arp's *On My Way* (1948) (A. Heath, *Abstract Painting, its Origin and Meaning* London 1953, p. 32).

66. The most important were Jay Hambidge, *Dynamic Symmetry in Composition* New Haven 1923, 1948; Matila Ghyka, *The Geometry of Art and Life* New York 1946; J. W. Power, *Les Eléments de la Construction Picturale* Paris 1933.

67. For a contemporary account of Constructionism's historical relations, see Anthony Hill, 'The Constructionist idea and architecture', *ARK* 18, November 1956, pp. 24–9. Hill ignored political content, writing 'The construction, far from being an exercise or research, is nothing more than the most advanced form of art work.'

68. *The Observer* 16 January 1955.

69. 'Abstract painting in England', letter to *The Listener* 13 September 1951, p. 427.

70. For historical precedents, see J. Beckett, 'The abstract interior' in N. Lynton *et al., Towards a New Art: Essays on the Background to Abstract Art 1910–20* London 1980, pp. 90–124.

71. K. Martin, 'Invention' 1956, quoted in A. Forge, 'On Kenneth Martin's writings' in Forge *et al.,* *Kenneth Martin* London 1975, p. 8.

72. Bowness & Lambertini, *Victor Pasmore* London 1980, no. 171.

73. K. Martin, 'An art of environment', *Broadsheet 2* July 1952, unpaginated.

74. 'I see nothing but confusion and social disaster on this road' [i.e. in individual action] ('On Constructive realism' in Bann, ed., *The Tradition of Constructivism* 1974, p. 236).

75. 'The Realistic Manifesto' 1920, quoted in H. Chipp, ed., *Theories of Modern Art* Berkely, Los Angeles and London 1968, pp. 325–30.

76. P. Martin, 'Analysis of selected works' in *Mary Martin* exh. cat. Tate Gallery 1984, p. 35.

77. A. Grieve, *New Beginnings* 1993, no. 53, p. 52.

78. A. Forge, 'On Kenneth Martin's writings' 1975, p. 7.

79. 'The primitive forces of kinetics are universal, they are within us and without. Therefore, through their use it is

possible to express life.' (K. Martin, 'Construction from within', *Structure* 6–1, Amsterdam 1964, reprinted in *Kenneth Martin* exh. cat. Tate Gallery 1975, pp. 12–13).

80. 'To begin by isolating fundamentals of motion – rotation, oscillation . . . – and then to use them in combination is to start not only from a beginning of forms but likewise of symbols.' (K. Martin, 'Movement and Expression' 1966 in A. Hill, ed., *Data: Directions in Art, Theory and Aesthetics: an Anthology* London 1968, reprinted in *Kenneth Martin* exh. cat. Tate Gallery 1975, pp. 16–18).

81. 'For me, construction, which has kinetic attributes, is a series of ordered and related acts consciously executed . . . Empiricism and intuition enter into the work in the choosing of the act, clear understanding may follow.' (Martin, 'Movement and Expression' 1966, in *Kenneth Martin*, exh. cat. Tate Gallery 1975).

82. Grieve reproduces a photograph of the first studio exhibition at 22 Fitzroy Street where the relief is hung so that its major horizontal appears to be a continuation of the picture rail ('Towards an art of environment', *The Burlington Magazine* November 1990, pl.15).

83. Martin, 'An art of environment' 1952.

84. Hill, 'The spectacle of Duchamp', *Studio Int.* January–February 1975, pp. 20–2.

85. Reproduced back cover, Grieve, *New Beginnings* 1992.

86. First exhibited in 1952 under the title of *Prototype for Commercial Reproduction* (*Ibid.* p. 48).

87. L. Alloway, ed., *Nine Abstract Artists* 1954, p. 4.

88. *Ibid.* p. 5.

89. Reproduced in *ibid.* pl.8.

90. For Frost's statement, see *ibid.* pp. 23–4.

91. Reproduced in *ibid.* pl.30.

92. Statement in *ibid.* p. 29.

93. R. Hilton, undated MS in the possession of Rose Hilton.

94. Reproduced in Alloway, ed., *Nine Abstract Artists* 1954, pl.28.

95. 'I am going in future to introduce if possible a more markedly human element in my pictures . . . I'm not going to be "afraid" of figuration any more.' (Hilton, letter to Frost, probably after February 1954; quoted in *Roger Hilton* exh. cat. South Bank Centre, London 1993, no. 16, unpaginated).

96. Reproduced in Alloway, ed., *Nine Abstract Artists* 1954, pl.51.

97. It is closely comparable to *Yellow and Black Composition* (1952/3), reproduced in *ibid.* pl.52.

98. Statement in *ibid.* p. 37.

99. *Ibid.* p. 11.

100. 'In St. Ives they combine non-figurative theory with the practice of abstraction because the landscape is so nice nobody can quite bring themselves to leave it out of their art.' (*Ibid.* p. 12).

101. L. Alloway, 'Description of "Dimensions" ', *Dimensions, British Abstract Art 1948–1957* exh. cat. O'Hana Gallery, London 1957, unpaginated.

102. L. Alloway, 'Personal Statement', *ARK* 19, Spring 1957, p. 28.

103. 'They are extra-intellectual communication that rely only upon the act of perception.' (R. Coleman, 'Dream worlds, assorted', *ibid.* pp. 30–32).

104. Coleman referred to photographs in *Vogue*, of a model posed in front of a painting by de Staël, taken during the artist's 1956 retrospective at the Whitechapel Art Gallery.

105. 'Comment', *ARK* 19, Spring 1957, p. 3.

106. Interview with the author, 5 February 1992 and seminar at the Courtauld Institute, University of London, 23 November 1990.

107. 'Critic's Choice', 1957, Arthur Tooth & Sons Ltd, London 19 September–5 October, nos 25–8.

108. See *Robyn Denny* exh.cat Tate Gallery 1973, illustration p. 13.

109. *Ibid.*

110. *Ibid.* p. 16.

111. Grieve sets the *Free Orthogonal Composition* among Hill's early 'Tachiste' paintings done as rapidly as possible ("Three second paintings")' (*Anthony Hill a Retrospective Exhibition* exh. cat. Arts Council 1985, p. 11).

112. 'The grid offered a paradigm of the security of mathematical measure, as it plotted order and coherence upon a chaotic residue.' (A. McNamara, 'Between flux and certitude: the grid in avant-garde utopian thought', *Art History* 15, 1, March 1992, pp. 60–79).

113. R. Krauss, *The Originality of the Avant-Garde and Other Modernist Myths* Cambridge, Mass. and London 1985, 1987, p. 13.

114. 'London: John Wells and Bryan Wynter', *Arts* (New York) November 1956, pp. 15, 73.

115. Rumney's gestural paintings were indebted both to Jorn and Pollock: he had seen the Guggenheim collection as a teenager. There is an analogy between *The Change* and Leslie Thornton's open *Screen*, constructed of plaster-coated lengths of wire in a roughly rectangular format, for 'This is Tomorrow' at the Whitechapel Art Gallery 1956.

116. McNamara writes of the grid as 'plotting an infinitely extendable set of relations within a dispersed spatial network' ('Between flux and certitude' 1992).

117. Interview with the author, 31 July 1989.

118. Exh. cat., New Vision Centre Gallery, London 1956.

119. 'John Plumb', *Architectural Design* January 1958, p. 28.

120. These paintings no longer exist but are recorded by transparencies.

121. Interview with the author, 18 January 1990.

122. I. Forbes White, 'John Milnes Smith and John Plumb', *Art News & Review*, 4 July 1959, p. 3.

123. In Milan in 1956 he met Asger Jorn and Enrico Baj and became involved with the *Mouvement pour un Bauhaus Imaginiste*, one of the forerunners of the Situationist International.

124. 'It is our thesis that cities should embody a builtin [sic] play factor. We are studying here a play-environment relationship. At this stage environment is of greater interest than the player . . . But, How would "A" play in London?' (Rumney, 'The leaning tower of VENICE', *ARK* 24, 1959. See also *ARK* 25, 1960 and *ARK* 26, Summer 1960).

125. 'Psychogeographical: . . . That which manifests, the geographical environment's direct emotional effects . . . Dérive: A mode of experimental behaviour linked to the conditions of urban society: a technique of transient passage through varied ambiances . . .' (I. Blaswick ed., *An Endless Adventure . . . An Endless Passion . . . An Endless Banquet. A Situationist Scrapbook* London 1989, p. 22).

126. Caption, *ARK* 26, Summer 1960.

127. See *Robyn Denny* exh. cat. Tate Gallery 1973, p. 27.

128. This project was abandoned, together with a Situationist scheme 'to study the effect of changing the colour of the Venetian Lagoon on the behaviour of visitors to the 1958 Biennale' (*Ralph Rumney* exh. cat. England & Co. 1989, p. 12).

129. L. Alloway, *An Exhibit* exh. cat. ICA, London 1957. The catalogue, a sheet of tracing paper with irregular black and red panels and blocks of print at various angles has no fixed orientation, in which it echoes the form of the installation. See also R. Morphet, *Richard Hamilton* exh. cat. Tate Gallery 1970, p. 34.

130. As had been the case with the Rothko exhibition in the

American pavilion at the Venice Biennale and the Tintoretto frescoes in the Scuola di San Rocco, Venice, both of which Denny had seen in 1958 (*Robyn Denny* exh. cat. Tate Gallery 1973, p. 27).

131. The *Austin Reed mural* and the mosaic mural at Abbey Wood Primary School in east London.

132. *Robyn Denny* exh. cat. Tate Gallery 1973, p. 27.

133. *The Guardian* 26 September 1959.

134. 'The mass media is influential not at the level of iconography and story, but at a level of spatial experience.' (Alloway, 'Making a Scene', *Art News & Review* 26 September 1959, pp. 2–3).

135. T. Ingold, 'The temporality of the landscape', *World Archaeology* October 1993, pp. 152–73.

136. 'For the first time in 10 years there was a festival flavour on the South Bank which reminded U.K. architects of the planning opportunities so far lost in that part of London.' ('News', *Architectural Design* 31 July 1961, p. 331).

137. British Aluminium, Cape Building Products and Pilkington Bros.

138. 'The group that came naturally to mind was the constructionists Kenneth and Mary Martin, Anthony Hill and John Ernest, who with Victor Pasmore have been making the relevant researches for some ten years.' (T. Crosby, 'International Union of Architects Congress Building, South Bank, London', *Architectural Design* November 1961, pp. 482–509).

139. A. Grieve, *Anthony Hill* 1983, pp. 40–2. See also A. Hill, 'The Question of Synthesis, Collaboration and Integration occasioned by the IUA Congress Headquarters Building', *Structure* 4th Series, 1, 1961.

140. 'Mary Martin says' in Crosby, 'International Union of Architects Congress Building' 1961, p. 503.

141. Ernest's *Mosaic Relief No 4*, 1966, in aluminium and plastic laminates in wood is one of a series of five pieces which present alternatives, possibly using permutations, to a grid system. (Information from Tate Gallery wallboard, 1994).

142. R. Morphet, *William Turnbull, Sculpture and Painting* exh. cat. Tate Gallery 1973, p. 45.

143. Crosby, 'International Union of Architects Congress Building' 1961.

144. For Hamilton's explanation of the imagery, see 'Richard Hamilton says' in *ibid.* p. 497.

145. *Ibid.*

146. *Ibid.*

147. This recognition extended to affiliates of the core group like Stephen Gilbert, John Ernest, John McHale, Gillian Wise and Peter Stroud.

148. Constructionism was to be the subject of an Arts Council exhibition organised by Alan Bowness in 1963; the British Council had already included the artists in several prominent exhibitions.

149. He agreed with the principal of 'This is Tomorrow', which had 'opposed the ideal fusion of the arts, but accepted their competitive, short-term conjunction' ('Principles', *Architectural Design* November 1961, pp. 507–8.)

150. This concept was theorised by Kenneth Martin and became the basis of much of his later work. See 'Chance and order', *One* October 1973; reprinted in *Kenneth Martin* exh. cat. Tate Gallery 1975, pp. 45–6.

NOTES TO CHAPTER 7

1. A. & P. Smithson, *Ordinariness and Light, Urban Theories 1952–60, and their Application in a Building Project 1963–70* London 1970, p. 84.

2. W. Chalk, 'Housing as consumer product', *Archigram* 3, 1963, reprinted in P. Cook, ed., *Archigram* London 1972, London and Basel 1991 pp. 16–17.

3. RBA Galleries, Suffolk Street; reviewed by Berger, 'For the Future', *New Statesman & Nation*, 19 January 1952, pp. 64, 66.

4. He named John Flavin, Susan Horsfield, Stewart Waghorn, Leonard Roads and Elizabeth Doelby (J. Berger, 'For the Future' 1952).

5. They reputedly felt equally shackled by the Kitchen Sink tag invented by David Sylvester for his article in *Encounter*, December 1954 (F. Spalding, 'Introduction', *The Kitchen Sink Painters* exh. cat. Mayor Gallery, London 1991, pp. 7–13).

6. Smith and Greaves in 1953; Bratby and Middleditch in 1954.

7. J. Spalding, *The Forgotten Fifties* exh. cat. Sheffield City Art Galleries 1984, p. 14; however, Jack Smith is quoted as pointing out that earth pigments were the cheapest (*Ibid.*)

8. Bratby stated that most of his table-top still lifes were painted in 1954 and depicted a table in his father-in-law's home in Greenwich. (*Ibid.* p. 53).

9. James Boswell, James Fitton and James Holland, the 'three Jameses', all worked for *Left Review* where they reestablished the tradition of political satire: '. . . we feel that we have broken away from the middle class and infantile code of good taste which has reduced English cartooning to emasculated illustration and religious hysteria' (James Holland, quoted in L. Morris & R. Radford, *The Story of the Artists International Association 1933–1953* Oxford 1983, p. 20).

10. For accounts of Peri, who arrived as a refugee from Berlin in 1933, see R. Watkinson & J. Lloyd in *Fighting Spirits: Peter Peri and Cliff Rowe* exh. cat. Camden Arts Centre, London 1987.

11. See Tate Gallery, *Catalogue of Acquisitions 1986–88* 1996, pp. 456–60.

12. David Sylvester recognised 'a consistent transformation, unblemished by passages of simplified naturalism' in Clough's work in 'Twentieth Century Form', at the Whitechapel Art Gallery, London in 1953 (Sylvester, 'Round the London galleries', *The Listener* 16 April 1953, p. 648).

13. See M. Yorke, *The Spirit of Place: Nine Neo-Romantic Artists and their Times* London 1988, pp. 237–42, 287.

14. D. Robbins, ed., *The Independent Group: Postwar Britain and the Aesthetics of Plenty* Cambridge, Mass and London 1990, p. 109.

15. '. . . ranging from the household to the multiple dwelling, to the neighbourhood unit, to the city . . . to the nationwide plan, and finally to the Continental plan . . .' (Le Corbusier, 'Tools of universality', *Trans/formation* 1, 2, 1951, pp. 41–2).

16. *Ibid.* Le Corbusier's response was to propose a reappraisal of 'the Continental plan, which offers a map conceived by men who wish to make possible the enjoyment of living-and-working in an environment that should satisfy universal norms'.

17. Judith Henderson ran the course for the sociologist, J. D. Petersen (C. Mullen, 'A journey around Nigel Henderson', in *Nigel Henderson*, exh. cat. Norwich School of Art Gallery 1982, p. 26). See also 'Notes towards a chronology based on conversations with the artist' in *Nigel Henderson, Paintings, Collages and Photographs* exh. cat. Anthony d'Offay Gallery, London 1977, unpaginated.

18. 'The imagery of bomb sites and destruction, atrophy and decay recurs throughout the Bethnal Green photographs. Children wander through the streets as if

through an aftermath.' (J. Lingwood, 'Nigel Henderson' in Robbins, ed., *The Independent Group* 1990, p. 77).

19. See A. Forty, 'Le Corbusier's British reputation', in *Le Corbusier, Architect of the Century* exh. cat. Arts Council 1987, pp. 35–41.

20. For a summary of the Smithsons' reformulation of Corbusian principles, see G. Whitham, 'Alison and Peter Smithson' in Robbins, ed., *The Independent Group* 1990, pp. 109–11.

21. A. & P. Smithson, *Ordinariness and Light* 1970, p. 43. In an article first published in French (*Vouloir* 25, 1927) and Dutch (*i 10* 1, 1, 1927) and republished in English in 1951, Mondrian argued for the application of neo-Plastic principles to urban architecture, proposing home, street, city as a single entity with the potential to become 'a sort of Eden', a collective social body that would subsume the individual. 'Home and Street must form a unity . . . Home and Street must be viewed as the City, as a *unity formed by planes composed in a neutralizing opposition that destroys all exclusiveness.*' (P. Mondrian, 'Home-street-city', *Trans/formation* 1, 2, 1951, pp. 44–7).

22. A. & P. Smithson, *Ordinariness and Light* 1970, p. 48.

23. A. & P. Smithson, 'But today we collect ads', *ARK* 18, November 1956, pp. 49–50.

24. A. & P. Smithson, 'House of the Future at the Ideal Home Exhibition', *Architectural Design* March 1956, pp. 101–2.

25. 'Man, Machine and Motion' opened at the Hatton Gallery, Newcastle in May 1955 and was on view at the ICA, London 6–30 July 1955. 'This is Tomorrow' was held at the Whitechapel Art Gallery in August 1956. It has often been pointed out that there was no such thing as 'an Independent Group exhibition' since the essence of the Group was the principle that each member acted individually (G. Whittam, 'Chronology' in Robbins, ed., *The Independent Group* 1990, p. 24).

26. 'Parallel of Life and Art', ICA 10 September–18 October 1953.

27. A medium not then established as fine art and more often associated with exhibitions of reproductions of Old Master paintings. Alex Seago comments: 'the staff of the School of Graphic Design [at the RCA] tended to look down on photography as a second-rate pursuit' (A. Seago, *Burning the Box of Beautiful Things: the Development of a Postmodern Sensibility* Oxford 1995, p. 142).

28. The catalogue dismissed conventional categorisation in favour of a more discursive system: the section headed 'Architecture' included entries for 'UNO Building', 'Detail, mask of Quetzalcoatl' and 'Different types of vegetable cellular tissue' (*Parallel of Life and Art* exh. cat. ICA 1953, unpaginated fold-out).

29. Subsequently the Smithsons aligned 'Parallel' with collage and the studied disorder of 'Patio & Pavilion' (1956), in a comparison of assemblage with designed objects, the latter represented by constructionist works of art and their own Economist Building (A. & P. Smithson, *Without Rhetoric: an Architectural Aesthetic* London 1973, p. 63).

30. A. & P. Smithson, 'The "As Found" and the "Found"' in Robbins, ed., *The Independent Group* 1990, pp. 201–2.

31. The phrase comes from the title of Alloway's article, 'The long front of culture', *Cambridge Opinion* 17 1959, pp. 25–6.

32. 9 August–9 September 1956.

33. A. Massey, *The Independent Group: Modernism and Mass Culture in Britain 1945–59* Manchester 1995, p. 96.

34. *Ibid.* p. 98.

35. R. Alley, in *Paule Vézelay, Paintings and Constructions* exh. cat. Annely Juda Fine Art, London 1987, unpaginated. Vézelay, whose real name was Marjorie

Watson-Williams, was deeply involved with the pre-war Ecole de Paris, and especially closely associated with André Masson. Living in London in the 1950s, she joined Groupe Espace in 1953 and immediately initiated a British branch.

36. L. Alloway, 'Introduction 1, Design as a human activity' in *This is Tomorrow* exh. cat. Whitechapel Art Gallery 1956, unpaginated; reprinted in *Architectural Design* September 1956, p. 302.

37. These details and a brief reference to the meeting with Vézelay are given in a letter from Robert Adams to Terry Frost, Tate Gallery Archive, undated but 1955. Adams recounted that he, Pasmore, Kenneth Martin and two architects had all immediately resigned from Groupe Espace, implying a personality clash with Vézelay, as much as a disagreement on principles. He suggested that Frost also resign (having apparently only very recently joined) and commented that neither Heath nor Hill would be prepared to join, as a result of Vézelay's attitude.

38. The *Times* critic recognised the dichotomy between 'an ideal style, a conscious purity of form' and certain sections which emphasised a social content, where the work was 'significant as a symbol, not a form' (9 August 1956).

39. Alloway, 'Design as a human activity' 1956.

40. *Ibid.*

41. *Ibid.*

42. The latter dominated Groups 5, 7, 9, 10 and 11. An exhaustive account of 'This is Tomorrow' is given in Robbins, ed., *The Independent Group* 1990, pp. 134–59. See also Massey, *The Independent Group* 1995, pp. 95–104.

43 Arranged by Theo Crosby, Germano Facetti, Edward Wright and William Turnbull.

44. Metaphorised by Turnbull's plaster sculpture, *Sungazer* and Crosby's space-frame roof structure, which was to be repeated on a larger scale in his 1961 IUA Congress building.

45. T. Crosby, 'This is Tomorrow', *Architectural Design* September 1956, pp. 334–6.

46. Hamilton maintains that McHale played very little part in the installation and that he was assisted mainly by his wife Terry Hamilton with Magda Cordell (*Collected Words 1963–1982* London 1982, p. 22).

47. *Ibid.* p. 22. Hamilton's themes were wittily converted into the signifiers that formed the installation. A passage with walls and floor of black and white dazzle stripes anticipated Op Art, flanked by a structure based on a funfair crazy house. Inside it, Duchamp rotoreliefs, a soft floor that emitted a scent of strawberries and a montage featuring Robbie the Robot from the MGM film *The Forbidden Planet* contributed to a 'randomised' concatenation of sensations and references. Robbie clasped an unconscious, nubile blonde girl. Tucked under her knee was the still from *The Seven Year Itch* showing Marilyn Monroe's unruly skirt, while the National Gallery's best-selling reproduction of van Gogh's *Sunflowers* was tacked alongside to underline the conjunction of high art and popular culture.

48. Interview with the author, 1 August 1989.

49. Groups 5 and 11, by John Ernest, Anthony Hill and Denis Williams, and Adrian Heath with John Weeks, were also constructionist and concerned with synthesis.

50. *This is Tomorrow* 1956, unpaginated. The statement was reproduced in rough script, without punctuation.

51. '. . . the "art of the as found" was made manifest' (A. & P. Smithson, 'The "As Found" and the "Found"' in Robbins, ed., *The Independent Group*, 1990, pp. 201–2).

52. 'Fundamentals of human habitat; a piece of the world (patio), and an enclosed space (pavilion), furnished with

symbols of human needs.' (A. & P. Smithson, *Ordinariness and Light* 1970 p. 120). A basic human shelter is illustrated in *ibid*. p. 33, with the caption: 'The minimal dwelling c.1950. Tram hut at Blackfriars Bridge, London'.

53. P. Smithson, 'This is Tomorrow', BBC Radio 3 Symposium, 17 August 1956, typescript p. 4 (TGA, TAV 234B).

54. G. Matoré, 'Existential space', *Landscape* 13, 3, 1966, pp. 5–6.

55. *Ibid*. pp. 5–6.

56. Each group made a poster. They are reproduced in Robbins, ed., *The Independent Group* 1990, pp. 122–3.

57. 'Man Woman Humanity History Food Newspapers Cinema TV Telephone Comics (picture information) Words (textual information) Tape recording (aural information) Cars Domestic appliances Space.' (Hamilton, *Collected Words* 1982, p. 24).

58. R. Banham, 'Introduction 2, Marriage of two minds' in *This is Tomorrow*, 1956, unpaginated. In his own introduction Alloway less poetically invoked 'the responsibility of the spectator in the reception and interpretation of the many messages in the communications network of the whole exhibition'.

59. Seago, *Burning the Box* 1995, pp. 112, 175.

60. Documented in detail in *ibid*. pp. 138–213, *passim*.

61. B. Glaser, '3 artists in New York', *Studio Int.* November 1965, pp. 178–83.

62. Alternatively, each tessera may be seen as representing a paint *tache*. Turnbull's painting, *Mask* (1955/6) is made up of *taches* which resemble elongated tesserae.

63. 'Contemporary architectural philosophy embraces a profound belief in our age and the material it offers' (Denny, 'Mosaic', *ARK* 16, 1956, pp. 18–20).

64. R. Kudielka, *Robyn Denny*, exh. cat. Tate Gallery, London 1973, pp. 19–20. See also Seago, *Burning the Box* 1995, p. 101.

65. D. Mellor, *The Sixties Art Scene in London* London 1993, p. 47.

66. *Evening Citizen*, Glasgow, April 17 1957, quoted in Kudielka, *Robyn Denny* 1973, p. 13.

67. Seago discusses Richard Smith's interest in ideograms and the long-standing exploration of 'words as pictorial objects' by members of the Graphic Design Department at the Central School (*Burning the Box* 1995, p. 100).

68. R. Smith, 'Figure/field work', *Art News & Review* 29 August 1959, p. 2.

69. '3 Paintings by Gustav Metzger', 14 Monmouth Street, London 30 July–19 August.

70. A. Wilson, 'papa what did you do when the nazis built the concentration camps? my dear, they never told us anything' in G. Metzger, *'Damaged nature; Auto-Destructive Art'* 1996, pp. 64–81. I am indebted to Andrew Wilson's essay for information on Gustav Metzger.

71. The event took place at 14 Monmouth Street on 4 November 1959 (C. Philpott, 'Chronology' in Metzger, *'Damaged Nature'* 1996, pp. 86–97).

72. Metzger's work became more overtly gestural after not having his paintings accepted for 'Metavisual, Tachiste, Abstract' in 1957.

73. 'Auto-Destructive Art', 4 November 1959.

74. 'Manifesto Auto-Destructive Art', 10 March 1960.

75. 'Auto-Destructive Art Machine Art Auto Creative Art', 23 June 1961.

76. Wilson, 'papa what did you do?' 1996, p. 72.

77. See J. Rydon, 'It's pictures from packing cases', *Daily Mail*, 12 November 1959.

78. 'Auto-destructive art is an attack on capitalist values and the drive to nuclear annihilation.' ('Auto-

Destructive Art', 23 June 1961). For the CND context of Metzger's work, see Mellor, *The Sixties* 1993, p. 33.

79. Conversation with the author, 20 February 1995.

80. Theo Crosby had invited Metzger to give a demonstration as a contribution to the 'Art and Technology' section of the Congress; he then tried to withdraw the invitation but Metzger refused to comply (Wilson, 'papa what did you do?' 1996, n. 13, p. 68).

81. In a statement made in court when, with other members of the Committee of 100, he was sentenced to imprisonment in September 1961, Metzger said: '. . . the situation is now far more barbarous than Buchenwald, for there can be absolute obliteration at any moment' (Quoted in *ibid*. pp. 71–2).

82. Clearly the fact that Metzger has amassed virtually no exhibitable works, in contrast to Latham who shows regularly, has contributed to this neglect.

83. Tate Gallery, *Illustrated Catalogue of Acquisitions 1976–8* 1979, p. 102.

84. *The Burial of Count Orgaz* (1586), San Tomé, Toledo.

85. J. A. Walker, *John Latham – the Incidental Person – his Art and Ideas* Middlesex 1995, p. 43.

86. J. M. Keynes, 'The Arts Council: its policies and hopes', *The Listener* 12 July 1945, pp. 31–2.

87. *Richard Hamilton* exh. cat. Tate Gallery 1992, no. 18, pp. 153–4.

88. Hamilton wrote a detailed description of the constituent images of *Glorious Techniculture* for 'Experiment in integration', *Architectural Design* November 1961, p. 497.

89. He subsequently cut off the upper section and modified the lower part. See entry for *Glorious Techniculture* in *Richard Hamilton* exh. cat. Tate Gallery 1992, no. 18, pp. 153–4.

90. A. & P. Smithson, 'But today we collect ads' 1956.

91. N. Whiteley, 'Toward a throw-away culture. Consumerism, "style obsolescence" and cultural theory in the 1950s and 1960s', *The Oxford Art Journal* 10, 12, 1987, pp. 3–27.

92. P. Cook, 'Introduction', *Living Arts* 2 June 1963, pp. 68–71. This issue of the magazine, published by the ICA, constituted the exhibition catalogue.

93. Cook, 'The key to the vitality of the city', *ibid*. p. 80.

94. Cook, Editorial, *Archigram* 3, 1963, reprinted in Cook, ed., *Archigram* 1972, 1991, p. 16.

NOTES TO CHAPTER 8

1. D. Lowenthal and H. Prince, 'English landscape tastes', *The Geographical Review* April 1965, pp. 186–222.

2. S. Schama, *Landscape and Memory* London 1995, p. 61.

3. Roland Penrose had suggested a landscape exhibition 'as a reply to Sir Kenneth Clark's contention that landscape painting was finished' (Minutes of Exhibitions sub-committee, 8 September 1955, TGA/ICA Archive). Forge agreed to make 'a selection of artists since the war and include all styles' (*Ibid.*, 15 November 1955).

4. A. Forge, letter to Lawrence Alloway, undated; TGA/ICA Archive.

5. 'The modern landscape artist has nothing to lose when he is told some unimaginable fact by a scientist, for he knows, when he turns to the scene in front of him, that he cannot define a cosmos in its terms but only in terms of himself.' (A. Forge, 'Some recent landscapes' in *10 Years of English Landscape Painting 1945–1955* exh. cat. ICA, London 1956, unpaginated).

6. Forge, letter to Alloway, undated, TGA/ICA Archive. The exception was Philip Sutton.

7. *Ibid.*

8. No titles appear in the catalogue but *Boulder Coast* was

listed by Gimpel Fils as a loan to the show as *Boulder Cliff*, the title under which it was shown several times (Gimpel Fils, 3 January 1956).

9. S. Daniels, 'Human geography and the art of David Cox', *Landscape Research* 9, 3, 1984, pp. 14–19.

10. Transcript TGA/TAV 297 B, BBC Third Programme, 28 July 1957.

11. 'The whole process of resolving the painting is one of physical activity, similar to walking round the dales . . . not [by] just that place being outside you like that, but your experience in it' *Ibid.*).

12. 'Order and chaos in landscape', *Landscape Research* 10, 1, 1985, pp. 2–8.

13. R. Williams, *The Country and the City* London 1985, *passim*.

14. '. . . the theme of a disappearing English arcadia in need of protection from the forces of modernism has been a powerful and conservative one throughout the twentieth century' (D. Cosgrove, *Social Formation and Symbolic Landscape* London 1984, p. 267).

15. W. G. Hoskins, *The Making of the English Landscape* Harmondsworth 1955, p. 299.

16. '. . . a well-cultivated sense of place is an important dimension of human well-being' (D. Meinig, 'The beholding eye' in Meinig, ed., *The Interpretation of Ordinary Landscapes* Oxford p. 46). 'Places are linked most of all with persons: a creator, designer, or author; a possessor, patron, or heir; an individual associated, either causally or fortuitously, by historical events or literary allusions.' (Lowenthal & Prince, 'English landscape tastes', 1965).

17. David Sopher variously cites the San Francisco cable-car and mediaeval heraldic devices for towns as evidence of a 'consensus that a particular component of the landscape stands for a place' (Sopher, 'The landscape of home: myth, experience, social meaning', in Meinig, ed., *Interpretation* 1979, p. 138).

18. C. Colvin, 'Introduction', *Paul Nash Places* exh. cat. South Bank Centre, London 1989, pp. 4–9.

19. D. Cosgrove, 'Geography is everywhere: culture and symbolism in human landscapes' in D. Gregory & R. Walford, eds, *Horizons in Human Geography* Towota, New Jersey 1989, p. 126.

20. For an account of the Great Bardfield group, see C. MacInnes, *Great Bardfield Artists* 1957.

21. T. Ingold, 'The temporality of the landscape', *World Archaeology* 25, 2, October 1993, pp. 152–74.

22. 'Sheila Fell – Notes' in *Sheila Fell* exh. cat. South Bank Centre 1990, p. 23.

23. D. P. Bliss, *Edward Bawden* Godalming 1979, p. 73. Bliss singled out Bawden and Aldridge as the leaders of the group.

24. MacInnes, *Great Bardfield Artists* 1957, unpaginated.

25. Carrington named the growth of the Women's Institute and the Young Farmers: 'genuine democratic activity in local affairs, surprising and a little distressing to those who managed them to their own satisfaction for a long time' (*Life in an English Village* Harmondsworth 1949, pp. 20, 22).

26. In his discussion of pastoral Sam Smiles refers to 'a nexus of belief that places the countryside within the context of a critique of society' ('Samuel Palmer and the pastoral inheritance', *Landscape Research* 11, 3, 1986, pp. 11–15).

27. T. Cross, *Painting the Warmth of the Sun: St Ives Artists 1939–1975* Penzance 1984, p. 66.

28. '. . . the influence of Wallis upon Nicholson . . . was to add sophistication and abstractness to his work rather than any superficial naivety' (C. Harrison, 'Notes on Ben Nicholson's development and commentary on selected works', *Ben Nicholson* exh. cat. Tate Gallery, London 1969, p. 15).

29. '. . . he was still sufficiently childlike to make the "s" at the end of his signature whichever way round he felt inclined to, and, when I showed him a reproduction of one of his paintings in a book, to push it away and remark: "I've got one like that at home".' (Nicholson, 'Alfred Wallis', *Horizon* January 1943, reprinted in M. de Sausmarez, ed., *Ben Nicholson, Studio Int.* special issue 1969, pp. 37–8).

30. *Ibid.* 1943, 1969.

31. Cross, *Painting the Warmth* 1984, pp. 73–5.

32. 'Introduction', *Voices* 2, 1946, p. 3. Val Baker, who was Welsh, later became editor of *The Cornish Review* and a cultural spokesman for Cornwall.

33. *Paintings from Cornwall* Penzance, British Library accession date 1950; *Britain's Art Colony by the Sea* London 1959.

34. J. Devlin, 'A serious pleasure', *Art, I*, 20 January 1955, p. 4.

35. A group of modernising artists, who included Marlow Moss, Cedric Morris, Lett Haines and Frances Hodgkins also worked in St Ives during the interwar years (D. Brown, 'Chronology', *St Ives 1939–64* exh. cat. Tate Gallery 1985, pp. 98–9).

36. Walter Gropius arrived in 1934; Gabo, Marcel Breuer and Moholy-Nagy in 1935 and Mondrian in 1938.

37. Brown, 'Chronology', 1985, pp. 100–1.

38. Wilkinson, 'Cornwall and the sculpture of landscape: 1939–1975', in Curtis & Wilkinson, *Barbara Hepworth, a Retrospective* exh. cat. Tate Gallery Liverpool 1994, p. 80.

39. He carried a photograph of it while he was serving in the RAF during the war (Lanyon, letter to Naum and Miriam Gabo, 11 June 1943; see M. Garlake, 'Peter Lanyon's letters to Naum Gabo', *The Burlington Magazine* April 1995, pp. 233–41).

40. 'The 11th one was the first *constructivist* one, it was *Construction with a Red Triangle*' (Mellis quoted in *St Ives 1939–64* 1985, no. 60, p. 167).

41. 'I dealt in squares, although inside the box there is a circle. From that circle I progressed (who could be better for a companion than Ben, whose name is synonymous with squares and circles!)' (Peter Lanyon, notes made in 1940, quoted in A. Lanyon, *Peter Lanyon, 1918–1964* Penzance 1990, p. 47).

42. Peter Lanyon, talk recorded for the British Council, 1963, quoted in *ibid.* p. 45.

43. '*White Track* exists within the context of European artists' interest in inferred and actual movement of objects across or within a field of activity' (Peter Lanyon, *Paintings, Drawings and Constructions 1937–64* exh. cat. Whitworth Art Gallery, Manchester 1978, no. 5, p. 9). *White Track* itself may have encouraged Mellis to work with comparable variations of wood colour and texture in pieces like *Construction in Wood* (1941).

44. The two constructions are reproduced in A. Lanyon, *Peter Lanyon 1918–64* 1990, p. 50.

45. It included some pre-war pieces, though the focus was on recent work. The earliest dated piece was Wells's *Still Life* (1930), no. 33 and the most recent his *Mobile* (1947) (unnumbered). For information on the Crypt exhibitions see D. Brown, *Cornwall 1945–1955* exh. cat. New Art Centre, London 1977, unpaginated and 'Chronology' 1985, pp. 104–5; P. Davies, 'St Ives in the Forties', *Artscribe* 34, March 1981, pp. 55–7; Cross, *Painting the Warmth* 1984, p. 85.

46. Cross, *Painting the Warmth* 1984, p. 84.

47. In the second show, in August 1947, Wilhelmina Barns-Graham replaced Bryan Wynter. Kit Barker, Barns-Graham, Berlin, David Haughton, Lanyon, Adrian Ryan, Wells, Wynter, Heron and Morris took part in

the final exhibition, though Morris's works were not catalogued (see *Catalogue of the Third Annual Crypt Exhibition* St Ives 1948).

48. P. Lanyon, letter to Gabo, February 1949, quoted in Garlake, 'Peter Lanyon's letters', 1995.

49. M. Rowe, 'John Wells and St Ives, c.1940–60: a study in the importance of place', unpublished MA Report, Courtauld Institute, University of London 1993, p. 25.

50. For an account of the founding and early history of the Society see Brown, 'Chronology' 1985, pp. 105–10.

51. It was open to lay membership and, initially, to people living outside Cornwall, but Pasmore, who became a member in 1952, was obliged to resign two years later when the rules were changed to exclude those who did not live locally (Brown, *Cornwall 1945–1955* 1977).

52. Philip James was a regular visitor; the Arts Council began to make a regular grant to the Society in 1950, when it also toured the annual exhibition of members' work; Hepworth's and Nicholson's participation in the Venice Biennale in 1950 and 1954 respectively was arranged by the British Council; from the mid-fifties the British Council regularly directed foreign dealers and critics to St Ives and facilitated their meetings with artists.

53. For the voting system proposed by Hepworth, adopted in November 1949 and the resultant resignations of Lanyon and others, see Brown, 'Chronology' 1985, pp. 106–8.

54. *Ibid*. p. 107.

55. *Ibid*. p. 106.

56. 'The St Ives school . . . has become the tool of an essentially abstract rather than realist movement . . . The school that has developed is due to the influence upon this society of Ben Nicholson and Barbara Hepworth' (Lanyon, letter to the *St Ives Times* 6 July 1956, quoted in Brown, 'Chronology' 1985, p. 108). In the early 1940s 'He [BN] had already begun to work towards what might eventually become the Penwith Society in 1949.' (M. Mellis, quoted in N. Lynton, *Ben Nicholson* London 1993, p. 177).

57. J. Lewison in *Ben Nicholson* exh. cat. Tate Gallery 1993, p. 69.

58. 'Chronology', *ibid*. p. 245.

59. V. Button, 'The war years' *ibid*. p. 58.

60. *Ibid*. pp. 60–1.

61. Button notes that this kind of landscape reference appeared in Nicholson's abstract still lifes as early as *1931–6 (still life – Greek landscape)* (*Ibid*. p. 61).

62. J. Barrell, 'The public prospect and the private view: the politics of taste in eighteenth-century Britain' in S. Pugh, ed., *Reading Landscape: Country – City – Capital* Manchester 1990, p. 23.

63. See Lanyon to Gabo, February 1949 in Garlake, 'Peter Lanyon's letters' 1995.

64. Made from blocks of Nigerian guarea wood given to her in 1954.

65. For Hepworth's own account of the generation of these images see *Barbara Hepworth: a Pictorial Autobiography* Bradford-on-Avon 1970, 1977, pp. 71–2.

66. Heron's review of Braque's 1946 Tate exhibition ('Braque', *The New English Weekly* 4 July 1946) was his first essay on the artist, followed by 'Braque', *New Statesman & Nation* 27 June 1953; 'Braque at the Zenith', *Arts* NY, February 1957 and *Braque*, a monograph, London 1958. With reference to *Harbour Window with Two Figures, St Ives: July 1950* he wrote that it, like 'all my paintings then and later, was totally unrelated to any painting ever made in Cornwall. It was largely based on the French masters I so admired . . .' (quoted in M. Gooding, *Patrick Heron* London 1994, p. 74).

67. '[Heron] was not tempted by the cold clarities of English abstraction . . . or by the constructivist austerities, however brilliant, of Gabo' (Gooding, *Patrick Heron* 1994, p. 47).

68. For discussions of content over formalism in Nicholson, see V. Button, 'The war years', 1993, pp. 59–62 and M. Garlake, 'Ben Nicholson', exhibition review, *The Burlington Magazine* December 1993, pp. 836–7.

69. Gooding, *Patrick Heron* 1994, pp. 53, 56.

70. '. . . this was the window occuring over and over again in my paintings of that period, whether we were actually in St Ives when I painted them, or at home at Addison Avenue, Holland Park. I probably painted more St Ives harbour window paintings in London than in Cornwall.' (*Ibid*. p. 74).

71. *Ibid*. p. 99.

72. cf. *Chemin de Fer au bord de la Mer, Soleil Couchant*, 1955, Whitechapel Art Gallery, London 1956, no. 2; reproduced *Nicholas de Staël* exh. cat. Tate Gallery 1981, no. 109, p. 129.

73. P. Heron, 'The abstract Pasmore', *New Statesman & Nation* 12 November 1949, pp. 547–8.

74. Frost made approximately nine works with this title *c.*1950, in various media and sizes. A collage of coloured paper on board called *Moon Quay* (1950) may have been exhibited in the first weekend show in Heath's studio (*Terry Frost* exh. cat. Belgrave Gallery, London 1989, no. 6).

75. Frost's association with the Fitzroy Street group led him to question the illusory nature of his painting while he was working for Hepworth in 1950/1. As a result he spent approximately nine months making collages and constructions instead of painting (E. Knowles ed., *Terry Frost* Aldershot 1994, p. 54).

76. Reproduced in L. Alloway, ed., *Nine Abstract Artists* London 1954, pl.8.

77. The clusters closely resemble an illustration in d'Arcy Wentworth Thompson's *On Growth and Form* Cambridge 1917, 1942 (fig. 239, p. 592) with which Frost was presumably familiar.

78. Alloway, ed., *Nine Abstract Artists* 1954, pp. 23–4.

79. 'Recollections and Movements', in *Terry Frost, Painting in the 1980s* exh. cat. University of Reading 1986, p. 18.

80. For an analysis of such relationships see E. Relph, *Place and Placelessness* London 1976.

81. Place may be defined in terms of human relationships rather than location. Place thus incorporates but is not identical with landscape (see D. Sopher, 'The Landscape of Home', in Meinig, ed., *Interpretation* 1979, pp. 129–49).

82. They are landscape as nature, habitat, artifact, system, problem, wealth, ideology, history, place and aesthetic (Meinig, 'The beholding eye', in *ibid*. pp. 33–48).

83. In a field with so many practitioners any selection is necessarily somewhat arbitrary. I have chosen to write about Sutherland, Hitchens, Gear and Lanyon because they exemplify the diversity of possible approaches to place; they cover between them a long chronological span and because they were all recognised by contemporary critics as significant landscape painters (see P. Heron, *Ivon Hitchens* Harmondsworth 1955, p. 11).

84. Relph, *Place and Placelessness* 1976, pp. 42–3.

85. G. Sutherland, 'Welsh sketchbook', *Horizon* April 1942, pp. 50–3.

86. '. . . I became aware that landscape itself, once one had ceased to think of it as being a view or scenic, was in a curious way like a great figure . . . there were other landscapes of the period – I mean such as the "Gorse on Sea Wall" – in which I was conscious of a kind of figurative element.' ('Landscape and Figures', conversation with Andrew, Forge, *The Listener*, 26 July, 1962, reprinted in

J. Andrews, ed., *Graham Sutherland Correspondences* 1979 1982, pp. 78–85).

87. '. . . the "Gorse on Sea Wall" was not specifically Welsh; I happened to see it there; I might equally have seen it on the North Downs . . .' ('Landscape and figures', in Andrews, *Correspondences* 1979, 1982).

88. Hitchens was born in 1893, Sutherland in 1903; Hitchens died in 1979, Sutherland a year later.

89. Sutherland's international status dated from 1952 when he provided the major British exhibition for the Venice Biennale; Hitchens showed in Venice in 1956 but his exhibition was overshadowed by Lynn Chadwick's Grand Prize for sculpture.

90. From 1940 to 1959 Hitchens held a solo exhibition every two years at the Leicester Galleries, only interrupting the sequence in 1945 for a retrospective at Temple Newsam House, Leeds, and in 1956 for the Venice Biennale. Between 1960 and 1976 he had nine solo exhibitions at the Waddington Gallery.

91. I. Hitchens, 'Notes on painting', *ARK* 18, November 1956, p. 51. Though not published until 1956, this text was essentially complete a decade earlier. The lack of references to Monet in connection with Hitchens's series perhaps reflects the decline in Monet's reputation in the decades after his death: 'Between 1930 and 1950 little was heard of the greatness of Monet, while his imaginative late works were generally decried.' (D. Cooper, 'Claude Monet' *Claude Monet* exh. cat., Arts Council 1957, p. 5).

92. '. . . a quantity of cool colour requires some warm colour to oppose it to preserve balance. This principle runs throughout – dark-light, warm-cool, up-down, in-out'. (Hitchens, 'Notes on Painting' 1956).

93. Derived from A. W. Dow's *Composition, a Series of Exercises in Art Structure* 1899. (P. Khoroche, *Ivon Hitchens* London 1990, p. 16).

94. 'The colour note of an object is essentially Itself. The representation of objects by their colour notation is one (only one) method of painting nature . . .' (D. Scrase, 'A theoretical letter from Ivon Hitchens to Maynard Keynes', *The Burlington Magazine*, July 1983, pp. 421–3).

95. Heron, *Ivon Hitchens* 1955, pp. 5 & 9.

96. *Ibid.* p. 6.

97. Hitchens, letter to Howard Bliss, Christmas, 1947, quoted in Khoroche, *Ivon Hitchens* 1990, p. 46.

98. Hitchens made a general criticism of contemporary painting for its lack of 'solid reality [where] the space between one object and another is of differing proportions, differing in tone and colour and significance. This is both mental and visual.' ('Notes on Painting' 1956).

99. '. . . the intention is to lead the spectator's eye *over* the canvas surface by an intentional redistribution of the tones and colours of nature and *into* the picture by the same means plus a reorganisation of the main planes of nature'. (Scrase, 'A theoretical letter' 1983).

100. '. . . diffuses the beam of attention even handedly across all the senses so we can take in whatever is around us which means sensations of touch and balance, for instance, in addition to all sights, sounds and smells'. (T. Hiss, *The Experience of Place* New York 1991, p. xiii).

101. *Ibid.* pp. 21–2.

102. 'Hitchens's special terrain centres on Petworth. It embraces a rich variety of the richest landscape in southern England.' (Heron, *Ivon Hitchens* 1955, pp. 9–10).

103. See Ann Bermingham on the naturalisation of labourers in Constable's paintings: 'This blending . . . naturalizes the laborers' presence in the landscape, and, by extension, it naturalizes the work they are shown performing there.' (*Landscape and Ideology: the English Rustic Tradition, 1740–1860* London 1986, p. 139).

104. Stephen Gilbert, a British artist who has lived in Paris since 1945, was a member of COBRA from 1948–51.

105. In 1950 Jane Drew suggested that the ICA hold a COBRA exhibition, which was agreed in principle, though it proved impracticable because of lack of money or suitable premises. (Management Committee minutes, 1 March 1950 TGA/ICA Archive).

106. Documented in R. Tillotson, 'Aspects of abstract painting in England, 1947–56', unpublished MA Report, Courtauld Institute, University of London, 1977.

107. '. . . the first of the younger generation . . . to command attention'. (B. Taylor, 'Spectacular variety', *The Spectator*, 24 February 1956, pp. 248, 250).

108. '. . . the fertility of that no-man's-land between the trenches of the abstract and the representational'. (D. Sylvester, *William Gear* exh. cat. Gimpel Fils, London 1948, unpaginated).

109. Though not Patrick Heron, who predictably objected to the non-spatial character of Gear's paintings. ('August exhibitions', *New Statesman & Nation*, 14 August 1948, p. 132).

110. *The Times*, 10 April, 1951; M. Middleton, 'Art', *The Spectator*, 13 April, 1951, p. 491.

111. When these paintings were first exhibited critics treated the titles as indicators of content in an intertextual relationship with the painted images.

112. *The Sunday Times*, 12 March 1950; the phrase 'recognisably Cornish' recurred four years later, with the addendum 'put through the mangle of a poet's imagination'. (*Ibid.* 28 March 1954).

113. Berger, 'Landscapes and close-ups', *New Statesman & Nation*, 3 April 1954, p. 436. Berger's poetic perception corresponds to the analytic categories described by Meinig in 'The beholding eye' 1979.

114. P. Lanyon, letter to Gabo, 3 December 1944. (Garlake, 'Peter Lanyon's letters' 1995).

115. 'It involves the whole complex of human relation to life. It is a mode of thinking, acting, perceiving and living. The Constructive philosophy recognizes only one stream in our existence – life (you may call it creation, it is the same). Any thing or action which enhances life, propels it and adds to it something in the direction of growth, expansion and development, is Constructive. The "how" is of secondary importance.' ('An exchange of letters between Naum Gabo and Herbert Read', *Horizon*, July 1944, reprinted in Read, *The Philosophy of Modern Art* London 1964, pp. 238–45).

116. Berger, however, recognised the historical significance of *St Just* (1952–3), as well as the problem that 'London or Venice Biennale gallery-goers' would not be aware of its local references, while 'the people of St Just who would, would not understand the picture'. ('Landscapes and close-ups', *New Statesman & Nation*, 3 April 1954, p. 436).

117. For discussions of the works that make up the series see A. Lanyon, *Portreath, the Paintings of Peter Lanyon* Penzance 1993, pp. 22–5; Garlake, 'The letters of Peter Lanyon' 1995 and 'Peter Lanyon's Generation Paintings' pamphlet, Tate Gallery, St Ives, 1994.

118. Lanyon described the *The Yellow Runner*, in which this imagery originated, as 'stockade as womb'. (A. Lanyon, *Peter Lanyon 1918–1964* 1990, p. 72).

119. H. Griffiths, *Peter Lanyon, Drawings and Graphic Work* exh. cat. Stoke-on-Trent City Museum & Art Gallery 1981, no. 43, unpaginated.

120. Unlike *The Yellow Runner*, in which the hill above Gunwalloe is represented, as it is in other images in the Generation Series. However, the hilltop which appears to be almost surrounded by sea can be seen in many parts of west Cornwall.

121. Though dated 1951 on the reverse in Lanyon's writing, he wrote to Hitchens late in 1952 that he had just 'constructed and executed Christ and the result is like the residue of a NAPALM bomb . . . I think I have at last painted a picture with no colour like glass'. The construction associated with *St Just* is made largely of colourless, clear glass. There can be little doubt that the letter (dated by a reference to Lanyon's forthcoming trip to Italy in January 1953) refers to *St Just*. The painting was first shown in 'Space in Colour' in July 1953. Since Lanyon remained in Italy until April, it appears that the painting was essentially complete by the end of 1952.
122. See *The Daily Telegraph* 22 September 1990 and J. Penhale, *The Mine under the Sea* Falmouth 1962, pp. 65–7.
123. 'Letters from Lanyon to Roland Bowden', *Modern Painters* Spring 1992, pp. 54–7.
124. Lanyon, letter to Roland Bowden, 16 December 1952, quoted in 'Letters from Lanyon' 1992. The dual imagery functions as a kind of simultanism, perhaps underwritten by Bergsonian philosophy, to which the potter, James Tower, had introduced Lanyon at Corsham. Causey quotes a letter to Paul Feiler (undated but 1952) in which Lanyon referred to 'a making immediate of a time process in space'. (*Peter Lanyon* Henley-on-Thames 1978, p. 5).
125. *Bojewyan Farms*, exhibited at Gimpel Fils in March 1952, when Lanyon was already working on *St Just*, also contains recognisable elements of the human body. *St Just* was conceived as the centrepiece of a notional polyptich, for which *Bojewyan Farms* would have formed the predella (*Ibid.* p. 17).
126. He wrote of painting *Porthleven*: 'In 1950 I faced a year's struggle in which I broke from my concern for structure only and attempted a more complex portrait of a place. About 12 constructions were made for this painting and set a pattern which I have followed since.' (A. Lanyon, *Peter Lanyon 1918–1964* 1990, p. 106).
127. 'When a miner comes out of the ground he comes to "Grass".' (Lanyon, letter to John Dalton, probably late 1952, quoted in *ibid.* p. 116).
128. Lanyon, letter to Gabo, 30 May 1947. (Garlake, 'Peter Lanyon's letters', 1995).
129. 'The new experience in landscape is one of journeying, inducing pattern by a process of movement in time . . . The final process of this constructed image is a revelation, a making outward, a giving of face, or of a surfacing of inner experience.' (Lanyon, undated text quoted in A. Lanyon, *Peter Lanyon 1918–1964* 1990, p. 289).
130. Quoted in *ibid.* p. 129.
131. In the possession of Sheila Lanyon, who also owns an undated lithograph by Treinen with similar imagery.
132. Though Scott saw a collection of *art brut* during his 1953 visit to New York.
133. Information from Sheila Lanyon.
134. Among the American artists whom he met on this trip were Rothko and Motherwell, with whom he later corresponded and who visited him in Cornwall, and de Kooning.
135. See A. Lanyon, *Peter Lanyon 1918–1964* 1990, p. 188.
136. P. Lanyon, 'Offshore in progress', *Artscribe* 34, March 1982, pp. 58–61.
137. A. Lanyon, *Peter Lanyon 1918–1964* 1990, p. 90.
138. '. . . belonging to a place and the deep and complete identity with a place that is the very foundation of the place concept' (Relph, *Place and Placelessness* 1976, p. 55).
139. Lanyon, letter to Roland Bowden, 20 April 1952, quoted in A. Lanyon, *Peter Lanyon 1918–1964* 1990 p. 280.
140. 'Peter Lanyon, Alan Davie & William Scott talking to David Sylvester of the BBC about their work', 19 June 1959, TGA/TAV 214 AB. Lanyon appears to have been describing what Hiss, quoting Arthur Deikman, called ' "a fluid body boundary" which can lead to "diminished self-object differentiation" ' (Hiss, *The Experience of Place* 1991, p. 21).
141. Lanyon wrote of *Solo Flight*, his first gliding painting, 'The red is the track of something moving over the surface of the painting, and at the same time, the track of the aircraft moving over the ground below.' (quoted in A. Lanyon, *Peter Lanyon 1918–1964* 1990, p. 194).
142. *Loe Bar* (1962) is an exception.
143. *Thermal, Soaring Flight, Solo Flight, Cross-Country* and *Drift* are examples of titles referring directly to meteorological conditions, techniques and the artist's personal experience of gliding.

NOTES TO CHAPTER 9

1. S. Arnold, 'Picasso and the ethics of art', *The Arts & Philosophy* 2, Autumn 1951, pp. 4–12.
2. A. Jefferson, 'Bodymatters: self and other in Bakhtin, Sartre and Barthes', in K. Hirschkop, D. Shepherd, eds, *Bakhtin and Cultural Theory* Manchester 1989, pp. 152–77.
3. It was painted when the theme of the Crucifixion was important for a number of artists, among them Sutherland and Roy de Maistre, and when Catholicism had a cultural significance as a locus of the stable and traditional. See especially Evelyn Waugh's *Brideshead Revisited* London 1945.
4. C. Lindey, *Art in the Cold War* London 1990, p. 136–7.
5. Both were widely distributed as print reproductions (*Ibid.* p. 113). *Saw Ohn Nyun* was the top-selling reproduction of 1961 (Anon., 'Reproduction Prints', *The Studio* April 1962, p. 153). In the early 1930s Kelly made at least nineteen paintings of this model alone.
6. N. Bryson, *Vision and Painting* Basingstoke and London 1983, p. 92.
7. *Ibid.* p. 94.
8. *Ibid.* p. 96.
9. *Ibid.*
10. Assumptions implicit in *The Studio*'s description of the subject as 'one of the Cambodian women the past-President of the Royal Academy took as subject matter after his trip to Asia as a young man' ('Reproduction Prints' 1962).
11. Lindey, *Art in the Cold War* 1990, p. 124.
12. Themselves 'determined by the fact that one does not see oneself as one is seen by others, and this difference in perspective turns on the body' (Jefferson, 'Bodymatters' 1989, p. 153). 'The Other, however, has a perspective on the subject that enables him both to see the external body that constitutes the subject's vantage point on the world, and also to see that body as part of that world.' (*Ibid.*, p. 154).
13. *Ibid.* p. 153.
14. See M. Yorke, *The Spirit of Place: Nine Neo-Romantic Artists and Their Times* London 1988, pp. 237–42; J. England, 'Introduction', *John Kashdan* exh. cat. England & Co., London 1989, pp. 3–4.
15. See R. Calvocoressi, *Reg Butler* exh. cat. Tate Gallery, London 1983, p. 19.
16. H. Read, 'Art in an Electric Atmosphere', *Horizon* May 1941, pp. 308–13.
17. 'Comment', *Horizon* January 1943, pp. 4–6. See also 'Comment', *Horizon* February 1942, pp. 74–5, where Connolly cited the attack on Gallimard in *Le Pilori* as an instance of the Fascist intolerance fostered by indifference to the arts.

18. M. Rémy, 'Surrealism's vertiginous descent on Britain', in *Surrealism in Britain in the Thirties* exh. cat. Leeds City Art Galleries 1986, p. 33.

19. H. Read, 'Art in Europe at the end of the Second World War', *The Philosophy of Modern Art* London 1964, p. 47.

20. W. Worringer *Formprobleme der Gothik* Munich 1911, trans. Read, *Form In Gothic* London 1927.

21. A. Stieglitz, 'The reproduction of agony: toward a reception of Grünewald's Isenheim altar after the First World War', *The Oxford Art Journal* 12, 2, 1989, pp. 87–103.

22. The German abbreviation for *Konzentrationslager*, used as the title of a publication issued *c.* June 1945 by the Office of War Information (R. Berthoud, *Graham Sutherland: a Life* London 1982, p. 126).

23. Correspondence with Robert Melville in preparation for *Graham Sutherland* London 1950 (TGA, TAM 67 67/16). The quotation from Aeschylus is often identified with Bacon; the two artists were close friends in the late 1940s and would have had such phrases in common. Sutherland quoted Aeschylus' 'Anxiety gnaws the human heart' later in the same notes with reference to his desire 'to express *in images* the outer chaos of 20th century civilisation'.

24. P. Hendy, 'Henry Moore', *Horizon* September 1941, pp. 200–6, reviewing Moore's Temple Newsam exhibition.

25. For an analysis of *genetrix* and *mater*, see F. Edholm, 'The unnatural family', in E. Whitelegg *et al.*, eds, *The Changing Experience of Women* Oxford 1982, pp. 166–77.

26. When the maquette was shown in the 'Study for an Exhibition of Violence in Contemporary Art' (ICA, London 20 February–26 March 1964) it was under the heading 'Violence observed in nature'.

27. F. Spalding, *Dance till the Stars Come Down: a Biography of John Minton* London 1991, p. 169.

28. *Ibid.* pp. 169–70.

29. Quoted by Spalding, 'John Minton: an artist in his time', in *John Minton: 1917–1957, a Selective Retrospective* exh. cat. Oriel 31, Newtown, Powys 1994, p. 15.

30. *Ibid.*

31. Spalding, *Dance* 1991, p. 169.

32. L. Freud, 'Some thoughts on painting', *Encounter* July 1954, pp. 23–4.

33. W. Townsend, quoted in *The Paintings of William Coldstream 1908–1987* exh. cat. Tate Gallery 1990, p. 90.

34. Lawrence Gowing described Coldstream's process as 'the system that maps the visual evidence' ('Remembering Coldstream' in *ibid.* p. 20).

35. T. Wilcox, in *The Pursuit of the Real* exh. cat. Manchester City Art Galleries 1990, p. 13.

36. Quoted in M. Evans, ed., *The Painter's Object* London 1937, p. 77.

37. Nos 28 and 30 in Ernst's London Gallery catalogue are described as *Fôret* (1925) (no dimensions given). Nos 925,6 & 7 (see W. Spies and S. & G. Metken, *Max Ernst Werke*, vol. 3 1925–29 Texas and Cologne 1976) carry the same title and date and recall Sutherland's *Armoured Form* (1950) (see D. Cooper, *The Work of Graham Sutherland* London 1961, no. 119a). Since 926 belonged to Paul Eluard and then to Roland Penrose it is the most likely model for Sutherland.

38. R. Alley, *Graham Sutherland* exh. cat. Tate Gallery 1982, p. 82.

39. Roger Berthoud, Sutherland's biographer, supports this, writing 'I am sure Gonzalez is one of those artists' artists whose influence tends to be underestimated. I should think it highly likely that G. S. was well informed about his work and had at least regular access to Cahiers d'Art.' (Letter to the author, 18 November 1994).

40. Gonzalez earned his living as a goldsmith; in the early summer of 1928 Picasso made visits to his studio to learn welding and in October the same year completed the metal sculpture *Head* and the metal-rod *Wire Construction* (Spies 66 and 71). See W. Spies, *Picasso Sculpture, with a Complete Catalogue* London 1972.

41. V. A. Ceoni, *Gonzalez* Barcelona 1973, p. 182.

42. Berthoud, *Graham Sutherland* 1982, p. 76.

43. *Cahiers d'Art* 1935, right side of p. 33.

44. *Cahiers d'Art* 1947.

45. See Cooper, *The Work of Graham Sutherland* 1961, nos 92c, 93a,b,c,d.

46. 'The atomic bomb is so powerful that with it, one plane can be expected to do as much damage as five 1,000-plane RAF raids did to Berlin.' (*The Daily Mirror* 7 August 1945).

47. *Reynolds News* 25 September 1945.

48. R. W. Clark cites the Frisch-Peierls memorandum and the opinion of Dr Maynord of the Institute of Cancer Research 'that a few micrograms of dust in the lungs may prove fatal', both dated 1940 (*The Greatest Power on Earth: the Story of Nuclear Fusion* London 1980, pp. 90, 109). Fantasy triumphed briefly with a rumour that scientific advances would soon permit life to flourish as never before in a tropical Britain protected from its natural climate by a gigantic atomic umbrella. (*The Daily Mirror* and *The Daily Express* 8 August 1945).

49. *The Era of Atomic Power* London 1946, pp. 59–60. 'Not only men and women, but the still-unborn, are victims of this terrible and unavoidable penetration' (C. E. Vulliamy, *Man and the Atom* London 1947, p. 137). A doctor serving with the US navy during the 1946 Bikini tests provided the best popular account of the possible effects of radiation (D. Bradley, *No Place to Hide* London 1949, *passim.*).

50. Vulliamy, *Man and the Atom* 1947, pp. 141–2.

51. D. Mellor, *A Paradise Lost: the Neo-Romantic Imagination in Britain 1935–55* exh. cat. Barbican Art Gallery, London 1987, pp. 75–6.

52. First published in book form in Vienna in 1913 and in English translation in New York in 1918.

53. S. Freud, *Totem and Taboo* London 1950, 1960, p. 76.

54. *Ibid.*

55. Mrs Rosemary Butler writes of Reg Butler in this context: 'He was fascinated by primitivism and anthropology, Picasso, African Art especially the Benin bronzes, Freud and Havelock Ellis. We have a much fingered copy of Totem and Taboo . . .' (letter to the author, December 14 1994).

56. Correspondence with Melville, TGA/TAM 67 67/16.

57. Sutherland, 'Thoughts on painting', *The Listener*, 6 September 1951, quoted in R. Alley, *Graham Sutherland* 1982, p. 108. Sutherland wrote: 'I think there is a distinction between the "thorns" done just before and at the time of the Crucifixion – and those done later. The former spring from the idea of a potential cruelty. To me they were *the* cruelty and were crucified in themselves . . .' (correspondence with Melville).

58. '. . . a balefully staring hybrid . . . with overtones of Max Ernst and Bacon' (Berthoud, *Graham Sutherland* 1982, p. 124). See Alley, *Graham Sutherland* 1982, no. 131, p. 113.

59. R. Melville, *Graham Sutherland* London 1950, unpaginated.

60. This first appeared in *Staring Tree Form* (1945) (D. Cooper, *The Work of Graham Sutherland* 1961, p. 46). The conformation on the left of *Chimère 1* is comparable to *Thorn Tree* (1945) (*ibid.*, pl.80) and anticipates aspects of the *Large Vine Pergola* (1948).

61. Said to have faded when the painting was shown at the Tate in 1982 (Alley, *Graham Sutherland* 1982, no. 131, p. 113).

62. They had both taken part in a group exhibition, 'Contemporary Painters and Sculptors', at Thos. Agnew, London in 1937, though Berthoud suggests that they may have met even earlier, through Roy de Maistre (*Graham Sutherland* 1982, p. 86).

63. See Sutherland's *Three Standing Forms in a Garden 11* (1952) and Bacon's *Study after Velasquez's Portrait of Pope Innocent X* (1953). See E. Van Alphen, *Francis Bacon and the Loss of Self* London 1992, p. 107 for a discussion of the 'curtain' in the latter.

64. Correspondence with Melville, TGA/TAM 67 67/16. Berthoud notes that Sutherland appears sometimes to have painted Bacon-like images before his friend and surmises that he may have seen canvases that were destroyed or paintings that were dated some time later (*Graham Sutherland* 1982, pp. 159–60).

65. Correspondence with Melville, TGA/TAM 67 67/16.

66. 'I'm just trying to make images as accurately off my nervous system as I can. I don't even know what half of them mean.' D. Sylvester, *Interviews with Francis Bacon* London 1975, p. 82; see also pp. 18, 43, 58, 59.

67. Cooper's dismissal of the *Standing Forms* as 'a private visual and emotional obsession' (*The Work of Graham Sutherland* 1961, p. 47) is characteristic of the silence which has surrounded the metamorphic theme.

68. They were 'enlarged from five of thirteen small maquettes of 1955, each roughly twelve inches high . . .' (S. Compton, *Henry Moore* exh. cat. Royal Academy, London 1988, no. 135, p. 237).

69. *Ibid.* nos 134, 135, p. 237.

70. The Tate had acquired Bacon's *Three Studies for Figures at the Base of a Crucifixion* in 1953 when Moore was a Trustee. Compton comments: 'It is tempting to imagine Moore's reading of these three sculptures as that Crucifixion.' (*Ibid.* p. 237).

71. J. Berger, 'Francis Bacon and Walt Disney', *About Looking* London 1980, pp. 112–13.

72. John Russell described it as 'anatomical Guignol' ('Round the Art Exhibitions', *The Listener* 12 April 1945, p. 412). For the impact of *Guernica* on Bacon, see M. Peppiatt, *Francis Bacon: Anatomy of an Enigma* London 1996, pp. 86–9.

73. *Ibid.* pp. 98–101.

74. H. Marlais-Davies, *Francis Bacon, the Early and Middle Years* New York 1978, p. 57. The Crucifixion was a long-lived theme for Bacon: he showed a *Crucifixion* in 'Art Now', October 1933, (reproduced in Read, *Art Now* London 1933, no. 61); he then made two more paintings of the subject (Marlais-Davies, *Francis Bacon* 1978, p. 19). In 1962 he painted *Three Studies for a Crucifixion*.

75. D. Sylvester, *Interviews with Francis Bacon* 1975, pp. 46, 112.

76. R. Penrose, *Wonder and Horror of the Human Head* London 1953, p. 20.

77. G. Deleuze, quoted by P. Adams, 'The Violence of Paint' in A. Benjamin, ed., *The Body* London 1993, p. 58.

78. E. van Alphen, *Francis Bacon* 1992, p. 80.

79. *Ibid.* p. 110.

80. 'I use that frame to see the image – for no other reason.' (Sylvester, *Interviews with Francis Bacon* 1975, p. 22).

81. '. . . the figures are portrayed in order to be watched by the viewer' (van Alphen, *Francis Bacon* 1992, p. 103).

82. D. Mellor, 'Existentialism and post-war British art', in *Paris Postwar, Art and Existentialism 1945–55* exh. cat. Tate Gallery 1993, p. 59. Bacon is recorded as implying that he did not favour an existential reading of his work (Sylvester, *Interviews with Francis Bacon* 1975, p. 82). Edita Wyzynska cites Melville, Sam Hunter, Nevile Wallis and Pierre Rouve as contemporary critics who considered Bacon an existential artist ('Critical reception of Francis Bacon's Painting in Britain 1945–1962', unpublished MA Report, Courtauld Institute, University of London 1990, pp. 31–2).

83. Sylvester, 'Francis Bacon' exh. cat. British Council, Venice Biennale 1954.

84. *Ibid.*

85. Mellor, 'Existentialism and post-war British art' 1993, *passim*.

86. J. Russell, *Francis Bacon* London 1971, p. 11.

87. Berger, 'Francis Bacon and Walt Disney' 1980, p. 114.

88. H. Read, 'New aspects of British sculpture' exh. cat. British Council, Venice Biennale 1952. Read was referring to T. S. Eliot's 'The Wasteland'.

89. Richard Calvocoressi suggests that with his drawings called 'Studies for Iron Sculpture', Butler was 'already beginning to absorb and transcend' Moore's example in 1946 (*Reg Butler* exh. cat. Tate Gallery 1983, p. 16). However, it is clear that these are outline drawings of Moore-like reclining figures rather than linear renderings like *Woman*.

90. *Ibid.* p. 16.

91. 'New aspects of British sculpture', 1952.

92. Melville, 'Personages in Iron', *The Architectural Review*, September 1950, pp. 147–51.

93. See also Calvocoressi, *Reg Butler* 1983, p. 9.

94. There is a similar ambivalence in Richard Hamilton's *Reaper* etchings. Also made in 1949, at the Slade, (A. Seymour, 'Introduction', *Richard Hamilton, Drawings, Prints and Paintings 1941–55* exh. cat. Anthony d'Offay Gallery, London 1979, unpaginated) they were inspired by Siegfried Giedion's *Mechanisation Takes Command* (*Richard Hamilton, Prints, a Complete Catalogue of Graphic Works 1939–83* Stuttgart and London 1984, n.21, p. 23), in which the author discussed the essential mediating role played by agricultural machinery in the relationship between nature and technology (Robbins, ed., *The Independent Group: Postwar Britain and the Aesthetics of Plenty*, Cambridge Mass. and London 1990, p. 55).

95. Left-hand illustration, *Cahiers d'Art* 1–4, 1935, p. 32. Mrs Rosemary Butler writes 'I don't think the drawings and sculptures by Julio Gonzalez influenced Reg in his iron sculptures and drawings . . . I am sure that Reg discovered the possibilities of iron as a sculptural material while he was working in Sussex during the war' (Letter to the author, 14 December 1994).

96. A. Bowness, *Lynn Chadwick* London 1962, unpaginated.

97. They were Adams, Armitage, Butler, Chadwick, Clarke, Meadows, Paolozzi and Turnbull, all of whom showed prints as well as sculpture.

98. H. Read, 'New aspects of British sculpture' 1952.

99. Alan Wilkinson writes: 'Thin, elongated standing figures were the subject of a number of drawings and sculptures of the late forties and early fifties, the most important being the bronze "Standing Figure" of 1950 (L. H. 290) which was based on a study in a drawing of *c*.1948 (L. H. Volume 1, p. 270).' (*The Drawings of Henry Moore* exh. cat. Tate Gallery and Art Gallery of Ontario 1977, p. 132). However, a version of the idea appears in drawings as early as 1937. See *Drawing for metal sculpture*, chalk and watercolour (1937), reproduced D. Sylvester ed. *Henry Moore vol. 1, Sculpture and Drawings 1921–1948* London 1944, 1957, p. 205 & A. Garrould, *Henry Moore drawings* London 1988, p. 66 in colour and *Page from a sketchbook* (1937) reproduced *ibid.* p. 65.

100. Calvocoressi, *Reg Butler* 1983, p. 11.

101. *Ibid.* pp. 22–3; R. Burstow, 'Butler's Competition Project for a Monument to "The Unknown Political Prisoner": Abstraction and Cold War Politics', *Art History*, 12, 4, December 1989, pp. 484–5.

102. *Ibid.* pp. 484–6.

103. Quoted in *ibid.* p. 477.
104. He repeated the head several times, most dramatically in the *Study for Third Watcher* (1954).
105. Calvocoressi, *Reg Butler* 1983, p. 65.
106. She showed *The Forest* (32); *The Bat* (33); *The Leaf* (34) and *Spider* (35), metamorphic images later described as a 'bestiary' (A. Pieyre de Mandiargues, *Germaine Richier* exh. cat. Hanover Gallery, London 1955, unpaginated).
107. *Le Diabolo* (1949) and *Le Diabolo Griffu* (1952) (R. de Solier, 'Germaine Richier', *Cahiers d'Art* 1953, pp. 123–9).
108. '. . . she asks not only how much damage the human body can endure and still remain human, but also how far the human body can be twisted into the shape of sub-human entities and still remain human' (Sylvester, 'On Germaine Richier', *Germaine Richier* exh. cat. Hanover Gallery 1955).
109. Calvocoressi, *Reg Butler* 1983, pp. 26–7. Mrs Rosemary Butler says of the relationship between Butler and Richier: 'I think the fact that Germaine Richier was a woman sculptor making surrealist sculpture interested him.' (Letter to the author, 14 December 1994).
110. '. . . a series of portraits whose truth is psychological rather than literary.' (Calvocoressi, *Reg Butler* 1983, p. 27).
111. M. Warnock, *Existentialism* Oxford 1970, p. 109.
112. The robot under discussion here may be differentiated by its active and often cinematic qualities from the lifeless, mechanical mannequin of de Chirico and the Dada artists. However, British artists were certainly familiar with these earlier works so that echoes of them may persist in the postwar period.
113. Hatton Gallery, Newcastle upon Tyne, May 1955; ICA Gallery, 6–30 July 1955.
114. R. Hamilton, *Collected Words 1953–1982* London 1982, p. 18.
115. Hamilton acknowledged the point in his introduction to the catalogue: 'The relationship between man and machine is a kind of union. The two act together like a single creature.' (*Man, Machine and Motion* exh. cat. Hatton Gallery 1955, unpaginated).
116. The first Sputnik flight took place in 1957.
117. R. Melville, 'Eduardo Paolozzi', *Motif* 2, February 1959, pp. 61–2.
118. M. McLeod, 'Paolozzi and Identity', in E. Paolozzi *Lost Magic Kingdoms and Six Paper Moons from Nanuatl* London 1985, p. 31.
119. F. Whitford, 'Inside the Outsider' in *Eduardo Paolozzi, Sculpture, Drawings, Collages and Graphics* exh. cat. Arts Council 1976, p. 9.
120. D. Ades, 'Paolozzi, Surrealism, Ethnography', in *Lost Magic Kingdoms* 1985, p. 62.
121. M. McLeod, 'Paolozzi and Identity', in *ibid.* p. 30.
122. *Ibid.* p. 41.
123. *Ibid.* p. 44.
124. L. Alloway, *The Metallization of a Dream* London 1963, p. 23.
125. J. Baas, 'John McHale', in Robbins, ed., *The Independent Group* 1990, p. 88.
126. D. Mellor, *The Sixties Art Scene in London* London 1993 pp. 107–17.
127. *William Scott: Paintings Drawings and Gouaches 1938–71* exh. cat. Tate Gallery 1972, p. 68. Scott's still lifes superficially resemble Bernard Buffet's, though since Buffet's first solo show was only in 1948 it seems likely that the distinctive appearance of Scott's paintings owed more to the print techniques that he learnt during his war service with the Royal Engineers.
128. A. Bowness, *William Scott: Paintings* London 1964, p. 8.
129. See A. Lewis, *Roger Hilton, the Early Years 1911–55* exh. cat. Leicester Polytechnic Gallery 1984, p. 4.
130. '. . . we involuntarily read a three-dimensional meaning:
we find a "subject".'(Heron, 'Paintings by Roger Hilton, at Gimpel Fils', *New Statesman & Nation*, 28 June 1952, p. 771).
131. A. Lewis, 'Chronology', *Roger Hilton*, exh. cat. South Bank Centre, London 1993, p. 109.
132. L. Alloway, ed., *Nine Abstract Artists* London 1954, p. 30.
133. Warnock, *Existentialism* 1970, p. 60.
134. Hilton and Gilbert had been close friends at the Slade, 1929–31. (Lewis, 'Chronology' 1993, p. 107).
135. In an undated draft letter to the *Guardian* Hilton wrote: 'the Stedilijk [sic] Museum in Amsterdam is perhaps the most go-ahead and enlightened in the world' (unpublished MS, collection Rose Hilton).
136. Hilton, statement in Alloway, ed., *Nine Abstract Artists* 1954, p. 29.
137. 'The struggle between the colours can be felt as a movement . . . The result is a dynamic tension which has reference to actual forces in the world and to real space . . . A man returns from the harsh clangour of the street, filled with the consciousness of class strife, of the oppression of the poor by the rich, of all the evils of the world. He steps into his room and there catches sight of another reality . . .' (unpublished MS, collection Rose Hilton).
138. P. Heron, 'Introducing Roger Hilton', *Arts* (New York), 31, 8, May 1957, pp. 22–6.
139. C. Harrison, 'Roger Hilton, the obligation to express', in *Roger Hilton* 1993, p. 26.
140. G. Limbour, 'Let the Material Speak for Itself', *Jean Dubuffet* exh. cat. ICA 1955, unpaginated.
141. Hilton, unpublished MS, collection Rose Hilton.
142. Hilton, letter to Frost, dateable to December 1955 through a reference to a review in the *Guardian* 3 December 1955; quoted by Lewis, *Roger Hilton, the Early Years* 1984, p. 60.
143. Reproduced in *Roger Hilton* 1993, no. 25.
144. cf. *Once Upon a Time*, no. 33 in *Roger Hilton* 1993.
145. *Ibid.* no. 26.
146. *The Observer* 29 June 1952.
147. Heron, 'Introducing Roger Hilton' 1957.
148. See David Sylvester's remark about Hilton 'painting with a mid-Atlantic accent' ('Selected exhibitions', *New Statesman & Nation*, 21 May 1960).
149. *William Scott* 1972, p. 70.
150. D. Robbins, ed., *The Independent Group*, 1990, pp. 64–7.
151. *Architectural Design*, October 1962, reprinted in *Collected Words* 1982, p. 36.
152. B. Friedan, *The Feminine Mystique* London 1963, p. 206.
153. Hamilton, *Collected Words* 1982, p. 44.
154. 'Irony has no place in it except in so far as irony is part of the ad man's repertoire.' (Hamilton, 'An Exposition of $he' in *ibid.* pp. 35–9).
155. Marshall McLuhan's *The Mechanical Bride: Folklore of Industrial Man* 1951, published in London in 1967, was circulating among artists in London in the late 1950s.
156. J. Clifford, *The Predicament of Culture: Twentieth-Century Ethnography Literature, and Art* Cambridge, Mass. and London 1988, p. 126.

NOTES TO CHAPTER 10

1. H. Read, *Contemporary British Art* London 1951, p. 25.
2. 'Every parish in the British Isles was affected and all 16,436 of them marked this in some way' (R. Francis, 'War memorials' in S. Nairne & N. Serota, eds, *British Sculpture in the Twentieth Century* London 1981, p. 63).
3. J. Wynter, *Sites of Memory, Sites of Mourning: the Great War in European Cultural History* Cambridge 1995, pp. 6–7.

4. *Ibid.* pp. 227–7.

5. For the record of attempts to find such a memorial form see J. Young, *The Texture of Memory: Holocaust Memorials and Meaning* New Haven and London 1993.

6. E. Relph, *Place and Placelessness* London 1976, p. 35. Among instances of 'placelessness' Relph cites amusement parks, shopping malls, Subtopia, reconstructed historical sites, restaurant and hotel chains (pp. 79–121).

7. 'Imageability: that quality in a physical object which gives it a high probability of evoking a strong image in any given observer'; 'It is that shape, color, or arrangement which facilitates the making of vividly identified, powerfully structured, highly useful mental images of the environment.' (K. Lynch, *The Image of the City* Cambridge, Mass. and London 1960, p. 9).

8. *Ibid.* p. 10.

9. See R. Cork, *Art Beyond the Gallery in Early Twentieth-Century England* New Haven and London 1985, pp. 249–96.

10. Cork, 'Overhead sculpture for the underground railway', in Nairne & Serota, eds, *British Sculpture* 1981, p. 95.

11. Architectural sculptors, of whom one of the most successful was Bainbridge Copnall, continued to provide swags, garlands and symbolic figures for important public buildings until well into the 1960s.

12. S. Kierkegaard, *The Present Age* New York 1962, p. 59, quoted in Relph, *Place and Placelessness* 1976, p. 126.

13. R. Melville, 'Contemporary sculpture in the open air', *The Listener* 10 June 1948, pp. 942–3.

14. 'It is being tried out as a public monument'; 'I can think of no other contemporary English example of monumental sculpture that remotely approaches its power' (Melville, 'Contemporary sculpture' 1948).

15. M. Garlake, '"A war of taste": the London County Council as art patron 1948–1965', *The London Journal* 18, 1, 1993, pp. 45–65.

16. Art critic for *The Architectural Revue*, the house journal of modernist orthodoxy.

17. Melville, 'Contemporary sculpture' 1948.

18. *Ibid.*

19. 'Sculpture as status symbol', *The Times* 3 October 1962.

20. R. Cork, 'An Art of the Open Air', in S. Compton, ed., *Henry Moore* exh. cat. Royal Academy, London 1987, p. 14.

21. This had become conventional and unimaginative following the resignation of the first Chief Architect of Peterlee, Berthold Lubetkin. 'The main part of the town, as so far built, is dreary in the extreme; the faults common to most of the new towns are present without the redeeming features possessed by some.' (J. M. Richards, 'Housing at Peterlee', *The Achitectural Review* February 1961, pp. 88–97).

22. *Ibid.* The subsequent addition of pitched roofs has weakened this parallel.

23. M. Martin, 'Artist and Architect' (1957), in *Mary Martin* exh. cat. Tate Gallery, London 1984, p. 26.

24. The Festival's administrative structure, established in March 1948, consisted of a Council of public figures in politics and the arts chaired by Lord Ismay. Its Executive Committee was the co-ordinating body for the Arts Council, the Council for Industrial Design, the Central Office of Information and the Councils for Science and Architecture. Below the Executive were the Presentation Panel and the Design Group.

25. In 1946 Mary Glasgow (then Secretary General of the Arts Council) suggested that the Council 'would rather like to have a chance of advising those responsible for music and so on at the Exhibition' (Memo to E. Hale, 2 December 1946, Arts Council archive).

26. Pooley, letter to Lord Ismay, 10 January 1949, Arts Council Archive.

27. F. Spalding, *Dance Till the Stars Come Down: a Biography of John Minton* London 1991, p. 156.

28. R. Berthoud, *Graham Sutherland, a Biography* London 1982, pp. 146–7.

29. M. Banham, B. Hillier, eds, *A Tonic to the Nation: the Festival of Britain 1951* London 1976, p. 102.

30. '. . . the key physical characteristic . . . is singularity, some aspect that is unique or memorable in the context' (Lynch, *The Image of the City* 1960, p. 78).

31. As Lynch indicates, the 'landmark cluster' creates a more effective reference than a single feature (*Ibid.* p. 101).

32. At £1,750 each; Dobson and Hepworth were each offered £500 though Hepworth's was later increased to £1,400 plus £400 for materials. Minor commissions were worth between £200 and £400 each (Arts Council, Art Panel minutes, 19 July 1949; P. James, memo to Art Panel, 9 May 1950; memo to A. Horn, 23 January 1950; Miss Popham, minute to Miss Rogers, undated but 1951).

33. 'The important point is that we cannot have Moore, Epstein, Dobson and Hepworth all together there as Moore and Epstein regard themselves as the two leaders in this, and of course their commissions are far greater than any of the others.' (Memo, P. James to D. Guthrie, 'Small FOB sculpture commissions', Arts Council/FOB files, 8 August 1949). Moore was less concerned than Epstein about siting and the demands of surrounding buildings (letter to Mary Glasgow, 26 May 1949, Arts Council/Sculpture Commissions).

34. Construction started on 26 July 1949 but because of strikes and shortages only 830 of 6,000 working drawings had reached the contractors by the end of the year (Banham & Hillier, eds, *Tonic* 1976, pp. 79–80).

35. Arts Council/Sculpture Commissions, 25 May 1949.

36. See 'The exhibition as landscape', *The Architectural Review*, special Festival issue, August 1951, pp. 80–104.

37. 'I have always felt that it is particularly the nature of sculpture to be inspired by the site . . . As the site conditions the form, the size and the material of the subject springs out of the formal solution quite naturally.' (Hepworth, letter to Mary Glasgow, 13 June 1949, Arts Council/Sculpture Commissions). However, in view of the delays she soon agreed to 'proceed with a free sculpture that will find its own home' (letter to Philip James, 21 June 1949, Arts Council/Barbara Hepworth Sculpture Commission).

38. Paolozzi has stated that it was inspired by a medical diagram of oral diseases and that its technique was adapted from Giacometti (R. Calvocoressi, *Reg Butler* exh. cat. Tate Gallery, London 1983, n. 23, p. 33).

39. '. . . this whole open-air enterprise . . . ought not to leave the impression that the public park is the only and striking alternative to the public gallery. There is a third pretext for keeping sculptors alive while we are building and town-planning . . . it might be interesting to proceed to the admittedly more difficult demonstration of sculpture in association with architecture' (F. Watson, 'Open-air sculpture at Battersea', *The Listener*, 24 May 1951, p. 846).

40. 'Not one of the larger sculptures on the South Bank is really successful. Epstein's *Spirit of Youth* is . . . a potboiler'. Moore's *Reclining Figure* achieved 'empty, if impressive virtuosity'; Hepworth's *Contrapuntal Forms* had 'the formal interest of a pair of coffins stood on end' (A. D. B. Sylvester, 'Festival Sculpture', *The Studio*, September 1951, pp. 72–7).

41. 'Whether or not it helps an artist . . . to have to meet the

requirements of a set *subject* when he is offered a commission, there is no doubt that it does help him to know what the *purpose* of the work is to be.' (*Ibid.*).

42. He cited as models Boccioni, Brancusi and the Constructivists (*Ibid.*).

43. 'It was pointed out to big industrial and commercial organisations, to Municipal Art Galleries, to other private and public bodies, the opportunity they have to celebrate the Festival year by acquiring works of a scale and importance which private patronage can no longer support' (D. Baxandall, 'Patronage of art and the Festival', *The Listener* 17 May 1951, pp. 788–90).

44. P. James, 'Patronage for painters, 60 paintings for '51', *The Studio* August 1951, pp. 42–7.

45. See *25 from 51: Paintings from the Festival of Britain* exh. cat. Sheffield City Art Galleries 1978, p. 27.

46. Baxandall, 'Patronage of art' 1951.

47. Arts Council, 'Festival of Britain Disposals', Arts Council Archive.

48. For the political implications of the Festival, see A. Forty, 'Festival politics' in Banham & Hillier, eds, *Tonic* 1976, pp. 26–38 and M. Frayn, 'Festival', in M. Sissons & P. French, eds, *The Age of Austerity 1945–51* London 1963, pp. 317–38.

49. J. Berger, 'The Unknown Political Prisoner', *New Statesman & Nation* 21 March 1953, p. 337–8.

50. *Ibid.*

51. He was the brother-in-law of Philip Johnson, Director of Architecture at MoMA, New York. He had served in the O.S.S. during the war. Penrose was keen to employ him for his contacts with industrialists which would facilitate fund-raising, but Kloman was said to be unpopular with the ICA staff, who found him unable to grasp its idealistic, informal nature (interview with Joan Edwards, November 1983).

52. The monument would be erected at Lake Success (ICA Management Committee minutes, 23 May 1951, TGA/ICA Archive). There is no indication of precisely where or when the idea originated, though there seems little doubt that it emanated from the United States.

53. R. Burstow, 'The limits of modernist art as a "Weapon of the Cold War": reassessing the unknown patron of the monument to the Unknown Political Prisoner', *The Oxford Art Journal* 20, 1, 1997, pp. 68–80, n. 54.

54. It included, as members of the ICA Management, Read, Gregory, Penrose, Rothenstein and Moore.

55. Joan Edwards interviewed by Dorothy Morland, 19 June 1978, transcript in TGA/ICA Archive. It appears that Eric Gregory and Penrose were aware of his identity at the time of the competition (see ICA Management Committee minutes, 6 October 1954).

56. *New York Times*, 25 February 1967. On 19 February 1967 the *NYT* carried a report on the mechanism of passing funds. The US government had established several ostensibly charitable front organisations, such as the Granary Fund of Boston, which was listed in neither the Boston telephone directory nor the Directory of Foundations. CIA money was put into the front foundation which then passed it to the charitable trust, which in turn made grants to designated recipients. These included over a period of several years the Boston Symphony Orchestra and the London-based magazine, *Encounter*.

57. Burstow, 'The limits of modernist art', 1997.

58. To 'all those men and women who in our time have given their lives or their liberty for the cause of human freedom' (Kloman, 'Introduction', *British Preliminary Exhibition for the Unknown Political Prisoner Competition* exh. cat. New Burlington Galleries, London 1953).

59. See R. Burstow, 'Butler's competition project for a monument to "The Unknown Political Prisoner"; abstraction and cold war politics', *Art History* 12, 4, December 1989, pp. 472–96.

60. Which received Arts Council prizes.

61. Joan Edwards, interviewed by Dorothy Morland, 19 June 1978 (TGA/ICA Archive).

62. For similar practices at the São Paulo Bienal, see M. Garlake, 'The British Council and the São Paulo Bienal' in The British Council, *Britain and the São Paulo Bienal 1951–1991* 1991, pp. 20–1.

63. *The Times* 24 March 1953.

64. *Daily Worker* 25 March 1953.

65. 'Of the 12 prize-winning works the least abstract is by Miss Hepworth, and her three monoliths are of course, very far from being in any way naturalistic.' (*The Times* 13 March 1953). 'An array wherein extravagant examples of abstract sculpture pullulate with devastating monotony.' (*The Daily Telegraph* 13 March 1953). *Le Soir*, Brussels referred to Butler's maquette as 'une composition abstraite'. 'Most of the skeletal entries . . . are abstract sculptures . . . the prize winners are Europe's leading abstractionists.' (*The Tablet* 21 March 1953). 'Es zeigte sich nähmlich, dass alle prämierten Werke rein abstrakte Skulpturen waren.' (*Sie und Er* 26 March 1953).

66. *France-Soir* 17 March 1953. See also *The Daily Mail* 19 March 1953.

67. *Aberdeen Evening Press* 24 March 1953.

68. *The Guardian* 21 March 1953.

69. Burstow, 'Butler's competition project', 1989.

70. Calvocoressi, *Reg Butler* 1983, p. 24. Calvocoressi saw a relationship between Butler's watchers and Moore's *Three Standing Figures*, which Butler had helped to carve.

71. See, for example, *The Guardian* 19 March 1953.

72. See A. Saint, *Towards a Social Architecture: the Role of School Building in Postwar England* New Haven and London 1987, chapters 4 and 5.

73. J. Forshaw & P. Abercrombie, *County of London Plan* London 1943, pp. 28–9.

74. In 1948 and 1951.

75. Saint, *Towards a Social Architecture* 1987, pp. 90–3.

76. Which implicitly maintained that familiarity with a work of art would breed appreciation. To some extent this has been borne out in practice: a remarkably large proportion of the pieces sited by the LCC are still in place, undamaged. Moore's *Draped Seated Woman*, on Stifford Estate, initially received with indifference, has been enshrined in local mythology as 'Old Flo'. (Information from Elaine Harwood.)

77. See M. Garlake, ' "A War of Taste" ' 1993.

78. Exceptions, such as the untitled abstract sculpture in metal, slate and wood (1962) by Bryan Kneale at Fenwick Place Estate, are rare.

79. Late in 1997 it was removed for up to three years while the surrounding area is redeveloped.

80. *Girl on a Round Base* (1964). See R. Calvocoressi, *Reg Butler* 1983, no. 64, p. 69.

81. *Jacob Epstein, Sculpture and Drawings* exh. cat. Leeds City Art Gallery 1987, p. 227.

82. *Ibid.* p. 276.

83. J. Stallabrass, 'The mother and child theme in the work of Henry Moore', in *Henry Moore – Mother and Child* exh. cat. The Henry Moore Foundation and Käthe Kollwitz Museum, Cologne 1992, p. 20.

84. *Ibid.* pp. 15–16.

85. 'Whether married women should be employed outside their homes has become the most topical issue concerning women in recent years.' (A. Myrdal & V. Klein, *Women's Two Roles: Home and Work* London 1956, p. xi). They pointed out that whereas 91 per cent of single women between eighteen and forty years and 80 per

cent of married women without young children had been employed during the war, by 1947 only 18 per cent of married women living with their husbands were working (p. 52). There was a sharp rise in married employment by 1951, so that by 1956 40 per cent of employed women were married, although their jobs were often part time and low grade, taken in order to afford consumer luxuries (M. Pugh, *Women and the Women's Movement in Britain 1914–1959* Basingstoke and London 1992, pp. 287–8).

86. The Village College, instigated by Henry Morris, Cambridgeshire's Director of Education, was to involve the whole family and thus the wider community, providing facilities for general cultural activities often lacking in rural areas (S. Compton, ed., *Henry Moore* 1988, no. 107, p. 224).

87. '... here was the chance of carrying through one of the ideas on a large scale which I had wanted to do' (Moore, letter to Dorothy Miller, reproduced in P. James, *Henry Moore on Sculpture* London 1966, p. 225). Because of the high cost to the artist of casting and materials, it was agreed that Moore might make three extra casts to dispose of himself, in addition to the smaller version produced in 1945 (*Ibid.*).

88. R. The trust was established in 1953, chaired by Sir Philip Hendy and funded initially by the Elmgrant Trust, with contributions from the Development Corporation, local industry, architects and builders, 'to acquire sculpture for the town' (F. Gibberd *et.al.*, *Harlow: the Story of a New Town* Stevenage 1980, p. 244).

89. R. Berthoud, *The Life of Henry Moore* London 1987, p. 261.

90. It has since been vandalized again and permanently removed from its position at the symbolic heart of the town.

91. Introduction, exh. cat., XXIV Biennale di Venezia, 1948.

92. Sir Victor Mallet, letter to Sir Ivone Kirkpatrick, 22 June 1948, quoted in British Council/Fine Art Committee Progress Report, 22 September 1948.

93. Supporters claimed that it attracted as much interest as the Turner exhibition, while right-wing critics used it as an excuse to attack the Cultural Convention and the directorate of the Palais des Beaux Arts for arranging a show by a foreign artist.

94. British Council/Fine Art Committee Progress report, 1 February 1950.

95. The British occupying forces wished to destroy the largest dock in Hamburg against German wishes.

96. Murray-Baillie, a member of the Monuments, Fine Arts and Archives branch, quoted in British Council/Fine Art Committee Progress Report, 11 July 1950. The exhibition was subsequently shown in Düsseldorf.

97. 'If art can express the peculiar humanity of a period in a spiritual form, then this expression is to be found in the work of Moore.' (*Die Zeit*, Hamburg, 22 March 1950, translated in British Council/Fine Art Committee Progress Report, 11 July 1950). 'What he experienced during the blitz we should be able to understand too'. (*Die Welt, ibid.*).

98. British Council/Fine Art Committee Progress Report, 8 May 1951. In 1952 the exhibition was incorporated into a larger sculpture show sent to Cape Town to celebrate the Van Riebeck tercentenary. The following year it travelled to Holland, Sweden, Norway and Denmark.

99. Three each for the *Madonna and Child* and the Stevenage *Family Group* and four for the Festival of Britain *Reclining Figure*.

100. Quoted in British Council/Fine Art Committee Progress Report, 1 July 1952.

101. With Epstein's *Catherine* and a cast of Frank Dobsn's *Fount*. Other participating countries were France, Belgium, Luxembourg, Denmark, Switzerland and Germany.

102. A cast of Moore's *King and Queen* was sold to the Middelheim municipal gallery, four works to the Stuttgart Staatsgalerie and a cast of the *Draped Reclining Figure* to São Paulo. The British Council assisted with the despatch of works to continental commercial galleries (British Council/Fine Art Committee, 10 February 1953).

103. As a result of cuts imposed on the Council in 1951, the exhibitions budget was reduced from £23,270 (1950–1) to £5,870 (1951–2) (British Council/Fine Art Committee, 8 May 1951). The exhibitions committee therefore decided to concentrate on events such as the Venice Biennale, where much of the cost was carried by the host country.

104. The event was initiated in 1946 as a theatre festival to mark the place of the worker in the new German state ('The changing image of the German worker: 40 years of the Ruhr Festival', *Kulktur Chronik* 4, Bonn 1986).

105. Moore showed a cast of the 1951 *Reclining Figure*, a maquette (1947) for the *Family Group* and *Head and Shoulders* (1950). The British Council Representative wrote of 'countless reproductions' in the press (Fine Art Committee minutes, 9 December 1952).

106. 'The work of Henry Moore ... represents all of us in our western impotence against mass and the machine ... man haunted by the machine taking refuge in the earth' (*Die Welt*, 22 March 1950; 'for us members of the machine age who know only too well the progressive mechanisation and dehumanizing effects upon our once-familiar world ...' both quoted in British Council/ Fine Art Committee 11 July 1950) (*Hamburger Echo*, 21 March 1950).

107. Shown Sonsbeek 1949, Germany and European exhibition 1949–50, Athens 1951 and Cape Town 1952.

108. The Barclay School group was shown in Germany and Europe 1949–50, South Africa and Cape Town 1951–2; the Harlow group at Recklinghausen 1954.

109. São Paulo 1953, Middelheim 1953 and 1955, Documenta 1, 1955.

110. São Paulo 1953, Sonsbeek 1955, Musée Rodin 1956.

111. 'It is a fundamental paradox that the political effect of cultural propaganda increases in proportion to its detachment from political propaganda, no matter how honestly and candidly the latter may be conducted and however wide the evidence it may win.' (Lord Lloyd, (Chairman of the British Council, 1937–41) letter to Lord Reith (Minister of Information) 16 February, 1940, quoted in F. Donaldson, *The British Council: the First Fifty Years* London 1984, p. 74).

112. C. Tennyson, Chairman, Central Institute of Art & Design, 'The shape of things to come', *The Listener* 5 March 1942, p. 297.

113. '... works which begin to express some aspect of a "lay" public feeling about particular places'; he cited Epstein's Cavendish Square *Madonna and Child* ('Public sculpture', *New Statesman & Nation* 4 July 1953, pp. 15–16).

114. L. Alloway, 'The siting of sculpture, 1', *The Listener* 17 June 1954, pp. 1044–6.

115. M. Middleton, 'Trouble at the Tate', *The Spectator* 20 March 1953, pp. 335–6.

INDEX

PHOTOGRAPHIC ACKNOWLEDGEMENTS

While every effort has been made to trace copyright holders, any further informa-tion on their identity would be welcome. In most cases the illustrations have been made from the photographs or transparencies provided by the owners or custodi-ans of the works. Those for which fruther credit is due are:

2, 3, 8 © Patrick Heron 1998 All rights reserved DACS; 5, 20, 81 © Royal College of Art, London; 10 © Estate of Ceri Richards 1998 All rights reserved DACS; 11, 102, 103, 104, 107, 110, 111 The Conway Library, Courtauld Institute of Art; 12, 22, 88, 96 © Eduardo Paolozzi 1998 All rights reserved DACS; 13, 61 Scottish National Gallery of Modern Art, Edinburgh; 14 Peter Garlake; 15, 35, 49 England & Co; 16, 46, 47, 92, 93 © William Scott Foundation; 19 the works of Naum Gabo © Nina Williams; 21 © Manchester City Art Galleries; 25 © The British Museum; 26 The Bridgeman Art Library, London; 27, 65 reproduced with kind permission of the Trustees of the Ulster Museum; 30 reproduced with permission of the Imperial War Museum, London; 44, 45, 91 © Estate of Roger Hilton 1998 All rights reserved DACS; 53 Ken Powell; 55 © Richard Hamilton 1998 All rights reserved DACS; 56 reproduced with the permission of Austin Reed Ltd; 58 © Crown copyright: UK Government Art Collection; 60, 64 © Angela Verren-Taunt 1998 All rights reserved DACS; 69 Tyne & Wear Museums; 77 Birmingham Museums & Art Gallery; 90 Albright-Knox Art Gallery, Buffalo, New York, gift of Magda Cordell McHale; 97 © Richard Hamilton 1998 All rights reserved DACS; 98, 99, 108, 110, 112 repro-duced by permission of the Henry Moore Foundation; 65, 103 © Alan Bowness, Hepworth Estate; 100, 101 © Hulton Deutsch Collection Ltd; 105 Ivon Hitchens estate.